DISARMING INTELLIGENCE

Disarming Intelligence

PROUST, VALÉRY, AND MODERN FRENCH CRITICISM

Zakir Paul

PRINCETON UNIVERSITY PRESS
PRINCETON & OXFORD

Copyright © 2024 by Princeton University Press

Princeton University Press is committed to the protection of copyright and the intellectual property our authors entrust to us. Copyright promotes the progress and integrity of knowledge. Thank you for supporting free speech and the global exchange of ideas by purchasing an authorized edition of this book. If you wish to reproduce or distribute any part of it in any form, please obtain permission.

Requests for permission to reproduce material from this work should be sent to permissions@press.princeton.edu

Published by Princeton University Press
41 William Street, Princeton, New Jersey 08540
99 Banbury Road, Oxford OX2 6JX

press.princeton.edu

All Rights Reserved

ISBN 978-0-691-25797-6
ISBN (pbk.) 978-0-691-25798-3
ISBN (e-book) 978-0-691-26153-9

British Library Cataloging-in-Publication Data is available

Editorial: Anne Savarese and James Collier
Production Editorial: Jill Harris
Cover Design: Karl Spurzem
Production: Lauren Reese
Publicity: William Pagdatoon
Copyeditor: Tash Siddiqui

Cover image: Gustave Caillebotte, *Halévy Street, View from the Seventh Floor* (1878), Hasso Plattner Collection / Museum Barberini

This book has been composed in Miller

10 9 8 7 6 5 4 3 2 1

CONTENTS

INTRODUCTION	Disarming Intelligence	1
CHAPTER 1	Gathering Intelligence: From Taine to Bergson	27
CHAPTER 2	Abdicating Intelligence: Proust and Narrative Form	52
CHAPTER 3	Testing Intelligence: Valéry Reconfigured	87
CHAPTER 4	Mobilizing Intelligence: Critical Neutrality at the *Nouvelle Revue Française*	129
CHAPTER 5	Situating Intelligence: Benjamin and Political Technique	153
EPILOGUE	Crises of Intelligence	185

Acknowledgments · 197
Notes · 199
Bibliography · 249
Index · 271

DISARMING INTELLIGENCE

INTRODUCTION

Disarming Intelligence

DISARMING INTELLIGENCE CHARTS a trajectory linking two moments in European thought through modern fiction and literary criticism. In Third Republic France, "intelligence" was a contested object for the sciences, one that differentiated the normal from the pathological. Around World War I, it emerged as a politically charged watchword in tense cultural polemics. Focusing on texts by Henri Bergson, Marcel Proust, Paul Valéry, and the critics of the *Nouvelle Revue Française* (*NRF*), this book shows how these writers questioned and transformed the values and meanings attached to intelligence. The reader will follow distinct steps in the struggle to control the signification of intelligence from the emergence of the term after its consecration by Hippolyte Taine and its reversal in Bergson, to its partial abdication in Proust's fiction, its crisis as faculty and class in Valéry, and its criticism in the pages of the *NRF*. Forays into essays by German thinkers extend this trajectory by emphasizing how the term was gradually displaced, almost vanishing from critical theory and literary criticism.

The book argues that a theoretical archive not often considered is central to the evolution and reception of modern French literature, thought, and criticism. Its aim will be to draw attention to how this literature negotiates a term whose banality and universality lend it much of its lasting fascination. The representation of intelligence in the works discussed necessarily differs, even as the concerns they express about the capacities and limits accorded to conscious rationality (especially in the creation and reception of literary works) endure. Many of the texts examined grapple with the difficulty of language to grasp and reveal the conscious and marginal workings of the mind. The belated temporalities of such recognition, that dilate and inverse the logical relation of cause and effect, will also be an underlying theme of analysis. Whether or not such representations can be mobilized to promote a national agenda or betray class interests becomes a politically divisive question. Constantly obliged to collaborate with other forces, to test its mettle and measure its worth, intelligence remains an embattled concept. These works do not always nor explicitly philosophize about intelligence but wrest new literary forms and critical attitudes from its demands for cogency.

Rather than considering intelligence to be an ideologically neutral or conceptually stable basis for understanding the operations of mind and matter, self and other, tradition and rupture, the writers and critics studied lay out its analytic excess and cultural overdetermination. In differing ways, Henri Bergson, Marcel Proust, Paul Valéry, the critics of the *Nouvelle Revue Française*, and Walter Benjamin suspend and reconfigure what the role and limits of intelligence might be. Shifting the emphasis from the anxious intelligence of subjectivity to the disarming intelligence of literary form, these writers and critics imply that "intelligence" is both less advantageous a faculty than it is usually taken to be and one that it is increasingly difficult to renounce.

From chapter to chapter, intelligence comes to light as the object of different types of knowledge, study, evaluation, engagement, and experiment. It moves among various fields—philosophy, psychology, literature, and critique—as it becomes a point of contention among competing assessments of cultural life and national character. Within this redistribution of the faculty, literature claims a manner of relating to intelligence capable of outstripping the insights of more methodic ways of thinking.

The literature of this period, roughly between 1870 and 1930, attempts to negotiate and displace the meanings of intelligence it inherits from the thought of the Third Republic, while also electing intelligence as a topic for narrative and analysis. Intelligence spurred the casting of a poetics and politics that did not simply abdicate analysis in favor of the irrational. Rather, these forms altered the place of literature within a wider range of discursive practices from the natural sciences and emerging social sciences to nationalist and partisan rhetoric.

The first chapter tracks how philosophers from Taine to Bergson sought to define intelligence as a semiotic faculty, while psychologists invented scales to measure its variation. Intelligence both separated individuals from one another and made them comparable. The reigning concept of mind was mechanical and prone to error, before it came to be contested by the emphasis spiritualism and vitalism lent to intuition. The second chapter analyzes Proust's novel arguments for demoting the faculty in favor of an experimental combination of intuition with intelligence. We then turn to Valéry's essays and notebooks, which serve as a testing ground for literature's pretensions to intelligence. Valéry recognized that the crisis in intelligence unleashed by World War I was not ephemeral, since cognitive faculties were assailed by technological and economic changes that came with the mechanization of everyday life. Yet he insisted that existing literary genres, especially the novel, failed to respond to these changes, thus creating the need for untried forms. The next chapter reconstructs the debate concerning the national and ethical character of intelligence in literary and cultural criticism around the First World War. The final chapter examines Walter Benjamin's critical essays on French writers in contrast with a dismissive relegation of intelligence to the free-floating literati by German thought. An epilogue briefly recasts the crises of intelligence by considering contemporary discourses about artificial intelligence.

Taken together, these studies argue that early twentieth-century French literature appropriated the category of "intelligence" from psychological and philosophical attempts to redefine an otherwise vague notion of understanding. The conceptual armature of Third Republic thought was disarmed in literary figuration, especially in works by Proust and Valéry, who displaced intelligence through formal, stylistic, and critical experiments. During this period, literature previously construed as the most distinguished use of language came under attack as only one of many forms of discourse, and an unproductive one at that. Challenged by new claims to objectivity—from the social and experimental sciences to the new media of photography and film—novelists and poets were forced to justify their intellectual existence in economies of intelligence. Although the poetics of the authors and critics studied here differ to the point of antithesis, they share a concern to negotiate a new stance toward thinking within literature and vice versa.[1] Studying the ambivalent senses of "intelligence" in French thought, along with its countering in early twentieth-century literature, offers a crucial corrective to apolitical views of modernism by revealing an ignored literary and aesthetic dimension to enduring cognitive, rhetorical, and political debates.

In French studies, the literary period roughly between the fin-de-siècle and the Front Populaire tellingly lacks a name. Often rejecting the umbrella term of "modernism," French-language critics use periodizations such as *l'avant-guerre, la grande guerre*, or *l'entre-deux-guerres*, invariably dividing the literary battlefield between an *avant-garde* and an *arrière-garde*. Such martial metaphors raise larger questions concerning the "bourgeois" status of literature and the tension between technique and commitment in a period in which writers seemed to have forfeited their right to exist.

Moreover, they implicitly recall the reciprocal entanglement of literature and combat in the French imaginary from Balzac, Baudelaire, and Flaubert onward. As Paris consolidated its economic power and cultural centrality in the "post-Napoleonic, proto-capitalist Restoration," it came to resemble a battlefield where "the way you win in its struggle is not by arms [...] but by insinuation, charm, gathering information, possessing social secrets."[2] By the interwar period, a committed left-wing writer like Paul Nizan could simply declare that the "culture of intelligence was an arm," one whose use-value was the object of intense class conflict.[3] In this context, the writers I study sought to disarm intelligence by dissociating it from its established regimens and associations.

The turbulent era studied here began with the Siege of Paris, leading to the French defeat to the Prussians in 1871 and the annexation of Alsace-Lorraine by the German empire; a spate of anarchist bombings and political assassinations followed as the political landscape was divided into competing doctrines of Boulangism, socialism, republicanism, xenophobia, revanchism, and nationalism; mass strikes, the experiment of the Commune, and its brutal suppression by Thiers, led to MacMahon's "republic of moral order"; the Panama Canal scandal and the Boulanger and Dreyfus affairs divided public opinion and spurred the appearance of the intellectual; peasants were transformed into Frenchmen through technological innovation, Hausmannization, the development of railroad networks, universal military conscription, and secularized school reforms; the aestheticized consumerism and café culture of Belle Epoque Paris, the separation of church and state in 1905, and the expansion of colonialism, and its *mission civilisatrice*, all became part of the identity of the Third Republic.[4]

The scientific moment, which largely displayed a positivist investment in experimental and empirical methods to capture the real, was soon challenged by a literary and philosophic culture that expressed increasing skepticism about the sovereignty of the intellect, as it pastiched the precision of laboratory culture and experimental protocols. When the Dreyfus affair introduced the figure of the "intellectual"—a kind of generalist of the intellect with public politics—the term was soon held in contempt. Much of the postwar pamphleteering across the political spectrum in 1919 constituted an attempt to reclaim some of the lost glory attached to the figure of the intellectual.[5] While this book is not a history of the intellectual, some discussion of the term is necessary at the outset, especially to frame many of the literary polemics discussed below.

On January 13, 1898, *L'Aurore* published Zola's open letter to President Félix Faure reproving the military state apparatus that falsely condemned

Alfred Dreyfus for counterintelligence on behalf of the Germans. A wave of right-wing outrage and anti-Semitic protests against Dreyfus and his defenders followed immediately, while the category of the "intellectual," called to co-sign the petition in his favor, was introduced, discussed, and immediately critiqued. Ferdinand Brunetière, the editor of the *Journal des deux mondes,* described the emergent class as "a kind of nobility, people who live in labs and libraries, this very facet is enough to denounce one of the most ridiculous deviations of our time, by which I mean the pretention to elevate writers, scholars, professors, philologists into supermen. Intellectual aptitudes, for which I certainly do not show contempt, only have relative value."[6] The very same day, *Le Temps* published a list of protestors, signed by scientists, academics, and writers, including Zola and Proust. For future prime minister Georges Clemenceau, such a disinterested movement of public opinion was a hopeful sign. For Maurice Barrès, Zola and the intellectuals were "rootless" (*déracinés*), lacking intuition, any sense of territorial belonging, not to say fully "French" blood.[7]

Lalande's influential dictionary of philosophy tellingly lists the pejorative implications of "intellectualism" as 1) a "reproach about thinking of things in a verbal, superficial way while imposing on reality, artificial, rigid frameworks which deform it as they claim to represent it; 2) the reproach of sacrificing 'life' that is, the natural prudence and fertility of instinct to the pleasure of critical thinking, which is a force for inertia, destruction, and inhibition."[8] Despite the vilification of their tendency toward excessive abstraction, intellectuals found a symbolic place in the public sphere. The left-wing intellectual, writes Foucault, became someone who had the right to speak as "the master of truth and justice [. . .] to make himself heard, as the representative of the universal [. . .] the conscience of everyone."[9] In the period between the fin-de-siècle and the Second World War—often intensified by the outbreak and aftermath of the First World War—contempt toward "intelligence" (and intellectuals as a class) resurged in waves of anti-intellectualism. At the time, many of the writers and intellectuals discussed below could neither successfully lay claim to the universal authority of their fin-de-siècle counterparts nor approximate the specialized domains of knowledge that emerged around World War II. The figure of the universal intellectual faded in favor of the specific intellectual, whose expertise in a precise field, no longer depended upon writing, but instead a shared ability to connect and politicize forms of knowledge.

The two defining events of the period, for the purposes of this study, remain the Franco-Prussian War of 1870 and the "Great War" of 1914–1918. The Franco-Prussian War often seems forgotten in descriptions of the ostensible hundred years of peace in Europe between the 1815 Treaty of Vienna and the First World War. While the war of 1870 spurred the reorganization of French society on every imaginable level to combat its perceived lack of precision, discipline, and order, and anxieties about a demographic decline in relation to Bismarck's newly consolidated Germany, the Great War unleashed an intense technical acceleration as trench, gas, and air warfare, shell shock, mutilation, and mass death created a traumatic break in narratives of positivism, rationalism, and scientific and cultural progress. In a passage that creates a complex analogy between obsession in love and war, Proust describes the Franco-Prussian War as a preoccupation that dominated the consciousness of the generation that lived through it, blinding them to its reality:

> People who were alive during the war of 1870, for instance, say that the idea of war ended by seeming to them natural, not because they did not think enough about the war, but because they thought of it all the time. And in order to understand how strange and momentous a fact war is, it was necessary that, something else wrenching them out of their permanent obsession, they should forget for a moment that a state of war prevailed and should find themselves once again as they had been in peacetime, until all of a sudden, against the momentary blank, there stood out clearly at last the monstrous reality which they had long ceased to see, since there had been nothing else visible.[10]

Only through forgetting and distraction does reality come into focus to the preoccupied mind, this passage suggests. Through his incorporation of World War I into his novel, Proust articulates the insight that just as modern war is not strategic but unforeseeable, truth is the accidental outcome of rectified error rather than methodic thinking. Proust's German translator, Benjamin, makes a not unrelated remark about the aftershock of the war which seemed to be less a naturalized obsession, than a devaluation in experience itself:

> Experience [*die Erfahrung*] has fallen in value, amid a generation which from 1914 to 1918 had to experience some of the most monstrous events in the history of the world. [...] For never has experience been belied [*Lügen gestraft worden*] more thoroughly: strategic experience has been contravened by positional warfare; economic experience, by the inflation; physical experience, by hunger; moral experience, by the ruling powers.[11]

Between these disasters, the status and role of the literary writer fluctuated from the decadent aesthete, the dilettante, the intellectual, and the anarchist to the anti-Semitic pamphleteer and the wartime nationalist, to name just a few of the more startling stances.[12] Although nearly none of the figures in this study were combatants, the conflicts of their time warped how they conceived of the act of writing itself.

Tracing the emergence of literary and critical discussions in this period allows us to better grasp the paradoxical heritage of contemporary theoretical discourse. Modern French literature, often dismissed as having purely formal concerns, deviates from models of criticism prevalent today. Reevaluating its literary-theoretical insights helps address a larger series of vexed questions: Who or what is deemed intelligent? What role does intelligence—whether understood as a mixture of will and conscious reason or studied intellectualism—play in the genesis of the literary work of art? How did these authors reconcile their creative vocations with fears that conscious intelligence might be an inimical force that kept them from writing such work, whose true sources remained unconscious? Should a literary intelligentsia work in the service of a national agenda? We cannot understand how French literature and thought conceptualizes literary creation and its psychic and political situation if we fail to grasp the innovative role and radical limits it lent to intelligence.

The Sword and the Mirror

In an essay on the nineteenth-century philosopher Théodore Jouffroy, the critic Charles Augustin Sainte-Beuve distinguished between two aspects of intelligence, reflection and action, comparing them to a sword and a mirror:

> Relative to objects of the intelligence one can behave in two ways. Every mind is more or less armed, in the presence of ideas, with the shield or mirror of reflection, and the sword of invention, of penetrating and restless action: reflecting and daring. Genius consists in the proportioned alliance of the two means, with the prevalence of daring.[13]

Sainte-Beuve suggests that everyone is "more or less armed" with intelligence, toward which one can adopt either of these two attitudes. Either one brandishes the reflective shield or mirror, or one wields the "sword of invention," using it to perform bold, penetrating feats. Genius does not choose between the two. As the image implies, intelligence can be martial, divisive, and aggressive, seeking to prevail against any obstacles or rivals. But it can also be reflective and defensive, returning an image of its surrounding environment without necessarily acting on it. The sword cuts, while the mirror exposes. Perhaps it was the seductive allusion to the story of Perseus, or else the neat dichotomy it offers, but Sainte-Beuve's aside about intelligence took on a life of its own. In the early twentieth century, writers as different as Benjamin and Julien Benda quoted the remark. For Benda, modern thinkers exalted *l'intelligence-glaive* and belittled *l'intelligence-miroir*.

Today, intelligence fills a different lexical space. In English, one thinks first and foremost of digital surveillance networks that gather and store massive amounts of information about individuals and collectives. Both sword and mirror, such "intelligence" purports to predict, protect, and respond preemptively to the moves of unnamed (internal and external) enemies. In French, these networks are referred to as *services de renseignements*, although the language of intelligence is increasingly used. Despite the importance of spying and military maneuvering around the Dreyfus affair, the current project does not address this aspect of intelligence due to the difference in lexical fields.[14] Secondarily, intelligence is artificial, the dream of an interactive mind-machine capable of maneuvering and supplementing, if not supplanting, the human body and its limited sensorium in increasingly seamless ways. On a pedagogical level, intelligence is the testing site that distinguishes between the innately gifted and talented, and those deemed unable to learn. Recent psychology invariably discusses conceptions of intelligence through metaphors rather than definitions. Its major currents—from Jean Piaget's genetic epistemology to Howard Gardner's multiple intelligences—rely on geographic, computational, biological, epistemological, anthropological, sociological, and systems metaphors.[15] The borders between these levels are rendered increasingly porous by contemporary regimes of artificial intelligence, data harvesting, and "societies of profiling."[16]

Notably absent from such military, artificial, pedagogical, and psychological registers is the literary. While one readily speaks about the intelligibility of a work, or the unintelligibility of a theory, it is rare to consider literary works themselves as possessing and affecting intelligence.[17] In late nineteenth- and early twentieth-century France, as I have been arguing, intelligence became a key category for examining the creation and reception of literary works in their syntactic, semantic, social, affective, and political modes.[18] The literary historian Jean David notes that in the early twentieth century intelligence enjoyed a role comparable to *raison* in eighteenth-century thought. During the Enlightenment, however, reason was used as a "weapon" (*instrument d'attaque*) against existing belief systems, whereas in the early twentieth century, "intelligence" was a hastily cobbled levy against a rising tide (*une défense contre une marée montante*) of inimical forces. As the historian of science Lorraine Daston notes, the general, quantitative, and putatively morally neutral notion of intelligence is "brashly modern."[19] While the term remains difficult to define, and even harder to measure or locate, its deleterious social effects as a regime of power are all too real. Recalling Alfred Binet's tautology that "intelligence is what is measured by intelligence tests," Pierre Bourdieu identifies a "racism of intelligence" as "the means through which the dominant class" produce a justification for their own privilege while excluding various others from power in the name of intelligence.[20]

French thought ascribes two modes of knowing to intelligence: knowledge as "potential or ability" and knowing as "simple possession of knowledge."[21] Littré's 1874 dictionary offers eight definitions of intelligence: these include the faculty or act of understanding; spiritual substance; an artist's capacity to produce effects; a rhetorical capacity to achieve certain results; communication among like-minded people; and a secret accord or unity or feeling.[22] While many of these meanings date back to the seventeenth century, the concept became "socially charged" in the post-Revolutionary period: as the intellectual historian John Carson writes, "champions of the Enlightenment and practical revolutionaries alike" used intelligence as a partial basis for social distinction that was no longer explicitly guaranteed by class.[23] Ceasing to refer to knowledge, it described either a shared or a personally possessed intellectual ability. From the nineteenth century onward, the concept shifted "from referring to a general faculty to [...] an individual attribute," from plural talents to a singular intelligence, and from limited to expansive cultural significance.[24] Even as man became an object of knowledge for the human sciences that targeted life, labor, and language, intelligence unraveled discourses of human exceptionalism and dignity.[25] In a more antihumanist vein, Georges Bataille declares: "The moment arrived, in the 19th century, when human intelligence brought to its highest degree of acuity stopped taking itself for the center and realization of the world. The feeling of infinite dignity was outstripped by those of distress and abandonment. Irony lay waste to dignity, hunger and passion made it hateful."[26] A Copernican revolution in intelligence led to the marginalization, not to say the abjection of the human.

The difficulty late nineteenth-century thinkers encountered in translating ancient terms that designate the capacity to think and know reflects the history of mind–body, human–machine, and nature–culture dualisms, as well as the consequent development of epistemology and metaphysics into national philosophical traditions. For Étienne Balibar, the Latin word *mens* is paradigmatic: during the early modern period it translates both *esprit* and *âme*, creating an epistemological and a theological current in French thought.[27] Intelligence, by contrast, stems from *intellegere*, suggesting that we are dealing with the ability to link or read otherwise disconnected elements together (*inter-legere* or *-ligere*).[28] Yet "etymology offers no protection," writes Maurice Blanchot, adding, not without irony:

> *Intelligere* alerts us to its dependency with regard to *legere* and the prefix *in*, and *legere* in turn opens onto the *logos* which, before it signifies language (speech, mark) expresses the gathering into itself of what has been dispersed inasmuch as it must remain dispersed. Dispersion and gathering in, such could be said to be the respiration of the mind, the dual movement that does not become unified, but which intelligence tends to stabilize so as to avoid the dizzying prospect of an ever-deepening investigation.[29]

This stabilizing force weakens the connection between intelligence and the spiritual dimension proper to *esprit*. While the association with divinity endured in the notion of a higher intelligence that could ground human thought, nineteenth-century "intelligence" largely adhered to the movement of life, rather than divine inspiration. Burdened with theological, revolutionary, and Idealist connotations, *esprit* increasingly designated collective historical consciousness, while the more malleable "intelligence" became a watchword in science and aesthetics.[30]

From 1870 to 1930, intelligence dominated the *esprit du temps*.[31] Scientists employed the term to locate pathologies before the wave of positivist psychological studies that culminated in the invention of intelligence testing.[32] The Ministry of Public Instruction chose Alfred Binet, an eclectic psychologist and a student of Jean-Martin Charcot, to devise a test to identify those unable to profit from compulsory education in a "normal" manner because of the state of their intelligence. Popularized and distorted beyond their original application, intelligence tests furnished a scale to evaluate and rank individuals according to mental fitness and adaptability, drawing attention to their supposedly innate qualities at the expense of their ability to learn.[33] Thinkers in fields from physiology and evolutionary biology to experimental psychology and philosophy fought to control the meaning of a term that paradoxically appeared at once universal and particular, republican and elitist, innate and acquired, measurable and incalculable.[34] Perhaps for this very reason, it promised to clarify the enigmatic nature of subjectivity and the movement of life itself.

The history of conceptions and regimes of intelligence is in many ways the history of exclusion. Part of the larger history of the subjectivization and naturalization of reason in modernity, Daston argues in the study alluded to above, "intelligence" in the nineteenth century became general, biological, innate, and unequal. Since well before the invention of intelligence testing, anyone who did not correspond to the neurotypical, adult, able-bodied European male was implicitly classed as less capable of freedom, citizenship, and made the object of the French republican *mission civilisatrice*, among other such regimes. Women, children, racialized and colonized minorities, the neurodivergent, and the working poor were excluded in varying ways that corresponded to and were naturalized by a host of categories invented by law, medicine, criminal anthropology, demography, biopolitics, and psychology. Naturalization here names "ways of fortifying various social, cultural, political, or economic conventions by presenting them as part of the natural order." Daston's work on the "naturalization of the female intellect" from Aristotle to Darwin provides a model for processes according to which norms of exclusion are reified through appeals to biological and physiological determinism, instead of acknowledging the socially constructed forces often at work behind such matrices.[35] Over time, women, as well as female animals, were cast as nurturing, mischievous, cunning, deceptive, emotive, curious, and malleable. At stake was the causal connection between sex and physiology, on the one hand, and mental and natural capacity, on the other.

> Eighteenth-century naturalizers distinguished sharply between the natural and the conventional but permitted the moral to pass freely between both realms, mingled the psychological with the somatic in both causal directions, and invoked education to correct or corrupt nature; nineteenth-century naturalizers barred the moral from the natural, made the body the causal substratum of character and intellect, and opposed obdurate nature to pliable nature.[36]

The ways that intelligence has been exploited as grounds for violent prejudice and domination has been extensively studied by scholars of this period, upending narratives—from positivism to contemporary neoliberalism—about the melioristic paths to realizing conditions of political equality given cognitive and epistemic diversity.[37] There would be many reasons for abandoning discussions of intelligence altogether, were it not for its persistent use and allure.

Critical discourse was not immune to the seductions of intelligence either. The cubist painter and art-critic Amédée Ozenfant speculates on the senses of "intelligence" in the early twentieth-century French critical idiom:

> What do they mean by intelligence? Many seem to confuse it with reason or logic, or with these two tools of intelligence. Or else does it refer to that clarity of mind, which some inspired people and idiots lack? Or else the faculty that "understands" the play of antecedents and consequences, and that educates you to anticipate, to handle causes lucidly in order to attain the effects one intends to produce? Certainly, a good, clear intelligence understands very well that its power is limited; it knows that it needs other faculties, like intuitive intelligence, to become global intelligence.[38]

Rather than settling on a definition of intelligence, Ozenfant worries over the shades of possible meaning that the term contains: reason, logic, lucidity, the ability to grasp premises and outcomes, the power of anticipating cause and effect. As we have seen, these nuances were fought over by nineteenth century psychology and philosophy.[39] Art criticism, like Ozenfant's, continues in this tradition and "intersects only erratically with English meanings of the same words."[40] Distinctions are upheld in English between intelligence and the narrower ambit of intellect, while the French tends to use the first term exclusively. Even when it is translated by its homonym, the slippery connotations of intelligence are often misplaced—a tendency that justifies our sustained examination of a single term.

This book explores the epistemic shift in which intelligence was used to transform the world of things into the world of signs. Contemporary to this metamorphosis, modernist literature is often considered a privileged nexus for thinking about the vexed relations between literature and philosophy. Critics have described the history of modern narrative form as undergoing an "inner turn," involving the collapse of outer space into inner psychic life.[41] Others evoke the "end of interiority." Rather than turning away from the real to the life of the mind, for Laurent Jenny, literature becomes a privileged space for the projection of inner life back onto the world.[42] The question remains how the perceiving mind and the perceived world are in turn represented in words, as literary artifacts, and whether such representation promises any knowledge about the nature of the mind or the world that is unavailable to other forms of thinking. The period under scrutiny further inquires whether literature is a form of thinking beholden to the kinds of agency, rationality, and cognitive structures as they were described by natural and social sciences or whether its singularity placed it on the side of inspiration and intuition.

Proust and Valéry both rejected the false dichotomies between intellect and intuition in their efforts to negotiate a place for intelligence within literary form. Proustian intelligence functions as the developing agent that makes the negative essence of experience available, leading up to the discovery of lost time and the apotheosis of art. But we should not charge Proust with his narrator's enthusiasms, nor conflate *À la recherche du temps perdu* with the fulfillment of a dogmatic aesthetic vocation. From the beginning, Proust sought to write a novel that acknowledged the fragility of intelligence, its manic overreach and diminished returns, in the hope of making its readers capable of desiring more than bedtime stories about redemption. Valéry's relation to flashes of insight were predominantely melancholic. For the poet, intelligence remains exposed to the passage of time and to political and technological crises, which would soon make literature unintelligible. Yet he, too, suggests that we may have no way of foregoing intelligence. Valerian intelligence transforms philosophical problems about embodied consciousness into linguistic performances across genres. Both the novelist and the poet-critic remind the "theoretical intelligence" of its bodily, finite, discontinuous condition, installing "a disorganizing sense of flux into its models of itself."[43] As French thought shifted its emphasis away from the nineteenth-century discourse on intelligence, contemporary writers folded intellectual analysis into literature, while polemicists projected it outward onto the world as a way of defending ultra-conservative values.

Charles Maurras—critic, politician, and theorist of the far-right monarchist movement *Action française*—offers a polemical, potted history of the course of French literature that divides up the centuries according to their reaction to the idea that literature possesses intelligence. In the seventeenth century, French writers were *la parure du monde* (the finery of the world) and lay no claim to specialized knowledge, let alone power. That disastrous conflation only occurred when royal authority was supplanted by the *homme de lettres*. Whether or not literature could offer any knowledge about the world, Europe fell under its tutelage during the age of revolution. The following century of failed revolutions, industrial and political, further divided the republic of writers into "hysterics"—who shut themselves in nonsense, and "industrialists"—willing to recreate any social milieu through a highly polished technical realism. Literature's desire for knowledge became increasingly anarchic, leading criticism to elevate intelligence over judgment, the latter understood as a discerning form of reason: "Intelligence was considered explosive, and anyone who lived by their intelligence appeared as a born enemy of real order."[44] In Maurras's conspiratorial account, the relation between the real and the imaginary was soon suppressed by the political confrontation between intelligence and sovereignty, democracy and monarchy. From the Dreyfus affair to World War I, writers were increasingly forced to pick a political faction. The refusal of the *NRF* critics to place literary criticism at the service of postwar French hegemony, as demanded by Maurrasians, led to an enduring transformation in criticism, critique, and literary paradigms.

However skeptically we consider Maurras's genealogy, underwritten as it is by his impenitent anti-Semitic and antidemocratic bent, it signals a distinction between intelligence, knowledge, and judgment.[45] Intelligence concerns the drive to apply teleological, cognitive thinking to singular situations in which origin and goal are not given. The writers and critics I study reveal how the relation between knowing and thinking is not simply a cognitive one, but rather a vacillation within and between judgments understood as a critical activity, and flair, an intuitive capacity to distinguish and discern. Setting literary works against the discourse on intelligence makes it possible to track not only how preconceived notions of intelligence are disarmed in literary figuration, but also how literature bears its own disarming notion of intelligence.

In this vein, the constellation of Proust, Valéry, and the critics of the *Nouvelle Revue Française*, as well as the thinkers from Taine to Bergson, to a lesser extent, might be read as elaborating a category of intelligent form. Their works do not always explicitly philosophize about intelligence but wrest new literary forms and critical attitudes from its demands for cogency. In doing so, they shift the emphasis from the world of the intelligent subject to the disarming intelligence of the literary. These writers and critics finally imply that "intelligence" is both less advantageous a faculty than it is usually considered to be and one without which it is difficult to narrate, describe, analyze, or relate to the world.

Disarming Intelligence

"Disarming Intelligence" should be understood in at least two ways, namely as a critical and a creative impulse. First, the armature or the weaponry of intelligence is taken apart in literary practice since literature, unlike logic, can play with alternatives that are not in contention.[46] The basic principles of non-contradiction, cause and effect, identity and difference that dictate logical thinking are suspended, opened to doubt, and free to be reassembled. The second sense of "disarming intelligence" is this literary play on possibility, which bears its own kind of knowledge. While philosophers must deal with the specter of necessity, literature, like rhetoric, can revel in modes of possibility.[47] This book thus aims to show how early twentieth-century French literature not only negotiates a specific place for "intelligence" in relation to other faculties, but also how it redefines and crafts its own understanding of "intelligence."

Attempts to reconcile historical and philological approaches to modern literature appeal to the notion of a distinctly artistic and literary intelligence, which would not be duped by language: "By teaching us not to be duped by language, literature makes us more intelligent, or intelligent in other ways. The dilemma of social art or art for art's sake becomes obsolete in front of an art that covets an intelligence of the world freed from the constraints of language."[48] Such claims, in this instance by Antoine Compagnon, do not, however, entertain the possibility that literature eradicates the fantasy of intelligence as a personal quality, property, or possession. Becoming more intelligent or altering one's intelligence demands a transformation or dissolution of existing relations to language. In a study on philology, Werner Hamacher emphasizes a "disarmed" technical apparatus that enables philology not to answer literary questions once and for all, but to seek answers other than the pre-existing ones: "Philology, where it deserves this name, responds to the questions, provocations, and attacks organized by literature *not* when it has an adequate technical arsenal at hand but rather when it is disarmed and must seek for other responses than those at hand."[49] Elsewhere he distinguishes between the history of literary and phenomenal events, noting: "History—namely, aestheticized history—is suspended in literary texts. And these texts articulate their historicality precisely by exposing the form of their speaking and the relation to their own prehistory as contingent [. . .]. Literature is the elucidation of the impossibility of writing literary history."[50] While my study draws on the history of ideas, its primary focus remains on the questions raised by the figural language of a constellation of literary and literary critical texts. In response to the questions, provocations, and attacks literature aims at intelligence, it seeks "other answers" than the ones offered by pre-existing arsenals, theories, and histories.

The puzzle remains that while literature exploits the expressive and affective potentials of language, it stays bound to the letter. A philosophical thesis can be rephrased in other words; a poem, as any critic soon discovers, cannot. In "The Perfect Critic," T. S. Eliot calls criticism the "disinterested exercise of intelligence." It is when we do not know enough that we tend "to substitute emotions for thoughts." Eliot declares that, ever since Aristotle, the critic has had "no method except to be highly intelligent, but of intelligence itself swiftly operating the analysis of sensation to the point of principle and definition."[51] What, one might ask, becomes of the world beyond the text and the critic? How do debates about the intelligibility of rhetorical and figural language bear upon ways of being? What are the interpersonal relational modes that literary intelligence enables, and more crucially, disarms?[52]

Literature, in this account, does not necessarily make us more intelligent, nor does it concern the irrational or unconscious primarily as surrealism and psychoanalysis might contend. Rather, it offers different ways of relating to intelligence, finding ways of questioning its falsely definitive categories, so that we can forget and rediscover what it is we thought we already knew, as well as what we failed to consider in the first place. This affordance is perhaps what makes it suspect.

Intelligence has a special place in the vaunted quarrel between literature and philosophy. "It is fair to say that since Plato's famous decision [to expel poets from the city] there has been consistent association of the poetic with a peculiar, mysterious, and even dangerous form of knowledge."[53] Although Stathis Gourgouris, like many others, describes this ancient contest in terms of a claim to knowledge, intelligence may precede the very division of poetry and philosophy into distinctive modes of knowing (whether *nous*, *epistemē*, *phronesis*, or *logos*). Poetry does not draw its aura of danger from knowledge as idea.[54] The idea belongs to the philosopher. The poet's knowledge is the knowledge of language, and her danger is the danger of traversing language without a reference either to the word or the world as a guarantor. Before Platonic philosophy invented the idea, and its dialectical machine counting out sophists and poets, it first repressed a certain kind of ruse. As Marcel Detienne and Jean-Pierre Vernant argue, the Greek word *mētis* (often translated as "intelligence") names a range of qualities from sophistry to the guile of Odysseus, from Oedipus' solution of the Sphinx's enigma to fishing and carpentry.[55] This *savoir-faire* or know-how was not knowledge or just knowingness, hence its preemptive exclusion from philosophy, unlike *sophia* or *nous*. The cunning deity rejected by philosophers was left to artisans, while rhetoricians and poets—from Homer to Oppian—founded the "stability of its terminology."[56] Metis, the forgotten goddess of intelligence, was soon replaced by her daughter: the regal, martial, and terrifying Pallas Athena, who gifted the mirroring shield to Perseus, allowing him to defeat the Medusa without meeting her petrifying gaze.

※

Modernity repeatedly returned to the category of intelligence in times of crisis when systematic philosophies faltered. The outbreak of the First World War triggered an acute interest in repressed forms of intelligence in relation to ethical questions across the West. In his influential 1915 essay, "The Moral Duty to be Intelligent," the American critic John Erskine discussed the ethical necessity of overcoming deeply entrenched Anglo-American cultural stigmas opposing intelligence and goodness: "The disposition to consider intelligence a peril is an old Anglo-Saxon inheritance."[57] The closer one came to Athens, Erskine suggested, the closer the good and the smart seemed to be. Meanwhile, the Dadaist Hugo Ball penned a wide-ranging polemic, *The Critique of the German Intelligentsia*, launching an attack on what he considered morally bankrupt currents in German thought from Reformation theology to his paranoic conspiracy of a "German-Jewish conspiracy to destroy morality," to which he opposed a pacifist, pietistic Rousseauist tradition.[58] While Erskine and Ball turned to the intelligentsia and their intelligence to defend the threatened moral fabric of the West, in France the debate took on an added accent of difficulty by being bound to the political and cognitive concerns particular to the Third Republic.[59] The crisis of values can be described as triple crisis of aesthetic value, cognitive faculties, and political ethos.

The earlier debate in nineteenth-century France concerned the divide between the empirical and natural sciences, on the one hand, and the "human" sciences, on the other.[60] The contested place of language was a key to understanding this rift. Any truth that could be expressed only through discourse was necessarily subject to the inherent relativity and ambiguity of speech. Thinkers after Étienne Bonnot de Condillac attacked the doctrine of faculties and innate ideas prevalent since Descartes, in order to argue that the origin of thought was speech and experience, rather than innate forms.[61] Taine took up Condillac's project to elaborate a theory of the sign, which was simultaneously a critique of the subject as imagined by post-Cartesian philosophy. The spiritualist tradition would, in turn, attack Taine, until his intellectualist realism was completely reversed by Bergson. It seems obvious that Proust and Valéry would be much closer to Bergson, rather than his now largely unread predecessors.

Yet the very idea that the truth about our selves is hidden from conscious investigation belongs not to Bergsonism, but to this longer tradition that speculates on the nature and limits of intelligence in language.

Alongside Taine's ambitions to adapt the methods of natural sciences to literature and philosophy, Sainte-Beuve attempted to derive the meaning of the work from the life of the author. Captured by the formula *tel fruit, tel arbre*, Sainte-Beuve's premise was that if one gathered enough "intelligence" about the life of a writer, their habits, experiences, and proclivities, then the secret structure of the work would be laid bare. Proust objected to this idea in the drafts for an early critical essay, *Contre Sainte-Beuve*, arguing that it was not the biographical, social self that wrote but a nocturnal, asocial other. This is one way to read the scandalous opening gambit of his preface, which announces a depreciation of intelligence and the kinds of truth it affords: "Each day I attach less value to intelligence" (*Chaque jour j'attache moins de prix à l'intelligence*).[62] Depreciating intelligence seems surprising for readers of Proust's novel because his narrative voice is identified with the hypertrophy of interpretive intelligence. Yet, as Deleuze notes, what matters in the *Recherche* is not so much what the characters think, but what forces them to think. Involuntary intelligence—triggered by memory, sickness, suffering, insignificance, the body, and random objects—is thus prized over the products of pure reason.

The Proustian narrator defers the time of writing in the hope that life will epiphanically reveal itself to him, thus keeping death at bay. And this fantasy is so powerful that what we call a Proustian experience still refers to the synesthesia that unleashes involuntary memory and restores a sense of being in and across time, otherwise occluded by the interested, analytic drive of intelligence. Likewise, the figure of Monsieur Teste incarnates Valéry's comparable fantasy of a power that renounces itself, having assured that it exists without entering the realm of art, action, or writing. Proust has often been read as elevating art over life, and Valéry as valuing art only when it renounces any likeness to the human. Yet their writing does not merely elevate or depreciate life in relation to literature. Rather they argue that life—full of belated, disarming intelligence—has a textual structure that begs for literary understanding. They use interpretation of the represented world as the central technique of narrative, which remains essentially conceptual, reflexive, and directed toward embodied consciousness, sensation, and feeling.

The "Absence" of French Modernism

Readers may justifiably wonder why this book does not relate its arguments about intelligence to the category of French modernism. After all, most of the works studied here are commonly deemed "modernist" in anglophone criticism. Yet my focus on intelligence puts pressure on the availability, if not the very existence, of French modernism as an explanatory category, which tends to occlude the narrative reconstructed here. As one commenter on the topic notes, "In France the word *modernisme* does appear during the twentieth century but generally refers to painting, the Catholic church crisis of 1907, tourist amenities that are not completely primitive, or [...] writers like James Joyce and William Faulkner."[63] While *modernisme* can characterize anything from Joyce to hotel plumbing, it does not delimit a literary period, genre, or movement, although it occurs occasionally in Huysmans's art criticism, or dismissive asides by Proust and Gide.[64] Bergson's works were placed on the Catholic index in 1914 when Pope Pius X condemned them for "philosophical modernism," recalling its theological use as a response to threatened dogma. French-language criticism, it is worth noting, largely eschews the category, preferring to speak either in terms of centuries, schools—symbolists, naturalists, surrealists, Dada, *esprit nouveau*, etc.—or to use military metaphors as periodization (*avant-garde* or *arrière-garde*, *avant-guerre* or *entre-deux guerres*).[65] The changing of the century is generally held to be more significant. One of the standard reference works in the crowded field of Proust studies is thus simply called *Proust entre deux siècles*.[66]

The *Recherche* is widely considered a quintessentially modern novel, which, to risk tautology, could only have been written when it was. Here modernity is construed less as an artistic phenomenon than an ensemble of factors effecting everyday life in the French Third Republic: expanded democracy, the reign of technical innovation and secular republicanism, experiments in painting and poetics.[67] Critics also emphasize the novel's devotion to style, its meta-theoretical bent, and the possible differences between the book the narrator intends to write and the one we read as traits of modernist textuality.[68]

While the terms *moderne*, *modernité*, and *moderniste* all exist in French, they refer to independent and distinct debates, as Vincent Descombes notes in a helpful lexical discussion. *Moderne* roughly indicates post-Cartesian thinking, an enlightenment alliance between natural science and human emancipation, the era of liberated subjectivity that the Germans refer to as *Neuzeit*. *Modernisme* refers to the Catholic theologians of the *Syllabus*, for whom it indicates "an attempt to reformulate dogmas to render them compatible with the modern 'mentality.'" Drawing on Anglo-American usage, he suggests *moderniste* may indicate an artist who feels the need to overturn traditional art forms, through a militant devotion to style (and perhaps Greenbergian medium specificity) as a will to break with the past, whereas Baudelairean *modernité* is opposed to antiquity and refers primarily to the conditions of life (*la vie moderne*) rather than a particular kind of art.[69] The *Salon de 1846*, Baudelaire's essay on the paintings of Ingres and Delacroix, defines *modernité* as the moment when the site of "heroism" shifts from officious civic and public life to the private and subjective sphere. Where does Proust belong on such a grid? Indifferent to the advent of the "modern," he seems to attach "no moral significance to historical evolution"; bound to modernity, historical events almost always appear as refracted private experiences in his novels; technically innovative, he does not commit to "modernist" style.[70] It is perhaps in his belated decision to include the First World War in his novel that Proust comes closest to the cyclical impulse of modernist historiography which finds renewal in decline.[71] As the Baron de Charlus mockingly notes, the very public that resisted "modernists in literature and art followed those of war."[72]

Contrast the absence of French modernism with the uncanny persistence of "discourses of modernity and modernism" which "have staged a remarkable comeback" in Anglo-Germanic criticism in the guise of "second modernity, liquid modernity, alternate modernity, countermodernity."[73] To this one might add the phenomenon of "death by prefix": "From Transpacific to Mediterranean, Pragmatic to Revolting, Digital to Slapstick, hardly a region, concept, technology, category of being, or historical movement has been excluded as a possible type of modernism."[74] Such designations seem caught at once in "the afterlife" and the arbitrariness of modernism. As Frederic Jameson argues, "any theory of modernism capacious enough to include Joyce along with Yeats or Proust, let alone alongside Vallejo, Biely, Gide, or Bruno Schulz, is bound to be so vague and vacuous as to be intellectually inconsequential."[75] While often understood as a crisis of temporality (a becoming time of space and vice versa), modernism also names a series of conundrums in the order of tradition and transmissibility: at once the triumph of the new, a way of discussing the now and the contemporary, it also denotes a desire for novelty that emerges as a reaction to the exhaustion of tradition and experience, for which antiquity suddenly seems to paradoxically incarnate the most intense form of infancy and novelty. Modernism instead reflects (and tries to distance itself from) fin-de-siècle decadence as it becomes cognizant of its own essential belatedness and unsustainable bid for actuality.[76]

The notion of the modern—or *modernus*—refers both to a break with the ancients, and to a "now" of writing.[77] "One is soon forced to resort to paradoxical formulations such as defining the modernity of a literary period as the manner in which it discovers the impossibility of being modern," writes Paul de Man.[78] Modernism, on the other hand, pulls together a host of -isms, as Daniel Albright suggests: Impressionism, Expressionism, Futurism, Cubism, Abstractionism, Primitivism, Imagism, Neoclassicism, Dadaism, Surrealism, Aestheticism, and Corporealism.[79] Derived from modernity, modernism—at once a reaction to and intensification of the modern—raises more objections than its usage has been able to resolve.[80] With various definitions dating back to the Reformation, the French Revolution, or the age of capital and industry, modernity has no reliable birth certificate either. In France, it can refer equally to the break with the ancients during the renaissance (the *querelle des Anciens et des Modernes* that pit Boileau against Perrault), the political and social upheavals of the 1789 revolution (later consecrated by Benjamin Constant's distinction between the freedom of the ancients and the moderns), or Baudelaire's transcription of modernity as a "transient, fleeting, contingent" impulse split between art and the eternal. The failure of the category to prevail may be one of its most distinctive traits. "The belief in the heroic negativity of the new and the newest," writes Hamacher, "has become so much part of the theoretical and literary-theoretical investigation in modernity that no one who repeats this axiom, no one who says that the foundation of modernity is failure, could ever risk failing."[81] In other words, when it comes to modernism and modernity, failure is the best bet: *qui perd gagne*.

Naturally, there are exceptions to the observation that modernism is an absent term in the French context. Valéry noted that any conventional periodization like "symbolism" may have been largely a retrospective projection.[82] Yet he used the term "modernism" to distinguish the zeitgeist in 1914 from the interwar period:

> Europe in 1914 had perhaps reached the *limit of modernism* in this sense. Every mind of any scope was a crossroads for all shades of opinion; every thinker was an international exposition of thought [...]. In a book of that era [...] we should have no trouble in finding: the influence of the Russian ballet, a touch of Pascal's gloom, numerous impressions of the Goncourt type, something of Nietzsche, something of Rimbaud, certain effects due to a familiarity with painters, and sometimes the

tone of a scientific publication [. . .] the whole flavored with an indefinably British quality difficult to assess![83]

Valéry's use of the word modernism responds to its classicist traces, which have become increasingly difficult to preserve from the destructive forces of modernity.[84] Albert Thibaudet, the leading critic of the *Nouvelle Revue Française,* too refers to modernism extending its reach to artistic form and criticism:

> Since Baudelaire and the Goncourt Brothers, there has existed in French literature a "modernism" which falls into none of the usual categories of classicism, romanticism, realism, or symbolism but which cuts across them all, combining sometimes the last three [. . .] opposing them at other times. Whatever the artistic form taken by such modernism, it bases such form on the avowed and potential principle that what is modern—the most modern possible and the most different from the traditional—should be sought and esteemed as a most desirable artistic aim, and that this modern, like the traditional which it opposes, is capable of formulating an ensemble, a system, a theoretic order, a complete and fertile formula for art. Thus, it affirms itself not only by its works but by its criticism based on those works.[85]

For Thibaudet writers from Baudelaire onward drew the hatred of professional criticism "because of the fact that they are not only moderns but theorists of modernism." Yet he adds that in 1920 the "passionate interest of such discussions" has past, leaving only minor skirmishes in its wake. What is noteworthy for the present discussion is the way in which "modernism" remains a speculative category that must be perennially reconstructed against more traditional periods and movements in the French context.

Recent studies and monographs speculate that if French modernism existed it was in 1913.[86] Excepting for a moment any reference to the *avant-garde,* who could count as a French modernist seen through the blurred lens of hindsight over a century later? Baudelaire, Rimbaud, Lautréamont, Mallarmé, Dujardin, Huysmans, Proust, Valéry, Jarry, Apollinaire, Gide, Segalen, Cendrars, Saint-John Perse, Larbaud, Cocteau, Colette, Cahun, Artaud, or Céline come to mind. Yet such a brief roster rings like a false totality to those attuned to the minor schisms of French literary history.[87] "The danger in attempting to open trade lines in both directions," that is, between modernity and modernism, "is, of course, that the institutional force behind modernism as something akin to a literary brand is so great that it risks swallowing the *NRF* as a whole," as

Anna-Louise Milne suggests. The specificity of the aesthetic and political positions and thick contexts of the journal equally suggest the facile nature of simply claiming it as a "modernist review."[88]

Proust, in this sense, is closer to the "classicisme moderne" of the *NRF*, and Valéry a post-Mallarméan symbolist, while Bergson represents the culmination of a Spiritualist and a Vitalist tradition of which he becomes the most famous exponent and critic. Yet one would be hard pressed to deny that Proust is a canonical modernist in the Anglophone world, just as Valéry (studied by critics from Edmund Wilson and T. S. Eliot to Wallace Stevens and Geoffrey Hartman) remains a key figure for modernist poetics.[89] More recently, Todd Cronan sets up Bergson and Valéry as key figures in a dialogue between the visual arts and affective critiques of representation.[90] Similarly, Hannah Freed-Thall brings together the figures in her innovative study of spoiled aesthetic categories from Proust to Ponge and Sarraute under the heading of French modernism, which is "particularly concerned with relations among art, social distinction, and everyday life."[91] It is worth recalling how readily Proust seems to find his place in comparative studies of modernist fiction, set somewhere between James, Woolf, Joyce, Mann, Musil, and Kafka. It is perhaps this critical, ironic tenor of modernism in English that its French cognate seems to lack. E. M. Forster—who does not really qualify as a modernist despite belonging to the Bloomsbury set—interrupts his discussion of the novel in English to declare that "no novelist anywhere has analyzed the modern consciousness as successfully as Marcel Proust."[92] This "success" we later learn, has to do with his "tricks with his clock," the "ravishing of the reader's memory," "flat" and "round characters," but above all the "internal stitching" of the novel which is bound together by its "waxing and waning" rhythms. The way Proust repeatedly fuses fiction and commentary, poetry and prose, focalization and montage make him the exemplary modern writer for Bloomsbury and beyond.

To be sure, the period Anglophone criticism calls "modernism" is deeply impressed by literature in French from Flaubert to Beckett, while the history of post-revolutionary France becomes an allegory of modernity, with its cycles of revolt and repression, and its antinomies of universality and particularity, classicism and romanticism, positivism and cultural imaginaries, rhetoric and terror. Compagnon suggests modernity is riven by five paradoxes: the superstition of the new, the religion of the future, a theoretical mania, the appeal to mass culture, and the passion for renunciation.[93] The *arrière-garde*, he adds, refuses the metaphysics of progress that underlies modernity. Turning from an avant-garde critique of language to philology, from Bergson's suspicion that the mind is oppressed by language to his conviction that only poetry could express *durée*, the *anti-modernes* incarnate anxiety toward modernity when it becomes institutional.

"French modernism" might be comprised by formal experimentation, new subject matter inspired by modernity, self-referentiality, and resistance to modernization.[94] Yet isn't such "French modernism," like "French theory," an auxiliary invention of translators and critics writing in other languages? The complicity of the two terms is suggested further by the anachronistic predilection of theorists writing in the postwar period for a prewar and interwar literary corpus. The absence of modernism as a heuristic category in French literary criticism, until quite recently, has meant that critics need to bring other contexts to bear on the period stretching from the Commune and the Belle Epoque to World War I, the Front Populaire, and Vichy.[95] The necessity of delimiting a context to read a corpus of writing that is not presided over by a concept like modernism means that criticism of French literature is perennially looking for alternative descriptive categories and periodizations, from the *style classique moderne* prized by Jacques Rivière's *Nouvelle Revue Française* to the *anti-modernes* and *arrière-garde* theorized by Compagnon and William Marx respectively.

Rather than rushing to find correspondences that would make certain writers in French look like modernists the present study leaves this literary space open. Worth tracking instead are the senses in which different thinkers used the word intelligence, and why they kept referring to such a mercurial category, at once overdetermined and underspecified, when other terms promised greater clarity and stability. It is tempting to conclude that the category of "intelligence" may be more pertinent than modernism for understanding the literary and critical experimentations of the period. Yet raising "intelligence" to a category that could rival, if not potentially supplant, modernism in its current classificatory and descriptive capacity is an undertaking beyond the limits of this study.

In a brief essay on Leopardi, Benjamin quotes Sainte-Beuve's distinction between the sword and the mirror, with which this introduction began. Putting a characteristic twist on the original citation, Benjamin recalls both arm and mirror, adding a piece of armor—a cuirass—to the pair:

> In a famous passage, Sainte-Beuve opposes *l'intelligence-miroir* and *l'intelligence-glaive*. This young man lost his sword at times. But he

stood fast, cased in armor. In this armor, the world is reflected, inverted and golden: *intelligence-cuirasse*.[96]

Noting that the poet tends to drop his sword, or his ability to make cutting distinctions, the critic disarms the poet of his *intelligence-glaive*. Yet, one remains dazzled by the overturned image of the world reflected in his armor—an image that demands to be read. Rather than limiting ideas of intelligence to reflection and invention, as Sainte-Beuve does, Benjamin gilds and inverts them. Neither merely acting nor reflecting, *intelligence-cuirasse* troubles the distinction by adding a defensive aspect to it. Gazing at the poet's armor the fascinated viewer sees an inverted world anew.

This introduction offered a series of interlocking frames for the main argument of my project: literature during the period "disarms" intelligence as a near synonym for a normalizing, logical form of thinking, and explores other versions of intelligence that introduce elements of uncertainty, possibility, and potentiality. In the pages that follow, readers will encounter ways of gathering, measuring, abdicating, testing, mobilizing, and situating intelligence. Chapter 1 studies the gradual emergence and consolidation of the term, subsequently contested by Bergson. Chapter 2 reads Proust's novel and criticism for the ways it both rejects and mobilizes the category. Chapter 3 turns to Valéry to analyze his abandonment of the literary to test its preconditions and pretensions to intelligence. While Proust seems to renounce intelligence, he cannot quite conceive of the literary without its involvement; the opposite holds in Valéry, for even as he tests it, his analytic bent keeps returning to lyrical, counterrealist, and quasi-political forms. Chapters 4 and 5 turn respectively to the *Nouvelle Revue Française* and Benjamin's essays to show how a neutral and political understanding of the French intelligentsia emerged during this period.

At this point, it is worth noting some issues this book does not address at any length. Readers may wonder how the lines of influence from figures like Taine and Bergson, who were in dialogue with considerably different sets of interlocutors, connect to Proust, Valéry, and the *NRF* in terms of empirical influence. Or else how the nineteenth-century novel, which was repeatedly claimed as a genre to rival and outdo other forms of institutionalized kinds of knowledge (science included), related to its twentieth-century iterations within and beyond France. Futhermore, what were the consequences in public discouse, so to speak, of the ways Proust and Valéry took up the discussions of intelligence, beyond those to be found in the reading of their work? As these lines of inquiry imply, intelligence as a topic, a quality of writing, and potential of literature and criticism raises more questions than any one study can hope to answer.

The fractured paths the present volume takes do not provide a definitive grasp on intelligence, which is less a concept in any fulsome philosophical sense than an enduring contest over the ways in which the fluctuating term is used. The accounts offered below are fractured and winding by design, mirroring the metamorphic quality of intelligence that drifts from psychology into literary–critical fields onward to the posthuman and artificial architectures, discussed briefly in the epilogue. Such a frame, this book wagers, could stand between the sword and the mirror, allowing for a less hostile, exclusive, and specular kind of intelligence.

CHAPTER ONE

Gathering Intelligence

FROM TAINE TO BERGSON

UPON CONSULTING THE definition of intelligence in the 1694 *Dictionnaire de l'Académie françoise*, one finds seven meanings ascribed to the term, all of which relate to human capacities of knowing. The equation of intelligence with "the faculty of understanding" or the "act of or capacity for understanding" had been well established since around 1500. The modalities of knowledge then ascribed to intelligence, as mentioned earlier, were basically two-fold: knowledge as "potential or ability" and knowing as "simple possession of knowledge."[1] In the early modern period, the faculty went from characterizing a universal capacity of understanding to a distinctive flair for invention, which made it a possible source for literary and philosophical innovation. Over time, however, intelligence stopped referring to knowledge, and became limited to a varying capacity to know. "By 1835," notes John Carson "'*intelligence*' had virtually ceased to refer simply to knowledge, instead suggesting either an absolute ability shared by all, or something relative that individuals could manifest in different measures."[2] Needless to say, this shift was not merely a lexical one, but a response to a wider transformation of the grounds of philosophical, scientific, and critical inquiry.[3] This chapter revisits the shifting meanings of intelligence briefly invoked in the introduction to offer an overview of the term during the latter part of the nineteenth century and the early twentieth century in philosophy and psychology. It first presents the scientific development of intelligence as a faculty that can be measured and whose quantification has broad political implications. The sections below then analyze the trajectory from Taine's understanding of intelligence as a "corrective force" that prevents the mind from erring to Bergson's creative force that opens the mind to speculation, with excursions in between to describe attempts to measure intelligence by Binet and Ribot. My goal is not only to describe the context in which intelligence became a problem for French thought, but also to frame the ensuing discussion of its literary–critical role.

The Second Empire, following the thwarted 1848 revolution, witnessed a thoroughgoing rejection of romanticism, and its cult of genius, in favor of empirical and critical inquiry: "The reaction of intelligence [or the intelligentsia] against genius [...] obliged a general critique against its predecessors, it seems that it placed all currents of production under the authority of criticism."[4] While philosophy sought to consecrate itself at the head of the of fields of knowledge in universities, it found itself mired in a conflict of the faculties. The clerical right criticized philosophers for their secularism, pantheistic tendencies, and reliance on the Germanic tradition, while those trained in scientific and medical disciplines criticized them for "political opportunism and theoretical incoherence."[5]

The institution of university philosophy was first incarnated by Victor Cousin and his doctrine of eclecticism, which fused German Idealism with Scottish Common-Sense Realism. Claude Bernard's experimental method and August Comte's positivism radically challenged this metaphysical focus with an appeal to laboratory observation of facts and positive laws. The École polytechnique and the École normale supérieure soon saw their graduates—Cournot, Renouvier, and Taine—gain popular intellectual if not institutional influence over the younger generations, one which often outstripped the professors of the Sorbonne. Félix Ravaisson and Charles Renouvier's "Spiritualism" remained rooted in the Cartesian "assertion of the epistemic and metaphysical primacy of thought," but without its mind–body dualism.[6] Spiritualist thinkers, led by Ravaisson, renewed the anti-empiricist legacy of François Maine de Biran. In the absence of translations of Hegel till the 1920s, neo-Kantian philosophy made inroads through the Idealism of Jules Lachelier and Émile Boutroux, while French philosophy of science experienced a golden age from Henri Poincaré and Pierre Duhem to Émile Meyerson and Léon Brunschvicg.

In late nineteenth-century France, the two principle avatars of intelligence were Taine and Renan. Renan, a philologist and orientalist by training prized for his prose style, was most well known for his best-selling and widely translated *La Vie de Jésus* (1863). His studies in Semitic history and the origins of Christianity were aligned with Taine's inquiries into the origins of contemporary France and the history of English literature, to the extent that their two names comprised a single, indivisible tetrasyllabic "Taine-et-Renan."[7] In Renan's description of dominant scientific culture, the "modern spirit" (*esprit moderne*) was essentially one of "reflective intelligence" (*intelligence réfléchie*).[8] Taine furnished the notion of intelligence with a scientific and social basis for the first time. Thibaudet, even as he deemed Taine's book *De l'intelligence* to be outdated in 1923, declared that Taine transformed "the world of things into the world of signs [...]. Taine contributed the philosophical files to the dossier. Renan the literary, social, and political ones."[9] After Taine and Renan, "intelligence" became the object of a complex semiotic appropriation as a literary and critical force.

A key shift occurred through Taine's work, which empirically analyzed intelligence as the mental capacity to register and interpret signs. His empiricism questions the existence of the faculty, replacing it with what Hilary Nias dubs an "artificial subject," a self produced by involuntary neural reactions and semiotic substitutions that stands at the limit of madness.[10] In this view, intelligence is only a guardrail that keeps the mind from falling into perpetual error. Taine separates the study of intelligence into the study of signs, as well as bodily, mental, and general knowledge, a division meant to reveal the "potentialities" of intelligence: sensation, memory, imagination, and language.

Taine's refusal to discern a deeper faculty underlying cognitive instances named by the umbrella term "intelligence" was mirrored by scientists who sought to measure its variation empirically. As mentioned in the introduction, Binet and Simon were charged with creating metrics inspired by psychophysics to measure the intelligence of schoolchildren. At the same time, Charcot, Janet, Ribot, and others fought over the possibility of unconscious or semi-conscious states of cerebration that, instead of reason, supposedly held the key to both scientific and literary creativity. In the age of novel hypotheses about reflex action, the double brain, cerebral topography, hallucination, and hypnotism, any claims made about the nature of mind were invariably the object of intense and often unrelenting debate.[11] The fervent interest in the terminology of the new psychology and philosophy of mind constituted a departure in a distinctly French literary and philosophic culture that still prized the capacity to express ideas in "everyday language" (*la langue de tout le monde*).[12]

Bergson, while deeply versed in scientific advances, was widely considered the philosopher who challenged the dominant meaning of intelligence and critiqued the larger culture of scientism. He reversed many of Taine's premises about the neurophysiology of the mind, while also arguing that human intelligence, a pragmatic drive to transform matter, had evolved beyond its scope. Instead of allowing one to adapt, it became a desiccating force that created an artificial gulf between consciousness and action by substituting "spatialized representations, identity, quantity, and discontinuity for the immediate data of consciousness revealed in intuition—duration, pure time, and memory."[13] To rehabilitate intelligence, one would have to locate its shared source within intuition, rather than separating the two aspects of mind in a gulf of abstraction.[14] The only way to save intelligence, Bergson insisted, was to think in a way that placed limits on its power, allowing embodied intuition to correct its usurpation over life. Focusing on intelligence—rather than the usual Bergsonian watchwords of intuition, *durée*, or *élan vital*—shows how the early view of intelligence set out in *Matière et mémoire* develops into a subtler, and finally more intriguing picture of the relation between intelligence and intuition in *L'Évolution créatrice*. Rather than placing them in binary oppositions, Bergson presents them as aspects of the same faculty of human understanding, which evolves over time from a common, now forgotten, origin. These two paths—the artificial and the vital—map out the looming cognitive and philosophic terrain for thinking about intelligence and its influence on modern French literature.

Examining the historical semantics of "intelligence" allows us to track its metamorphosis in meaning, from a universal ability to know, through a particular capacity that individuals possess with varying degrees of intensity, to a shared evolutionary force that can be honed through practice. Rather than imposing a typology on intelligence, this chapter explores its signifying structure, whose meaning and value, as Taine insists, is always "a function of the cultural system in which it occurs."[15] Taine's reduction of mind to machine, and the related restriction of the self, can be read as a move away from the use of figural language to describe thought toward the measured observation of nervous, cognitive, and semiotic functions. For Bergson, on the other hand, intelligence is an analytic, essentially practical approach to the world, which precludes access to qualitative forms of life, unless it yields to creative intuition.

Measuring Intelligence

Throughout the nineteenth century "*l'intelligence* comes to represent the very spirit of the scientific mind, methodically gathering all kinds of information to bear upon its investigations of the objective world."[16] The sciences at the intersection of psychology and the emergent social sciences appropriated intelligence as a topic, whose social and political applications soon became clear. Taine's refusal to see a deeper faculty behind the cognitive instances named by "intelligence" was mirrored by those who sought to measure its variation empirically. In 1860, Gustav Fechner published his groundbreaking treatise on psychometrics. Fechner sought to demonstrate, *pace* Kant, that the human mind was just as open to measurement as the material world. The mathematical notation underlying this idea declared, "equal relative increments of stimuli are proportional to equal increments of sensation."[17] If one could measure the stimuli, Fechner concluded, one could also eventually provide a quantifiable model of mental states and their intensities. Taine took Fechner's study as the sign that the "pincers" of science had finally captured their most resistant subject: man.

> Science at last approaches man; it has gone beyond the visible and palpable world of stars, stones, and plants to which it had been contemptuously confined—it now challenges the soul, armed with exact and piercing instruments whose precision and whose reach have proved themselves over three hundred years of experience.[18]

Using these "exact and piercing instruments," *De l'intelligence* sought to offer both a "psychology of intelligence and a theory of knowledge."[19]

Taine's views on psychological heredity were developed by Théodule-Armand Ribot. He accredited Taine's treatise with having provided an experimental version of *Erkenntnistheorie*, its more abstract German predecessor. Ribot "investigated the pathology of mental attributes or conditions—attention, will, personality—since these pathologies were the perceived equivalents of nature's experiments on humanity."[20] His studies expounded two central claims about psychic life: "Psychic individuality is merely the subjective expression of the organism," and "the self [*le moi*] only exists at the condition of varying continuously."[21]

Influenced to varying extents by Broca, Lamarck, Spencer, and Galton, Ribot was the proponent of theories of unalterable cultural and racial difference, as well as inherited dispositions as illustrated by the transmission of nervous and mental diseases.[22] His early positions shifted from an anthropologically deterministic, physicalist stance on human nature to one that acknowledged environmental factors such as the ones studied by Durkheim, some of whose work he published in the *Revue philosophique*. "While Ribot emerged from the shadow of physical anthropology, he retained assumptions of cultural anthropology. The inequalities of intelligence and character were due to a 'primitive' stage of cultural development, if not to racial aptitudes."[23] Yet his 1900 *Essai sur l'imagination créatrice*, writes the literary historian Michael Finn, was "almost Proustian in its relegation of the rational intelligence to an organizational rather than an investigative role in the creative process."[24] With his heady mix of determinism, attunement to environmental and social factors, as well as the dynamic role of the unconscious, Ribot reflects a series of wider transformations in the theory and practice of the human sciences.

His range was matched by Binet, who not only invented the first IQ test, but authored a series of studies on suggestibility, alterations of the personality, double consciousness, animal magnetism, chess, and child psychology which "spared no effort to investigate nearly every physical, anatomical, and physiological correlation to intelligence—from head measurement to physiognomy to handwriting—even though he never studied race and did not commit himself to hereditarian interpretation."[25] He was also the first to use the term "fetishism" to describe sexual proclivities and "perversions," and wrote popular psychological thrillers for the stage, whose performances he would attend in disguise to observe audience reactions.[26] As mentioned above, the French Ministry of Public Instruction chose Binet to devise a test capable of identifying any student who "because of the state of his intelligence was unable to profit, in a normal manner, from the instruction given in ordinary school."[27] Compulsory public education in France made such criteria of identification necessary for teachers to be able to differentiate among the growing ranks of new students between those who had lacked proper instruction and those who had developmental difficulties.[28] One of Binet's notable definitions of "intelligence" brackets sensibility, emotion and will, to call it the "faculty of knowledge, which is directed toward the outside world, and which labors to reconstruct it as a whole, from the small fragments given to us."[29]

In previous studies, Binet had come to express increasing skepticism toward the connections made by Paul Broca and other craniometrists tying intellectual superiority to cerebral size.[30] He turned away from the associationism he defended in his early work, *La psychologie du raisonnement*, to question the relations of thought and images through a method of "controlled introspection," which led to the hypothesis of image-less thinking. Thus, the 1903 *Étude expérimentale de l'intelligence* posits that "relations, judgments, attitudes etc." cannot be reduced to imagery. Binet's view of thought, as Piaget notes, was largely unconscious: "As for knowing what these acts of thought [. . .] consist of, Binet reserves his opinion, confining himself to noting the relationship between intellectual and motor 'attitudes,' and concludes that, from the point of view of introspection alone, 'thought is an unconscious activity of the mind.'"[31]

| DIFFÉRENTES ÉPREUVES | ÉCOLES DE M. L. ET DE M. M. SITUÉES A PARIS RUE DES RÉCOLLETS ET RUE SAMBRE-ET-MEUSE |||||
| | AGE DES ENFANTS |||||
	7 ans.	8 ans.	9 ans.	10 ans.	12 ans.
6 ans.					
Distinguer matin et soir....	10	10			
Définir par l'usage......	10	10			
Copier losange.........	9	10			
Compter 13 sous simples...	9	10			
Comparer 2 figures esthétiques.	9	10			
7 ans.					
Main droite, oreille gauche..	8	10			
Décrire une gravure......	7	10			
Exécuter 3 commissions....	7	10			
Compter 9 sous simples et doubles.............	4	9	10		
Nommer 4 couleurs.......	4	9	10		
8 ans.					
Comparer 2 objets de souvenir.	4	8	10	10	
Compter de 20 à 0.......	3	9	10	9	
Indiquer lacunes figures...	3	8			
Donner date du jour.....	4	8	10	10	
Répéter 5 chiffres........	2	5			
9 ans.					
Rendre sur 20 sous.......		4	10	9	10
Définir mieux que par l'usage.		3	6	7	7
Pièces de monnaie.......		2	10	9	9
Mois................		2	8	10	9
Comprendre des questions faciles...............		2	9	9	10
10 ans.					
Ordonner poids.........		1	5	6	
Copier dessin mémoire....		2	4	5	
Critiquer phrases absurdes..			4	5	8
Loger 3 mots en 2 phrases..			3	5	8
Comprendre questions difficiles..............			3	3	7
12 ans.					
Suggestion de lignes.....			2	3	
3 mots en 1 phrase......			2	4	8
60 mots en 3 minutes.....			2	4	5
Définitions abstraites.....			1	2	4
Phrases désarticulées.....			1	4	7

FIGURE 1. Results of a Binet-Simon Test (1911).

The empirical tests devised with Théodore Simon at the *Société Libre pour l'Étude Psychologique de L'Enfant* purposely separated bodily measurements and learned skills from intelligence. "It is the intelligence alone that we seek to measure, by disregarding, in so far as possible, the degree of instruction the child possesses [. . .]. We give him nothing to read, nothing to write, and submit him to no test which he might succeed by means of rote learning."[32] Instead, the Binet-Simon test focused on the practical, adaptive skills of the children being tested. The various tasks students were asked to perform—from pointing to parts of their body, copying a diagram, and telling time to defining words and finding rhymes—were in turn classified according to age groups. An age-based classification allowed Binet to focus neither on the genetic heredity of a child, nor their potential academic future, but an ability to carry out a series of actions relative to coevals at present. How a child performed relative to those with the same chronological age determined whether they were dubbed "advanced," "normal," or "retarded," producing a provisional "mental age." In 1912, Ludwig Wilhelm (later William) Stern, a German psychologist who happened to be Walter Benjamin's uncle, argued that "mental age should be divided by chronological age, not subtracted from it, and the intelligence *quotient* or IQ was born."[33]

Translations of the test were soon taken up by Americans from Henry H. Goddard, Lewis Terman and Charles Spearman, who followed in the footsteps of English social eugenicists like Francis Galton to make adapted versions of the test a widely applied tool to control and classify members of society from workers and schoolchildren to immigrants and the mentally unfit. Galton's notion of "hereditary genius" had sought to justify the concentration of political and cultural power in a few families in Victorian Britain, while his reconstruction of "fossil IQs" ludicrously ranked historical figures based on accounts of their childhood precociousness. Racist uses of intelligence testing can be placed in a continuum from phrenology, Galton's eugenics, atavism, and craniometry to Herrnstein and Murray's *The Bell Curve*. From the standpoint of evolutionary biology, the inaccuracy of socially conservative arguments, which attribute differences in performance on IQ testing to biologically innate rather than environmental factors, is based on a set of false assumptions. Stephen Jay Gould lists them as the view that there can be a single meaningful number given to intelligence; that it can be used to rank people in a single order, which is correlated with social attributes (income, criminal history); that it is highly heritable, and that it is effectively unchangeable. If any one of these premises is falsifed, then the reified, exclusionary theory of intelligence falls apart.

Binet had already objected to such views in his 1901 study, *Les idées modernes sur les enfants*: "Some recent philosophers seem to have given their moral approval to these deplorable verdicts that affirm that the intelligence of an individual is a fixed quantity, a quantity that cannot be augmented. We must protest and react against this brutal pessimism; we will try to demonstrate that it is founded on nothing."[34] Binet's "common sense" theory of intelligence was informed less by philosophical or experimental claims of this period than by his everyday observation of his two young daughters. His definition of intelligence testifies to an emphasis on practicality over abstract reasoning:

> It seems to us that in intelligence there is a fundamental faculty, the alteration or the lack of which, is of the utmost importance for practical life. This faculty is judgment, otherwise called good sense [*le sens commun*], practical sense, initiative, the faculty of adapting one's self to circumstances. A person may be a moron or an imbecile if he is lacking in judgment; but with good judgment he can never be either. Indeed, the rest of the intellectual faculties seem of little importance in comparison with judgment.[35]

Binet clearly emphasizes judgment, along with common sense, initiative, auto-critique, and the ability to adapt to circumstance, over anything resembling specialized intellectual prowess or cultural knowledge. He was especially wary of the discriminatory uses that could be made of his tests, insisting that any such scale "does not permit the measure of the intelligence, because intellectual qualities are not superposable, and therefore cannot be measured as linear surfaces are measured." To believe otherwise would be to fall prey to the error of the expert graphologists who confirmed that Dreyfus was a traitor:

> It is really too easy to discover signs of backwardness in an individual when one is forewarned. This would be to operate as the graphologists did who, when Dreyfus was believed to be guilty, discovered in his handwriting signs of a traitor or a spy.[36]

As Binet's analogy suggests, any discussion of intelligence, however innocuous it seems, is never far from becoming a politically charged conflict over the interpretation of signs and attributions of agency. Binet's contributions increasingly placed emphasis on practical measures to counter the material disadvantages faced by the indigent. Like Ribot, he cast doubt on the "stages of civilization" view that equated the "primitive" mind to the "sensory intelligence" of childhood.[37] Why deprecate others, he asked, "when the novel and above all poetry" presuppose the writer has "the soul of a child?"[38] Literary imagination, his rhetorical question implies, not only remains closer to the sensorium of childhood, but also escapes the strictures of testing.

While Binet moved beyond craniometry, his test carried traces of its statistical and instrumental approach to intelligence.[39] The translation and widespread misapplication of a written version of the test in the United States, spearheaded by eugenicists like Goddard, would have confirmed his worst suspicions. The IQ became a marker of "inborn" intelligence, an entity quite unlike anything imagined by its French originators.[40] Binet, who had brought intelligence to bear on the fetish, had effectively invented a fetish for intelligence. While scientists had claimed that intelligence could be measured, it became evident how the influence of social milieus disrupted the scientificity of their entreprises. Notions of intelligence that refused to recognize the exclusionary effects of class, race, and gender were merely tools of political repression. For those who recognized these factors, lingering doubts emerged that there were dimensions of intelligence which escaped the measurement of tests.

From Equality to Distinction

Long before the fin-de-siècle scientific discourse of intelligence emerged as a measurable faculty with significant political applications, the notion of intelligence was widely used yet marked by ambivalence. Intelligence was torn in two opposite directions: one binding it to equality, the other to distinction. Either it appeared to be a universally shared faculty of human understanding, or a particular quality of understanding which belonged to a select few who applied it methodically, thus avoiding the errors that came from an uncritical reliance on sense experience or abstract reasoning. Unsurprisingly, Descartes is the early modern source of this distinction since he presents intelligence both as the shared capacity to think (*bon sens*), and a kind of distinction that arises from a methodical approach applied to thinking (*la méthode*). First, the faculty is treated as a shared ability to think; and second, the philosopher reacts to this axiomatic equality.[41] Cartesianism seems torn between a democratic idea that the particularity of intelligence does not matter, since anyone can transcend limits through the application of a universal method, on the one hand, and his suggestion that not everyone is equally suited to philosophy, on the other.

Intelligence continued to hold sway in the post-Cartesian psychological and spiritualist traditions of French philosophy.[42] Following the broader question about the origin of knowledge (how it is possible to know anything), ways of thinking and writing about intelligence were being transformed from its early modern origins. The translation of Locke's *Essay* delivered a considerable blow to the possibility of innate ideas entertained by Descartes. Following Locke, Condillac argued that there were no innate ideas, and that words and speech constituted the sole origin of mental life and knowledge. In his *Dictionnaire des synonymes*, Condillac defines intelligence as follows: "From *inter* and *legere*, reading between. The faculty to see, to grasp things as they really are. Cf. *Bon sens*. Hence, the name for the substance that sees. God is the supreme intelligence."[43] Intelligence is likened to insight, the ability to "see things as they are," and common sense, grounded by divine knowledge. In the *Essai sur l'origine des connaissances humaines*, Condillac overturns many of Descartes's arguments concerning innate ideas, invoking his own reading of the British empiricists. In a significant section of the *Essai*, defining various modes of understanding, Condillac distinguishes between *bon sens* and *intelligence*, in terms of degree:

> Good sense and intelligence consist in conceiving and imagining, and they differ only in regard to their objects. For example, to understand that two and two make four or to understand an entire course of mathematics is equally to conceive, but with the difference that one is called good sense and the other intelligence.[44]

If the difference between *bon sens* and intelligence can be ascribed to the "nature of the object being dealt with," then their uses can also be distinguished in terms of the novelty they allow one to perceive and imagine. "Thus it seems that the object of good sense is found in what is easy and ordinary, while it pertains to intelligence to conceive or imagine things that are more composite or new."[45] Intelligence enables creative elaboration. By limiting intelligence to the complex and the particular rather than the common and universal, Condillac breaks with the Cartesian legacy.

Condillac's claim that ideas are primarily linguistic suggests that innovative or complex ideas require the use of intelligence rather than common sense. Literary language, which seeks to transform our relation to signs and language itself, would thus be a critical site for intellectual breakthroughs. This model of literary invention would take distance from pre-individual or unconscious models of composition gathered under the antique tradition of genius or inspiration.

By the end of the nineteenth century, the ambivalence of intelligence yielded to another idea: that it destabilizes the very coherence of self. Influenced by Condillac, Taine develops a theory of the sign that ties the possibility of perception to the apprehension of the smallest stimuli. The subject that emerged from such perceptive practices was constantly threatened by hallucination, yet also laid open to unprecedented possibilities of self-understanding. It seemed likely that the true self was an unconscious one.

True Hallucination

Thus far, I have invoked Taine's work as part of the scientific approach to intelligence. Yet much of the originality of his conception relies on a "hallucinating" self, a notion that had great influence on literary figures. Taine's view of intelligence radically limited the purview of mind while simultaneously making it the ultimate theater of human endeavor. No fewer than seventeen editions of *De l'intelligence* appeared between 1870 and 1933. Experimental scientists like Binet and Ribot may not have invented the intelligence test without Taine's prior speculative contributions. Bergson's recalibration of intuition relative to intelligence also reveals a strategic dimension when seen as an attempt to overturn Taine's influential project. For Taine, intelligence does not possess the perceptive, critical, or creative role it is habitually accorded. Rather it is a corrective, at times repressive, force needed to steer perception away from a perpetual risk of hallucination and error.

After the decline of positivism, Taine became a leading figure in French philosophical circles.[46] He quickly distanced himself from the official thinkers of the day, criticizing Adolphe Garnier, François-Pierre Maine de Biran, and especially Cousin for their eclecticism.[47] Admired by contemporaries from Nietzsche to Mill, Taine's unorthodox career eventually led to his election to the Académie française in 1878. His larger *zoologie de l'esprit humain*—spanning aesthetics, criticism, as well as cultural and social history—adapted the methods of natural sciences to aesthetics without using explicitly metaphysical foundations.[48] His program for modern aesthetics was to define the nature of each art historically rather than dogmatically, that is, not by imposing precepts but by discerning "laws."[49] The triad he employed to make literary history scientific—*race, milieu, moment*—purported to be a systematic consideration of the hereditary, national, sociological, and historical conditions in which a work was written. This method culminated in his *Histoire de la littérature anglaise*. Each work could indeed be situated in the era from which it emerged, which Taine, in a Hegelian turn of phrase, called its "general state of Spirit (or Mind)."[50] As the critic increasingly understood the political upheavals of the age through the movement of spirit and natural law he came to eschew dissident political views and turned inward to explain the workings of mind.[51] "We are banned from political life," he declared, "the only way is pure science or pure literature."[52]

Taine saw his work as part of a tradition established by Étienne Bonnot de Condillac, Antoine Destutt de Tracy, Hermann von Helmholtz, Herbert Spencer, John Stuart Mill, and Alexander Bain.[53] He professed that his book contained the root of all of his historical and moral ideas. His epistemology offers a restricted theory of the subject, presenting knowledge as a sequence of "events" inexplicable in terms of *esprit*. However, it casts doubt upon the existence of intelligence, suggesting that the mind is constantly at the threshold of madness, and intelligence is limited to restricting associative chains of images. Mind only stumbles upon truth in error: "Thus our mind hits the mark, though its aim is bad."[54] Taine places error in lieu of method. His eccentric system—inspired by evolution, anatomy, physiology, the second law of thermodynamics, literary criticism, and narrative fiction—depicts intelligence as a drive to conform to one's surroundings, one whose insights are at best partial and random, at worst blindly destructive.

The Tainian subject receives impressions via sensations, which form images in the mind. These images become phantom sensations, less fleeting once memorized. While hallucination can overpower reflection, Taine concluded from reading Alfred Maury's *Sleep and Dreams* (*Le sommeil et les rêves*) that ordinary reflection is perhaps nothing other than the mind holding delirium at bay.[55] Taine's materialism elevates the matter of mind over spirit, while casting doubt on the reliability of sense experience. He makes the startling claim that all mental operations are akin to nascent hallucination, based on the premise that consciousness is inherently exposed to perceptual error: "Thus, external perception is an internal dream which proves to be in harmony with external things; and instead of calling hallucination a false external perception, we must call external perception *a true hallucination*."[56] Without naming Taine, Bergson later contests his view with a common-sense account of perception which contends that memory renders such experiences indistinguishable from perception, obviating the need to cofound perception with hallucination.[57]

Reducing perception to "harmony" with the outside world implies that mental representations are verifiable images that correspond to real objects. Instead of bracketing hallucinatory experiences as exceptions, Taine uses them to postulate the workings of regular cognitive processes, likening them to a broken clock that can reveal the mechanism of one in working order: "In general, any singular state of intelligence must be the subject of a monograph; because one must see the uncalibrated clock to distinguish the counterweights and the cogs that we notice when the clock is working properly."[58] As he wrote elsewhere, human beings are basically mad, their bodies sickly by nature, and any glint of sanity or health is a happy accident.[59] Taine concludes that normalcy is a state of equilibrium won by warring against delusions, dreams, and false memories. Instead of being critical or creative, intelligence plays a corrective, at times repressive role: it steers perception away from a perpetual risk of erroneous images.[60] Intelligence emerges when weak ideas and stray perceptions are crushed by the evolutionary need to adapt. As such, its role in the policing of the self is unmatched.

As Bertrand Marquer rightly argues, Taine's insistence on the pathological aspect of intelligence to define its normal function is reflected in the "clinical fantastic" forged by writers like Edgar Allan Poe and Guy de Maupassant, a genre centered on the "halluciné raisonnant" capable of lucidly narrating delirium.[61] Prone to the shock of original sensations, writers and artists required "prolonged [study] by a psychologist friend," just as Taine chose to study Flaubert.[62] At once subjects and scientists, artists know more about hallucination and perception than the average person. A novelist is "a psychologist who naturally and involuntarily puts psychology at work [. . .]. He loves to represent feelings, to feel their connections, their precedents, their consequences."[63] Literature was henceforth understood as the transcription of the "logic" of beings and events: "As a general rule, therefore, whatever interests us in a real personage, and which we entreat the artist to extract and render, is his outward or inward logic; in other terms, his structure, composition and action."[64] Just as classical painting could reveal the logic of the body, for Taine, the realist novel became the exponent of the logic of relations, not a replica of reality.

De l'intelligence develops Taine's ongoing investigation into involuntary psychology and symbolic language, shifting the study of intelligence from a faculty to a theory of the sign.[65] A sign is defined as that which in present experience "suggests the idea of another possible experience."[66] Thinking occurs through abstract names or nouns (*noms abstraits*) which enable the mind to grasp general ideas and associations that exist prior to and independently of it.[67] Taine's nominalist theory of the sign is suffused with hidden *petites perceptions* that both enable and threaten the subject's agency. These sensations congeal into tendencies that make naming and acting possible, accounting for the "higher operations" of human intelligence.[68] For William James, Taine's semiotic theory names substitution as a "cardinal logical function" for the first time.[69] While the substitution of signs for perceptions and images enables general knowledge, judgment and recollection reduce the influence of illusory images. The substitutive linguistic structure of cognition makes reality intelligible to human understanding. The human mind is a storehouse of images and clichés, for which language furnishes words and names as functional substitutes.[70]

Taine divides his subject into the study of signs and of bodily, mental, and general knowledge. Reduced to its elementary state, knowledge consists in facts governed by laws of contiguity and resemblance. Taine proceeds from simple perceptions into complex ones, memories, and beliefs to account for universal concepts and judgments. The analytic part of his work focuses on elements of knowledge, arguing that signs are always more or less faded images, themselves substitutes for sensations. Thought approaches reality through such images. The synthetic part focuses on the nature of these mental images through laws of iteration, decay, and destruction.[71] This division enables him to track how intelligence constructs complex "moral events" from its elements: language, imagination, memory, and sensation.[72] Fragile and tentative, these elements are connected and made measurable through sensation.

Not only are there no innate ideas, Taine argues, but there is also no innate self to be found in consciousness. The mind is an apparatus to record and reorder sensations:

> There is nothing real in the self save the series of occurrences. Of varying aspect, these are in their nature all alike, and can be reduced to sensation, which [...] reduces to a set of molecular motions.[73]

Taine compares the neurophysiology of consciousness to a dance. The "self" is a large-scale rhythmic illusion produced by a multitude of minute neural events and linguistic signs. The repetition of synaptic connections produces varying units—words, lines, pages—that Taine calls *clichés*.[74] This photographic metaphor explains the persistence of psychic events. In such cases, the cliché has receded to a memory trace, which is revived years later by an accidental sensation, setting off the dance again.[75] Memory is defined as an "absent sensation," which persists after the fact.[76] What Taine describes as involuntary cerebration, a spontaneous resurrection of a supposedly lost image or instant, is akin to what Proust later develops into involuntary memory.[77]

Taine alters the meaning of intelligence by defining knowledge in "mechanical and materialist" terms: "The novelty of my book is to be entirely composed of small facts, significant cases, individual observations, descriptions of psychological functions, atrophied or hypertrophied."[78] The technique of collecting facts and cases allowed him to implicitly criticize the eclectic spiritualist tradition and approach intelligence without the metaphysical arsenal of *substances spirituelles, passions de l'âme, essences, facultés,* or even interiority. Instead, he proposes a *science des faits* that deals only with *connaissances*, links the study of intelligence to physics and physiology, and produces a new image of mind: "A flow and a beam of sensations and impulses, which, seen from another side, are also a flow and a beam of nervous vibrations, this is the mind."[79] Taine presents a general science of observable facts that could demystify the human mind. Thanks to discoveries in psychophysics, he claimed to be able to reconstruct an entire theory of elementary affects, going beyond the limits of the moral world, and reimagining the relations between molecular transformations and thought. Such materialist bluster is aimed at the Cartesian doctrine of faculties, Kantian limits on inquiries into the genesis of intelligence, and Cousin's eclecticism, which considered intelligence to be a quality that stems from an unknowable source.

As we have seen, *De l'intelligence* argues that sense perceptions and internal images are in constant conflict, and that perception is comparable to hallucination. Yet the opposition between image and discourse and between rational and representative functions of mind blurs as Taine's treatise proceeds. Taine's theory of the sign, the name, and the influence of subconscious stimuli suggests that the larger part of oneself lies beyond reach. The conscious self is incomparably smaller than the hidden one. His psychology splits between surface and depth, positing two ideas, two wills, and two agents in everyone, beyond which looms a greater threat of disaggregation.[80] This doubling works on memory and perception, too. Consciousness, in short, becomes the belated recognition that the initial access to reality—whether as name, sign, or memory—has been error, and requires the repression of the illusory impression to restore true perception. Intelligence is this corrective force. "The human mind is then a theater where many different plays are performed at once, on different levels, only one of which is lit up."[81] Intelligence rushes constantly to redirect the lighting to what it momentarily thinks is the correct stage, where the right play is being performed, leaving the rest of the theater in the dark.

Contra Taine

Taine and Renan's rationalism began to decline after the shock of the French defeat in the Franco-Prussian War in 1870. By the 1890s, it had been replaced by a new intellectualism, armed with a Thomist epistemology, whose various currents were incarnated by Charles Maurras, Maurice Barrès, and Charles Péguy.[82] Posterity was not kind to Taine, accusing him of "materialism, positivism, scientism, and pessimism."[83] Valéry exiled Taine—alongside Sainte-Beuve and Ferdinand Brunetière—to a class of "chattering mutes" prone to asking the wrong questions and providing no answers.[84] Such dismissals suggest both how far French thought cut itself off from its nineteenth-century roots, and how challenging Taine's views remained. While his critics made their voices heard, his thought exercised tacit influence on Proust and Saussure, who contested and elaborated on his theories of involuntary memory and the sign.[85]

Although a formidable critic and historian of literature, in *De l'intelligence* Taine had reduced literature and art into case studies for understanding the workings of intelligence. Literature had become an exemplary instance from which general laws could be extrapolated. But the watchwords of nineteenth-century criticism—biography, morality, and influence—now appeared as obstacles veiling the work itself. As William Marx notes, Valéry was one of the leading figures who brought a formalist approach to French poetics, indicating a way out of the dead-end of criticism based both on "erudition" or "etiology" (the desire to find external causes to account for the form and content of a text) and "impressionism" (a criticism that privileges the personal and affective reactions of the reader).[86] I turn to Valéry at length in chapter 3.

The move to formalism was enabled, in part, by Bergson's account of the "intensity of psychological states" in the 1899 *Essai sur les données immédiates de la conscience* (*Time and Free Will*). Bergson argued that qualitative criticism was necessary to explain affective intensity, which could not be accounted for in quantitative terms: every change in a psychological state was a change in qualitative nature. Moreover, Bergson denied the artwork any transcendental aesthetic qualities. The spectator sympathized with the feeling expressed in or produced by the work of art—he vacillated on this point—but this feeling remained purely subjective.[87] Bergsonian aesthetics broke with the post-Kantian tradition that linked any judgment of taste to an aesthetic universal.

The implication critics drew from Bergson's thesis was that one could no longer measure psychic events or works quantitatively, let alone classify them on a scale. The subjective and qualitative singularity of aesthetic experience called for explication, rather than discrimination: texts became immanent objects of knowledge, rather than judgment.[88] Until then, as Valéry wrote, the function of criticism had been to "compare the incomparable."[89] With the collapse of a quantitative psychology founded on what Bergson considered linguistic misapprehension, the path had been cleared for a philosophy of movement. The difference between Valéry and Bergson's projects, Thibaudet suggests, resides in their varying technical ability and willingness to systematize their intuitions: "Valéry may not be able to organize his intuitions like a philosopher, lacking technique, because the anti-technique that counts as pure philosophy for M. Bergson, only comes to the light of intelligence through a more rigorous and far-flung technique, at the antipodes of a technique, a purer philosophy. But above all Valéry does not want to organize them into a philosophy."[90]

Despite an adherence to the idea that the poet or the novelist could reveal structures of interiority hidden from ordinary consciousness, Bergson's inherently skeptical attitude toward the ability of transitive language to capture subtleties of mind and the flux of the real announced a new crisis in philosophy, literary criticism, and creation. Art, for Bergson, attempts to show us "in nature and in ourselves, inside and outside of ourselves, things that do not explicitly strike our senses and our consciousness."[91] Furthermore, his elevation of intuition reveals its tactical dimension when seen as an attempt to overturn Taine's view of intelligence.[92] The difficulty of reconstructing a dialogue between Taine and Bergson can be attributed to the latter's studied avoidance of naming his predecessor. In *La pensée et le mouvant* (1934), he criticizes Taine and Mill as empiricists who mistake the partial elements of psychological analyses for fragments of the self, accessible only to philosophical intuition. In his correspondence, we find letters thanking contemporary scholars for studies about Taine's work, especially concerning his psychology of intelligence. Bergson was undoubtedly Taine's most important critic: he argued from the outset that a new qualitative approach was necessary to explain affective intensities, which could not be measured otherwise. With the collapse of empiricist psychology, the path was clear for Bergson's vital science.

Bergson's Leap

Bergson's "intuitive method" develops from the place and limits he accords to intelligence. Intelligence is both opposed and complementary to intuition, the latter defined as "instinct become disinterested, self-conscious, and capable of reflecting upon and indefinitely enlarging its object."[93] While "intelligence" remains a marginal term in Bergson's vocabulary—as opposed to central ones like *intuition, durée, mémoire,* and *élan vital*—it marks many junctures that make creative thinking not only possible but necessary. Grasped in time, intelligence is not the paralyzing, self-interested, hallucinatory analytic tendency Bergson criticizes at first, but a force for action in the material world, no longer separated from the world by a self-imposed gulf. While Bergson is usually understood as rejecting intelligence in favor of a spiritualist notion of intuition, this section challenges this common interpretation. It shows how Bergson displaces and nuances the notion, revealing its complexity, instead of rejecting it outright. As we will see in the following chapters, this movement parallels the way in which Proust, Valéry, and the critics of the *NRF* refuse to leave intelligence to scientific and political culture, working instead to reveal its capacities and imperfections.

The *Essai sur les données immédiates de la conscience* (1889) argues for the givenness of the world against the Kantian claim that the transcendental aesthetic mediates all experience.[94] Bergson raises intuition over positivist attitudes that use quantitative, rationalistic inquiry to approach ostensibly natural phenomena. The scientific attitude—which elevates the quantitative over the qualitative, extension over duration, and space over time, when studying the external world of things and the inner world of signs—reifies intelligence. Bergson argued that such binary oppositions needed to be overturned, especially when it came to the study of inner phenomena.[95] Discursive intelligence flattens psychic reality into a "homogenous milieu" to make it intelligible. Bergson jostles the habitual activity of intelligence as the guarantor of facts, fixed elements, and homogenous space, exposing it to the flux of unformed inner phenomena.[96] Furthermore, he stresses the methodological point that scientific models relying on language falsify our picture of psychic life. Bergson reverses Taine's view by arguing that rather than false concepts giving rise to insignificant words, words themselves impede our understanding.[97]

Matter and Memory (1896) continues the attack on associationist psychology and the dream of cerebral localization, while addressing the bodily structure of memory. Although this work discusses Ribot's experimental psychology in *Les maladies de la mémoire*, it also invokes Taine's view of the brain as a "polypus of images."[98] Bergson argues that the brain—even if the observer were gifted with superhuman intelligence, armed with the keys to the kingdom of psychophysiology—would only yield information on bodily movements being prepared at any given instant, rather than explaining consciousness. To think otherwise would be akin to attempting to reconstruct a play based on the exits and entrances of actors on stage as viewed from the wings.[99] Although Taine remains unnamed, Bergson's recourse to a theatrical metaphor makes his target sufficiently clear. Bergson argues that memory is not perception to a lesser degree, nor is perception a more intense form of memory as Taine thought.[100] Moreover, the mind is not the location of consciousness in any philosophically significant way. Intelligence is a shuttling between levels of consciousness, Bergson claims, adopting Taine's view that its activity is best captured in resemblance and juxtaposition. *Matter and Memory* shows how intelligence tends towards spatial forms, whereas intuition hews to the *durée*, i.e. the subjective lived experience of duration rather than the time measured by clocks. This distinction explains why intuition seems capable of linking our understanding to the real, overcoming the gulf stipulated by intelligence. While intelligence remains in Bergson's view analytic and spatial, precluding access to intuition, he attempts to articulate the grounds for "intellectual intuition," the perception of metaphysical reality deemed impossible by Kant.[101] As Frédéric Worms comments, Bergson aims less to "raise intelligence to a specific intuition than to re-immerse it in the temporal intuition through which its object, like any real object, is given to it."[102] Intelligence is obliged to find its source not in the intuition of the *durée*, but within its own relation to the surrounding world, always already there.

These reflections were given practical relief in "De l'intelligence," a speech Bergson gave at the Lycée Voltaire in 1902.[103] Describing an acquaintance who became an eminent physician without showing diligence or intelligence in his youth, Bergson asserted that the intellectual faculty was inherently plastic, subject to transformation by effort and concentration. Unlike the prizes awarded at the ceremony, intelligence was not meted out once and for all. Bergson wanted the students not to confuse the flowers of intelligence with their source. Education does not constitute intelligence; it increases and directs its "elasticity." True intelligence, he argued, is what allows one to "penetrate what we study, touch its depths, draw its spirit toward ourselves and feel it affect our soul."[104] Neither knowledge, nor the ability to reason and reach general conclusions, intelligence is a voluntary form of attunement of mind with the object at hand: "It is an exact adaptation of mind to its object, a perfect calibration of attention, a certain inner tension that at the right moment gives the necessary force to promptly grasp, strongly grip, and durably retain."[105]

In *L'Évolution créatrice*, Bergson refines the relation between intelligence and intuition, presenting them as aspects of the same faculty of human understanding, which evolved over time to valorize the instrumental, directed traits that came to be known as intelligence. As Georges Canguilhem argues, like all Bergsonian concepts these traits are the "fulfillment of a tactic of life in relation to its milieu."[106] Rerouting the concept through its evolutionary history, its primordial *élan vital*, Bergson "reverses the hierarchy between epistemology and biology [. . .] and resituates intelligence as a limited part of the process of life," in which, writes Suzanne Guerlac, it acts as "a specialized adaptation of the mind in the service of useful action."[107]

Bergson's reversal of intelligence is captured in his rewriting of the Platonic allegory of the cave.[108] Neither turned toward the shadows nor blinded by the sun, human intelligence is less a gaze than a force pulling us along whatever paths it chooses to furrow. It needs the resistance of the ground to feel its own potency, a task to direct its impulse. The constitutive irony of intelligence seems to be that while it is uniquely suited to execute specific activity, it fatally oversteps these bounds, gradually taking over the management of life. Intelligence evolves to exceed its limits.

Intelligence and intuition are entangled in life and only analysis separates them. Bergson imagines philosophy as an effort to mobilize thinking within the totality of living forms, a goal that gradually moves intelligence from a place of isolated dominance in order to experience its genesis again virtually: "The intellect [*l'intelligence*], being reabsorbed back into its own principle or source [*principe*], will relive its own genesis in reverse. [. . .]. [But the undertaking] will consist in an exchange of impressions that, correcting each other and being layered upon each other, will end up dilating humanity in us and making it such that humanity transcends itself."[109] Intelligence, from Bergson's evolutionary point of view, is not an approach to life as a whole, but a protean tool meant to enable adaptation. By allowing humans to act and understand the context of their action simultaneously, intelligence creates the illusion of being at home in the world. But it is at home among things, shares its "logic" with inert matter, and can maintain its position only if it reifies its relations with life. Intelligence equally distorts relations to time by spatializing it. Bergson concludes that intelligence, "*characterized by a natural incomprehension of life*," is only "at ease in the discontinuous, the immobile, the dead."[110]

A Vital Science

As we have seen thus far, rather than pit intelligence against intuition, Bergson marshals intelligence to further the creative impulses of intuition. *L'Évolution créatrice* (1907) analyzes the faculty of acting contained within the faculty of understanding. Instead of working toward an accurate representation of life, "our thought, in its purely logical form, is incapable of conceiving the true nature of life and the deep meaning of the evolutionary movement."[111] Intelligence taken as logical thinking is at odds with life's moving nature. Yet it remains entangled with intuition, which explains why it cannot simply be rejected. The opposite of intelligence is emotion, Deleuze suggests, the kernel that allows one to differ from "intelligent individual egoism" and "quasi-instinctive pressure."[112] It is not difficult to see why any intellectualist approach to intelligence—however empirical—would fail to produce anything more than a mirror of itself. Minds surely evolve to adapt to matter, yet this evolution invariably entails a failure to adapt to life, which becomes a spur for intelligence to break with intellectual habit, embodied *habitus*, and self-interest.

Bergson's argument criticizes dominant modes of thinking about intelligence more than it attacks intelligence itself. As he notes, we can never transcend intelligence since intelligence alone allows us to picture what lies beyond it. Before Bergsonian epistemology can elaborate an evolutionary science of life, it must first dethrone intelligence. Like vegetal and animal life, intelligence and instinct (a tendency he sees as belonging to animals that becomes unavailable to humans as they evolve) are opposing yet complementary forces: "There is no intelligence in which we do not discover traces of instinct, and above all, no instinct that is not surrounded by a fringe of intelligence."[113] Instinct tarries within the domain of intelligibility, leading to the false conclusion that instinct and intelligence belong to the same order, differing only in scale and intensity. Bergson specifies that the co-presence of intelligence and instinct should be ascribed to their strange complementarity. As mentioned above, instinct is a form of intuition that has become disinterested and self-reflexive. Despite the Janus-faced aspects of mind, whose essence can only be distorted by rigid definitions, schematizations of Bergson's distinctions are possible. For example, intelligence is the mind's knowledge of itself, intuition, the attention mind pays to its dealings with matter; intelligence is the knowledge of forms, while instinct targets matter; intelligence fabricates imperfect instruments, instinct exploits mechanisms; intelligence is a questing form common to higher vertebrates, instinct a kind of unconscious flourishing common to swarms. Intelligence uses mobile signs; instinct, adherent ones. Intelligence remains naturally deficient since any act of satisfaction creates new needs. By focusing on the structural lack at the core of intelligence, Bergson shifts it away from a state of presence, being or plenitude. Intelligence is indeterminate, intuition immediate. Intelligence concerns the transformative effects hypothetical and actual conditions have on objects, as well as the relations between them. It finds an exit: "The essential function of intelligence will be to sort out the means of dealing with any circumstances whatsoever."[114] In a rare positive definition, Bergson describes intelligence as a structuring and deconstructive force: *"the indefinite power of decomposing according to any law whatsoever and of recomposing into any system whatsoever."*[115]

Bergson's paradox concerning the main impulses of mind captures many shades of difference between intelligence, intuition, and instinct: *"There are things that intelligence alone is capable of looking for, but will never find by itself. Instinct alone could find these things, but it will never go looking for them."*[116] Intelligence is incapable of finding what it seeks precisely because it divides the real according to its self-interest, splitting the continuous world into a world of images, instead of immersing itself in continuity. Intuition is closer to such "reflection" than to instinct or feeling.[117] The underlying question remains why intelligence is drawn to the discontinuous rather than the mobile. Its original orientation is practical, directed towards inert objects, and their manipulation in space. It is only when this kind of knowledge is applied to theoretical problems that it misfires. "Pure theory," Bergson concludes, would require a fidelity to movement rather than stasis, but intelligence is "designed for something else entirely." Only when it violates its own tendencies, taking an "unnatural" distorted posture, can it think through the true continuity and mobility of life.[118] Intelligence invariably reduces the foreign to the familiar, the different to the same, and the new to the known. Yet theory without intelligence is absurd. The only answer to the aporias of intelligence is action. There is no intelligible proof that intelligence can function off its own terrain. Bergson sums up his attitude toward intelligence in an image of expulsion:

> You can speculate as intelligently as you wish upon the mechanism of intelligence, but this method will never allow you to go beyond it. You will obtain something that is increasingly complex, but not something superior, nor even something simply different. It is necessary to rush in headlong and, through an act of will, drive the intellect out of its home.[119]

Where, one might ask, is intelligence at home? Bergson's answer, which should come as no surprise, is the world of unorganized matter, to which the "latent geometrism" of intelligence responds. Being at home in the world of things explains why intelligence tends to reify vital relations, living beings, and life itself. Nor is this regrettable, as "life" only yields its secrets when handled like an inert object. In such passages, Bergson's "new idiom" enables a "return to a self-conscious subjectivity" that overcomes "the deliberate suppression of the self by Taine."[120] The nomadic thinking that results when intelligence becomes mobile is part of another chapter in French thought, from Blanchot and Levinas to Deleuze and Derrida, which valorizes the critical potential of errancy and difference.

Philosophy, as Bergson understands it, is neither systematic nor a pragmatic approach to life. Rather it is an intervention that aims to examine the living without any "ulterior motives for practical use by freeing it from the forms and habits that are properly intellectual."[121] Rather than attributing objectivity to the scientific method, Bergson identifies science with action taken upon inert objects. The object of philosophy is to "speculate, that is to say to see." This identification of speculation with vision is hardly anodyne. Yet, what is perhaps more remarkable about this passage is how vision is not considered to be a habitual human capacity. In its quest for insight, pure intelligence blinds us more often than it allows us to see. If matter and mind emerged from a shared origin, then any return to it necessitates transcending, if not disarming intelligence. Bergson describes such a movement, arguing that vitality itself depends upon a transcendence of intellectuality through feeling (*sentiment*):

> The deeper the feeling and the more complete the coinciding, the more the life it places us back into reabsorbs intellectuality (by going beyond it). Since the essential function of intelligence is to link together the same with the same, only facts that can be repeated are entirely adaptable to the framework of intelligence. Now, intelligence probably gets, *après coup*, some hold on real moments of real *durée* by reconstituting the new state from a series of views or snapshots taken of it from the outside and that resemble as much as possible what is already known. In this sense, the state contains intellectuality as a "potentiality" so to speak.[122]

The essential function of intelligence, recalling its oft-invoked etymological sense, is to link the same to the same. Hence, Bergson concludes, only repeated events enter its framework fully. The iterative structure of the reasoning mind alienates it from space. "Space is not as foreign to our nature as we imagine, and matter is not as completely extended in space as our intelligence and our sense represent it."[123]

Bergsonism thus identifies two correlated aspects in intelligence. These two aspects constitute its "essential ambiguity" and can be mapped onto the divide between matter and mind. Intelligence and matter are co-constituted. One cannot have ascendancy over the other, since that would imply finding a source for intelligence in an already existing material order, or accounting for the phenomenal world through the pre-existing categories of intelligence.

This chapter has tracked the transformation of intelligence from a universal ability to know to a specific capacity that individuals possess with varying degrees of intensity. Rather than impose a typology on intelligence, it has sought to explore its structure as a complex word, one whose full meaning and value, as Taine insists, always depends on the cultural moment in which it occurs. Taine's reduction of mind to machine, and the related restriction of the self, can be read as a move away from the use of figural language to describe thought toward the observation of nervous, cognitive, and semiotic functions—ones that were quantified and measured by laboratory psychology. For Bergson, intelligence is an analytic, essentially practical approach to the world, which precludes access to qualitative forms of life, unless it yields to creative intuition.

Part of the difficulty in gauging Bergson's influence in and since the interwar period derives from the considerable shadow his thinking casts on his era in retrospect. Gide was aware that the entire period in French letters would one day seem Bergsonian. A journal entry from 1924 declares:

> What I dislike in Bergson's doctrine is all I ever thought without his saying it, and everything that is flattering, even caressing to the mind. Later on, his influence on our epoch will be thought to be seen everywhere, simply because he himself belongs to the epoch and constantly yields to the trend. Whence his representative importance.[124]

From Taine to Bergson, as this chapter has demonstrated, ways of thinking and writing about intelligence evolved significantly. Whether or not an author from this era was Bergsonian becomes a moot point, when we consider, with Gide, how Bergson's fidelity to movement became representative of his time. The outcomes of this transformation resonate in Proust's novel, in Valéry's essays and *Cahiers*, in the criticism of the *Nouvelle Revue Française*, and their common quest for new ways of writing about, and often against, intelligence.[125]

CHAPTER TWO

Abdicating Intelligence

PROUST AND NARRATIVE FORM

AMONG THE MANY QUESTIONS Proust's characters ask each other in his novels, at least one brings the conversation to a halt. In Madame Verdurin's salon, the aggressive Comte de Forcheville bluntly confronts the reserved Charles Swann, a man known for his good taste and discretion: "Now, Swann, what do you mean by intelligence [...] does it mean a gift of the gab, does it have to do with how people manage to worm their way in?"[1] The question is particularly pointed given Swann's Jewish heritage, and Forcheville's implication that he has managed to usurp a place for himself in high society. Swann remains quiet, aware that any definition he offers will fail to satisfy his audience, merely fueling their mockery instead. His silence arrests the rhetorical contest his hostess has been trying to stage between him and his social and romantic rival.

Even after the conversation resumes, Forcheville's unanswered question remains hanging in the air. It remains deeply unclear what qualifies as intelligence in this fictive world. The nature of intelligence had long been a concern for the novelist. Following Proust's understanding, use, and thematization of intelligence allows us to renew our reading of the *Recherche*, especially the way in which it conceives of artistic processes. The attention that readers have inevitably given to the dramatic claims for involuntary memory and epiphanic moments needs balancing by the long unfolding of a narrative that explores life as a text to be deciphered. Intelligence in Proust is by no means abandoned—it is rather, as I argue, belated: it comes into play as the work of analytic mind in the aftermath of the encounter with occulted signs of experience.

When Antoinette Faure, the daughter of the future French president, asked Proust to take a questionnaire in her diary, her curiosity about his favorite qualities in men and women elicited the following answers: "Intelligence, moral feeling" for the former, and "gentleness, unaffectedness, intelligence" for the latter.[2] Proust's answers betray little hesitation about his preferred quality, while the order implies a gendered difference in valuation. I argue that the novel he would write as an adult tells a story about intelligence. Its narrator struggles over thousands of pages to discover his vocation as a writer, gradually realizing that intelligence must abdicate its place as the primary faculty to create works of literature. Instead, it must collaborate with other powers that allow the transcription of experience in its minute specificity, from which laws can be extracted in turn. The priority of intelligence determines whether it acts as a force of sterility and conformity, or a spur to writing and thought.

The effort to abdicate the primacy of intelligence is part of Proust's larger attempt to reclaim ground that the novel had lost to the positivist and experimental sciences on the one hand, and decadent and symbolist poetics on the other. The growing popularity of "intellectualized and ideological literature" that followed left little room for the kind of fiction he prized.[3] One might expect that Proust or his narrator would elect a poetics of irrationality instead of one of intelligence. Yet, Proust remains adamantly opposed to the formal presence of "obscurity" in literature.[4] Instead, his novel shows how intelligence slowly discovers its limits, and the need to give up its place as the dominant faculty, yet continues to play an essential role in the development of impressions and events into insight. For both Proust and his narrator, the possibility of capturing experience depends upon the novel's ability to find the right attitude towards intelligence. When intelligence reigns, it can only test its stance against itself, remaining distant from the transformative vision of the self and the world revealed in the work of art, which Proust unabashedly calls the "truth." As the novel repeatedly shows, however, the real difficulty lies in the absence of an adjudicating faculty, once intelligence has been deposed. Instead of sovereign intelligence, we encounter a range of interpretive and inventive capacities that allow the narrator to situate himself in a fluctuating world of signs.

This chapter studies the novelist's complex, evolving, and easily misunderstood views about literary intelligence to show how Proust honed a hybrid form that allowed him to open channels between the critical essay and the novel. Beginning with *Contre Sainte-Beuve*, I describe Proust's ambivalence toward intelligence, both in his critical writings and above all as a structuring force for the fictive world of the *Recherche*. Analyzing the arc of the diminished primacy of intelligence renews our sense of the covert sources of knowledge with which it must collaborate. Examining the vicissitudes of dethroned intelligence moves us away from chronocentric and teleological readings cribbed from the theories of *Le Temps retrouvé*, the final volume of the novel, towards ones that acknowledge the vast passages in the novel where it seems nothing happens. Since neither the sovereignty of intelligence nor its mere abdication prove to be tenable postures, Proustian intelligence is often relational, renegotiating itself vis-à-vis other forces in the work. While it seems that Proust challenges and dismisses the notion of intelligence, the novel deploys the term with multiple connotations. The frequent use of the notion may not seem like contestation, yet it is precisely in its semantic drift that the concept becomes unusable in the ways discussed in the previous chapter. While Proust was certainly a reader of Taine and Sainte-Beuve, he was less familiar with Bergson and keen to distinguish his fiction from the philosopher's thought. In short, while one might expect a simple refusal of the notion of intelligence, scrutiny of the novel shows what a major role it plays.

There are good reasons to doubt the wisdom of attributing to Proust a favorable view of intelligence. Intelligence, he argues, is not the faculty best suited to capture the past impressions at the core of the artist's experience of creativity. Yet, without its assistance writers could never begin to create, since the elusive raw material of past experience is not at their disposal. The role of intelligence in the genesis of the work of art is bound to be duplicitous, functioning both as an impetus and an obstacle to the truth the artist seeks, and for his desire to write. Suddenly, young Proust's preferred quality gains an unforeseen aspect by keeping the adult from accessing unclouded impressions of past happiness, ones that seem to have been locked away in chance objects, forgotten sensations, and fleeting landscapes. Conscious knowledge about the past proves powerless in such a situation, since only memories that surface on their own possess any force for breaking the bonds of habit.[5]

It bears recalling that Proust's argument with Beuvian criticism concerns the validity of conversational and biographical methods that sought to isolate the intention of a writer. For Christopher Prendergast, studying this polemic in detail shows that "there is more than one straw man in Proust's relentlessly aggressive sparring with Sainte-Beuve."[6] He adds that "Proust's hostility to Sainte-Beuve" is due as much to his "aesthetic of the 'unfinished' as his insistence on the separation of biographical and creative selves."[7] For the purposes of the present argument, however, it is his invocation of intelligence that bears consideration. Anecdotes from the lives of authors that Sainte-Beuve relished in reporting were irrelevant for Proust. The essence of the work of art is not to be sought in the social life of the writer, in which he appears as his habitual, volitional, intelligent self. Instead, writing is the activity of a solitary, unknown, nocturnal figure. Once the psycho-biographical route is barred, any literary singularity must be located in the writing itself, where the sense of the "pure past" is resuscitated through fortuitous experiences of involuntary memory. The elusive sensations of involuntary memory do not promise discursive knowledge. They must be unraveled by the same intelligence that hinders the capturing of forgotten sensations, delaying the instinctive recreation of lost worlds by offering counterfeit substitutes in exchange.

Writers of fiction cannot simply renounce intelligence once and for all. Abdicating is an ongoing gesture that never reaches completion. Intelligence can only momentarily abdicate its crown to other powers such as involuntary memory, instinct, impressions, or perception. Proust argues that writing must begin with intelligence, even if the contributions of conscious intelligence are outstripped by what unconscious forces make us think.[8] Intelligence conspires to keep one from accepting painful truths about the possibility of love, friendship, sociality, and meaningful communication, which nonetheless break through in upheavals of being.

Reading *In Search of Lost Time* as a novel in which intelligence is carefully staged enables us to reinterpret the ordering and play of signs it proposes. As Deleuze contends, the novel is not merely a series of books about time lost and regained, as it is commonly read.[9] Rather, it dramatizes the struggle to make imperceptible signs perceptible in the quest for truth. Roland Barthes adds another dimension to this deciphering quest, which, in Deleuze's powerful readings, by turns Platonic and anti-logocentric, seems too clearly directed at "stripping human truth of appearances superimposed by vanity, worldliness, and snobbery."[10] For Barthes, there is a logic of Proustian discourse, a structural inversion or reversal that affects time, social mobility, laws of self, sexuality, identity, memory, and even truth: this ethos of inversion structures the worldliness of Proust's world.[11] Departing from this dual emphasis on signs and reversible structures, my reading shows how in an essential part of the novel discursive intelligence disarms itself, overcoming its defense mechanisms in order to allow the untold truth to emerge—a truth it then deciphers and elaborates.

For Proust, the privileged domain for such disarming intelligence is literature, especially the novel, as it delves into the lives of men and women, unveiling truths hidden from investigations marshaled by conscious intelligence. Literature thus becomes a singular form of research that aims at broadening our perceptive powers, otherwise hemmed in by memory and identity.[12] Perceptive powers can only serve in the quest for truth on the condition that intelligence be held subordinate to them, later analyzing and translating what they first describe without its interference. The focus on Proust's critical ideas about intelligence in the first section ("Intelligence Failures") shifts to an analysis of his novel's theories about its role in art, especially music and painting, in the second section ("Experimental Faith"). The third section ("A Brilliant Contest") builds upon the first two by drawing attention to Proust's intricate staging of deferred intelligence in high society.

Intelligence Failures

It is easy to recognize the intelligence of the Proustian narrative voice. As Empson quips, "much of Proust reads like the work of a superb appreciative critic upon a novel which unfortunately has not survived."[13] Yet taking "intelligence" as a point of departure provides a way of reimagining the *Recherche* precisely as a novel. It allows us to look beyond the critical cleft between "philosophic" readings that focus on the theoretical discussion of time and memory, "cultural" readings that study sexuality, class, and politics, and "aesthetic" readings that unravel the role of music and art. These seemingly discrete elements can be connected through a subterranean network of intelligence.

Intelligence suggests a third term to a significant binary in contemporary Proust studies: redemption and reparation.[14] The redemptive reading of Proust that supposedly ends in the apotheosis of art, after the circles of sociality and love turn out to be wasted time, began to be contested by queer critics from Leo Bersani and Eve Kosofsky Sedgwick onward. The omnipotence of art in the redemptive account seemed to ascetically deny so many pleasures of relationality that the novel develops yet cannot quite embrace. The reparative reading—against the paranoid possessiveness of the narrator, most evident in the Albertine cycle—shifts focus to the world beyond the subject in Proust. Yet a third way is elided or presumed by this binary opposition between aesthetic redemption and sociality or worldly reparation: the disarming of intelligence in writing. It is important to restore the particularity of writing to accounts of Proust's novel, to discern how the writing of and in the novel we read differ from the theoretically hyperbolic claims it makes in the name of art (which it often uses as a metonym for writing). Furthermore, its incessant depiction of erring intelligence considerably undermines accusations that it forecloses relational possibilities. Rather than taking the dead ends and vicious circles the narrator encounters at face value, the novel asks us to imagine alternatives.

Proust welcomed his editor Jacques Rivière's attempts to systematize his thinking by confirming that his work was a dogmatic construction, whose axioms lay encrypted in the text of his novel.[15] However we consider the critical analogies Rivière went on to establish in his essays between Freudian psychoanalysis and the Proustian "intermittences of the heart," his gesture allows us to isolate a specific dogma concerning "intelligence," or rather its failures, from Proust's earliest writings onward.[16] What he meant by "intelligence" is far less certain. English translations largely avoid the issue by using the word "intellect," recalling an established philosophical opposition between "intuition" and "intellect." Such familiarity robs us of the chance to examine the complex modes of "intelligence" as they are developed in Proust's novel. There are compelling reasons for staying with "intelligence," even if it turns out to be a false cognate in English. At the very least we should be aware of its foreignness: as I argued in chapter 1, the term we have been tracking has a fraught history in French thought from Cartesian disputes to the wave of positivist, psychometric, materialist, and spiritualist treatises influential in the Third Republic.

Much of this contest of meaning arises from the reference to a range of abilities, for which the word postulates a single source. Emile Littré's 1877 dictionary, as mentioned in my introduction, helps name these abilities. The Littré considers "intelligence" as a faculty of understanding; clear and easy comprehension; mind (*esprit*) insofar as it conceives; a mental substance (*substance spirituelle*); the act of knowing; the artist's capacity to produce and reproduce medial effects (such as chiaroscuro in painting, or dialogue in theater); a linguistic capacity of obtaining a certain result through choices made in speech; an animal's vivacity; communication among like-minded people; and finally, a secret accord or unity of feeling.[17] Beyond these semantic differences—which can be grouped into the epistemic, aesthetic, and social—one should be sensitive to the syntactic subtlety of the French *intelligence*, often used as a "transitive" noun to designate the understanding of a specific area, situation, or field, whereas in English it is almost uniquely used to denote a subjective faculty rather than a form of knowledge.

While lexicologists analyze words by separating them into their possible meanings, such meanings remain in conflict each time a word is used. To decide which one of these meanings Proust was referring to in general would be arbitrary. Our inquiry begins with the considerably more challenging premise that Proust knowingly mobilizes a host of meanings attached to this complex word since its emergence as a subject of scientific and philosophical discourse, and his characters use it with no less circumspection in their evaluation of themselves and each other. This variation informs his ambivalent attitude towards the resources of "intelligence."

In "Contre l'obscurité," an early polemic against the influence of symbolism, Proust argues that words do not share the same status in philosophy and literature.[18] Attempts to systematically infuse literary works with ideas only leads to a double obscurity: the obscurity of ideas and images. He analyzes this "aesthetic error," common among young writers at the time, as an error concerning the "logical faculty." While a literary work can expose "a philosophy," it only does so through its "artistic potential." Writers use words poetically, attending to their "figure," "harmony," and the "charm of their origin." They appeal to the imagination and sensibility as much as to reason. In short, the "evocative power of a word" (*pouvoir d'évocation*) must equal its "potential for strict signification" (*potentiel de stricte signification*): "Words are not pure signs for the poet."[19] Here Proust makes the surprising claim that philosophy initially has the right to appear obscure, due to its technical use of language and its appeal to logical faculties, but that the poet has no such right. Instead of requiring an introduction to a specialized vocabulary, the poetic use of language must be transparent.

If poets or novelists first appeal to the "logical faculty," they run the dual risk of creating "nearly unintelligible" literature, while also falling short of the "rigorous and defined" use of language in "metaphysics." "How does it happen that a concern for logic confers the right to be obscure? Why is logic not on the side of clarity?" asks Vincent Descombes. Commenting on this passage, he writes: "The philosophers whose lessons Proust may have learned did in effect teach that man possesses, in addition to his 'sensitive' (and therefore 'poetic') faculties, a group of 'logical' faculties. These powers of conceptualization and reasoning Proust regularly refers to as *intelligence*. Professional philosophers prefer to speak of *reason*."[20] For Descombes, Proust's use of "intelligence" can be equated to "logical faculties," leaving the "sensible faculties" free for the literary and the aesthetic, while reason becomes the preserve of professional philosophy. Such synonymy, however, is far from self-evident. It cancels the power of evocation that surrounds *intelligence* in French, beyond its "potential for strict signification." More importantly, it veils Proust's careful redistribution of the logical and sensible faculties within his novel.

To be sure, when criticism deals with a narrative universe as vast as *In Search of Lost Time* it can hardly expect to unlock its secrets through a magic word. Instead, the work becomes an endlessly explorable space in which pre-existing notions of meaning are deported and inverted.[21] One has to "decipher the literary word not as the dictionary explains it, but as the writer constructs it."[22] In the exemplary case of *intelligence*, meaning is not merely deported and reversed, but repeatedly emptied, belated, abdicated, and disarmed. A repertoire of possible meanings emerges for Proust's *intelligence* through its uses: consciousness itself; the will, to a lesser degree; common sense or ordinary sanity; a concept-hungry analytic drive; the opposite of instinct; and received ideas. The most insistent of these is doubtless the inquisitorial impulse or the will to know. However, notes Michael Wood, such categorization itself seems "an act of the arid, classifying intelligence, a symptom not a cure."[23] Any critical attempt to decipher the sense of *intelligence* in Proust must attend to its dramatization, without yielding to the lure of pre-emptive definitions.

For Proust, unlike Taine, art and literature were practices, and not conceptual activities. As such they were "unintelligent." Similar stances in romantic and positivist philosophies of art allow us to grasp the importance of Proust's criticism of intelligence. The critique of intelligence addresses not only Sainte-Beuve and Taine, but philosophers in general. It is not a "trial of rationality" but of the incapacity to think art outside of the realm of philosophy. For our purposes, the critical implications of *Contre Sainte-Beuve* are thus two-fold: art is freed from rationality as an impetus to writing; art becomes an object for the novel. Proust's etiology of a vocation includes the discovery that writing can include a figurative reflection on the status of the work of art, which does not require supplementary discourse to be intelligible. Indeed, the truth of a novelistic account is greater precisely to the degree that it allows the narrator to inscribe moments of frustrated insight and "dull sensation" (*sensations obscures*) into his quest.[24]

Unsurprisingly, Proust did not think philosophers were particularly good readers of his novel. In a footnote to an essay on Flaubert's style, published in 1920, he complains that philosophers misunderstand his prose primarily because they take his words in their current meaning, rather than in a historical register, as he attempts to use them. His willful confusion of timely and untimely meanings begs an obvious question: what does an author of the late nineteenth century intend when he uses words in a consciously anachronistic manner? The only example we are given of such a word, prone to being misread by philosophers, is *intelligence*:

> But the French seventeenth century had a very simple manner of saying profound things. When I try to place myself in its lineage in my novels, philosophers object to my use of the word "intelligence" in its contemporary meaning, etc.[25]

Proust's footnote goes on to recall what French schoolchildren used to learn about Descartes in philosophy class. The possibility that the thinker could be read ironically, thus suspending his egalitarianism, was introduced into the French pedagogical tradition by Joseph Reinach, a French politician and Dreyfusard, who wrote numerous set-texts for courses in French rhetoric.[26] As such, how one reads "bon sens" acts as what Barthes might call the "zero-degree" of Third Republic Cartesianism:

> I know that Descartes began with his "good sense" which is nothing other than rational principles. We used to learn that in class. How can M. Reinach [...] not know, and how can he believe that Descartes showed "a delicious irony" in saying that good sense is the best shared thing in the world. In Descartes this means that the stupidest man uses principles of causality despite himself etc.[27]

Here *bon sens* means nothing other than "rational principles," and thus Descartes's remark refers to the fact that even the "stupidest man" unknowingly relies on "principles of causality." The distribution of common sense, a question at the core of French philosophy since Descartes, becomes increasingly difficult to discuss, as words have lost the "simple capacity to say profound things" since the early modern period. The loss of this capacity to designate is accompanied by a broader hermeneutic suspicion.

Now Proust claims he writes in the "simple" and "profound" manner of seventeenth-century French as opposed to using words in their contemporary meaning. "Contemporary meaning" could refer to use of a word in ordinary language, but also to the definitions currently favored by philosophers. Given Proust's use of *et cetera*, one could imagine he had other examples of such word-concepts in mind. However, the elliptical sign could also suggest that Proust's views on intelligence could be developed further, given the indications provided in the note, and its ongoing figuration in the *Recherche*. The footnote to the Flaubert essay suggests that Proust's novel emulates a "very simple manner of saying profound things" in order to outstrip the insights afforded by concepts. Yet intelligence and stupidity turn out to be entangled postures toward rational principles. Flaubert—despite, or perhaps because of, his war on "bourgeois stupidity" (*bêtise bourgeoise*)—had been taxed with stupidity by several eminent critics, from Brunetière to Thibaudet, who located his *intelligence* and ideas in his correspondence with Louise Colet rather than his fiction. Proust's response sought less to defend Flaubert's intellect than to recall his grammatical and stylistic innovations.[28] In the preface to Paul Morand's short story collection *Tender Shoots* (*Tendres stocks*), he focuses further on how the unconscious is materialized in Flaubert's impersonal descriptive technique: "intelligence [...] tries to become the hammering of a steamboat, the color of foam, an island in a bay [...]. This undulation is transformed intelligence, which has fused with matter. It gets into the hedges, the silence, and the woodland light."[29] In large parts of the *Recherche*, from nature to high society, intelligence takes us into the silence, the hedges, and shimmering undergrowth of language and thought.

Critics from Julia Kristeva and Vincent Descombes to Miguel de Beistegui and Joshua Landy have offered sustained accounts of Proust's relations to philosophy.[30] Luc Fraisse has written a richly documented examination, drawing attention to the influence of Cousin, Darlu, Séailles, Tardes and Bergson in addition to Descartes, Leibniz and Schopenhauer.[31] In light of these works, my point is not to reevaluate the critical influence of philosophy on Proust's novel, nor to declare it magically free from the influence of earlier periods. Proust's response to this double operation, as the next section argues, was to draw analysis into the novel, to the point of supplanting the narrative voice, and thus inaugurating the possibility of the novel having a heterogenous relation to philosophy. "Once Proust's idealism is noticed it seems to appear in nearly every line of his great novel," writes Edmund White, adding "but if he was a philosopher, at the same time he had more faith in the senses and in memory than in the intellect to experience ultimate truths."[32] The somewhat simplified picture of Proust's philosophical sources—often considered to be a mixture of German Idealism drawn from reading Schopenhauer and Schelling, French spiritualism via the teachings of Alphonse Darlu, and the English aestheticism of Ruskin—ignores the equally formative influence of positivism, especially Taine. *Contre Sainte-Beuve*, the variants and manuscripts that constitute Proust's first critical venture, might have easily been dubbed *Contre Taine*.[33] He singles out the thinker for his specious "intellectualist conception of reality [that] limited truth to science."[34] Against this positivist reduction, Proust enacts a theory of the involuntary sign which becomes available to the novelist seemingly through the unconscious—whose very existence was the object of a heated debated in the era. Rather than leaving psychologists to study and reduce creativity to abnormality, Proust argues for the role of a novelist as observer of involuntary and coded signs that resist empirical capture.

Exceptional creativity was traditionally the province of genius rather than intelligence. As early as 1908, Proust turns away from Schopenhauer's view that pure objective intuitions of "genius" require "the perfection of the mind and in general everything that can favorise its activity in the physical constitution."[35] Instead of health, Proust valorizes the insight offered by the sick body:

> The powerful intuitions of my mind, even on an evening when I am exhausted or dead. Principles of renewal that is truth. As a spiritual man one freezes like others.[36]

As Deleuze would later argue, novelties in style are born not of health or adaptation, but of an irremediable weakness. A disposition closer to sickness allows one to leave conventional modes of perception, in which each object seems inscribed within a larger network of meanings and associations, toward a reconsideration of how words, facts, and objects might be related. One moves from relations of necessity to ones of possibility. Proust's attention to bodily experience to renew the truth marks a turn away from Schopenhauer's *The World as Will and Representation*, according to which the inner disposition of genius "comes from outside." Rather than rely on a teleological account of nature, Proust turns to Nerval, and the romantic stylistic device of describing singular moments, which are no longer "subordinate to a philosophical referent but built on a literary model."[37]

Proust's "critique of intelligence" repeats the distancing function of the early pastiches that he wrote to purify his style of influences from Balzac and the Goncourts to Taine and beyond.[38] Various narrative themes, too, come together here: "sensible impressions" provide access to "the essence of art" insofar as they belong to an "un-intelligent activity." One of the main interpretive difficulties lies in the status we accord the transformed literature of "laws and ideas" discovered at the end of the novel. Leading up to, and possibly opposed to these laws are the fragmentary, non-systematic, and frustrated moments of insight, in which intelligence is only capable of "a logical truth, a possible truth." The artist's work, as a well-known passage from Proust reads, is to reverse the labor carried out within us every minute by "*amour propre*, passion, intelligence, and habit." Intelligence for the writer, unlike the scientist, comes second, in a belated position, after experiment and experience.

The preface and drafts for *Contre Sainte-Beuve*, from which the novel would germinate, remains the classic passage for Proust's view of intelligence:

> Each day I attach less value to intelligence. Each day I realize better that it is only outside of it that the writer can recapture something of our past impressions, that is, reach something of himself and the sole matter of art. What intelligence gives back to us in the name of the past is not the past. In reality, as it sometimes happens to the souls of the deceased in certain popular legends, each hour of our life, as soon as it dies, embodies and hides itself in some material object. There it remains captive, forever captive, unless we happen to encounter the object through which we recognize it, we call it, and it is set free. The object in which it hides—or the sensation, for every object is sensation in relation to us—we could very well never encounter it. And thus, there are hours of our life that will never be resuscitated.[39]

This passage makes a series of crucial claims about the inferiority of intelligence, but only in relation to objects. External objects, rather than interiority, are instilled with the power to capture "past impressions," and "each hour of our life" is hidden away in an unlikely place. In the Proustian mythology, part of this is due to our inadvertence in being observers of our lives. Objects instead offer sensations to us, the intensities of which are dulled by habit. The difference between intelligence and perception, can be recast in terms of vision and language. For Proust, Deleuze writes, "*intelligence tends towards objectivity, as perception toward the object* [...]. For perception supposes that reality is to be *seen, observed*; but intelligence supposes the truth is to be *spoken, formulated*."[40] This difference persists until the narrator realizes that truth does not need to be spoken to become manifest. It can be found in involuntary signs and external phenomena. Moreover, this tension suggests why intelligence cannot have (sequential or hierarchical) primacy over perception because if it merely speaks about the past without translating what is encrypted in the object, it loses any claims to objectivity.

Not that mere objectivity is the goal here. Unlike his predecessors, Proust is interested in objectivity only in order to free the real from the burden of an epistemic function, restoring its aesthetic, figural, and affective dimensions. In this sense, the artist defers using the explanatory intelligence to regain a primacy of vision, while the writer relies on belated intelligence to rectify errors of perception. Intelligence depends upon the information inscribed in all kinds of cognitive and existential errors, without which it cannot function. Nor can it simply invest objects with significant memories, for this very process of investment weakens the force of the impressions being consecrated. Our incapacity to store memories in not a passive failure. The past is only present in those objects where intelligence has not sought to incarnate it. "Intelligence not only loses the past," writes Wood, "it actively misplaces it."[41] One is tempted to conclude that only the forgotten is truly memorable.

The value Proust accorded to intelligence—expressed in terms of *prix attaché* (price attached)—recalls the perennial problem of reconstructing the author's views out of the novel, a critical activity to whose perils we are alerted by another sentence which also speaks of a *prix*: "A work in which there are theories is like an object on which one has left a price tag."[42] Writing about Proust's theories of intelligence must negotiate between the diminishing returns he attaches to criticism and theory for its incapacity to liberate memory from matter, and the scorn his narrator seems to pour upon the idea that one might distill theories from artworks in order to evaluate them as one would check a price tag.[43] His initially hostile stance towards intelligence accrues nuance throughout the *Recherche* from the early volumes to the last, *Time Regained*. It is noteworthy that Proust interrupted writing an early novel, *Jean Santeuil*, to finish his long-delayed essay on Sainte-Beuve, a project that finally sent him back to fiction, this time to the first volume of the *Recherche*, *Swann's Way*. His indecision between criticism and fiction suggests that he was perfecting an experimental style that would create channels between two genres. This third genre might be called *recherche*: a novel form of intelligence and an intelligent form for the novel cast in an inimitable narrative voice.[44]

In 1909, Proust found a form that allowed him to open secret paths between the critical essay and the novel. He did so by writing in such a way that his intelligence could "accommodate and transcend" the suffering he had just experienced in "absolute form," after his mother's death. Barthes comments:

> Now "intelligence" (a Proustian word) [...] if we follow the romantic tradition, is a power which traumatizes or desiccates affect; Novalis called poetry "that which heals the wounds of the intellect"; the Novel can do this too, but just not any novel: a novel which is not written according to Sainte-Beuve's ideas.[45]

By attributing Proust's discovery of a narrative form to the need to mourn his mother, Barthes falls into the kind of biographical reading that Proust dismisses in *Contre Sainte-Beuve*.[46] It is not necessary to situate the genesis of the novel in Proust's pain to argue that the *Recherche* is written to transform the relation of intelligence to suffering.

Such a transformation produces a triple effect in Proust's novel on the literary and stylistic level. First, intelligence distorts the fabric of the fictive world—the way the narrator errs in the social, erotic, and artistic spheres, only later understanding their impact. Second, although the narrator's discovery of his vocation is bound to his apprehension of time and memory, his ability to write nonetheless depends on the value he attaches to his capacity to think analytically. This leads him to distinguish between instrumental and critical forms of intelligence, rejecting the former and accepting the latter, up to a point. Third, on the syntactic level of the phrase, paragraph, even the arc of the entire novel, there is a concerted effort to delay the recognition of what is being described as far as possible. Belated intelligence exposes the temporal structure of intelligence as a faculty, and a form of insight, unlike supposedly atemporal notions of "truth," "knowledge," or "meaning." Furthermore, it questions the conventional narrative of historical processes in which causes and effects are closely linked, rather than reversed, sundered, anachronic, or dilated. Intelligence, the novel suggests, survives only when the desire to know adapts to time as a medium of radical alteration.

Tracking the abdication of sovereign intelligence from Proust's early critical writing through the *Recherche* offers a way of reimagining the forces that structure and fragment his fiction. This incomplete abdication creates a covert route through the Proustian network of lost time. The next section reconstructs some of Proust's arguments against the primacy of intelligence in the quest for truth and its translation into art. Intelligence adulterates our impressions by usurping a place for itself before perception, which itself invariably fails to register the essence of objects. For Proust, otherwise imperceptible signs only make themselves known when such domineering reason is distracted or occupied. These signs are forceful because they harbor elements of the pure past, which intelligence has not invested with value or worn out through repeated reflection. Seemingly insignificant details can turn out to be hieroglyphs of truth. But only the artist can rescue this truth with the added contribution of intelligence, which now comes second, contorting itself into an unusual stance. Such a reordering is catalyzed by painful shocks that remind us how far we have strayed from the truth in the clichés of ordinary life. In its defensive mode, intelligence holds such shocks at bay since it has no fidelity to truth. Instead, it works to uphold the apparent integrity and consistency of a sense of self. Only those ready to sacrifice notions of selfhood can explore truths we ordinarily spend our lives actively ignoring or interpreting away. The greatest works of art can also catalyze and dislocate intelligence. Paradoxically, the best preparation for the creation of such works, according to the Proustian mythology, is time whiled away.

Experimental Faith

Proust's detour into criticism allowed him to articulate some of the most troubling aesthetic problems for both artist and spectator, writer and reader: Can we judge aesthetic works without the standards of reasoning intelligence? How does an artist begin to create except under the control of intelligence? If intelligence is obliged to acknowledge its inferiority to impressions, are all its truths necessarily tainted? An alternate version of the preface I have been discussing contains helpful clues:

> Although every day I attach less value to criticism, and even, if I must admit it, to intelligence because more and more I believe it to be incapable of that recreation of reality which is everything in art, it is to intelligence that I turn today in order to write a critical essay. Sainte-Beuve.[47]

Recognizing that intelligence is particularly at a loss to spur aesthetic creation does not amount to renouncing its critical potential:

> After all, we have to ask intelligence to establish the inferiority of intelligence. For if intelligence does not deserve the supreme crown, it is intelligence alone that is capable of awarding it. And if it has only second place in the hierarchy of values, there is nothing else capable of proclaiming that instinct occupies the first place.[48]

While intelligence alone can recognize its inferiority and demote itself from first place, it creates a void that is seemingly incapable of being filled. Once intelligence abdicates its crown, it can no longer name instinct as the sovereign faculty.

Intelligence overthrows itself once it recognizes that knowledge is not proprietary. Things that are "clear before us do not belong to us," and "what one knows does not belong to oneself," as Proust's narrator says in two closely related phrases late in the novel. It is because there is no proprietary link between abstract knowledge and the individual that the truths of intelligence are secondary to the truths of experience, instinct, impression, or involuntary memory. Proust never denies that there are truths of intelligence that are of considerable value, but since they are limited to the realm of knowledge, they can never be authentically our own.[49] The arbitrariness of ideas formed by pure intelligence is what makes them even less compelling according to the narrator: "Ideas formed by pure intelligence only have a logical truth, a possible truth, their election is arbitrary."[50] Moreover, pure intelligence cannot be "profound," since one does not plumb the depths to attain it.[51] Only those truths that are rescued from obscurity affect us.

Adulterated intelligence homes in on truth, coming to correct habitually erroneous perceptions. Instinct, impressions, and intelligence continue their play well into the *Recherche*. There is a "changing attitude to intelligence which involves us at last in what appears to be a flat contradiction" for critics who pit the following claims against each other: "for instinct dictates our duty and intelligence furnishes pretexts for avoiding it"; "Where life encloses it, intelligence breaks out [...]. Intelligence does not experience those closed situations of a life without issue."[52] Cocking draws attention to how intelligence vacillates between being a force for avoiding duty and for breaking through life's impasses. The changing attitude towards intelligence is part of a meta-fictional narrative that structures the *Recherche*, especially *Time Regained*, which offers "not a circumstantial account of how he [Proust] came to write the novel, but an attempt to tidy the process of creation as he experienced it into a system and to read it in terms of his idealist preconceptions."[53] Rather than seeing the end of the novel as a belated effort at systematicity, we can consider it a lure for reading that seeks to stabilize the meaning of intelligence. Proust does not necessarily share his narrator's idealist preconceptions. The novel the narrator vows to write in *Time Regained* could not be the one we have just read. What we have at the end of the novel is not a contradiction, but rather Proust's persistently complex use of a shifting word in several different ways. The novel constantly delays the arrival of recognition and meaning. Everything from its elaborate narrative arc down to the style and length of its sentences has trained the reader to set aside preconceptions about the nature of intelligence and to track its unfurling instead.

Intelligence that collaborates with other forces at the end of the *Recherche* does so with the consciousness that it cannot access "involuntary feelings," which are the true sources of the laws governing human experience. Intelligence cannot preside over an excavation of such feelings but can be surprised by them. Consider the suffering after Albertine's disappearance that makes the narrator realize that he has loved her all along—an affection that was impossible to realize in her captive presence since she merely serves as a motif for his jealous curiosity.[54] After her death, this truth is itself inverted through mourning. The narrator is shocked to realize that what he considered love, or desire, was a side-effect of habit. An earlier example of such a disarming recognition is Swann's discovery that Odette is not "his type" before they are married. The *Recherche* could, of course, be read as a series of love affairs that wear themselves out and turn themselves inside out: between Swann, Odette and Forcheville, between the narrator and Gilberte, then Albertine, and finally Charlus and Jupien, Morel and Saint-Loup. The narrator condemns high society and love at first because they are sources of lost time, only to partially revalorize them through their resurrection in art, which puts the haphazard, the waste, and the excess insight that was never available for experience, to work. Such a setting-to-work requires intelligence. This intelligence, as I have been arguing, only functions as afterthought, making sense out of life's misrecognitions and unexpected blows *après-coup*. Involuntary intelligence, which animates the narrator's analytic digressions on all manner of topics, is the kind that enthralls many readers of Proust. Its unexpected sources are the sick body, the traveler, the chattering socialite, the snob, the jealous lover, the insomniac, and the lonely child. This is the zone in which the narrator carries out his research.

Chance encounters with affects, stray impressions, and instincts do more to uncover the true laws of nature for the artist than the tacit accord—the *intelligence*—which presides over friendship and philosophy: "The dumbest people [*les êtres les plus bêtes*], in their gestures, their remarks, their involuntarily expressed feelings, manifest laws that they do not perceive themselves, but that the artist surprises in them."[55] Surprising general laws in particular bodies and singular situations becomes the narrator's *modus operandi*. To prepare, he tries to minimize the charge of intelligence in perceptive modes, moving from more to less intention: from looking to seeing, from listening to hearing, and from speaking to chattering. The remainder of this section tracks how artists in the *Recherche*, especially painters and musicians, excel to the extent that they can abdicate intelligence in order to perceive nature, discover laws, and create percepts and affects. Art germinates from the "rare moments when we see nature such as it really is, poetically."[56] Only after seeing nature poetically, rather than intentionally, do artists use intelligence to extend and expose the impression that can last a mere instant. By doing so, they expand the perceptive powers of their audience, leading it beyond both fashionable notions of taste and the clichés in which they are promoted.[57]

Artists, in this account, do not reason, rather they seize hold of laws expressed through impressions, symptoms, gestures and half-stifled feelings.

Much critical attention has been lavished on the visual arts in Proust—sculpture, painting and photography—and the techniques they offer for capturing impressions. But the lengthy figurations of painting in Proust do not mime the visual arts as much as they use vision as a means to renew writing.[58] Proust inherits much of his notion of "creative intelligence" from Ruskin, who opposes it with the power to perceive and represent the real, which is held captive by unadulterated sense impressions.[59] In *Modern Painters*, Ruskin emphasizes how far an artist like Turner had to set his intelligence aside before looking at the world and beginning to paint: "I say that he 'thinks' this, and that he 'introduces' that. But, strictly speaking, he does not think at all. If he thought, he would instantly go wrong; it is only the clumsy and uncreative artist that thinks."[60] In *The Elements of Drawing*, Ruskin speaks of the "innocence of the eye" necessary for painting:

> The whole technical power of painting depends upon our recovery of what may be called the innocence of the eye; that is to say a sort of childish perception of these flat stains of color, merely as such, without consciousness of what they signify—, as a blind man would see them if suddenly gifted with sight [. . .]. We go through such processes of experiment unconsciously in childhood; and having once come to conclusions touching the significance of certain colors, we always suppose that we *see* what we only know, and have hardly any consciousness of the real aspect of the signs we have learned to interpret.[61]

It comes as no great surprise that amongst the many artists who populate Proust's world—Bergotte, La Berma, Vinteuil, Morel—it is the painter Elstir who provides the paradigm of the "innocence of the eye":

> The effort made by Elstir to rid himself in the presence of reality of all the notions of his intelligence were all the more admirable, since this man who before painting, made himself ignorant, forgetting everything out of integrity (for what one knows is not one's own), had an exceptionally cultivated intelligence.[62]

Recall that one of Littré's definitions for intelligence is the capacity to create medial effects. To say that Elstir has an "exceptionally cultivated intelligence" as a painter suggests a virtuoso capacity to imitate and manipulate styles from the history of painting. Yet Elstir seems to momentarily repress any such mastery before painting. Instead of embellishing reality, his effort consists in ridding himself of this ability to relate to tradition in favor of ignorance, which spurs his brushstrokes more intensely than impersonal knowledge.

After translating Ruskin's *Bible of Amiens*, Proust remained fascinated by the possibility of recovering the "innocent eye," of bestowing sight on the blind (and the seeing), and the child's wonder to the ironic adult. Anyone having a truly aesthetic experience risks facing the world with a scrambled sensorium. Bergotte, the young narrator's mentor, dies while looking at the little patch of yellow wall in Vermeer's *View of Delft*. The patch forces his gaze, "like a child drawn by a yellow butterfly he wants to catch."[63] The momentary return to the innocence of the gaze leads the dying novelist to the realization that he should have written as Vermeer painted, adding multiple layers of color to his phrases to "make language precious in itself." Literary style, Bergotte's death suggests, is a quality of vision akin to color in painting—a vision worth suffering to recover from the strictures of intelligence.[64]

In the lessons on literature the narrator gives to Albertine, he schematizes the connection between different kinds of artistic intelligence as the reversal or the disruption of the logical and cognitive relation between cause and effect:

> Mme de Sevigné, like Elstir, like Dostoevsky, instead of presenting things in logical order, that is to say, by starting with the cause, shows us first the effect, the illusion which strikes us. This is how Dostoevsky presents his characters. The actions seem as deceptive to us as those effects of Elstir's in which the sea appears to be up in the sky. We are quite surprised to learn that some sullen person is really the best of men, or vice versa.[65]

The reader or the spectator of an artwork is struck by illusion before understanding its cause and receives the impression before it is translated by intelligence. Art delays the moment understanding lays claim, if at all, to experience.

The spectator's intelligence throughout the *Recherche* is emptied by painting, reading, and, above all, music. What painting does to sharpen the perception of space, music does for time and memory. Music, Beckett declares, is the catalytic element in Proust. It is a short jump from the deadly *petit pan* and Bergotte's ideal sentences to the enchanting *petite phrase* and its promise of happiness. Swann's initial encounter with the phrase in Vinteuil's sonata leads him to a "happiness that was noble, unintelligible, and precise," thus augmenting his sensibilities.[66] Years later at the Saint-Euverte soirée, Swann rediscovers Odette's love for him, as well as the fact that it will never return to the same musical phrase. Listening allows him to still the abstractions of intelligence that only harbor false fragments of the past. Stumbling upon his past through Vinteuil's music, he recognizes the impotence of his intellect and realizes that even as he recalls the notes, he is "reasoning this way not about the phrase itself but about simple values substituted, for the convenience of his intelligence, for the mysterious entity he had perceived."[67] He does not try to translate the music of the little phrase into language; instead, he simply replaces it with thought. Later still the narrator, listening to the Septuor, describes Vinteuil's compositions "as free from analytic forms of reasoning, as if it were carried out in the world of angels."[68]

Whether or not the Proustian listener can grasp the non-analytic core of music reveals much about how intelligence is construed. Angelic reasoning recalls Leibniz's definition of music as "occult arithmetic in which the spirit is unaware that it is counting, as it does many things in confused or insensible perceptions which it cannot notice through distinct apperception. For those who believe that there cannot be anything in the soul of which it is unaware are mistaken."[69] Yet Proust's music theory, Beckett contends, resembles less that of Leibniz than Schopenhauer, as the latter "rejects the Leibnitzian view of music as 'occult arithmetic,' and in his aesthetics separates it from the other arts, which can only produce the Idea with its concomitant phenomena, whereas music is the Idea itself, unaware of the world of the phenomena, existing ideally outside the universe, apprehended not in Space but in Time only, and consequently untouched by the teleological hypothesis."[70] In Schopenhauer's distinction between intuition and intellect, only the former offers us immediate access to the essence of things, while the latter constructs a rational representation of the world through concepts. Anne Henry and Jean-Jacques Nattiez have meticulously traced what this distinction means for Proust in relation to the mimetic hierarchy of the arts, confirming Beckett's initial suggestion that music is catalytic. The process it catalyzes moves from a first provocatively nebulous perception to an intelligent examination of the mysterious power of the work that inevitably substitutes simpler values in its place, and finally, the liberation of a seemingly unrelated, transcendent truth.[71]

Albertine, for one, seems aware that such catalytic reactions occur while listening to music. She repeatedly chooses to play works on the pianola that are unfamiliar to the narrator. The passage that analyzes her choice of musical programs also articulates intelligence in relation to "attention" and "reflection":

> [Albertine] chose pieces which were either quite new or which she had played to me once or twice, for, beginning to know me better, she was aware that I liked to propose to my attention only what was still obscure

to me, and to be able, in the course of successive renderings, to link to one another, thanks to the growing, but alas! distorting and alien light of my intelligence, the fragmentary and interrupted lines of the construction first almost buried in the fog [...]. She guessed at the third or fourth repetition, my intelligence, having grasped, having consequently placed at the same distance, all the parts, and no longer having to exert any effort on them, had conversely spread and immobilized them on a uniform plane [...] she knew that the moment when the working of my intelligence had come to dissipate the mystery of a work, it was very rare that it had not, during its baleful task, picked up some profitable reflection in compensation.[72]

Decoding a new piece of music, placing all its obscure lines on the same plane, allows the narrator to vaguely reflect upon something else, arriving at an unexpected insight at the end of what he deems an otherwise off-putting task.

Consider this passage alongside the description of a painting by Elstir, which restores the impossible vision of the Carquethuit port to the narrator. Intelligence functions like an opportune dab of paint on a canvas that reunites disparate perspectival lines, just as it reveals the underlying structure of musical works.[73] Yet it is worth noting that in this passage the narrator seems implicated in a process of dissipating, rather than in structuring works of music. He aims to dispel their mystery, annulling the distance between fragmentary lines, while profiting from his preoccupied intelligence to discover some unheard truth impossible to attain through rational thinking.[74]

In the rare instance when impressions are allowed to surface without intellectual surveillance, intuition forms truths that would otherwise go unremarked. Allowing for imperceptible signs to become perceptible is the counterintelligence work performed by the artist:

This work of the artist, this struggle to discern beneath matter, beneath experience, beneath words, something that is different from them, is a process exactly the reverse of that which, in those everyday lives which we live with our gaze averted from ourselves, is at every moment being accomplished by vanity and passion and intelligence, and habit too, when they smother our true impressions, so as entirely to conceal them from us, beneath a whole heap of verbal concepts and practical goals which we falsely call life.[75]

Not only is instinct opposed to intelligence, rather intelligence—along with self-love, passion and habit—arms the artist with motives for shying away from instinct, since it knows that instinct would undermine its reign. And despite such subterfuge, the reign of intelligence is not absolute. In the *Recherche*, as mentioned above, the narrator comes to admit that intelligence is no longer his primary epistemic or heuristic resource. Instead, it becomes a principle for translating the shuttling passage between impression and expression, placed at the core of the work of art: "was not the recreation by the memory of impressions that had then to be deepened, clarified, transformed into equivalents of intelligence, was not this process one of the conditions, almost the very essence of the work of art?"[76]

Proust's narrator discovers the epiphanic structure of time, and his vocation to write, by speculating on a series of sensuous upheavals that make him attentive to the fabric of experience. It is analogical, rather than logical thinking, which allows him to discover the laws of style linking two seemingly discrete events or experiences in *Le Temps retrouvé*:

> True life, life finally discovered and illuminated, the only life that as a result is really lived, is literature; this life that, in a sense, at every instant inhabits all men as well as the artist. But they do not see it, because they do not seek to clarify it. And thus their past is weighed down by innumerable clichés that remain useless because intelligence has not "developed" them. Our life, and also the life of others; because style for the writer, color for the painter, is not a question of technique, but of vision. It is the revelation, that would be impossible by direct and conscious means, the qualitative difference that there is in the way that the world appears to us, a difference that, if art did not exist, would remain the eternal secret of each person.[77]

Although it seems to elevate the rarefied word of literature over life, this passage also extends a literary structure to the everyday. It thus offers a series of capital claims for Proustian poetics: Literature alone can express qualitative differences of perception. The style of a writer is attributed to this secret quality of their vision, but such vision depends on how well "intelligence" translates impressions into expressions. Although intelligence can be an obstacle to accessing impressions in Proust's photographic metaphor, it is also the fluid that develops the clichés of life, which would remain unseen without it.[78]

Given his supposedly dwindling faith in intelligence, Proust never abdicates it entirely, or never stops abdicating it, since there would be no way of doing so, once and for all. It is the very incompleteness of this movement that affords intelligence its role in his novel, as a point from which he is forever parting. Such departures take on an experimental and experiential quality, a testing against life, which leads to the repeated recognition that "other powers," although higher, require the connivance of intelligence. The narrator realizes as much once Albertine disappears:

> But [...] the fact that intelligence is not the subtlest, the most powerful, and the most appropriate instrument for grasping the truth, is only one more reason for beginning with intelligence, and not with an unconscious intuition, not with a ready-made faith in presentiment. It is life itself that, little by little, case by case, allows us to notice that what is most important for our heart, or for our mind, is taught us not by reasoning, but by other powers. And then it is intelligence itself which, acknowledging their superiority, abdicates, by reasoning, in their favor, and accepts the role of becoming their collaborator and servant. Experimental faith.[79]

The task of the artist is to perceive what lies buried beneath the junk-heap of false concepts called "life." Here it is life itself that allows one to gradually notice that what matters is not taught by reason, but the collaboration of other powers with an abdicating intelligence. Breaking with Pascal's maxim about faith and the "reasons of the heart that reason does not know," the novel places hearts and minds on the same side. "Experimental faith," as Wood aptly comments, is "an extraordinary two-way signpost, pointing to a form of belief which would have the empirical caution of science, and a science which would be willing to take the risks of belief."[80] In one of his preparatory notebooks, Cahier 57, Proust clearly pits sensibility against intelligence, only to arrive at the conclusion that even if the vital impulse is not intellectual, it requires intelligence to attain the generality that remains inaccessible to sensibility alone, for "if intelligence is not capable of life, sensibility is not capable of the general."[81]

Speaking of Madame de Cambremer in *Sodom and Gomorrah*, the narrator recalls a phrase from Leibniz: "A philosopher who was not modern enough for her, Leibniz, said that the journey is long from the intelligence to the heart."[82] In his *Essays on Theodicy*, Leibniz distinguishes between understanding the truth and the will to the good by explaining that any perception of a truth is an affirmation of truth, whereas perception of the good requires the will in order to act in accordance with it. This, he comments, is "the reason why our soul has so many means of resisting the truth which it knows, and that this passage from mind to heart is so long, especially when understanding proceeds to a great extent only by faint thoughts [*pensées sourdes*]."[83] Proust's tenacity lies in insisting that one cannot begin with faint thoughts themselves, but that one must begin with reasoning intelligence precisely because it is not the most well-calibrated instrument for perceiving them. As this miscalibration is made known to the conscious mind, it comes to recognize the *pensées sourdes* that have made silent advances toward the secret truths of the heart and mind.

In a rare interview given to *Le Temps* in 1913, Proust said the following about the delicate yet necessary place of intelligence in literary and artistic creation: "If I allow myself to reason thus about my book, it is because it is to no degree a work of reasoning, its most minor elements were provided to me by my sensibility, I first glimpsed them in my own depths, without understanding them, having as much difficulty in converting them into something intelligible, as if they had been as foreign to the world of intelligence as, how should I put it, a musical motif."[84] It is only by restaging or recalling such "deep impressions" foreign to the world of intelligence that intelligence captures and translates them.

I would now like to offer a few examples of a peculiar narrative device from the *Recherche*—akin to Viktor Shklovky's notion of "defamiliarization" and Ian Watt's "delayed decoding"—that gives a stylistic example of this translation: a description is offered without the reader being conscious of what is being described and the intelligible name of the object is only furnished at the end of a circuitous passage. Consider the following:

> A little tap on the windowpane, as though something had struck it, followed by a plentiful light falling sound, like grains of sand being sprinkled from a window overhead, gradually spreading, intensifying, acquiring a regular rhythm, becoming fluid, sonorous, musical, immeasurable, universal: it was the rain.[85]

The syntax of this passage studiously avoids presenting things in logical order. As a result, the reader's intelligence is suspended in an attempt at deciphering until familiarity solves the puzzle. Another passage that uses this technique describes the insomniac narrator waiting for dawn, mistaking the last gas lamp for the first rays of sun, and only then realizing, to his horror, that it is midnight and that all his suffering is still to come.

In one of the most striking instances of this technique, belated intelligence takes on a political edge, where it relates to the dynamic of anti-Semitism and philo-Semitism that Proust explores in French society.[86] The scene occurs at the seaside resort of Balbec:

> One day when we were sitting on the sands, Saint-Loup and I, we heard issuing from a canvas tent against which we were leaning a torrent of imprecation against the swarm of Jews that infested Balbec. "You can't go a yard without meeting them," said the voice, but here there is

a plethora of them. You hear nothing but, 'I thay, Aphraham, I've chust seen Chacop.' You would think you were in the Rue d'Aboukir." The man who thus inveighed against Israel emerged at last from the tent, and we raised our eyes to behold the antisemite. It was my old friend Bloch.[87]

This passage changes in meaning radically once it turns out that the speaker is Bloch, the narrator's snobbish friend, who conceals his Jewish heritage behind a posture of aestheticism. Elsewhere in the novel, he adopts the Anglicized moniker Jacques du Rozier, not hearing the echo with the rue des Rosiers, a central address for Parisian Jews. This passage, notes Maurice Samuels, creates a kind of *mise-en-abyme* by which the narrator can distance himself from the self-hating Jew, while the narrator himself, mocking Bloch's tirade, repeats the structure *ad infinitum*.[88] The stability of meaning is here opened to multiple and marginal narratives through the delayed revelation of the speaker. This passage should be read in dialogue with the larger depiction of Jewishness in Proust, especially in relation to the Dreyfus affair, where "intelligence" is merely a compliment paid to someone who has the ability to rise above personal prejudice and see the matter impartially—i.e., who happens to agree with you.[89] It offers too an instance of Proust's "Jewish" humor, which Deleuze suggests, should be opposed to Socratic irony because it always places intelligence *after* encounters, rather than "anticipating, instigating and organizing" them.[90]

It is easy to forget today how threatening Proust's style appeared to contemporaries, some of whom excised his novel from the space of literature, relegating it to the domain of experimental psychology. Critics from Céline to Benda hastily grasped his "demeaning" of intelligence and attacked it with different degrees of viciousness. Partisans of French intelligence claimed that directing intelligence was the only way to conserve "ethical" values—family, nation, and state—against the corrosive powers of thinking. The nation's literature was meant to provide an intelligent defense of such values in uncertain times, rather than endlessly interpret how they came to be instituted as self-evident. In his polemic against "pure literature," *La France byzantine*, Benda singled Proust out as an anti-intellectual writer, one whose sole interest lay in his extraordinary capacity for psychological observations, from which he, and, above all, his devoted readers, remained incapable of abstracting any overarching laws of consciousness. Proust's work, in Benda's account, amounted at best to a massive case study meant for clinicians and specialists: "Those who have drawn valid consequences from these observations are those who, in the silence of the laboratory, considered them with sangfroid, not with the panic of revelation, knew how to sort them out, grouped them according to a method, elucidated them through others, interpreted them scientifically. It is through them that Proust served psychology, not on his own and even less through his literary critics."[91] In short, Benda wanted to reverse Proust's inversion of intelligence, reinstating its primary "scientific" position à la Taine. Yet this very distinction between science and literature was a fulcrum for Proust's upheaval. In a passage discussed above, the narrator writes, "an impression is for the writer what an experiment is for the scientist—with this difference that in the case of the scientist the action of the intelligence precedes the event and in the case of the writer it follows it."[92] Benda was at least willing to recognize the acuity of such observations. Proust provoked even greater repulsion from foreign critics.

In 1929, when the German Proust translation being prepared by Franz Hessel and Walter Benjamin was brought to a halt, the critic and philologist Kurt Wais issued the following judgment. Wais's description of Proust is difficult to read for its anti-Semitism, homophobia, misogyny, and eugenicist vitriol. It remains worth citing, however, since it captures a great deal of what was considered threatening about Proust's endeavor:

> A real explosion of the stable, firmly rooted form the novel [...] was undertaken by two non-full Frenchmen, the half-Jew Marcel Proust and André Gide, who was brought up in the gloomiest Calvinism [...]. In Proust's hands, personalities [...] crumble into inconsistent individual traits [...]. He who himself has not been moved cannot move others. The hundred figures remain phantoms, whose blood he silently sucks in his neurotic monologue *À la Recherche du temps perdu* (which swelled from the three volumes originally planned to thirteen): effeminate men and masculine women around whom he flutters with the hair-splitting chatter of his endlessly piled-up similes and whom he analyzes with talmudical ultra-intelligence. Indeed the stale air of the darkened sick-room, for fifteen years, the incubator of this evil-minded, dainty hair-splitter, whose sole concern revolves around the penetration of strata of society that are closed to him, the inquisitive microscopy of the problems of puberty and the morass of outrageously depraved sexual perversions which Proust has in common with most of Europe's Jewish literary men [...] all this will probably keep away from this work any present-day reader who is not a neurologist.[93]

It is shocking, but not surprising, how swiftly the qualities latter-day critics ascribe to Proust—everything from his non-normative views on sexuality and gender to his minute investigations of intentionality and non-intentional states—serve here as signs of intellectual and moral degeneracy for Wais.[94] It is no accident that the heart of this transformation contains an accusation of Proust's "talmudical ultra-intelligence." For Wais, Proust's intelligence is a "hair-splitting chatter" unable to rise beyond its perverse obsessions. Between the Third Republic and Vichy France, arguments against the perversity of intelligence were never a purely anodyne, literary affair. From the Dreyfus affair onward, as Arendt argues, Proust's society witnessed the transformation of the "crime" of Judaism into "vice" of Jewishness, which could only be eradicated in the Nazi view.[95]

During World War II, René Étiemble defended Proust against all charges of anti-intellectualism and mysticism which claim that Proust abandons the principle of causation for "Talmudic style," itself speciously considered a failure of reason in this historic context. Étiemble shows that throughout his work Proust was harassed by thoughts and actions that implied the scandalous disappearance of causality. Being in love, for instance, was to be faced with a "monster in whose presence we are just as disoriented as before an individual for whom the principle of causality hardly exists and who would later turn out to be incapable of establishing links between one phenomenon and another."[96] Étiemble recalls the path from likeness to law: "The truth will only begin at the moment when the writer will take two different objects and posit their relation, which is analogous in the world of art to that unique relation of causal law in the world of science."[97] Intelligence develops involuntary associations but cannot discover these associations on its own. It must flutter around men and women, attending to their "chatter" to expand its field of research. Wais could hardly recognize this because he mistook the genre of the *Recherche* for a "neurotic monologue."[98] As the final section of this chapter argues, it is nothing of the sort. Rather, it often takes the form of verbal contests whose layered significance often remains latent, coded, or deferred.

A Brilliant Contest

Proust may have been the first novelist to conflate his characters entirely with their manner of speaking.[99] The *Recherche* repeatedly shows that social relations are embedded in linguistic relations, from professional jargon and familial sayings to regional accents and spurious etymologies. The social and spiritual zoology dreamt of by the nineteenth century, from Taine to Saint-Beuve, could ironically only be realized in the pages of a novel that restricted its intelligence of human nature to actions, words, and gestures from which it extrapolates general laws. Although Proust and his contemporaries revel in the contest of meaning behind the use of the word, *intelligence* comes to mean the calculating, willful use of reason, which the novel (read against the grain) unravels into a repertoire of nondominant modes of receptivity to the world as it gradually renounces the primacy of intelligence.

That Albertine, Gilberte, Charlus, Jupien, Madame de Guermantes, and several aristocrats are all distinguished by their intelligence suggests how many competing senses Proust associates with the quality: intellectual curiosity, political conviction, wit, taste, bookishness, self-deprecation, and pragmatism.[100] Saint-Loup's amoral intelligence is mistaken for a moral quality by the narrator, while the Duchesse de Guermantes regrets that her nephew does not have the "intelligence" to retain the stupidity inherent to his aristocratic milieu, as instead, he reads Nietzsche and Proudhon and yearns for an "open intelligence" ("He talks to you about Morocco," she complains to her husband, "it's appalling"); the scathing Guermantes wit is compared to a regional specialty like rillettes from Tours or biscuits from Reims; Madame de Villeparisis becomes a social pariah due to her intelligence, more suited to a second-rate writer than a "femme du monde"; Charlus is considered intelligent despite his "vices," before being considered more intelligent because of them; Jupien, who runs a bordello, seems intelligent like a "man of letters"; Cottard, an excellent physician, cannot treat intelligent patients; while Brichot, the Sorbonne professor and lexicologist, is considered intelligent for showing a fashionable contempt for his profession. Finally, the condescending Princesse de Parme praises the young narrator because he wears American rubbers to protect his soles in bad weather: "Voilà un homme intelligent."[101]

Speaking is one way, perhaps the primary way, that people in salons signal their intelligence. The writer instead becomes the one who records and analyzes the ways people try to sound smarter or more lovable, or merely different from each other. To listen to ways of speaking is to register the speaking subjects' quests for distinction.[102] Proust's narrator often speculates about the relative intelligence of people he knows, since it seems only intelligence can democratize their otherwise highly hierarchical social relations. Being invited, recognized, and allowed access to a social sphere beyond one's own depends upon how intelligent one is perceived to be. Cognitive elitism becomes a sort of pseudo-meritocratic response to social hierarchy. As Descombes notes, everyone from the servants to the socialites in Proust is trying to answer a deceptively simple question: who is invited by whom?[103] Here, intelligence functions as an *idée reçue* in the Flaubertian sense, accounting for much of the novel's social comedy. Odette, for instance, is deemed not to be intelligent by Swann, a judgment whose misogyny critics echo without questioning. Instead of taking Swann at his word we might see what this posture enables Odette to accomplish. She describes herself as lacking intelligence, not because that is how she feels, but because it is chic to be self-deprecating, *cela faisait bien*. However, she manages to beguile Swann precisely because of his intelligence. At the end of the novel, she ends up near the apex of the social world in ways that suggests she is crafty at the very least, possessing the kind of cunning that comes from being disempowered.

Swann confuses life and the novel in his doomed affair with Odette. This error is caused, in no small part, by his misdirected intelligence; rather than writing his book on Vermeer he turns Odette into a Botticelli:

> Then, too, he belonged to that category of intelligent men who have lived idle lives and who seek a consolation and perhaps an excuse in the idea that this idleness offers their intelligence objects just as worthy of interest as art or scholarship could offer, that "Life" contains situations more interesting, more novelistic than any novel.[104]

Idleness stalks the narrator too, whose life often repeats patterns from Swann's. He is consoled for his listless ill-health by the literary idol of his youth, Bergotte, who tells him: "Our friends were telling me that you have been ill. I am very sorry. And yet, after all, I'm not too sorry, because I can see quite well that you are able to enjoy the pleasures of the mind."[105] Whether or not the narrator can enjoy his still dubious gifts at this point, before sickness catches up with him, depends on how he chooses to spend his time. Bergotte's acknowledgment of his intelligence is a source of many intricate conversations between Gilberte, the narrator, and his parents, especially his father, who fears this appreciation from a mind considered frivolous by men of the world like Norpois, whose intelligence is supposedly respected by Bismarck. The narrator's father veers between indulgence and contempt toward his *genre* of intelligence: "The contempt which my father had for my kind of intelligence was so far tempered by affection that, in practice, his attitude towards everything I did was one of blind indulgence."[106] Much later, the narrator questions Bergotte's judgment by skeptically dissociating pleasure from his sterile intelligence: "As for the 'joys of the intelligence,' could I call by that name those cold observations which my clairvoyant eye or my power of accurate ratiocination made without any pleasure and which remained always infertile?"[107]

During his first dinner with Bergotte, shortly after being disappointed by seeing the actress La Berma on stage, despite her great reputation, he speculates that there are perhaps no genres of intelligence but only a shared seat in an audience that is watching the same play: "For my intelligence must be one—perhaps indeed there exists but a single intelligence of which everyone is a co-tenant, an intelligence towards which each of us from out of his own separate body turns his eyes, as in a theatre where, if everyone has his own separate seat, there is on the other hand but a single stage."[108] This remark suggests that what is reified as an individual or even class-based intelligence is instead an embodied, perspectival, provisional, or situational one. The "play" of intelligence itself opens up the register of performance, repetition, and varying degrees of receptivity. The mind was often likened to the theater in this period—the image recurs in Taine, Binet, and Bergson, as discussed in the previous chapter—yet Proust adds to its theatricality. Intelligence is now reimagined as a collective attention to the same stage.

When it comes first, intelligence is "conscious, intentional, conceptual, deceptive, practical, able to deal only with dead objects or moments."[109] A disarming intelligence instead teases out the potential implications of surreptitiously registered mobile signs. This is something that the narrator discovers as a young man thanks to Françoise's condemning gaze, when he is frantically orchestrating his encounters with the Duchesse de Guermantes—a figure who loses nearly all interest for him, despite her *esprit d'Oriane*, once he begins talking to her. He realizes that the essential is not said through words, but remains unsaid, folding itself into gestures. It is only in the opening cruising scene of *Sodome et Gomorrhe*, the fourth volume of the *Recherche*, that that he understands the meaning of the glint he sees in the Baron de Charlus's eyes in Balbec, an "understanding" later intensified by his voyeurism in Jupien's bordello. Such belated intelligence is contrary to the kind of intelligence that Proust condemns at the beginning of *Contre Sainte-Beuve*.

After his epiphany in the Guermantes library, at the end of the novel, the narrator realizes the necessity of receding into language to be alone with his impressions, or whatever he can salvage of them. It is an established axiom in Proust studies that the narrator discovers that spending time talking with others ironically turns out to be the perfect training ground for solitude. But what a focus on talk about intelligence adds to this picture is that the solitude necessary for writing can only be gained once one begins to renounce the fantasy of sounding smart in social settings, whether as procrastination or compensation for not writing.

One could develop the relation of belated intelligence to the violence of speech at length, showing how it hinders then forces the narrator to approach truth. Chatter turns out to be a scintillating, yet necessary, waste of time, but the alchemy of art does not guarantee its elevation into truth. The Goncourt pastiche in *Le Temps retrouvé* is exemplary in this sense: it elevates but also falsifies the "verbal jousting" (*joutes verbales*) of the Verdurin salon. At most, the end of the novel throws an Orphic gaze backwards to confirm its recognition of what is being lost. Walter Benjamin underscores the destructive aspect of chatter in Proust's work: "It was Proust's aim to design the entire inner structure of society as a physiology of chatter. In the treasury of its prejudices and maxims, there is not one that is not annihilated by a comic element."[110] Finally, this predominance of chatter becomes a propaedeutic to the spiritual exercise of self-isolation and self-absorption, the greatest since Loyola, which Benjamin reads in Proust: "the overloud and inconceivably hollow chatter which comes rolling out of Proust's novels is the drone of society plunging down into the abyss of this loneliness."[111] The emblem of an isolated society is Swann's hysterical, chattering body alone in his carriage, rehearsing diatribes against the Verdurins once he realizes that they are abetting Odette in her liaisons with other suitors. While the "physiology of chatter" points to Proust's attempt to provide an ethnology of the Third Republic, this "hollow loneliness" announces the attitude the solitary writer takes toward it.

A curious dinner scene *chez* Madame Verdurin, alluded to at the outset of this chapter, suggests how the minutiae of Proust's text resist our most tenacious attempts to schematize his views on intelligence. The editors of the *Pléiade* edition slyly dub this passage from *Swann in Love* "definition of intelligence" in their index, and we are in on the joke, once we find nothing definitive in it.[112] Swann has taken to defending a duchess, La Trémoïlles, much to the chagrin of the Verdurins, since she belongs to an aristocracy to which the middle-class couple of self-styled aesthetes have no access. Madame Verdurin sees Swann as an infidel preventing her "from creating a complete moral unanimity among the little clan." Hence her snobbish desire to reduce the prestige of his judgment before the others. Once Swann declares the duchess "intelligent", the jousting between Swann and Forcheville begins:

> "It all depends on what you call intelligence" said Forcheville, who felt it was his turn to shine. "Now, Swann, what do you mean by intelligence?"
> "There you are!" cried Odette, "that's the sort of big subject I'm always asking him to talk to me about, and he never will."

"But, but..." protested Swann.

"What tripe!" said Odette.

"Tripe with onions?" asked the doctor.

"As you see it," Forcheville went on, "does intelligence mean the gift of the gab, does it have to do with how people manage to worm their way in?"[113]

Odette's exclamation functions both as intellectual curiosity and flirtation, while Cottard's pun, a mark of tired wit, is still part of being a good social performer. Forcheville, a count who belongs to the same social circle as Swann and is a rival for Odette's favors, corners his interlocutor, needling him for a definition. Swann is no match for his insinuating, quick-witted tone. When we first meet him, the narrator's aunt doubts whether Swann is intelligent at all, since he avoids "serious" topics in conversation, limiting his interjections to specify the dates of a painter's death, correct a book's title, or offer precise details about recipes. Swann hides his erudition, which he has never been able to transform into a work. Instead, he opts for nuance. We return to the dinner table when the Sorbonne professor Brichot interjects:

"There is," said Brichot, hammering out each syllable, "a rather curious definition of intelligence by that gentle anarchist, Fénelon..."

"Listen!" said Mme Verdurin to Forcheville and the doctor. "He's going to give us Fénelon's definition of intelligence. Most interesting. It's not often that you have a chance of hearing that!"

But Brichot was waiting for Swann to give his definition. Swann did not answer, and by evading them spoiled the brilliant contest that Mme. Verdurin was rejoicing at being able to offer Forcheville.[114]

Brichot's brandishing knowledge that is not his own is another challenge to Swann, trying to tease him out of his reserve. Yet, Swann has understood that only silence can neutralize the situation, spoiling the "brilliant contest" of terminologies and definitions. Swann's eloquent silence refuses to take a stance towards intelligence—which demands that one take a side—at the risk of appearing dumb. The inability to say what one means does not get one very far in Proust's salons. Forcheville may be right in equating intelligence with a facile, manipulative capacity to use language to reach calculated aims: to worm one's way in. The irony of this early scene is intensified at the end of the novel when Forcheville marries Odette, after Swann's death, and adopts Gilberte, leaving her a fortune and a title worthy of Saint-Loup's hand.[115] Thus Swann's rival unknowingly, or perhaps intelligently, allies the two paths leading out of Combray toward Swann's house and the noble Guermantes residence, considered antinomic by the young narrator: *le côté de chez Swann* and *le côté de Guermantes*.

Here it is worth following Brichot's allusion back to Fénelon, who was most famous for his novel *Les Avéntures de Télémaque*, a 1699 addition to *The Odyssey* that staged intelligence as a form of protean adaptation. At the turn of the century, Fénelon was part of a set of philosophers whose classic style was considered a model to set against the influence of German philosophy.[116] A commentator on Descartes, Fénelon went on to write a *Treatise on the Existence and Attributes of God*, completing what he construed as the project of the *Metaphysical Meditations*.[117] For Fénelon, God was "universal intelligence" and "infinitely intelligible" and our ideas "are a perpetual mingling of God's infinite being which is our object, and of the limits He gives always and essentially to each creature."[118] One cannot identify which definition Brichot meant to allude to in Mme Verdurin's brilliant contest. The allusion to Fénelon ushers us into Proust's larger discussion of a possibly higher spiritual order, which we intuit through other powers and which would guarantee the superiority of art, rather than there being only material nullity, as the most skeptical intelligence claims. For Fénelon, the absence of a higher spiritual order destroys the meaning of human intelligence. If there is no higher intelligence to decipher in nature, then individual intelligence is faced with a void. Such a void cannot be the object of intelligence. Thinking alone offers no guarantees for Fénelon; only divine intelligence can ground existence.

Proust expressed his affinity for the seventeenth century's philosophical idiom. As we discussed above, the distribution of intelligence and common sense was a question at the heart of French philosophy since Descartes. It was however becoming increasingly difficult to discuss, since words had lost their simple capacity to say profound things since the early modern period. Brichot's allusion to Fénelon, read alongside Proust's claim that he used "intelligence" in its seventeenth-century valence, repeats the difficulty of defining what his narrator describes as "foi expérimentale," namely the collusion of an abdicated intelligence with covert sources of knowledge. Misunderstandings of the word and its ends arise from the currency or the untimeliness of its use.

In 1922, shortly before his death, Proust responded to a survey addressed to leading literary figures. The editors asked whether the "renewal of style" in modern literature was leading to hermeticism, a "crisis of intelligence" worth denouncing. The continuity of style was owed to, rather than undermined by, its perpetual renewal, Proust argued, yet he also distanced himself from writers who sought out formal innovation for its own sake. Rather, he emphasized the necessity of hewing to the real, translating its impressions.[119] In a similar survey, a year earlier, he had clarified his goals for the novel in terms of pure intelligence:

> To say one last word about the so-called novel of analysis, it must in no way be a novel of pure intelligence, according to me. It must be drawn from the unconscious, to make it enter into the domain of intelligence, while trying to keep it alive, to avoid mutilating it, or making it suffer the slightest possible loss, a reality that the light of intelligence alone, it seems, would be enough to destroy. To succeed in this salvage work, all the forces of mind, and even the body are not enough.[120]

Acknowledging the embodied mind and the accidental nature of insight become essential points of departure for the novelist. Unless the light of intelligence is used tactically and belatedly in the dramaturgy of art, it threatens to blind us to the play.

Proust's attitude towards transcendent foundations, that would preclude such blindness, changed during his career as a writer as he actively weaned his art from a dependence on faith: "For God, whose absence in *À la Recherche* [François] Mauriac has deplored, is named in *Jean Santeuil* as the sanction of the beauty that is also truth; it was later that Proust exercised his intelligence to the utmost to do without the sanction, while keeping the value of experience."[121] For Shattuck, experimental faith was "Proust's wager," a "double declaration of faith in the material and the spiritual, in the intelligence and in 'other powers.'"[122] One might juxtapose "Proust's wager" to "Swann's gambit" understood as an evasive strategy. As Swann's silence suggests, the desire to define "intelligence" once and for all mistakes the nature of the problems it poses. These are not questions that can be answered conceptually, or even discursively, they require an oblique figuration in which multiple definitions are given voice in a brilliant contest that proceeds by fits and starts, throughout the novel. Such a privileging of the literary over the critical should not suggest that anything in Proust is ineffable. On the contrary, he struggles—with "all the forces of mind, and even the body"—to recover a place in the novel for everything dismissed or unregistered as ineffable experience. How this recovery is expressed proves to be the perceptible difference between reading Proust and his necessarily more schematic critics.

As this chapter has shown, Proust continually nuances his emergent definition of intelligence in the various contexts in which it occurs. Intelligence must be disarmed, losing its primacy, to become disarming, enabling the possibilities of art. From the Verdurin salon, where Forcheville teases out Swann's idea of intelligence, to Elstir's studio, where the painter empties his gaze of intelligence, or the stage where La Berma performs with an intelligence of diction, the novel offers ways of reconsidering the critical and creative function of intelligence. It gradually refutes the long-held notion that intelligence resides uniquely in the mind as a private property, showing instead how it emerges through a complex network of aesthetic, political, and personal investments in the world. Proust's writing thus becomes a singular form of fictive "research" that aims at broadening our perceptive and expressive powers, otherwise kept hemmed in by habit, voluntary memory, and intelligence. Such powers can only be exercised on the condition that intelligence is held subordinate to them, later expressing what they first perceive erroneously. The failure of the narrator and so many Proustian characters to obey this condition is what makes them worth talking about.

CHAPTER THREE

Testing Intelligence

VALÉRY RECONFIGURED

COMPARE TWO IMAGES OF Paul Valéry. The first is a 1913 oil painting by Jacques-Émile Blanche that shows the poet and critic in a reflective pose.¹ This realist portrait, housed in the Musée des Beaux-Arts in Rouen, captures much of Valéry's now outdated image—as Mallarmé's last disciple, a poet silenced by his demands for pure language who becomes the Bossuet of the Third Republic. He strikes us as a monumental figure, to be sure, but one who for that very reason is largely unread, if not unreadable, today. The other image, which is more difficult to find, and is reproduced here, comes from the 1945 illustrated edition of "Cimetière marin" by the Italian painter Gio Colucci. A few sparse lines and curves here evoke several figures, from a sailboat to the outlines of a skull or sphinxlike face, but also resist figuration. Hardly a portrait of Valéry in any conventional sense: looking at it one is forced to imagine what in Valéry's writing may have provoked Colucci to sketch such an image. Perhaps this Valéry moves away from realism, from symbolism, and academicism toward other potentialities of sound, sense, language, and thinking.

Valéry holds a strange position in French literary history, especially when it is told in English. His diffuse presence as a critical authority on aesthetic questions and yet relative absence as a figure of literary study, outside specialist circles, can be attributed to the untranslatability of his lyric poetry, and to the massive, non-systematic quality of his prose writings.² It is hard to reconcile Valéry's absence from current critical Anglophone discussions with his unimpeachable position in the post-Mallarméan moment in France. His words engraved on the entrance to the Palais de Chaillot testify to his status as the lapidary laureate of interwar

FIGURE 2. Gio Colucci, "Untitled," 1945. From Paul Valery, *Cimetière marin* (À l'enseigne de la Trirème, 1945).

France.[3] His critical concerns were evident to Walter Benjamin and later Theodor Adorno, who both draw on his writing in their aesthetic theories. This chapter makes a case for reconsidering Valéry as a poet-critic, prose writer and a critical theorist of literary "intelligence."

The advantage of approaching his oeuvre from this acute angle is that it helps one avoid the usual pitfalls that await readers, who all too often ratify the common image of the reactionary classical poet. Instead, Valéry emerges in the pages that follow as a figure attuned to the changing ground of literary production. He was deeply affected by the historical, mediatic, political and economic reversals taking place as he traced a distinct path for the emergence, figuration, and disfiguration of French "intelligence." Not only an aesthetic antithesis to Proust, as Adorno suggests, the poet-critic's fragmentary writings expose the dominant premises of the period concerning literary form. Valéry's doubts about the potential of the novel as a genre made Proust's belated intelligence, as analyzed in the previous chapter, an impossibility to him. He takes interest in testing literary intelligence as an alternative to the demands of fiction. One of his aphorisms describes intelligence as the faculty of recognizing one's own stupidity (*sottise*). This attitude should be read as part of his larger rejection of the stultifying demands of realist aesthetics, and an elevation of the potentiality of language over the work itself. As I show, his attitude toward the intentionality of the artwork varied from an early radical intentionalism to an equally adamant anti-intentionalism.[4] The former is marked by a desire to direct the reader's reactions through strict formal control, whereas the latter is characterized by a relinquishing of authority over the interpretation of his own works.

Daniel Oster helpfully divides the arc of Valéry's career into two phases of formalism.[5] The first was a technical phase influenced by the legacy of Poe, Mallarmé, Rimbaud, and symbolism. Valéry's claims during these years anticipated many tenets of structuralist poetics, from defining literature as a metalanguage to reading poetry as a generation of forms. The poetics of this first phase posited the work as a closed entity, mirroring the supposed determinism of the material universe. His perfectly constructed sonnets can be read as an attempt to write closed works. Valéry's second formalism shifted from the "certainties of mechanism to the anxieties of indeterminism," to borrow the phrase Suzanne Guerlac uses to describe the wider epistemic shift in scientific discourse.[6] As Oster remarks, Valéry's metaphors and analogies no longer aimed to reveal the secret structure of reality but counted as possible mental operations within a larger spectrum. This second phase focused on the force of language, rather than forms, especially in the unforeseeable effects of literary language upon readers. The closed work now became an open act capable of transforming, reproducing, marginalizing, but above all, interrupting the mind of the reader. The hypothesis of two phases in Valéry's work is admittedly heuristic. From his very first critical essay, "De la technique littéraire," he is conscious of the "force of language," and reflects on a poetics capable of producing a given effect on the reader.[7]

I add to this picture by showing that, despite his fluctuating formalism, Valéry remained committed to the idea that the real is formless. Rather than representing reality, literary language, in prose or verse, ought to voice its recognition of its singular point of elocution. Instead of resulting from an act of cognition based on the supposed immediacy of consciousness, literary insight results from pushing the "tension between contingency and the law of construction to the breaking point."[8] The fault of the realist novel resides in its epistemic claim to objectivity, falsely obtained at the cost of silencing or erasing its own poetic origin. Valéry avoided what he deemed to be inane sentences in his own prose, a style inherited from both Mallarmé's *crise de vers* and his own break with the Mallarméan dream of The Book. Neither entirely prose nor verse, his language is unnameable. Rather it is a fragmentary, paratactic enunciation of intelligence. It takes self-consciousness and self-variance as its object, making opinions, actions and feelings appear contingent and alien, rather than personal and affective. Lacking conventional plot- and character-driven interest, it belongs to the genre of the *histoire sans récit* or the *récit sans histoire* ("story/history/plot without narrative" or "narrative/history/plot without story") exemplified by the *Monsieur Teste* cycle. Its counterrealism attends to the artifices of interiority and swerves between the processes of the mind, the body, and the world (*corps-esprit-monde* or CEM as Valéry writes in the *Cahiers*). Valéry deflates the Cartesian notion of a universally shared faculty into a personal myth of intelligence. He defines "intelligence" as the power of substitution or translation in language, situating its interest in potentiality rather than actuality.[9] Its avatar is the inhuman figure of Edmond Teste, who abjures his considerable intellectual powers in order to remain sovereign.

The political valences of Valéry's thought came to the fore in his recognition that the literary object was obsolete, and that literature, philosophy, and indeed intelligence itself would soon become a relic of a culture belonging to the past. His awareness of the marginality of Europe—heightened by a series of wars from the first Sino-Japanese conflict to the Second World War—was translated into a set of "quasi-political" essays dealing with the "crisis of intelligence." The difficulty of defining intelligence, both as an intellectual process and a literary phenomenon, was recast as a political problem capturing a range of social and historical changes, from the rise of new media to the Bolshevik Revolution.

This chapter begins by comparing Proust with Valéry on aesthetic form. Reading *Monsieur Teste* alongside the notebooks, it then analyzes the innovative relation between two kinds of intelligence and crisis as described by Valéry: the "Seeking-Intelligence" and "Finding-Intelligence" (*Intelligence-Recherche* and *Intelligence-Trouvaille*).[10] Forays into other texts, including his fragmentary tales and essays, elucidate understudied points of Valéry's own unique method for "testing" the limits of intelligence. The lens of "intelligence" shows the remarkable consistency of Valéry's literary and philosophical concerns despite the heterogeneous scope of his writing.

Afterhours at the "Valéry-Proust Museum"

Proust and Valéry were near contemporaries. Adorno's 1953 essay, "Valéry-Proust Museum," to which the title of this section alludes, argues for the theoretical significance of juxtaposing two figures who remained largely ignorant of each other's work. Rather than a study of influence, any comparison between Proust and Valéry becomes a reflection on the intelligibility of the work of art and its afterlife in the historical conditions of its decay. Jacques Rancière's more recent invocation of Proust and Valéry also casts them as a conceptual couple in French criticism: Valéry was not only the aesthetic antithesis to Proustian poetics, but also an opponent to the novel's potential as a literary form.

Proust had read little Valéry, and the poet–critic almost entirely ignored the *Recherche*. Some clarification concerning their level of mutual ignorance might be illuminating at the outset to better distinguish between their literary critical projects.[11] Although Proust had published a programmatic article, "Against Obscurity" ("Contre l'obscurité"), that targeted symbolist poetics, he reserved critical judgment upon the 1917 publication of *La jeune parque*, a poem Valéry had himself described as a "long poème obscur." He did however discuss the poet's work in his correspondence, arriving at the conclusion that Valéry had "rediscovered Malherbe via Mallarmé" (*retrouvé Malherbe en traversant Mallarmé*), suggesting a crossing of classical form with symbolist syntax.[12] After the "Cimetière marin" appeared in the June 1920 volume of the *NRF*, Proust dedicated a copy of the first part of the third volume of the *Recherche*, *Le Côté de Guermantes I*, with the inscription: "To Monsieur Paul Valéry who in Le Cimetière Marin has captured the abstract in a mobile concreteness as no one had until now."[13] Arresting the abstract in concrete movement is more than an alluring formula; it is a remarkably accurate description of Valéry's poetics in this period of his writing.

After Valéry became a consecrated poet, having published *La jeune parque* in 1917 and *Charmes* in 1922, he drew Proust's critical attention. Responding to a fragment titled "Eupalinos ou l'Architecture. Dialogue des Morts," which purports to be a lost Platonic dialogue published in the *NRF*, Proust addressed a few paragraphs of his "À propos de Baudelaire" to refute the poet's vision that placed the creative gesture in line with the "blind work of nature" (*travail aveugle de la nature*). For Valéry, a creative gesture was an illuminated act (*un acte éclairé*) that functioned like nature, which abridged its working in such flashes. Proust replied that for every "harmonious" artist who created in continuum with nature and vivacity, there was an unnatural fecundity founded on illness—one that was in rupture with the natural order. He placed Baudelaire, Dostoevsky, and himself in the latter group constructed against Valéry's vision of creativity and deemed them capable of far more than a single poetic act: they "create something of which not a single paragraph could have been accomplished by a whole line of a thousand artists in fine health."[14]

Proust did not participate in the homage to Valéry organized by the literary review *Le divan* in 1922, despite being repeatedly solicited to do so. He claimed it was impossible as he had not yet found an excuse for his longstanding silence—"I have yet to apologize for my silence before such a great poet for which I would have preferred to substitute a laudatory voice."[15] On the other hand, Valéry did contribute to the special commemorative issue of the *Nouvelle Revue Française* for Proust, but only to confess his near total ignorance of the novelist's oeuvre: "Although I have scarcely read a single volume of Marcel Proust's great work, and though the very art of the novelist is an art that I find almost inconceivable, I am nevertheless well aware, from the little of the *Recherche du temps perdu* that I have found the time to read, what an exceptionally heavy loss literature has just suffered; and not only literature but still more the secret society composed of those who in every age give the age its real value."[16]

Despite, or perhaps because of, such incapacity to conceive of the art of the novelist, he declares that the interest of the *Recherche* lay precisely in its fragmentary quality (an insight Barthes and Blanchot would later appropriate): "The interest of his works lies in each fragment. We can open the book wherever we choose; its vitality does not depend on what went before, on a sort of *acquired illusion*; it depends on what might be called the *active properties* of the very tissue of the text."[17] Valéry's ignorance of the complex sequence of events and relations described in the novel allows him to identify fragmentary textual activity as the truly innovative aspect of Proust's work. The last words of his essay attempt to situate the Proustian narrative voice in the French tradition: "As for the means he used, they are undoubtedly derived from our finest tradition. It is sometimes said that his books are not altogether easy to read. But I never fail to reply that we must bless the difficult authors of the day [. . .]. At the same time as readers that they win for themselves, they give them back to Montaigne, to Descartes, to Bossuet."[18]

While that essay may conclude on a laudatory note, recognizing Proust as the training ground for a reader's intelligence, a preparation for difficult reading as such, Valéry simultaneously announces the rising tide of unintelligibility, one that threatens to foreclose the possibility of understanding canonical writers: "All these great men talk in abstractions; they reason; they probe deeply; in a single sentence they may express the entire substance of a complete development of thought. They are not afraid of the reader; they do not count their own labor nor his. Given a little more time, we shall no longer be able to understand them."[19] In private, Valéry was keen to demarcate himself from what he suspected was a shared research program in Proust, given their interest for liminal states of consciousness whose implications for human cognition were not merely "literary." Following a reflection on his own bad, or extremely selective, memory in his notebooks, Valéry remarks parenthetically, "(The fact of Proust shows that this is not merely a literary condition.)"[20] Elsewhere, he writes that he felt he was unlike Proust, who drew the substance of his need to write from the world itself. In a 1935 letter to Germaine Pavel, author of a comparative study on the two authors' treatment of sleep, Valéry declared that what separated him from the novelist, despite their shared interest in psychology, somatism, sleep and dreams, was their relation to time in general, and lost time in particular:

> I imagine Proust had an excellent memory and enjoyed reviving the finest details as one colors the fibers of neurons for the microscope. I have a bad memory. I forget events as if they could have happened to someone else. I have no childhood memories. In short, for me the past is abolished in its chronological and narratable structure. I have the indomitable feeling that it would be a waste of my time to regain lost time.[21]

Could narrative persist formally if the past were abolished, made unavailable as a chronological and narratable structure? Valéry's prose forms are particularly intriguing insofar as they move beyond the literary obligation to narrate the past. And yet it was the same Valéry who, in 1922, the year of Proust's death, writes: "Imagine that one awakes in the middle of the night and one's whole life is revived and speaks to oneself [. . .]. Sensuality, memories, landscapes, emotions, bodily feelings, depth of memories."[22]

There is no shortage of critical writing on the two authors under scrutiny. Beginning with Ernst Robert Curtius, the novelist and the poet have also served as the frame for comparative studies of twentieth-century French literature.[23] Walter Benjamin, too, juxtaposed the writers, especially for their comparable approach toward the "aporetic" experience of beauty. Benjamin isolates Proust and Valéry's respective attempts to reproduce this impasse in language:

> Beauty in relation to *nature* can be defined as "that which remains true to its essential nature only when veiled." [. . .] If one attempted

to reproduce this aporia in the material of language, one would define beauty as the object of experience [*Erfahrung*] in the state of resemblance. This definition would probably coincide with Valéry's formulation: "Beauty may require the servile imitation of what is indefinable in things." If Proust so readily returns to this object of experience (which in his work appears as time regained), one cannot say he is revealing any secrets. It is, rather, one of the disconcerting features of his technique that he continually and locquaciously builds his reflections around the concept of the work of art as a copy, the concept of beauty—in short, the hermetic aspect of art.[24]

Building on Goethe's claim about the veiled nature of beauty, Benjamin redefines beauty as "the object of experience in the state of ressemblence." He notes that while Valéry speculates on this indefinable aspect of things, and Proust attempts to regain it through involuntary memory, in both instances, the essential core of beauty remains veiled or hermetic. By maintaining the emphasis on the veil, Benjamin distances Proust and Valéry from instances of revelation or epiphany.

For Adorno, comparing Valéry's *Le problème des musées* with the passages on museums and trains stations in the *Recherche*, especially *À l'ombre des jeunes filles en fleurs*, allows one to question the afterlife of the work of art—namely, the possibility of its still being legible, visible, or audible after years of conservation and exposition.[25] He turns to Proust and Valéry, whom he calls the "two authentic French poets of the last generation," and their opposing positions toward the museum and the museum-like (the *museal*). For Valéry, the troubling surplus of masterworks at the Louvre is precisely what keeps a visitor from the pleasures (*délices*) of aesthetic judgment. Instead, the museum becomes a mausoleum for culture, indeterminately juxtaposing great works without signaling the singular "mental event that raised them out of those surroundings."[26] A visit to a museum inevitably ends, in Adorno's account of the Valérian position, in confusion: "One does not know why one has come—in search of culture or enjoyment, in fulfillment of an obligation, in obedience to a convention. Fatigue and barbarism converge. Neither a hedonistic nor a rationalistic civilization could have constructed a house of such disparities. Dead visions are entombed there."[27] Valéry compares the anarchy of the museum with the patent absurdity of listening to ten orchestras at once. The exhaustiveness of the archive soon exhausts the intelligence of the visitor.

Proust—or at least the Proust Adorno reconstructs from the narrator's positions on the question in the *Recherche*—is diametrically opposed to

Valéry's dismissal of the museum. Proust's narrator experiences the caesura of history that separates one work from another, an artist from an audience, and a book from its commentary, when traveling from one place name to another (*d'un nom à un autre*). Given the emphasis on distance and departure, it is no accident, notes Adorno, that Proust's key sentences on the museum are encrypted in a passage on train stations. The metaphoric connection between the museum and the train station is set to work in a description comparing the ominous sky glimpsed in the Gare Saint-Lazare to those above crucifixion scenes in paintings by Veronese or Mantegna. Both spaces are withdrawn from "the conventional and superficial unity of objects of action." They become symbolic bearers of death in the form of ancestral departures and the "new and perishable universe" created by artists.

The intersection in Valéry and Proust's writing on the museum for Adorno lies in the investment of happiness (*délices*; *enivrante joie*) that they expect the artwork to yield.[28] Their positions diverge due to their initial standpoint, that of the creator and the consumer respectively: "Valéry feels himself at home in the studio; Proust strolls through an exhibition. There is something exterritorial about his relation to art, and many of his false judgments, as in questions of music, denote traces of the dilettante until the end [. . .]. But he moulded this weakness into an instrument of strength as only Kafka could."[29] Proust's intelligence as a critic lies in the concerted naïveté of his amateur's gaze. For him, works of art become "part of the life of the person who looks at them, an element of his own consciousness."[30] By appropriating the artwork to consciousness, Valéry and Proust question how to present and represent art, in an attempt to discover which frame could possibly stay the rising tide of unintelligibility.

Adorno's staging of this polemic is itself a repetition of the exchange Proust and Valéry have concerning the nature of the artistic gesture: to what extent is art an offshoot of vitality, an abridged version of nature? In *Eupalinos ou l'architecture: dialogue des morts*, Valéry mourns the death of the *archē*, the organizing principle that made architecture possible and gave an intelligent principle for selecting and exposing artworks. Without this principle, as he notes in *Le problème des musées*, works of art are exposed to error:

> Their mother is dead, their mother Architecture. So long as she lived, she gave them their place, their use, their constraints. They were refused the freedom to err. They had their space, their well-defined light, their subjects, their alliances. . . . As long as she was alive, they

knew what they wanted ... —Farewell this thought says, I will go no further.³¹

Once such an archaic principle withdraws, art becomes vulnerable and exposed to error. Valéry symbolically leaves his own thinking incomplete, the fragmentary dash serving as a virtual farewell to canonical aesthetics.

We find a recent variant of the Proust–Valéry polarity in *La parole muette*, Rancière's inquiry into the contradictions of literature. Here Proust seems to come down squarely on the side of intelligibility. Obscurity can be ascribed to an insufficient translation of impressions to expressions. Consider the following passage from *Le Temps retrouvé*:

> A writer reasons, that is to say, he goes astray, each time he lacks the strength to force himself to make an impression pass through all the successive states which culminate in its fixation, its expression.³²

"In order to be able to understand this phrase, and the function of the 'myths' of literature themselves," Rancière writes, "we ought to set it into contrast with the constantly varied declarations of one of Proust's contemporaries, who, in both public and private texts, waged an endless war against literature in the name of literature's own requirements."³³ His Valéry, like Adorno's "conservative" critic, argues for the interest of classical art: "The appeal of classical art may well consist in the series of transformations it calls for, if things are to be expressed in conformity with the *sine qua non* conditions imposed on the author."³⁴ This conditioned, regulated notion of the classic throws Proust's passage from impression to expression into question. For Valéry, writes Rancière, "the virtue proper to classical art was the line by which an 'idea' distanced itself in order to become song."³⁵ The transformation of thinking into song is rule-bound; the desire for sense is diverted through the arbitrariness of sound. Hence, the distinctness of art is held up against the seriousness of thought and the illusory coherence of history.

Valéry argues in *Tel quel* that the harmony of classicism is itself a thing of the past. The voice, which acted as the condition of possibility of literature, is no longer its guarantor:

> For a very long time, the *human* voice was the basis and condition of *literature*. The presence of the voice explains the earliest literature from which classical literature took its shape and its admirable *temperament*. The whole human body was present *under* the voice, upholding and ensuring the equilibrium of the "idea" ...

> There came a day when we could read with our eyes without spelling, without hearing, and literature was completely transformed.
>
> Evolution from the articulate to the touched—from the rhythmic and linked to the instantaneous—from what a group of listeners accepts and demands to what a swift and eager eye, roving freely over a page, can cope with and take in.[36]

Instead of placing the epistemic rupture between voice and text, Proust chooses to place it between the potential of history and the potential of metaphor, a choice that allows him to imprison the myth of the book in genesis deep into his book itself.[37] Valéry's distinction between the time of the speaking body and the time of writing leads to his annotation of the possibilities of thought and writing, rather than writing works of literature. The "suspicion" about the possibility of literature and the withdrawal of the *oeuvre* before a more fundamental undoing or *dèsoeuvrement*, Rancière argues, is not a discourse born out of historical trauma, or political demystifications of discourse in the 1940s. Instead, these mid-century topoi found in Paulhan, Blanchot, Gracq, and others emerge from the contradictions of literature already at work in Proust and Valéry.

Valéry was drawn to the practice of poetry largely as a formal exercise in constraint. He typically prizes the process of composition—what he calls its "program"—over the resulting poetic work, which remains open to interpretation and perpetual modification. His prose fell into two large categories: the essays that were commissioned by various journals and editors and the private auroral speculations in his *Cahiers*. As Malcom Bowie writes, "no great European poet has provided his readers with a richer prose hinterland than Valéry in his notebooks, essays, dialogues, lectures, and occasional writings."[38] Prose offered him a form free of the constraints of meter and enjambement in which he could reflect on the significance of his writing and thinking.

This division in Valéry's oeuvre recalls Benjamin's apothegm about romantic novel criticism: "the idea of poetry is prose."[39] However, the reverse seems equally apt for the poet, more indebted to classicism than romanticism: the ideal of his prose is poetry. If the best poetry strives to be lyric poetry for Valéry, then prose too, once it recognizes its limits, is bound to take on a lyric aspect. However, the voice underlying his poetics does not unify a human subject.[40] Voice instead underscores the fragility and ruptures of the intelligent self, which Valéry considered a reflexive effect of consciousness. His attack on prose, the topic of the following section, targeted narrative forms, such as the nineteenth-century realist novel, which laid claims to objectivity without acknowledging the fracture between the self and language.

Valéry's Attack on Prose

Both as a poet and a critic, Valéry seems to have hated prose and its devices. This section refines our image of Valéry as an enemy of certain kinds of prose, while drawing on his poetics to account for his antagonism towards narrative genres. His hatred of prose was further exaggerated and instrumentalized by writers and critics, particularly André Breton, Maurice Blanchot, and Jean Paulhan, who inaugurated new critical idioms, working through the legacy of Mallarmé. Stepping back from this reception, this section then rearticulates Valéry's considerably more nuanced theory of prose, drawing on the significant work done by Judith Robinson and Michel Jarrety.

Valéry's devaluation of the *romanesque* can only be understood in light of his own prose production, especially *Monsieur Teste*. Benjamin speculated that Teste was the secret exponent of Valéry's larger project meant to destroy two widely held poetic axioms: that writers are intelligent and that intelligence is irrelevant to the poet.[41] Destroying these two clichés about intelligence means moving beyond Valéry's repulsion to prose and exposing literature to another kind of intelligence, which is anything but self-evident and has nothing "human" about it. After Dante's *Divina commedia* and Balzac's *Comédie humaine*, Valéry sought to compose a "*Comédie intellectuelle*, which had not yet met its poet."[42]

Although I will be focusing on Valéry's prose, the site of his thinking about intelligence, his work is first prized as a poet.[43] Most of his early published work was composed of lyric. His intellectual verse uses the incantatory or "charming" phrase to elevate sound over sense, or revel in the delay in between.[44] For many critics, Valéry's theory and practice of poetry destabilizes traditional modes of thought and signification.[45] Merleau-Ponty considers Valéry's conception of literature a "pure exercise of intelligence" entirely outside of the "exercise of life."[46] Thibaudet describes Valéry's major poetic theme not as a conflict between body and soul, but the very annihilation of material reality in a contest between the "spiritual reality of the body" and "the other spiritual reality of consciousness."[47] He defines Valéryan "intelligence" as "a potentiality of forming relations" between things that do not exist. Geoffrey Hartman further specifies that Valéry used "every means to retard in us that faculty of the intellect often named induction, by which we are enabled to make a quick or conventional guess at the referent of a phrase."⁴⁸

This aesthetic of threatened and delayed meaning, somewhat like Proust's, was born out of Valéry's larger interest in the formal qualities of language that "suspend hasty rationality or commonplace recognition." The famous "silence" roughly between 1896 and 1916, during which Valéry wrote only for himself, contributed to his aura as a solitary genius without an oeuvre, a legend ripe for Nathalie Sarraute's satire in *L'Enfant de l'éléphant* (even though his prose anticipated the *nouveau roman*'s narrative stripped of commentary and psychology).⁴⁹ During this period, Valéry reflected on literature's paradoxical situation, which could neither be identified with rationality, nor merely forgo it. Were it to become purely rational, a variant of mathematical or logical notation, its literariness would disappear. And if it became a hermetic use of language free from the strictures of thought, it would be powerless to face the conditions of social domination surrounding it.⁵⁰ The explorations of such paradoxes, at the heart of the aesthetic, made Valéry a predecessor for postwar thinkers, from Adorno and Derrida to the *Tel Quel* group, intent on locating the limits of thought in figural language.⁵¹

Countless fragments testify to Valéry's relentless skepticism concerning the practice of writing, and the value of literature in particular. In *Tel quel* we are asked: "Could a man of ruthless and profound intelligence apply himself to literature? From what angle? And where would he situate it in his mind?"⁵² The series of questions could easily be reversed: what does it imply about someone's intelligence if they happen to be profoundly interested in literature? What if they willingly suspend disbelief while reading an attempt to depict reality through the device of an impersonal omniscient narrator? Such belief in the signifying power of fiction is what Valéry dubs literary superstition, all forms of which have a common basis in forgetting the linguistic basis of literature: "This is what I call all beliefs that share a forgetting of the verbal condition of literature. Hence the existence and *psychology of characters*, those living beings *without entrails*."⁵³ The imprecision of the most common terms of literary analysis—the existence and the verisimilitude of characters, referential fidelity, psychological realism in the novel, even literary analysis itself—are sources of confusion. For Valéry, one might as well be talking about the Mona Lisa's nervous system or the Venus de Milo's liver. His persistent unwillingness to admit the mimetic potential of fiction, or to partake in a shared vocabulary of aesthetics, stems from the same axiomatic reversal of form and content at the basis of many of his topical judgments: "LITERATURE:

What 'form' is to anyone else is 'substance' to me."[54] The inversion between *forme* and *fond* signals Valéry's radically particular critical idiom. His notion of form, it has been suggested, suspends understanding in favor of sheer visibility or radiance, thereby restoring a sense of possibility to the object being contemplated.[55]

Given his self-consciously idiosyncratic attitude toward the authority of fiction, it is fitting that the poet's most famous pronouncement on the matter is not to be found in his writings.[56] Instead, André Breton attributes it to him in the 1924 Surrealist manifesto, invoking Valéry as a celebrity witness in his trial against the realist attitude from Aquinas to Anatole France—a tradition he condemns wholesale for its hostility towards all intellectual or moral development, and its promotion of literary mediocrity mirrored by the rise of the novel:

> As a cleansing antidote to all this, M. Paul Valéry recently suggested that an anthology be compiled in which the largest possible number of opening passages from novels be offered; the resulting insanity, he predicted, would be a source of considerable edification. The most famous authors would be included. Such a thought reflects a great deal of credit on Paul Valéry, who some time ago, speaking of novels, assured me that, so far as he was concerned, he would continue to refrain from writing: "The Marquise went out at five." But has he kept his word?[57]

Significantly, it turns out that Valéry's statement about the marquise was a promise, a vow of abstention.[58] Breton's inquisitional tone is quick to question the eminent writer's continued relevance: Had he kept his word, or had he also slipped into novelistic banality?[59] Breton condemns the lack of ambition of novelists whose reliance on "pure and simple informative" syntax turns fiction into an arbitrary collection of details, descriptions, and commonplaces that leave no discretionary powers to readers, except the power to stop reading.[60] While Valéry was remarkable for his resistance to realism, he may well have betrayed the intensity of such commitments in subsequent prose writings.

Breton's equation of fiction to a reduction of the reader's freedom is a tactic echoed in Valéry. In the preface to *Histoires brisées*, his experimental fragmentary tales, which I will discuss later, he formulates the distinction between poetry and prose in terms of the agency accorded by a work to its reader:

> Every literary work is from moment to moment exposed to the reader's *initiative*. From moment to moment, he can react to his reading by

making substitutions which will affect either the detail of the work or its evolution. The background, the narration, and the tone of voice can all be more or less altered, while less or more delicately preserving the effect of the whole. Almost all art consists in persuading the reader to forget his own powers of intervention in comprehensively forestalling his reactions, in hedging them in through the discipline and perfection of the form. Every story can admit one or more denouements quite other than that which is actually provided; it is much more awkward, by the way, to manipulate at will a well-made poem.[61]

The arbitrary form of the novel requires readers to forget their power to intervene—perhaps, here a synonym for intelligence—whereas the formal perfection of poetry limits and channels their possibility to do so. Valéry holds the formal contingency of the novel, and his overwhelming sense of contingency as such, responsible for distracting him from narrative path or the *voie du récit*.

The impossible sentence Breton attributes to Valéry—*La marquise sortit à cinq heures*—is phrased in the *passé simple*, almost as if it were aware of its historical charge.[62] The *passé simple*, an aorist, for Benveniste is a verb without speaker, which narratologists identify as an exclusively narrative form. As narrative voice, such a sentence is neither true nor false, yet to function it demands belief in the signifying power of fiction, just what Valéry is unwilling to accept.[63] The two examples mentioned in the Surrealist manifesto—the anthology of inane first sentences, and the proscribed sentence—are part of a larger argument about the power of arbitrariness and the reduction of agency afforded that make it impossible, for Valéry, to situate himself in a narrative universe as a reader, let alone to begin writing fiction. Teste shares Valéry's contempt for the novel: "I am not made for novels or plays. Their great scenes, rages, passions, tragic moments, far from exciting me, strike me as shabby outbursts, rudimentary states in which every sort of nonsense is let loose."[64] Narrative fiction is the place where "being is reduced to stupidity" (*sottise*), Teste declares.[65] Valéry set a different course for his writing, with the aim of recognizing and reorganizing the self.

Fiction's basic appeal to reality proves trivial at best, and its methods for depicting this reality are even more bereft. What Valéry doubts is the truth-value so commonly accorded to the practice of reading and writing about the lives of others. This truth-value is even more threatened to the extent that a fictional work is complete. As he puts it in one of his most decisive literary axioms: "a work is always a fake" (*une oeuvre est toujours un faux*). It has no corresponding author who works under a single moment of inspiration; rather it is the result of many contradictory impulses and combinatory movements cobbled together into a whole. Hence its constitutive duplicity: the more fiction seems complete, the more it has falsified to gain the appearance of closure. It is to this theory of falsehood that I would now like to turn.

Valéry's devotion to perfection as a writer and a rhetorician was deeply intertwined with his skepticism about the formal truth of literature. According to Blanchot, Valéry's commitment to form betrays a prior defection from art itself, which he conceives of as essentially arbitrary:

> Valéry sees only arbitrariness and conventions in the means and effects of art, and that is because he denies the real value of the form that he asserts and whose demands he observes: there can be perfect writers only because perfection has no truth for him.[66]

In his larger argument, Blanchot echoes Paulhan's claim that the essential secret of surrealism—its *raison d'être*—was a will to refute Valéry's aesthetic theory. The latter amounted to an ultimatum between conscious acts of composition and the falsehood of the *chef d'oeuvre* on the one hand, and madness, the trance, and authenticity of worklessness on the other.[67] Valéry chose the masterpiece and the masterpiece triumphed over his skepticism, in Blanchot's view, reducing it to a light, brilliant, and rather vain state of mind.[68] In a curious turn of events, Valéry's distate for impersonal, omniscient realist fiction—initially a reason for the avant garde to cautiously celebrate the poet laureate, quickly turned him into the *bête noire* for a generation of critics that sought an exit from the dead end of formalist criticism.

Valéry distinguished sharply between poetry and prose, or more precisely between lyricism and fiction. For the distinction is not so much one of genre, but of the linguistic-enunciatory conditions of the text, the choice between the impersonal *il* and an irreducibly singular *je*. Valéry reverses the passage Blanchot (following Kafka) later proposes as the quintessential movement of writing literature, leaving the domain of the "I" for the neutral, third person. The difference between the two conceptions comes from the subject position they identify with narrative voice—*je* or *il*. First-person speech retains a relation to the other—what Teste calls the rival intelligence—as it is addressed from within a polarity of the speaker to the "you," at least implicitly present, which guarantees some degree of significance to what is said through listening. This model of address, of voice, is intrinsic to poetry for Valéry, and ought to become the ambition of prose.

Poetry becomes the future of prose, a future that can only be attained if prose is honed to its essence, moving beyond the task of communication or imitation. Before this transformative effort, prose is a transitive medium: "In fact, meaning, which is the tendency toward a uniform mental substitution, unique and resolutive, is the object, law, and limit of existence of pure prose."[69] Prose disappears once its message has been delivered, Valéry argues, and if it is prose, its message can always be delivered by other means. Indeed, this transmissibility is one of its identifying features: namely the ability to be expressible by another piece of writing.[70] Poetry conversely does not perish, or transmit anything; rather it creates a singularly expressive state:

> There is no question in poetry of transmitting to one person something intelligible happening within another. It is a question of creating within the former a state whose expression is exactly and peculiarly what communicates it to him [. . .] as a result such a reader enjoys very great freedom as to ideas, a freedom analogous to that which music allows to the hearer.[71]

Distinctions between pure poetry and pure prose abound in Valéry's published and unpublished works, and only rarely does he comment on the various hybrid forms that exist between these two extremes, such as the prose poem or poetic prose. To schematize the dichotomy that emerges from these pages one might say that poetry is a necessary exercise whose limit is algebraic, while prose is an artificial, contingent instrument whose limit is music.[72] Poetry is perpetual beginning, whereas prose is development. Prose remains unfinished, but the crafted verse is complete. When prose is finished, it becomes verse. In his "Propos sur la poésie," Valéry cites a remark by Racan to Malherbe in which the difference between the two kinds of writing is likened to the difference between walking and dancing. The speed, rhythm, end, and direction of walking—or prose—are determined by intention and determination, whereas dancing—or poetry—is an end in itself that involves no real displacement.[73] Even the physical attitude of the reader varies for Valéry, as the novel makes him forget his body and throws him into a "crisis of gullibility" (*crise de crédulité*), while poetry restores a somatic sense of being alive.[74]

However these distinctions strike us, it is important to move beyond their opposition, as Jarrety shows, towards the series of underlying tensions between lyricism and fiction, *poiesis* and *mimesis*, the performative and the constative, *discours* and *récit*.[75] Likewise, it is worth noting a historical nuance in the argument against the novel. The epistolary novel and eighteenth-century *conte* were never objects of contempt for Valéry. His attack on prose is addressed particularly towards the nineteenth-century realist novel exemplified by Balzac and Flaubert. Their narrative voice is anything but a voice, their fiction is not addressed: it has no point of view, no enunciation and this absence does not engage the reader's attention but demands credence in the performance of imitation. Valéry's refusal of realism is a refusal of this sacrifice of the intellect demanded of both the reader and the writer. His premise remains that the real is incoherent and formless, whereas perception is singular—a situation that makes mimesis impossible and relegates representation to a counterfeit regime of language. However, this should not suggest that literature could ever simply be the bearer of truth. Rather, only when it acknowledges the lyric singularity of its enunciation can literature distinguish itself from philosophical and historical claims to veracity. Fiction generates unbearable propositions such as *la marquise sortit à cinq heures* in its quest to mimic "objective truth," understood as shorthand for fidelity to reality in the accrual of detail.

A fragment from the *Cahiers* describes Valéry's ideal novel, which he equates with the diary of everyday events:

> Why could a "novel" not be the diary of someone's day [...] a *certain way of looking at things* [...] the incoherent sequence made up of substitutions of moments and quite distinct phases.[76]

Although this description recalls aspects of works written by Joyce, Svevo, Woolf, and Musil, among others, the fragment does not suggest that Valéry is referring to any of them. During this period, he became increasingly interested in the uncertainty and relativity of the material world, and this passage, too, suggests that his attention to the intensities and vectors of the everyday meant to question the ability of fiction to represent the real.

For Valéry, words can only engender words, never unmediated truth, which, as Colin Davis writes, he considers little more than "a means to an end, an expression of the will to power, or a metaphysical obfuscation resulting from a lack of precision or rigor."[77] In her reading of the *Cahiers*, Judith Robinson shows how skeptical Valéry remained towards the capacity of language to express truth. All too often systematic attempts at enunciation, whether in literary or philosophical realism, were undermined by the vagueness of words, which created false, and even worse, insoluble problems. The task of thinking thus becomes to limit the number of illegitimate questions that have their origin in a misuse of language—especially the deification of words into unimpeachable concepts that reign over matter, and the resulting anthropomorphism of understanding. Valéry's definition of a philosophical problem is a problem that one does not know how to enunciate properly and the analytic goal he set for himself seems to have been not one of resolution or solution, but construction and enunciation: "As for me, I spent my life looking for formulations rather than solutions."[78] Finding an *énoncé* is another name for the process of destroying the truth claim of a question, thereby laying it open to a new order of linguistic performativity.

There is then a third way between the representative *parole brute* and the poetic *parole essentielle*—to recall a Mallarmean distinction—a secret prose that can only be unveiled by denouncing its more common variant. This unnamable prose is neither entirely prose nor entirely verse. Unlike the novel that is bound to become an arbitrary list of human events chosen for their capacity to distract the reader, the prose of intelligence has no human interest. It takes either the form of a *histoire sans récit* or a *récit sans histoire*. These two modes of Valérian prose could be described further as a counterrealism that is concerned with the constructed character of interiority rather than the depiction of sociality, privileging the particular, living detail, and a collection of fragmentary tales that take liberties with the independent existence of the real world by elevating mental plasticity over external reality. Written in this vein, Valéry's most famous exponent of the life of the mind, and its limits, was Monsieur Teste.

Teste, Testis—*Valéry's "Inhumanism"*

Many of Valéry's abstract claims about the imitative structure of thinking and the arbitrary violence of language are given voice in *Monsieur Teste*. Benjamin discerned the implications of Valéry's secret critical project to recognize the articulations and limits of thought. In 1931, in a tribute to the poet on his sixtieth birthday, Benjamin wrote:

> Valéry sets out to explore the writer's and especially the poet's intelligence [*der Intelligenz des Schreibenden, zumal des Dichters*] like an inquisitor, and calls for a break with the widely held view that it is self-evident that writers are intelligent, as well as with the even more widely held view that intelligence is irrelevant to the poet. He himself possesses intelligence of a kind that is anything but self-evident. Nothing can be more disconcerting than its embodiment: Monsieur Teste [...]. However human Monsieur Teste feels himself to be, he has taken to heart Valéry's aperçu that the most important ideas are those that contradict our feelings. He represents, therefore, the negation of the "human."[79]

In *Monsieur Teste* there is no enumeration of detail and no "human" interest. Instead, we are confronted with a dehumanizing desire for an authentic voice, emerging from a quest for precision, rigor, and purity. Teste is only interested in the facility or difficulty of what can be known or achieved. The uniqueness of his voice is produced artificially through a series of para-textual devices, including the friend who knew Teste, an archive of family letters, and his logbook.

As a text, *Monsieur Teste* refers to a series of writings published as a volume in 1926, the earliest of which was written in 1895. Valéry describes Teste's inception as follows: "Teste was created—in a room where Auguste Comte spent his early years—at a moment when I was drunk with my own will, and subject to strange excess of self-consciousness. I was affected with the acute malady of precision. I was straining toward the extreme of the reckless desire to understand, seeking in myself the critical limits of my powers of attention."[80] Valéry willfully tested the "critical limits" of his "powers of attention" in a room associated with the tutelary figure of systemic thinking and philosophical positivism whom he unravels into a fragmentary allegory of testing.

In addition to being the third-person present singular indicative of the verb *tester*, Teste's name recalls an older form of *tête* (head). It also echoes the Latin *testis*, both "witness" and the generative, genital organ. Commenting on this etymology, Giorgio Agamben notes that *testis* derives from an archaic Latin form *tristis*, which means "the third standing by." Teste as a third, Agamben suggests, stands between the observing eye and the world, even the "I" and itself, as a kind of second-degree self.[81] Oster adds that the first name "Edmond" could be read as an anagram of "demon" or a cipher for "monde," while the common sobriquet "monsieur" is a marker of his "vulgarity."[82] This wealth of possible meaning is perhaps why Valéry's narrator calls Teste none other than the "demon of possibility."[83]

Beyond a personification of intellectual vigilance, one could hardly describe Teste as a character: "There is no known likeness of Monsieur Teste."[84] "More than a character," notes Jeffrey Mehlman, Teste is "the consolidation of an option to abandon poetry as deleterious to intelligence."[85] Precisely because of his unique interest in what one *can* do, Teste does very little: he dines at the same café each night, speculates on the stock market, hardly acts, never falls in love (a confirmed bachelor, he is later married), distrusts words, speaks infrequently, and falls asleep after inviting the narrator to smoke a cigar in his home. It is easier to place Teste using family resemblances: Poe's Dupin, Balzac's Louis Lambert, and Huysmans's Des Esseintes, mixed with elements from Da Vinci and Descartes.[86] *Monsieur Teste* might equally be read as a drug narrative, an abnormal transcription of consciousness as intoxication, which "duplicates" Baudelaire's *Paradis artificiels*.[87] Teste could serve as a precursor to Brecht's Herr Keuner, Musil's *Man without Qualities*, and certain figures in narratives by Beckett and Blanchot.[88] "Teste incarnates Valéry's relation to narrative," Vincent Kaufman suggests, "but also his paradoxical relationship to literature in general, if indeed literary practice presupposes the affirmation of an identity or a singularity."[89]

We encounter Teste's mind during an evening he spends in the company of the narrator. The anonymous narrator, who cannot abide *bêtise* (which only roughly designates stupidity), is convinced that Teste has discovered hidden laws of thinking.[90] His memory allows him to retain impressions that the imagination alone is unable to construct. In short, he recognizes the importance of "human plasticity."[91] Teste extends Valéry's inquisition of received ideas. He spends his free time considering the temporality of freedom itself: "The delicate art of duration, time, its distribution and regulation [. . .] this was one of Monsieur Teste's great experiments [. . .]. He was a being absorbed in his own variations [. . .] who commits himself without reservation to the frightening discipline of the free mind."[92]

The status of *Monsieur Teste* as fiction remains vexed. Valéry comically deflated it as "the story of a guy who thinks."[93] In the *Cahiers*, he describes Teste somewhat more grandly as an "intimate apostle of consciousness" and "a mystic and physician of—pure and applied—Self-consciousness."[94] As the narrator remains unnamed, and Valéry himself often speaks of a fantastical encounter with Teste, nothing assures or prohibits us from believing that Valéry could be the narrator of the *récit*. Continuing Proust's autofictional game that places an unnamed narrator as a witness at the center of the text, Valéry claims to discover a series of axioms about the intelligibility of literature and life, thinking through and against his persona. Harassed by the conventions and constraints imposed by others, and by selfhood upon consciousness, Teste tries to purify his thinking of *idées reçues*. The violence that he inflicts upon himself often takes the form of a reduction. Significantly, he despairs of reading, burns his papers, and possesses no books.

At the origin of any reputation, Teste quips, there is a fault, an original sin, or a *faux pas* that gets the literary world talking: "Every mind said to be powerful begins with a mistake that makes it known. In exchange for the public's dime, he gives the time required to make himself noticeable."[95] At the theater, he observes how the reactions provoked by art reduce the individuals in the audience into an unintelligent, undifferentiated mass. There is almost nothing to be said, in this case, as there is nothing that differentiates one person from another: "One is *beautiful*, extraordinary, only to others! *They* are eaten by others!"[96] Since art is made to belong to a great leveling movement, the essential task of writing becomes one of self-immolation and alienation from artfulness. Aesthetic experience has nothing to offer to the extent that spectators of art are consumers of language, in Teste's view, consumers themselves consumed by the language of others. Jean-Luc Marion calls Teste's gaze "idoloclastic"—it cannot "attest any idol," instead putting "to the test what it beholds as one holds an enemy to the ground, in order to test him."[97] Unlike the shared attention to a unique stage, Proust's image for intelligence, Teste's intelligence evaluates the audience instead.

Valéry considered depicting the death of his alter-ego but found each possible death would risk a more dangerous fall backwards into novelistic arbitrariness.[98] Contrary to such false closure, Teste remains a figure of potentiality:

> All that I do and think is merely a Sample of my possibility. Man is more general than his life and his acts. He is *designed*, as it were, for more eventualities than he can experience. Monsieur Teste says: My possibility never leaves me.[99]

This possibility presumes blankness. Here is what Teste's nondescript room looks like: "I have never had a stronger impression of the *ordinary*. This was any room, like 'any point' in geometry—and perhaps as useful. My host existed in lodgings of the most usual sort."[100]

In his isolation, Teste remains conscious that he lacks a sparring partner, a rival who could force him back into life:

> It is not living to live without a living resistance, without objections, without that prey, that other person, the adversary, that undifferentiated remainder of the world, both obstacle and shadow of the self—another self—a rival, irrepressible intelligence—an enemy as best friend, that divine, that fatal and . . . and intimate . . . hostility.[101]

It is unclear how Teste would encounter or evaluate rival intelligence, let alone dialogue with it, since he considers speech as the bearer of non-knowledge. In his formula: "If we knew, we would not speak—we wouldn't think, we wouldn't talk. Knowledge is foreign to being itself."

If language holds no promise of clarifying the nature of being, then intelligence becomes a strategy of deviation, in which the mind swerves away from itself, its memories, and specially the suffering body. Physical pain becomes Teste's true rival. His bedtime constitutes the only turning point in the story: the encounter between painful sensation and an already irritated intelligence. On a stylistic level, Teste's coughing interrupts his thinking, as ellipses fragment the text. The effect of parataxis makes each instant in his presence an abrupt beginning. Valéry's text stages interruption through a reflection that is itself interrupted. Rather than making thinking somatic, Teste renders the life of the body conscious.[102] *La soirée avec Monsieur Teste* and *Studies on Hysteria* both appeared in 1895.[103] Whereas Freud and Breuer transform the idea of hysteria into unconscious symptoms through hypnosis or repression, notes Jean Starobinski, Teste reverses the hysterical process, making his pain a mental thing.

This counter-hysterical movement might be used to characterize Valéry's narratives, whether in the *Teste* cycle or the *Histoires brisées*, which he began but never finished, as a rule. Unlike the "surrealist idolatry of the powers of language," as Oster helpfully recalls, Valéry considered "literature as a deliberately anti-paranoid activity."[104] Rather than forming relations, his prose is paratactic—a fragmentary leaping from one lyric enunciation of sensation become intelligence to another. The goal of these works was to create a rupture between novelistic fiction that is a representation without origin—the view from nowhere—and a discourse that opens onto statements of reality (even if they are imaginary), not by attempting to say the real but by offering a sensible and singular relation to it. It is hardly accidental that Valéry named this relational mode the life of intelligence: "The life of intelligence offers an incomparable lyrical universe, a whole theatre in which neither adventure, passion, suffering of a very particular kind, nor comedy, nor anything human is lacking."[105] In the *Cahiers*, he admits that intellect was the only relation that allowed him to invest in an object: "The things of the world interest me only as they relate to the intellect, for me, everything relates to the intellect."[106] This intellectual relation tends toward the universal and negates the singular. Yet, as the unique instrument for approaching the world, it marks one of the limits of Valéry's entire enterprise. "This point of view [of the intellect] is false, since it separates the mind from all other activities, but such abstract operations and falsifications are inevitable, every point of view is false."[107]

The "prose of intelligence" makes few claims on its readers' credulity because it does not obscure its point of view. As suggested above, it vacillates between a *histoire sans récit* or a *récit sans histoire*, whose motto might be the first sentence of *Agathe, or the manuscript found in a brain* (*Agathe, ou le manuscrit trouvé dans une cervelle*), "the more I think, the more I think" (*plus je pense, plus je pense*). In this fragment, which was supposed to represent Teste's nocturnal thoughts, we witness the birth of conscious ideas as syntax itself:

> They ascend, original; in a meaningless order; mysteriously moved toward the admirable noon of my presence, where burns, as it best may, the sole thing that exists: the any *one*.[108]

This passage shows how concertedly Valéry extended Mallarmé's reflections on the restricted *technique de vers* to a generalized *technique quelconque*.[109] In doing so, Valéry leaves us with traces of what the interplay of intelligence and voice—the paradigm of his poetry—would look like as a very particular kind of non-mimetic, antidiegetic narrative. As Atsuo Morimoto notes, this voice has multiple facets—erotic, existential, or ideal—and each time Valéry "constructs a voice" distinct to the piece of writing at hand.[110]

To what extent did Valéry succeed in liberating prose from its dependence on representation? His work moves from the impersonal generality of the human towards the inhuman singularity of *l'une quelconque*: "I don't know why [. . .] authors are praised for being human when everything that makes man greater is inhuman or superhuman and one cannot deepen anything without quickly losing this impure commerce, this mixed view of things called humanity."[111] The trouble with representation, then, is its beleaguered humanism.[112]

When Valéry made such trenchant claims, he was a *"rhétoricien à l'état sauvage,"* to borrow Paulhan's phrase about him. This meant that he was often mistaken, and that his repeated errors composed a system: a machine whose operation could be studied to reveal its regularity. Perhaps it was an antiliterary war-machine, as Paulhan suggests. But there is also another possibility. The "attack on prose" described in the previous section should not invoke a uniquely military metaphor, a campaign to defeat the adversary once and for all. Rather, it might invoke a musical term. An attack in music is how one strikes a string to produce a note, the intensity at the beginning of that note, as well as the parameter used to determine the speed at which a sound reaches its maximal intensity. Valéry's attack is a singular way of striking the tense cord separating fiction from lyricism to produce unheard sounds, driving prose to its sonorous intensity.

Intelligenti Pauca: *Reading the* Cahiers

"Intelligence—articulated sensibility—in many dimensions—however *intelligenti pauca?*—this little bit is a hyper-sensibility—nothing yields all. Thus waiting, thus hidden organization."[113] Intelligence in Valéry's criticism is almost indistinguishable from intellectual crisis. The hyper-consciousness of the young symbolist poet slowly translated into a wide-ranging intellectual examination of European cultural practices and their imminent demise. This section explores a small selection from the vast archive of Valéry's notebooks to show how the term "intelligence" connects his reflections on the potentialities of fractured subjectivity to growing political concerns.[114] Instead of being a "pure poet" cut off from the world, Valéry tracked unprecedented social transformations within the negativity of his struggle with language.

Valéry, like Proust, and Mallarmé before them, underwent a mental crisis that was a formative influence in self-understanding. Reading a letter Proust wrote to a schoolteacher in 1888, his biographer Jean-Yves Tadié refers to the student's confession of his inner life since his teenage years, marked by an unbearable level of self-consciousness. Proust describes the "exhaustion and despair" caused by the constant doubling, which robs him of his supreme source of joy, his literary existence.[115] The analytic demise of pleasure can be attributed to the unrelenting gaze of self-consciousness.[116] For Tadié, Proust and Valéry suffer from the same psychosomatic malady, which becomes creative consciousness over time.[117]

While this analogy may be compelling in terms of Valéry's poetry, it is less convincing when applied to his prose and journals. Rather than transforming crippling self-consciousness into creative work, these texts diverge from self-consciousness in endless critical variations that refuse to be enclosed. These are the *Abweichungen* or deviations to which Adorno devotes his essay.[118] To describe the deviant object of Valéry's inquiry, he glosses one of his key terms: "*Rhumbs*—the gradation marks on the compass rose, as well as the angle between one of these marks and the meridian, hence the deviation of a course from the north, what Valéry has in mind is 'swerves from the governing direction of the "set" of my mind.'"[119]

Intelligence, in Valéry, may be nothing other than the force that allows a mind to swerve away from itself. As an entry in the *Cahiers* signed by Teste expresses the matter, intelligence solicits incessant redefinition.

Teste: Intelligence, the mind, everyone defines these inescapable myths in their own way—offering and refusing them to themselves at one point or another.—The idea that comes to me this morning—put it like this: Intelligence is the potential for *substitutions* (insofar as *better* suited). The problem would be: In place of one proposed set of things or circumstances—substitute another such that ... etc. *and thus what was not possible, becomes so*. The role of languages in intelligence then seems very clear. It's a characteristically fundamental substitution. Substitution of words and things. To understand is to effect a substitution-translation.[120]

Equated with translation, intelligence amounts to "the capacity to substitute words and things." Understanding proves to be an operation of linguistic "substitution" until the unclear becomes clear, or the impossible seems possible.

Valéry's *Cahiers* comprise ceaseless experiments in writing and reformulating obstacles of and for intelligence, with and against Teste. His dual research program, as Bowie notes, questions "the subject matter and problem-solving techniques characteristic of philosophy, mathematics, natural science, and the fine arts," as well as "thinking itself and [...] the place occupied by thinking beings in the order of nature."[121] One finds entries on the relation between "intelligence" and memory, nerves, hunger, boredom, sleep, awakening, automatism, animality, variation, substitution, economy, dreams, distraction, habit, rational choice, discernment, instinct, articulate feeling, drawing, skepticism, the ability to recognize stupidity and the limits of intelligence. Yet it would be a fundamental misconception to consider "intelligence" as one of Valéry's themes—instead, it remains a force that problematizes the possibility of isolating a theme in thinking in the first place.[122] In this vein, it is necessary to place "intelligence" in the larger nexus of Valéry's interest in reflexivity.

A striking 1915 letter from the poet to Pierre Louÿs invokes the vicissitudes of reflexivity and the multiplicity of the self. Describing the experience of looking in a mirror, Valéry boldly identifies "all of psychology" with the delay experienced between thought and action, impulse and reflex, self-consciousness and image:

> You see yourself obeying with a delay. Compare this to what happens when you are looking for a word or a "forgotten" name. All psychology is this delay, what one could paradoxically dub: what happens between something [...] and itself.[123]

This peremptory claim appears less so when placed in the larger context of reflex theory that flourished in the second half of the nineteenth century. As Valéry wrote elsewhere in the *Cahiers*: "I was dominated by the idea of functioning. I think the Act-Reflex type was the fundamental fact."[124] The influence of phenomenology and psychoanalysis on French thought largely occludes the distinct tradition of metapsychology and reflex theory that Marcel Gauchet has described as the "cerebral unconscious."[125] Attending to reflexes enabled thinkers to demolish the falsely static essences that had dominated psychology: notions like "self," "mind," or "faculty." A list to which we might well add reified versions of "intelligence." In the period, reflexology served as the basis of psychology alongside sensorimotor theory, a context that proves key to reading the *Cahiers*.[126]

Throughout the *Cahiers*, Valéry took self and consciousness to be effects of a system, rather than a cause, although his position went from one of reductionism to increasing complexity. Moreover, he systematically investigates everything that seems to escape the grasp of his own awareness. Consciousness arises from unconscious patterns of cerebration and recedes: "The substance [of psychic life] is *functioning*, and what we observe, the veil."[127] The principal difference between reflex actions and mental functions resides in the direction of the impulse. Psychic relations proceed in both directions, so to speak, from action to reflex and vice versa: "The nascent state of the reflected is the reflex."[128] Valéry sought to extend the eventuality, possibility, and virtuality of psychic life as such, as Hartman notes, "recalling the emergent yet unrealizable character of consciousness, a state where intense expectation is not as yet betrayed by event."[129]

While exploring the relations between language, sensibility, memory, affectivity, and artistic creation, Valéry hewed to his alternative to the unconscious and the Freudian complex: the "implex."[130] First appearing in the notes of the *Cahiers*, before being introduced in *L'idée fixe or A Dialogue at the Seaside* (*L'idée fixe ou Deux hommes à la mer*), a dialogue ostensibly about treating anxiety addressed to the medical profession, the *implexe* was theorized in Valéry's work from 1908 to 1920. Not a neologism, it had been used by French psychologists before to designate psychic virtuality. "By *Implex* I mean that by which and in virtue of which we remain contingent, conditional," writes Valéry.[131] An ensemble of abilities and potential powers, the implex comprises our capacity to act, react, and understand. As Benedetta Zaccarello explains, the implex operates like a sedimented habit that never rises to consciousness; it orients the subject to select certain stimuli over time, thus influencing action, cognition, and memory.[132] A reactive network, the *implexe* feeds on subjective experience, while remaining formless itself.

The implex emerges from the sensorimotor theory shared by thinkers like Ribot, Binet, and Bergson.[133] Keen to distinguish his coinage from Janet's anthropomorphic notion of the "subconscient," Valéry rejected the idea of a secondary personality capable of different perceptive and intellectual judgments:

> For them [psychologists, etc.] they [unconscious and the subconscious] are meant to signify some inconceivable hidden springs of actions—at times they stand for sly little inner goblins, marvelous tricksters, who can guess riddles, read the future, see through brick walls, and carry on the most amazing industry inside our hidden workings ... No, the *implex* is not *activity*, quite the contrary. It is a capacity. Our capacity for feeling, reacting, doing, understanding—individual, variable, more or less known to us—and always imperfectly and indirectly (like the sense of tiredness)—and often misconstrued.[134]

Despite his resistance to psychoanalytic, psychological, and philosophical systems, Valéry understood literature had not yet turned its attention to the tropes and metaphors that made thinking about self-presence and consciousness possible. The *Cahiers* respond to this lack in their impossible attempt to map Valéry's "intellectual implex."[135] The poet reminds philosophers, Derrida observes, that philosophy is written, while philosophers remain philosophers precisely insofar as they forget this verbal aspect of their activity.[136] In his reading, the three-fold consequences of Valéry's resistance to philosophy are: a break with the circular regime of self-presence based on a speaking and listening voice; an insistence on the formal character of philosophy; and a practice of philosophical writing no longer oriented and watched over by the "law of meaning." Yet, literature cannot afford to ignore the nature of consciousness as a subject or relegate it to the philosophers:

> But up to the present, literature has not, so far as I am aware, paid much attention to this immense treasure house of subjects and situations [...]. What are we to make of terms that cannot be precisely defined unless we re-create them? *Thought, mind* itself, *reason, intelligence, understanding, intuition,* or *inspiration*? ... Each of these terms is both a means and an end in turn, a problem and a solution, a state and an idea; and each of them, in each of us, is adequate according to the function which circumstances impose on it.[137]

Valéry's critique of spontaneous meaning, and his parallel interest in the dynamic virtuality of mind, made intelligence a term to which he would return more than once. Both as a means and an end, a problem and its resolution, a state and an idea, intelligence demanded to be put to the test.

The measure of intelligence, Valéry writes, lies in the speed of felicitous, unprecedented, and non-premeditated responses:

> The measure of "intelligence" is in the promptness of felicitous, unusual and spontaneous *responses*—What does *felicitous* signify here (Sometimes the person who's just uttered such a response is hard put to account for it—(cf. commonplace inspiration)). This, at last, is one of those manifestations which prompts the use of the word "intelligence."[138]

Intelligence appears to be a reflex, a fitting response that is hard to justify rationally. Invention, it follows, is the result of "unique personal *understanding* of things" which allows one to see the world differently. An intelligent answer, or an invention, appears self-evident once it has been uttered, but the process that leads up to the discovery of this obvious solution remains mysterious to most. This disposition, this mixture of feeling and understanding, which enables rapid, unexpected responses, is dubbed intelligent in ordinary language. The secrecy of the highest intelligence (of a Bonaparte or a Leonardo), Valéry speculates, has to do with the capacity to discover new relations between things whose "law of continuity" escapes us.[139] Once this relation is found, deciding the proper course of action is as simple a feat as comparing two lengths.

In his most sustained entry concerning "intelligence," Valéry describes his caustic tendency to test everything against it as his most desperate impulse. This dense, dynamic passage deserves to be quoted at length as it takes us through the potentialities attributed to "intelligence": it is a miraculous transformative force, a remedy against boredom and suffering, a replacement for impossible pleasures, a principle for making distinctions, and a perpetual search.

> My most desperate, most certain impulse was the one that expressed for me, alone and without any other rigor, these words: everything by intelligence, everything replaced, fought, attacked, defended by intelligence. This noun, what meaning did it have?—To be sure, that is what I first called this the power to change water into wine, to occupy boredom, to cut off the roots of pain, the mixture of analysis and imagination— the will to suppress, either by substitution, observation, or enlargement

that disfigures without touching them—the thoughts, hours, difficulties, or phantoms—when these formations were against me. Rather than the pleasure that one can only have impurely, mixed with fears—came the idea—the ersatz. I would simultaneously tend toward composing the real and the imaginary and never confusing the idea and the feeling, the sign and the thing. I wanted to reconstruct everything respecting this distinction, *in a pure state*—the distinct, even the formless and the vague of which I made a category—and I desired the wealth of new combinations that result in the right division of components, operations, forces [. . .]. There was something of a religion in this utterance. My separating and distinctive power.[140]

Intelligence emerges in these lines as a quasi-sacred effort to reconstruct everything based on a prior distinction between the idea and sensation, the sign and the thing. The very capacity to think according to such an original opposition becomes the guarantor of the "right cut" and "the proper division" between elements, operations, and forces.

The potential of intelligence lies in its analytic power, its ability to separate and institute binary oppositions.[141] The unfettered ambition of Valéry's own experiment quickly outstripped its means:

A most remarkable thing. My means fell short of these ambitions. I knew it. I was often desperate. At times, I told myself that this insufficiency was on the contrary favorable to my clarity. To grasp itself better my intelligence *had* to be for the most part simulated, volitional, and thus more clearly felt by me. [. . .] Besides I always sought difficulty, because ease is automatism—occurs without thought. The domain of intelligence is everything left unregulated or unresolved by automatism. It is not defined (for me) by the *finding*, but by the *seeking*. Once in its usual state (itself!) it derides what it finds and what it has found. It is faithful to *quid agendum* and to *nihil reputans actum*.—It happens that this disposition or education affects its powers, makes it discover insurmountable difficulties in yesterday's ease, paralyzes it before almost nothing.[142]

The incapacity of intelligence to correspond to its project paradoxically reveals its character and its limits. Attacking a larger problem than one can resolve is a way of forcing intelligence to become aware of itself and its own limits, which would otherwise remain unconscious and unobserved.[143] Hence, the temporal bias of Valéry's own intelligence that disregards past exploits, while adhering to the task to come.

This last thought—which parenthetically introduces the division between *Intelligence-Recherche* and *Intelligence-Trouvaille*—argues that the searching kind of intelligence can become petrified by its past exploits, paralyzed before nothing.[144] Elsewhere in the *Cahiers*, Valéry formalizes the difference between the two kinds of intelligence as follows:

> There is a Seeking-Intelligence, and a Finding-Intelligence, one of demands and one of answers. Some have a mind that is always awake and questioning. They find resistances, exciting stops on all sides where others don't worry. The latter—who are not always the same— produce products that are sometimes without cause and not expected by themselves. They are constantly inventing. Sometimes, they only find the question after the fact for the answer which occured to them.[145]

Intelligence splits into seeking and finding, questions and answers. The inventors often discover the questions after the answers, inverting the temporality of research into a retroactive *après-coup*. The resistance, blockages, and arrests usually associated with sterility excite a certain category of thinkers, while others remain uninspired. For Valéry, these obstacles and inventions suggested a new art of writing capable of making broken tales out of fragmentary thinking.

Broken Tales

Although Valéry's disparate oeuvre ranges from verse, dialogues and librettos to essays, notebooks, and translations, my unique focus in this section will be on his abstract tales posthumously collected as *Histoires brisées*, since they best expose what I take to be his counterrealism. Counterrealism should be understood here not only as a resistance to the demands literary, philosophical, and aesthetic realism places on the reader's intelligence, but also a fragmentary form of writing that presents an alternative to its tenets. Instead of renouncing the real, Valéry's counterrealism multiplies the potential modes of approaching it through the language of the senses.

In order to speak of counterrealism, one must first agree, however provisionally, on some sense of realism. Commonly considered a historical periodization, a pervasive set of literary techniques that come to define the novel as a genre itself, the use of plot, dialogue, and description to capture symptoms and surfaces of social life, realism is invariably placed in a series of oppositions that come to define it. Peter Brooks relates realism to *res-ism*, or thing-ism, suggesting how far "realist literature is attached to the visual, to looking at things, registering their presence through sight." He adds that realism, as "a label we apply to a period and a family or works, very much belongs to the rise of the novel as a relatively rule-free genre that both appealed to and represented the private lives of the unexceptional—or rather, found and dramatized the exceptional within the ordinary, creating the heroism of everyday life."[146] For Fredric Jameson, historical realism devolves as novels move from social demystification toward the representation of subjective experiences, slowly leading to the inward turns of "modernism" and the literary representation of affect.[147] The "realist vision" and the "antinomies of realism" that Brooks and Jameson respectively explore show realism to be richer and more dialectical than its critics presume. Yet, the aspect of realism that Valéry objects to can be taken, for the purposes of the present discussion, as the attempt to represent and expose the causal and affective logic of subjectivity and sociality in narrative.

Valéry's experiments in the posthumously published *Histoires brisées* enact and extend his critique of realism, training readers to question the arbitrary authority of the real. His "counterrealism" exposes the constructed character of interiority in fragmentary tales. First published in *Le Figaro littéraire*, *Histoires brisées* appeared as a volume with Gallimard in 1950. Valéry began writing the tales when visiting Catherine Pozzi in 1923. He was at a crossroads in his career after the death of Edouard Lebey, for whom he worked as a private secretary. His motivations to try his hand at narrative were economic as much as they were poetic, spurred by a letter from Gaston Gallimard in which the editor told him: "write me a cerebral and sensual novel and I will shower you with gold."[148] Gide, too, had asked him to attempt to write a novel. He responded with characteristic derision: "As for the sensual and cerebral novel, just the thought of physically writing a book drives me nuts."[149] To Gallimard, however, he responded with more subtlety, announcing his experiments in prose, while also confessing his inability to meet the editor's expectations for a conventional novel.[150] The novel imposed itself on Valéry as a timely genre from which he might profit. He never wrote one, but this inability recalls his lifelong quest for a secret prose form, which could be as learned and rigorously composed as verse.[151] His imagination refused to swell to populate a fictive world. Instead, he chose the *conte*, as it seemed detached from truthfulness and allegiance to reality by its self-consciously fictive nature.

Valéry wrote many of the fragments collected in *Histoires brisées* in the *Cahiers*, later marking them as a part of a series, not unlike a composer writing variations on a theme. The series can be classified as those invoking mythic female figures (Calypso, Hera); the insular tales (Robinson stranded on his island; the rites of an island society called Xiphos); the thoughts of Rachel, Sophie, Teste's niece, and an unnamed slave; and finally, Acem, an androgynous oracular figure (whose name encrypts the CEM or *corps-esprit-monde*). Each of these series proves a kind of opening, an opportunity for Valéry to begin writing, to present the reader with a "cerebral and sensual" experiment, which does not lend itself to narrative development. These tales, as critics have remarked, are not merely unfinished, they are unfinishable by design. Often elliptical, circling around the enunciation of a secret, the tales break off precisely when they risk saying the unsayable, to better preserve it as an enigma.

Consider a few themes from the *Histoires brisées*. Calypso and Héra describe the conditions of possibility for the apparition of divine beauty, as seen by the male gaze of Gozon, a double for Valéry. After taking love and beauty from the canon of novelistic leitmotifs, he turns to the equally influential genre of the "Robinsonade," imagining a castaway on a desert island. The "Robinson" fragments deal with the potentiality of what one can do, think, and create when material necessity has been met yet one is cut off from the supports and supplements of everyday society. If no man is an island, Valéry wonders what insularity does to one man: "Robinson amidst his worldly goods became a man again, that is to say a creature of indecision, a being not to be defined in terms of its circumstances alone."[152] After securing his material survival against the elements, Robinson is faced with his mind. "Without books, without writing, Crusoe re-creates his intellectual life [. . .]. This Crusoe must contemplate human affairs and consider them *sub specie intellectus*."[153] A Cartesian without the security of thought to find certainty, Robinson is relinquished to his previsions and his provisions: "Crusoe ends by having created his own island."[154] Yet he continues to err in time, an errancy in the past that cannot be the theme of a narrative for Valéry, which is where the text breaks off.

The arts of memory, which serve as the source of narrative, are rejected in "The Slave." The slave, who is the happiest of philosophers, mocks both stories and storytellers:

> Memories are lies, and stories are fit only for children. Listeners to tales are more simple-minded than those snakes the charmer induces to sway to the bewitching flute: they obey the word, they surrender to its illusions, they are cold or hot or shuddering or exalted, shieldless before the arms of language. For them, the phrases are real creatures, sentences are events![155]

Obliged to speak to a queen, who holds him captive, the slave is forbidden to evoke the past, and thus one day falls into silence, having exhausted all his tales, doctrines, and anecdotes about the heroic adventures and illustrious lives. This is when he discovers his true calling:

> I shall sing the senses. It is the senses that are truth, the senses are purity. For the real object in itself signifies nothing and alludes to nothing. Not to memory, nor to interpretation, nor to reason. But the senses, present sensation, immediate objects, in these lies profundity.[156]

The slave's epiphany could easily stand as a description of Valéry's undertaking in many of these fragments and in his verse.

There is a paradoxical return to vision here, as the slave and Valéry both elevate what the eye sees to the source of understanding. But rather than narrate what the senses perceive, Valéry sings the senses themselves. The fragments from Emma's journal, describing her relation to her body, or Rachel, a few pages that undertake a phenomenology of love, offer the most lyrical examples of this song of sense. A different series that plays on place rather than subjectivity describes the customs of Xiphos. The name of the island recalls the Greek for sword and by derivation the term used in ancient Athens for decapitation. In a temple, a decapitated head, reminiscent of the Sybille, metes out justice and judgment, declaring *Cogito, non sum*.[157] On Xiphos, we are told, everything is a sign, and nothing is insignificant. Their gods do not demand fidelity but incredulity. Inhabitants of the island suffer from sicknesses like "anastrophe" where "after performing an action its victims immediately performed its opposite—or else its simulacrum."[158] Other suffer from "egophobia," losing the ability to say "I" or "me." And the beggars beg not for money but for ideas, style, verse, love, or esteem. Monasteries are filled with those who take vows of silence out of contempt for language. Poets and mathematicians offer "menticures" to sharpen one's language and hone one's mind, while philosophers are content to repair broken porcelain vases. One can go to a shop to improve the intonation and the timbre of one's voice, to avoid vulgar words, or forget ideas that are not one's own. The only legal punishment on Xiphos strips the condemned of their identity and furnishes them with another, including a new family, a past, and a personality other than their own.

The narrator of "Acem" lends voice to Valéry's counterrealism when he declares:

> But reality is simply what it is, in other words precisely what denies or conceals itself from phrasing: no one can say where it begins or ends,

and to claim to represent it is as idle an attempt as that of the painter, who depicts faces of objects by means of strokes unknown to nature, where are neither lines nor planes . . . [159]

Reality does not possess "traits" or "traces" that would make it representable, the narrator implies, and one can imagine his author's wry acquiescence.

Whether echoing a person's inner thoughts or the mores of an insular society, Valéry's tales bear a completely different relation to the real than novelistic conventions would dictate. Valéry comes closer to Borges or Calvino in what Brian Stimpson aptly calls his counterfictions. The *Histoires brisées*, for Stimpson, "display the same intense alliance of the physical and the mental that characterizes the poetry, but the notion of aesthetic closure is constantly subverted as the stories articulate the very impossibility of resolving the tensions between mind and body, between self and other, order and disorder."[160] These counterfictions take the self and the senses as their subject, expanding not into narrative and plot, but folding into a style of writing that enacts a discontinuous relation to the real. Speaking about counterrealism rather than counterfiction underscores this nuance: full of shifting perspectives, inconsistent narrative voices, temporal uncertainties, largely bereft of structure, plot, and causality, Valéry's broken tales exploit the arbitrariness of language leaving us with another vision of the real.

Valéry's private and fictive examination of intelligence forced him to confront the economic and political changes that made disinterested intellectual research—whether literary or scientific—seem like a relic of an unattainable past. In his "Remarks on Intelligence" ("Propos sur l'intelligence"), an influential essay published in 1925, Valéry addressed the fate of a paralyzed, yet productive, intelligence. In continuity with his poetic and counterrealist project, he imagines a quest for political clarity as a rubbing of the mind's eyes, organs made of words. The words that retain his attention are "crisis" and "intelligence." The concluding section of this chapter examines the ambitions of Valéry's "quasi-political" prose.

The Outlook for Intelligence

Intellectual crises are particularly difficult to analyze because their logic remains hidden—they occur in the "kingdom of dissimulation." Valéry defines crisis as the passage from one regime to another, more precisely:

the passage from one particular mode of functioning to another, a passage made perceptible by signs or symptoms. During a crisis, time seems to change its nature, duration no longer gives the same impression as in the normal state of things. Instead of measuring permanence it measures change.[161]

Coupled with the notion of crisis, intelligence requires redefinition as it may be disrupted by new underlying causes.

Yet, as I have argued in this chapter, intelligence is resistant to definition and only seems to take on its meaning in resistance to another term—Valéry's range of alternatives includes sensibility, memory, instinct, and stupidity. As we have seen, it has been variously considered a faculty, a degree of a faculty, and the entirety of mental activity. Moreover, the word underwent a shift in interwar Europe: "During the last few years this word, already encumbered with several quite different meanings, has, by a kind of contagion frequent in language, contracted a new and entirely foreign sense."[162] Considering these changes, Valéry cleaves intelligence into two categories revealed by the crisis: a "faculty" and a "class." The rest of the essay minutely unfolds the implications of the *crise d'intelligence* in terms of economics, technics, time, profession, and pedagogy. Questioning intelligence means questioning its critical passage from one sensible regime to another:

> The phrase *crisis in intelligence*, then, may be understood to mean the deterioration of a certain faculty in all men, or only in those most gifted in the faculty, or who *should be*, or again as a crisis in all the faculties of the average mind, or further a crisis in the *value* and prestige of intelligence in our society, present or to come. And finally, it may also be seen, if we include the new meaning borrowed from the Russians, as a crisis affecting a class of persons with respect to the quality, the number, or the living conditions of its members.[163]

Putting pressure on his titular phrase, Valéry pursues these five distinct ways of understanding the crisis—universal cognitive decline, the decline of the intellectual elite, the crisis of the average mind, the crisis in the value of intelligence, and the crisis of an intellectual class—suggesting in passing that any crisis involves such a generation of ambiguous meanings out of an overdetermined present.

Inquiring whether "average intelligence" has increased in the modern world demands an ecology of the everyday, paying special attention to how habits are conditioned by the intervention of technology. Valéry comments, for instance, on the remarkable progress of insomnia. The global effect of technology is meant to alleviate the cognitive burden experienced in daily life: we are instantaneously *shown* things that previously had to be *understood* over time.[164] Intelligence becomes intoxicated by its addiction to energy and speed. As a result, the force of attention, the capacity for continuous mental effort, slow work, even sleep may diminish. Valéry wonders whether writers will possess the constancy to develop their own style faced with economic pressures to produce and publish works that appear innovative. Nothing seems less certain in this configuration than the survival of literary practice.

On the political, military and socio-economic front, the figure of the self-sufficient man is threatened by systems of complexity and the diminution of natural resources: "We are witnessing the dying out of the *man who could be complete*, as well of the man who could be materially self-sufficient."[165] Machines adapt humans to their own uses, while technocrats produce and reify the subjects that they govern: "Not a single mortal is left unswallowed into the structure of these machines, to become an object of their functioning, a nondescript element in their cycles. The life or death, the pleasures and works of men are details, means, incidents in the activity of these beings, whose rule is tempered only by the war they wage against each other."[166] Such forces collectively transform intelligence as a faculty, forcing it to acquire and shed properties, leading to a potentially "permanent deformation of mind," not to mention a "new definition of man."

> Among living intellects [*intelligences*], some spend themselves in serving the machine, others in building it, others in inventing or planning a more powerful type, and a final category of intellects spend themselves in trying to escape its domination. These rebellious minds feel with a shudder that the once complete and autonomous *whole* that was the soul of ancient man is now becoming some inferior kind of *daemon* that wishes only to collaborate, to join the crowd to find security in being dependent and happiness in a closed system that will be all the more closed as man makes it more closely suited to man. But *this is to give a new definition of the human.*[167]

The life of the mind is determined by its interactions with—or its conscription within—the closed system of technology.[168] Any "rebel" intelligence that Valéry suggests might resist domination is herded into a "nebulous" socio-political class dubbed the *intelligentsia*.

The social sphere in the Western world is constituted like a machine with universal ambitions for its reign: "*It cannot put up with anyone whose duties and circumstances are not precisely specified.* It tends to eliminate those individuals who from its own point of view seem aberrant."[169] The intelligentsia, as a class with an indefinite function, becomes a prime candidate for elimination or reconfiguration. Admitting that all human endeavors require intelligence, Valéry subdivides the intellectual class into the fungible and the nonfungible, those who possess use-value and those who do not. To schematize: the crisis of intelligence is a trembling that affects a universal mental faculty; or uniquely a meritorious or social category; a crisis of all the faculties of the average mind; a crisis of value attributed to this faculty; a newly named historical class exposed by the Russian Revolution. The difficulty of clarifying which of these factors—the personal, the intellectual, the cognitive, the economic, or the political—is the constitutive or determining one, let alone how each factor warps the other, is itself another way of describing the crisis in intelligence.

The withering away of the senses of intelligence was inevitable for Valéry, for as he announces at the opening of "La crise de l'esprit," in 1919 even Europe recognizes its mortal condition: "We later civilizations, we too know that we are mortal."[170] What made Europe's admission of mortality remarkable was precisely its previously unprecedented cultural capital, historical hegemony, and intellectual freedom, which carried an aura of immortality, separating it and imposing it upon the rest of the world. Valéry sums up "European achievement" in a hyperbolic formula: "the most intense power of radiation combined with an equally intense power of assimilation."[171] This power to emit and absorb ideas is challenged by the crisis of intelligence to the extent that Europe's future is uncertain, torn between isolation and hegemony:

> Will Europe become *what it is in reality*—that is, a little promontory on the continent of Asia? Or will it remain *what it seems*—that is, the elect portion of the terrestrial globe, the pearl of the sphere, the brain of a vast body?[172]

Valéry's eurocentrism is indissociable from his intellectualism. The notion of culture, intelligence, and masterpieces are entangled in an immemorial relation with the "idea of Europe." The crisis of intelligence thus entails a crisis of eurocentrism. The same history that allows Europe to appear as the head of a vast body, rather than the cape of the Asian continent, enables its decapitation. The global spread of European science and technology, through commerce and conquest, renders Europe susceptible to being overcome: "Must such phenomena as democracy, the exploitation of the globe and the general spread of technology, all of which presage a *deminutio capitis* for Europe . . . must these be taken as absolute decisions of fate?"[173] The *capitis diminutio* (decrease of the head), as it is usually called, is a term Roman jurists used to designate the loss, reduction or alteration of an individual's legal status or rights, especially the right to liberty, citizenship, and family.[174] Valéry extends the meaning of the term to suggest Europe's shrinking significance in political and economic terms. Derrida places Valéry's thinking about the crisis in a "singular configuration" with Husserl and Heidegger.[175] He locates the shared features of their otherwise divergent thinking in the opposition of *esprit* or *Geist* and nature, meant to place history on the side of spirit. Europe, it appears, is not a geographical or historically delimited zone, but a spiritual configuration. Hence, the crisis facing Europe is a crisis in the devaluation of spirit.[176]

Valéry remained convinced that Europe had never had a politics worthy of its greatest minds. His critique of colonialism consists in a rebuke of the tendency of European nations to disseminate their technical knowledge and capital in brutal territorial wars. Scientific intelligence was betrayed by economic and military competition, political idiocy, and idiotic policy.[177] This critique of colonialism lies closer to a form of "hypercolonial Euro-capitalism," to borrow Derrida's phrase. Just as the sciences tended to proceed from certainty to uncertainty, determinism to crisis, historical powers dissipated their capital in a kind of political entropy. The violent loss of intellectual energy described here, however, is part of Valéry's larger "politique d'esprit."

The ongoing crisis in the sciences, from mathematics to quantum mechanics, brought about a loss of an ancient ideal of unity.[178] Universality itself seemed to be in the process of decomposition, while causality no longer held the power to account for phenomena:

> The particular crisis in the sciences, which now seem to despair of their ancient ideal of explaining the universe as a unified whole. The universe is breaking up, losing all hope of a single design. The world of the ultramicroscopic seems strangely different from the world as an agglomerate mass; in the former, even the identities of bodies is lost . . . Nor shall I mention the crisis of determinism, that is to say of causality.[179]

At the same time, science was destroying Cartesian certitudes that nature was capable of being methodically grasped and mastered.[180] However, the very incomprehensibility of the cosmos seemed an apt metaphor for the critic to describe the effect of unseen forces on the masses:

As natural causes produce hail, typhoons, and epidemics, so intelligent causes affect millions of men, the great majority of whom submit to them as the vagaries of the sky, the sea, the earth's crust. When intelligence and will act upon the masses in the manner of blind, physical causes . . . *we have what is called politics*.[181]

Politics is the reduction of intelligent and volitional causes into blind force. Elsewhere, Valéry warily describes politics as the art of keeping people from meddling in what concerns them, then forcing them to decide on matters they do not understand.[182] While the principle of causality seemed increasingly inapplicable to the indeterminate and relativistic world of particles, the real causes affecting millions of people were naturalized as disastrous phenomena akin to the weather.

Valéry's vision of the French mind linked it to universality, while a wider European spirit comprised the confluence of Mediterranean, Greco-Roman, and Christian traditions: an active, disinterested form of curiosity, a happy mixture of imagination and logical rigor, a non-pessimistic skepticism and an unresigned mysticism.[183] Hesitant to foretell Europe's future, he nonetheless formulated a "fundamental theorem" about its political significance in an increasingly globalized world: "I have claimed that the imbalance maintained for so long in Europe's favor was, *by its own reaction*, bound to change by degrees into an imbalance in the opposite direction."[184] The reasons Valéry argued that Europe would fall prey to its own energies are best sought in a short text set in a lighthouse on the banks of the Yalou River in China—the site of a momentous naval battle during the Sino-Japanese war.[185]

In an 1899 letter to Gide, Valéry described "Le Yalou" as a kind of "Teste in China." The text, which was finally published in 1938, confirmed Valéry's impulse to think beyond national boundaries. The dialogue introduces an anonymous figure to a Chinese sage, learned in writing and military strategy, who explains both why Western power is impotent and why European politics remain caught in cycles of revolutionary violence. The sage locates Europe's "most exquisite error" in its adulation of intelligence, a monstrous quality of mind that he considers inherently threatening to law and order.

> To you, intelligence is not one thing among many. You neither prepare nor provide for it, nor protect nor repress nor direct it, you worship it as if it were an omnipotent beast. Every day it devours everything. It would like to put an end to a new state of society every evening.[186]

Rather than descending from a higher spirit governing the world, intelligence is compared to a beast set to devour all that exists. The voraciousness of intelligence pits the individual against social order and tradition, revealing an anarchic quality of mind.

> A man intoxicated on it believes his own thoughts are legal decisions, or facts themselves born of the crowd and time. He confuses his quick changes of heart with the imperceptible variation of real form and enduring Beings.[187]

The intoxicating character of introspection pits it against laws. "Chinese tradition" preserves itself against such perils, the sage suggests, since each person is connected to prior and successive generations in a "fabric of the dead and of nature." Limits are forcefully placed on science and experiment, in favor of tradition and inheritance. Even ideographic writing is designed to exert political control over the masses and limit intelligence to a class of men of letters: "But our form of writing is too difficult for it. It is political. It conceals ideas [. . .]. All the powers of the intelligence therefore are left to the lettered class, and an unshakeable order is founded on difficulty, and on the mind."[188] From its traditions to its characters, Valéry's China, notes Christopher Bush, is less "a narrative of things past but an achronic epistemic grid that precludes anything like what we might think of as history or even an experience of time."[189] The constitutive difficulty of such a static system maintains the very order that is supposedly corroded by a democratic Western intelligence.

The sage ascribes the anxious cast of the European to a fear of "blood and time" in an arresting passage: "For your ideas are terrifying and your hearts weak. Your acts of pity and cruelty are absurd, committed with no calm, as if they were irresistible. Finally, you fear blood more and more. Blood and time."[190] The crises coursing through Europe from the fin-de-siècle to the interwar years left Valéry wondering whether, in such an "anguishing" and "exciting" moment of history, human intelligence could survive, let alone continue to possess the same character and limits. Interruption, incoherence, indifference, and shock instead become the ordinary conditions of life. Due to the very ambiguity of the term, he does not provide any definitive responses about the future of intelligence; instead, he keeps sharpening how the question is articulated. Teste contemplates the waters of the Yalou River at the end of the dialogue: "The individual then feels deeply related to what passes below his eyes: water."[191] Rather than narcissistic liquidation, his gaze on the flowing surface of the river suggests that an alternative organization of tradition and its transmission, one that collectively and forcefully limited the place accorded to intelligence, could contain a power of continuity unavailable to the European mind. Rather than being continuous, European thought resembles a gap, a spacing that could soon come to an end. "Who knows if our culture is not a hypertrophy, a gap, an unsustainable development, which one or two centuries will have been enough to produce and exhaust."[192]

This unfinished transvaluation of the value accorded to intelligence makes it difficult to inherit Valéry's critical project today.[193] In *Six Memos for the Next Millennium*, Italo Calvino makes a case for doing so:

> Among all the values I would like to see passed onto the next millennium, there is this above all: a literature that has absorbed the taste for mental orderliness and exactitude, the intelligence of poetry, but at the same time that of science and philosophy: an intelligence such as that of Valéry as an essayist and a prose writer.[194]

What the "intelligence" of Valéry as an essayist and a prose writer *could be* remains open to contention. What would it mean to inherit a "value" that is constantly undermining itself through a series of crises? The present reading of Valéry has argued that it means inheriting a series of variables and tests for intelligence, as well as the task of deciding which senses of intelligence one is leaving behind.[195]

Valéry's prose—from *Monsieur Teste* to the fragments in the *Cahiers*, from the broken tales to the quasi-political writings—delimits a testing ground to gauge the potential consequences of allowing various forms of intelligence to decay. The intense literary and critical reaction to the First World War would make such a critical project both more urgent and divisive. This chapter has tracked Valéry's aesthetics and poetics in his prose fiction, criticism, notebooks, and political essays, in which he measures the literary against the demands of his own intelligence. While his image remains caught between Blanche's modern classicism and Colucci's abstract formalism, with which this chapter began, it becomes one whose contours can now be reconfigured.

CHAPTER FOUR

Mobilizing Intelligence

CRITICAL NEUTRALITY AT
THE *NOUVELLE REVUE FRANÇAISE*

THE FIRST WORLD WAR transformed the relations of literary production, cultural criticism, and political praxis.[1] The outbreak of the war suspended many of the debates between conservatives and moderns that had marked the intellectual landscape of the Third Republic, creating consensus around the necessity of placing all the nation's material and moral resources in its defense—an unexpected *union sacrée*. After the war, many of the repressed debates about the extent to which culture should be tied to national interest resurfaced with renewed force. Many of these polemics, as discussed in the previous chapters, crystallized in how "intelligence" as a word, faculty, and class could be understood. Torn from its influential role in Third Republic psychology, science, and philosophy, intelligence was recuperated by aesthetic, literary, and political discourse during and after the war. The changes in its uses shed light on interwar polemics that pit the French nationalist right against the more equivocal, and at times left-leaning writers, studied here. This chapter contends that the disinterested critical idiom and aesthetic program associated with the *Nouvelle Revue Française*—namely "modern classicism" (*le classicisme moderne*) incarnated in *NRF* style (*le style NRF*)—emerged as a response to the conflation of aesthetics and politics by Maurrasian nationalists.[2] The meanings of intelligence in this context move from intellectuals as a hotly contested class during the interwar period to an ostensibly neutral form of critical acuity. The *NRF* transformed the critical essay—placed under the dual aegis of Bergson and Montaigne—to make it both the prose translation of a contemporary "ideological lyricism" and an anachronist renewal of an early modern genre, which would seem increasingly untimely after the war.[3]

The pages below track how the conflict of interpretations around the key term of "intelligence" determined the course of the review's editorial policy and critical agenda. The fate of the *Nouvelle Revue Française*—situated between extreme right nationalism and radical avant-garde groups, while belonging to neither—clouds many familiar narratives about modern criticism. The suspension and reprise of the journal questions the complex nature and the impact of the First World War on literary figures, as well as their self-understanding of intellectual responsibility.[4] More than a literary review, as Maaike Koffeman notes, the *NRF* was an "anthology of the best contemporary writers, a talent agency, a forum for debate, a quality brand, and above all a certain conception of literature."[5] Even contemporaries thought that the *NRF* possessed a uniquely perceptive critical voice, which allowed it to recognize and publish a series of works that transformed French literature, especially the novel.[6] Addressed to the literati and the intelligentsia, the review became a successful venture as it accrued "symbolic capital," which translated into commercial success, up to a point.[7] On an institutional level, the review secured its dominant place in twentieth-century French literature by establishing its own publishing house (Gallimard), curating an influential series of colloquia and cultural events (the "Décades de Pontigny" led by Paul Desjardins), and opening a theatre (the *Théâtre du Vieux-Colombier*) that staged literary works by French and international authors associated with the group.[8] The group consisted of André Gide, Marcel Drouin, André Ruyters, Jean Schlumberger, Jacques Copeau, Gaston Gallimard, and Jacques Rivière. Paul Claudel, Paul Valéry, Marcel Proust, Albert Thibaudet, Roger Martin du Gard, and Alain Fournier were allies in different periods.

Known for their aestheticism, disinterestedness, and commitment to "pure literature," there was little reason to expect drastic critical change from the "circuit" of writers and critics surrounding André Gide.[9] Yet most of them claimed to have been deeply affected, if not transformed, by the war, which killed Charles Péguy and Alain Fournier. And while other combatant writers wrote harrowing testimonies of what they witnessed in the battlefields, reactions were far from limited to those who were there in the flesh. Malcolm Bowie succinctly describes the spectrum of literary positions provoked by the war as follows:

> In prose and verse, a multitude of established writers recorded their personal reactions to it, and a significant number of newcomers

discovered their literary vocation in the trenches or during the German air raids in Paris. Some of these texts were pro-war rallying cries, others were private expressions of shock or sorrow, and still others were internationalist and pacifist in their sympathies. While Barrès was writing the nationalistic journalism later collected in his compendious *Chronique de la Grande Guerre*, Romain Rolland was appealing for solidarity between German and French intellectuals in his *Au-dessus de la mêlée*. After the armistice a period of philosophical, moral, and political stock-taking began and in due course produced its own rich crop of essays and treatises.[10]

Gide's journal describes how many of the *NRF* critics who were deemed unfit to serve compensated for their distance from the frontline by living in a state of heightened alert: "For those who are mobilized, wearing a uniform allows them a greater freedom of thought. For us who cannot wear a uniform, we are mobilizing our minds" (*c'est l'esprit que nous mobilisons*).[11]

When the *NRF* reappeared in June 1919, under Rivière's newly minted editorship, the only apparent mark it carried to indicate the five-year interruption in its publication were two discreet words on its iconic beige cover: *nouvelle série*. Attempts to reconstruct the debates surrounding the appearance of this "new series" show how the critical posture of the *NRF* changed in relation to historical events, turning from a defense of artistic autonomy to an immanent conception of both creation and criticism. Rather than embracing the nationalist agenda of *Action française*, and the reactionary classicism of its master theorist Charles Maurras, the *NRF* sought to defend a *classicisme moderne* that combined a reverence for tradition with a taste for innovation. Latent tensions concerning the task of the critic came to the fore when the supposed political neutrality of the *NRF* was disturbed both by internationalist intellectuals and French ultra-conservatives.[12]

This chapter documents this story through the lens of intelligence and the various aesthetic and political values that were attached to it, beginning with Charles Maurras's 1905 *Future of Intelligence* (*L'avenir de l'intelligence*). Along with Pierre Lasserre, Maurras opposed the order of classicism to the anarchy of romanticism—itself a cipher for the ideals of the French Revolution—as the first step toward articulating the monarchist political program of *Action française*.[13] It would be hard to overestimate the importance of Maurras's discourse at the time. His polemic provides a conceptual matrix against which we can situate both the *NRF*'s prewar stance towards the role of "intelligence" in analytic criticism, and its postwar "demobilization" under Jacques Rivière. The next section focuses on the stunted experience of the *NRF* critics during wartime. Rivière's crucial experience as a prisoner of war in Germany, as recalled in *The German* (*L'Allemand*, 1918), informed his controversial reprise of a neutral cultural policy after the war. The final section examines the intense contest to control the meaning of "intelligence" in 1919. It analyzes a series of critical exchanges around Henri Barbusse and Romain Rolland's pacifist manifesto in the left-wing newspaper *L'Humanité*, and Henri Massis's reactionary manifesto for an "Intelligence Party" (*Parti de l'intelligence*). Rivière avoided both positions by placing a "tautological" conception of both creation and criticism at the core of the *NRF*, one that refused to define the literary in any terms other than its own. Rivière's critical and editorial attitude is based on intellectual neutralization, which disarms the goal of thinking by suspending it between two identical terms. Invocations of intelligence thus shifted from designating the fiercely contested class during the interwar period to a kind of autonomous literary–critical acuity capable of defusing polemical public discourse.

Maurras and The Future of Intelligence *(1905)*

Most discussions of conservatism versus modernity in French cultural studies end up forever re-enacting the *querelle des anciens et des modernes*. In its fin-de-siècle iteration, ancients are Catholic, conservative traditionalists who favor the preservation of social, political, and intellectual hierarchies and champion the model organization of the seventeenth century. Moderns are secular individualists who suffer under the strictures of such classicist aesthetics, yearn for the liberating self-expression of romanticism and the revolutionary representations promised by the eighteenth century.[14] Reading Maurras, one sees how he reorganizes these postures through a new rhetoric of "intelligence," understood mostly as the intelligentsia.[15] Maurras's elevation of politics to the primary consideration in any intellectual endeavor characterizes his methodically reactionary mindset.[16]

Dedicated to René Marc Ferry, the founder of the defunct review *Minerve*, Maurras's tract framed itself as a narrative of French cultural decline. Its title recalls both Taine's *De l'intelligence* and Renan's *L'avenir de la science*, while it lays the groundwork for the *Action française* critic Pierre Laserre's *Le romantisme français*, which synthesized and enlarged Maurras's anti-romanticism, as well as his attitudes toward intelligence at large.¹⁷ Maurras argues that a new redistribution of energies was overwhelming the living conditions of the average person, a domination which one could only ignore if "dumb like a conservative or naïve like a democrat."¹⁸ *Les honnêtes gens*—whoever they were—were now dead. The rise of mass literacy and the industrialization of cultural production eradicated the enlightened love of literature and letters: "The notion of a certain superior play of wit is completely lost."¹⁹ The omnipresence of readers was predictably held responsible for a decline in reading. Ferdinand Brunetière's popularity at the École normale supérieure and his contributions and eventual editorship of the *Revue des deux mondes* were the emblem of the scandalous passage of culture from the right to the left, as young intellectuals supposedly no longer read Descartes or Augustine, let alone understood Racine.²⁰ Maurras was quick to dismiss such developments as symptoms of a systematic transformation. Instead, he drew a more absolute line of demarcation: "But what does it matter [...] barbarians are barbarians, our friends are our friends!"²¹ Tautology, as we will see, would also play a surprising role in Rivière's aesthetics after the war. Rivière curated what counted as Gallimard style for the immediate postwar period. His editorial practices gradually expanded to become an attempt at forging a European spirit, whose necessity was made evident by the trenches and killing fields. I will only note here that the political division of the world into barbarians and friends, which serves as Maurras's point of departure, takes the form of an assertion of French identity, centered around the monarchical ideal. What began as a set of reactionary aristocratic, antirepublican, xenophobic, anti-Semitic, and monarchic political positions was soon translated into an ideal of classical Latinate style, one that, in turn, reflects the very politics from which it stems.²²

In Maurras's hands each century takes on a distinct character, which can be traced backwards and projected forwards. He deduces the Reformation from the Renaissance, the Revolution from the Reformation, romanticism from the Revolution, and the Republic from romanticism.²³ Such a secular lineage attempts to account for the impasse faced by the French writer in 1905, a decisive instant when he is bound to choose between the avatars of "gold" and "force."²⁴ Maurras quotes Georges Clemenceau, who became prime minister the following year, to specify the nature of the shift in the contemporary period: "The sovereignty of brutal force is disappearing [...] we are hurtling towards the sovereignty of intelligence."²⁵ This supposedly disastrous change in the nature of sovereignty—which he describes elsewhere as the "reign of the spirit over the masses"—only makes his fundamental appeal all the more urgent: "The moral question is returning to the social question, no mores without institutions."²⁶ If the nature of sovereignty morphs into an intellectual one, then the intellect must be policed and protected from the influence of foreign and local factions. Writers gradually became dangerous figures given their combined moral power over public opinion and economic instability.²⁷ In the seventeenth century, writers were nothing more than ornaments (*la parure du monde*), whose role was to "soften, polish and amend the general mores [. . .] please the public and entertain each other." They governed nothing.²⁸ In the eighteenth century, the disappearance of royal authority did not yield to the power of the people: "The heir to the Bourbons is the Man of Letters [. . .]. The revolutionary era marks the highest point of literary dictatorship."²⁹

In the nineteenth century, the rise of capital, empire and industry frustrated the newly usurped power of the writer: "The natural flow of literature follows the natural divagations of the age that came before; but the series of military, economic and political facts contradict these divagations one by one."³⁰ This contradiction gives rise to a new double desire within nineteenth-century literature for anarchy and insurrection. Hugo and Béranger prop up the military by lending it a false air of liberalism, George Sand mystifies the just grievances of the proletariat, while Balzac and Zola become "industrial" realists. On the other, the literature of the *cénacles* or coteries becomes "hysterical," "isolated," and "insurrectional."³¹ Increasingly hermetic in form, the literature and criticism of "intelligence" methodically broke with a reading public:

> More concerned by *intelligence* (that was the word which was used) than judgment, criticism served and favored this inclination so that instead of correcting himself by drawing closer to better models of his race and his tradition, a Gautier became more Gautier and yielded fatally to his sin, which was the mania for description without measure; a Balzac, a Hugo only made efforts to resemble themselves, that is to say, to distinguish themselves by their own characteristic eccentricity. The gap had to grow between the average well-brought-up, literate public and the writers the century gave it. They almost all began not to be unknown but to be deemed bizarre and incomprehensible.³²

This crucial passage introduces the idea of a criticism that elevates intelligence above judgment as its primary criteria. Such a priority leads writers to resemble themselves more intensely—note the near tautology of "a Gautier becomes more Gautier"—to demarcate their brand of writing on the literary marketplace. But more acutely, this break with better models and aesthetic judgment inevitably leads to their eccentricity, incomprehensibility, their constitutive bizarreness; what our current critical idiom would likely valorize as singularity. Maurras intuits a political problem in the emergence of literary singularity, as literature no longer plays the part of a unitary linguistic, national, or ethical model. By the same token, the writer becomes an essentially duplicitous figure, subtracted from the order of dominant forces, laid open to the influence of capital: the "intelligent" agent is inimical to order.[33] "Intelligence was seen as an explosive, and those who lived by their intelligence appeared to be the born enemies of real order."[34] If order depended on the separation of political power from literary legislation, then the figure of the intellectual could only pose a threat.

Placed in an increasingly adversarial stance, losing ground to industry and finance, intelligence, taken both as a faculty and class, is called upon to choose between "force" and "gold." If it can no longer be the primary "force" of the nation, which is overwhelmed by technical innovations, and the movement of international capital, then it must recognize its demotion, and collude with the ancient philosophical and religious traditions of the nation, which form a defensive line that stretches from agriculture and the army to the clergy, and even certain historical financial interests. For Maurras, this constellation calls on "intelligence" to determine its own relation to the coming age:

> The future is fear or hope. But one can fear justly and hope misguidedly. Where the precision of science does not reach, the delicate appreciation of judgment and reason, a mixture of intuition and calculation can discern and grasp what promise and menace are worth.[35]

The onus placed on this volatile mixture of judgment and reason, intuition and calculation, amounts to nothing less than differentiating "promise from menace" in an increasingly unforeseeable future. For Maurras, criticism could only assume this prophetic function if it chose to anchor itself to institutions, to reject finance ("the representation of strength without the signature of the strong") and to ally itself to "the free fatherland, one that can only be upheld by virtue of Blood."[36] The true function of "French intelligence" was to see and make visible whichever regime would be the best, in order to choose it with authority, and ally other forces to its cause. Maurras's *L'avenir de l'intelligence* sets the intellectual, political, and affective stage that critics of the *NRF* would stumble upon. As Thibaudet noted, the master thinker of *Action française* had honed his political rhetoric as a literary critic:

This thinking too shaped its rhetoric, and before that its logic, in literary criticism. It drew both the problem it found and the spirit of the solutions it furnishes from the commerce of aesthetic forms and norms [...]. Having clarified the literary idea of tradition and order, it carried out its analysis, used its instrument on the religious and political order.[37]

The appeals of the *NRF* critics to "intelligence" in criticism cannot be understood, and indeed would not have been articulated in such terms, without the "commerce of esthetic forms and norms" as launched by *L'avenir de l'intelligence*. Maurras's defense of classicism was less a specific literary program than a wholescale attack on myriad forms of political and aesthetic upheavals—from the post-revolutionary republic to fragmentary romantic prose and symbolist poetry. The *NRF* critics, especially Thibaudet, countered this narrative through the notion of *classicisme moderne*, which placed classic and romantic aesthetics in a complex intellectual continuum. Many of the battles that the *NRF* faced in the foundation, mobilization, and demobilization of the review could be traced back to the terms of this 1905 polemic.

Gide & Company

Apart from Gide's charisma, a group of gifted young critics, and Jean Schlumberger's considerable family fortune, there were few early signs of the illustrious future that the *NRF*, and its publishing house run by Gallimard, would come to enjoy in the interwar period.[38] From its foundation the group refrained from expressing its self-conception in manifestos, seeking instead to remain free of the influence of intellectual schools and political tendencies. As Rivière later reflected, it was neither to "announce any literary gospel nor to proclaim the coming of a new school" that the group gathered and founded a review.[39] The desire for aesthetic autonomy was suggested by its unassuming title, which did however contain two telling qualifiers: *Nouvelle* and *Française*. Novelty meant turning against the waning legacies of romanticism, naturalism, and symbolism, as well as rejecting both the ongoing neoclassical revival and the avant-garde provocations of Dada. The adhesion to a distinctly "French" tradition could be understood as an elevation of the analytic function of criticism, which rejected the vocabulary of inspiration, subjective feeling, and spontaneity, focusing instead on technical constraints, the objective qualities of the literary work of art, and the critical effort to explain its affective hold. The theoretical impersonality—later associated with Paulhan and

Blanchot—was initially an editorial policy of anonymity. None of the writers from the journal were reviewed in its pages, and some of their most important declarations came as unsigned notes. A problematic aim, given the diversity of opinion, was the aspiration to hone a collective critical voice that could contain the central convictions of all.

Benda's portrayal of Gide offers an arch description of *l'esprit NRF* as a whole: "entirely enamored with doubt, 'availability,' anxiety, fervent for precious thought, sybilline logic, verbal esotericism, contemptuous of the affirmed, the sharp, the rectilinear."[40] Schlumberger, the review's first editor, explained its relation to its time by distinguishing between two kinds of aesthetic problems in his "Considerations," which opened the inaugural issue in 1909:

> In art, there are circumstantial and essential problems. The former are renewed once every fifteen or thirty years or every half-century, depending on whether they are a matter of fashion, taste, or mores. The more ephemeral they are, the more they attract attention. When it comes to essential problems, they are never the order of the day. Each artist confronts them, alone in the most decisive moments of his life. But he knows the anxiety of isolation; he doubts the vitality of his work, he interrogates the ancients and the masters anxiously, which takes him back to the very principles, to the primary matrices of all artistic creation.[41]

By opposing perennial questions to ephemeral ones, Schlumberger divides criticism into a higher form of questioning and everyday commerce. The essential questions are not necessarily reflected in critical fashions but encountered in the anxious, isolated practice of writing. In Schlumberger's account, circumstantial problems create literary groups, while vital problems, the ones discovered in writing, spark literary friendships. They give rise not to a "unity of taste, but of method, not of genre, but of style."[42]

The closest the group came to having a slogan was in borrowing Du Bellay's Renaissance motto: *défense et illustration de la langue française*, while broadening the signification of each term. In Schlumberger's gloss, *langue* meant not only language, but culture; *française*, was not a declaration of exclusivity, but a heightened responsibility towards what was happening within the country; *défense* meant a "physiological response, a reaction of a living organism to all good or bad influences"; and finally, *illustration* was a process of clarification. New French criticism further acknowledged that although one may not be able to spur genius which "alone gives rise to glory, and appears only at its own hour," it nevertheless falls on each reader "to explain, extend and surround it in an atmosphere of admiration and intelligence."[43] For Rivière, the work was an event that first invaded the critic's being—an attack of momentary blindness—followed by a speculative retreat examining the cause of such a loss of vision, followed again by a return to an overwhelmed self. Gide added the immanent criterion of aesthetic judgment: "Art must find its own sufficiency, its end and its perfect reason within itself."[44] Appeals to order, history, ethics, or politics were ruled out from the start: the contemporaneity of the work was only valuable insofar as it could retain some degree of actuality to come. History, ethics, politics, and even aesthetics up to a point, were now subsumed under writing.

Looking back at the journal, Rivière described the *esprit NRF* as the vital ability to remain open-minded, while nonetheless promoting distinct new directions in literary practice:

> It had this marvellous double property: firstly, of not excluding anything a priori, of not casting anathema on any genre or any art form, and secondly, of all the same indicating a direction, of encouraging new tendencies. [. . .] Joining the *Nouvelle Revue Française* was like receiving a badge, not of perfection, but of life; anyone accepted into its pages received proof that their efforts had meaning, and that they had turned to the future.[45]

Whether through the editorial activities of Gallimard, Jacques Copeau's theatrical productions at the *Vieux-Colombier*, or the ten-day long meetings at the Abbey of Pontigny, the *NRF* strategically welcomed a spectrum of art forms and genres, while securing leading authors and critics to contribute to its prestige. Moreover, Thibaudet noted that the writers around Gide comprised an "academy of the novel," in which "the novel was summoned to reflect on itself," especially its formal qualities, in order "to find the evolutionary lines of its genre."[46] The real "adventure" of the novel according to Rivière, notes Koffeman, was not to be found in explicit themes, but in its capacity to unearth hidden zones of human thought and motivation.[47]

Given this double stance of tradition and innovation, the *NRF* was able to attract both cultural nationalists and the poetic avant garde, rolling opposing aesthetic and political tendencies into their own intellectual style. The French playwright, novelist, and *NRF* critic Henri Ghéon dubbed the resulting synthesis *classicisme moderne*. This apparent oxymoron was meant to signal "a profound respect for tradition with a renewal of literary themes and techniques."[48] Rather than yielding to Maurras's polemical opposition of classical and romantic form, the *NRF* critics sought to locate the analytic and poetic qualities of classical style in a continuum with modern literature.[49] Classicism, for Thibaudet, was a form of intelligence: "a conscious force that discerns, ranks, and disciplines."[50] There was no reason to rob modern literature of its critical potential—especially as regulator of intelligence—which had cyclically recurred in Greek, Latin, and French thought: "Can the notion and taste of the classic, as fertile regulators of our intelligence, as means of our criticism, as principles of our judgment, provide us today with the elements of a positive foundation? Can they once again become an aesthetic 'institution'?"[51] Any possibility of elevating *classicisme moderne* into an "aesthetic institution" would soon be interrupted by the outbreak of the war. While the prewar *NRF* separated the aesthetic and the political, the experience of the war made the two spheres indissociable. Lines of demarcation that seemed distinct became blurred once more.

Considering their staunch aestheticism and evident political indifference, the reaction of the *NRF* to the outbreak of the war is even more striking. Nearly all the contributors of the review were caught up in the whirlwind of war, which they saw as a redemptive moment, a liberation from the dead ends of their civilian careers and domestic lives. Conflict, as Yaël Dagan notes, promised a new system of values, representations, norms, and language: a change in the critical climate.[52] General mobilization concretized the change in sensibility they had been calling for. Instead of trying to persevere despite the catastrophic turn of events, the *NRF* stopped publishing immediately in 1914, as if the conflict annulled their critical stance. As Schlumberger wrote in a letter to Gide, it would have seemed almost despicable, assuming they had been able, to publish nonsense about Madame de Guermantes during the war. While Gide sought to distance himself from intensified literary "nationalism," writes Michel Winock, "the *Nouvelle revue* decreed [the qualifier] *French* [...] was immersed in a feeling of patriotic complacency that garnered it sympathy from l'Action française."[53]

An irruption of national feeling, *la passion de la France*, in Rivière's words, came to disorient "intellectual cosmopolitanism" and "the vague indulgence for foreign forms of thinking." This newfound susceptibility to national sentiment was coupled, for many writers, with a religious awakening. The suspension of critical activity involved a displacement, rather than dissolution, of aesthetic categories onto the field of "life" or "experience" itself. Yet, as Benjamin remarked, those "who returned from the battlefield had grown silent—not richer but poorer in communicable experience."⁵⁴ Rivière, who did not experience the battlefield for long, was an exception in this sense. His reflections on national character and intellectual temperament, written in a German war camp, would influence the editorial politics of the *NRF* obliquely yet decisively when he became the director of the review after the armistice.

Rivière's Wartime (1914–17)

Mental mobilization meant being constantly attuned to news from the front, reading all the available newspapers and discussing them endlessly, starving for signs of intelligence. In *Le Temps retrouvé*, the narrator, at first uniquely interested in the war, comes to see it as a monumental distraction drawing writers away from literature into partisan, social and ideological causes. "So many humanitarian, patriotic, internationalist and metaphysical conversations. No more style, I used to hear, no more literature, life."⁵⁵ Rivière, who was enlisted, deemed barracks life "terrifying stupid" (*d'une bêtise terrifiante*) and "atrocious," the war "horrible," yet even its aftermath offered "anyone who has a taste for psychology [...] a spectacle both intoxicating and hopeless."⁵⁶ Rivière had a lot of time to observe the spectacle, since he was captured after four days of combat and made a prisoner of war in Saxony. His experience seems closer to the one depicted in Renoir's *La grande illusion* than to the spate of gruesome early war novels such as Barbusse's *Le feu* (1916), Paulhan's *Le guerrier appliqué* (1917), or Dorgelès's *Les croix de bois* (1919).

Renoir's film resonates here through the series of national and class-based stereotypes that structure it. More significantly, set as it is in 1914, the only trench in sight is the tunnel the prisoners of war dig to escape, their motivations to do so ranging from boredom and the spirit of contradiction to a kind of aristocratic pragmatism. When the guards carrying out a search for contraband tear up an edition of Pindar in Greek that belongs to a French teacher and translator, he can only exclaim, "Ils sont vraiment trop bêtes!" The war, which lasts longer than anyone expects, is said to democratize everything from ways of speaking to microbes and diseases, which had previously followed fin-de-siècle class lines. The "grand illusion" of the title refers to the naïve hope that such a large scale internecine European conflict would be the last.⁵⁷

Returning to Rivière with this picture in mind, his wartime writings seem less idiosyncratic. Later published as *L'Allemand: Souvenirs et réflexions d'un prisonnier de guerre*, the captive critic undertook a sincere analysis of what he calls the synthetic, universalizing spirit of the

Germans in comparison with the analytic cast of the French mind.⁵⁸ Full of dualisms, *L'Allemand* is of at least double interest. It can be read both as a memoir of Rivière's wartime obsessions, and a record of the qualities he considered distinctly French reconstrued negatively through the portrait of the German disposition (or the lack thereof).⁵⁹ Difficult to read for its premise that "national character" can be analytically demarcated along political borders, it is nonetheless crucial for any understanding of the editorial politics of Rivière's *NRF* after the war. Rivière's wartime speculations about the relation—and separation—of aesthetics and politics made it impossible for him to adhere to the nationalist classicism of the Maurrassians, who directly challenged the critical neutrality of the *NRF*.

Rather than a document of testimony, *L'Allemand* is perhaps best read as a psychic construction that calls to be deconstructed.⁶⁰ Doing so allows us to understand how the meaning of *français* and *intelligence* before and after the war could hardly be the same. Although it takes the form of a series of remarks about national mentalities, historic, linguistic, and gestural differences, it ought to be deciphered as a compendium of Rivière's oppositions between reflection and action, judgment and potentiality, strategy and timing, intelligence and flair. These pairs—the first series of which are valorized as French, the second derided as German—amount to a composite self-portrait of the critic. Agamben places Rivière in a lineage of critics (alongside Max Kommerell, Gianfranco Contini, Félix Fénéon, and Walter Benjamin) who "resolve the work's intention into a gesture" rather than approaching it on the philologico-hermeneutic (interpretive) or physiognomic (historical or natural contextual) level.⁶¹ While this may hold true for Rivière's criticism, *L'Allemand* equally pertains to the sphere of "physiognomic" criticism, which situates the work in the order of historical and collective imaginaries.⁶²

To exceed his position as prisoner, Rivière sought to see himself through his captors' eyes. He attributed the variance between French and German character to a series of sensorial differences: the linear French relied on vision, primary evidence and tended to particularize; whereas as the melodic Germans were dominated by hearing, open to indefinite variation, and constantly surpassing the individual.⁶³ Rivière thus considered the ultimate French art to be drawing, while the German one was music. In a reversal of Rousseau's position that man was naturally good, Rivière argued that the wartime actions of both nations showed how man was essentially *méchant*. Axiomatic evil meant that the intelligent subject was faced with a constant imperative to survey its actions and thoughts. Rivière describes this hyper-vigilance he discovered as a prisoner:

Account for all the consequences of this, I say. Always represent to myself, in advance, the weight in effort and suffering of each sentence that I may utter. Mentally translate each one of the impulses of my mind in terms of realities.[64]

Rivière equated intelligence with a nearly impossible foresight of the real consequences of psychic activity, which he vowed to analyze and translate into prose.[65] His greatest fear during and after the war remained the possibility of allowing the conflict to saturate language. In a particularly evocative image, he likens his anxiety about the perils of speech to those of the soldiers who were afraid of attracting an enemy bombshell if indiscreet chatter betrayed their position. Rivière recognized the difficulty of such moral translation during the war given the impossibility of thinking accurately and with justice, *penser juste*. The ballast of war, which warped the gravitational field of ideas, made all thinking viciously circular:

> And I came to the idea that during wartime all thought is subject to a kind of gravity. The passions of each individual, even deeper his race, his nationality form a star, around which his reflection, drawn by an invisible influence, can do no better than to turn. In reality, one no longer thinks [. . .] one snaps up everything that can encourage you in your system in passing, and the rest, one doesn't see; it slides by your nose, without any hint of the disorder that it could create in your representations.[66]

If thinking from the "racial," class-based, or national point of view is bound to go in circles, Rivière is equally skeptical about the possibilities of revolt, or fantasies of pacifist elevation above the force of gravity. Instead, he aspires to view both self and other through an emptied gaze (*l'oeil dépouillé*). The resulting image of the German character, needless to say, is far from objective. To the Germans he attributes a formidable will and equally formidable indifference: "They are nothing—they desire, expect, and pretend nothing."[67] This dispassionate intensity is essentially disoriented and amorphous, and easily susceptible to being manipulated by stronger forces: "Such severe inertia of feeling cannot fail to have consequences for intelligence. The indifferent heart leads the German to an inability to distinguish between ideas, a weakening of his values."[68] The French possess innate moral distinctions that allow them to make judgments, in Rivière's view, whereas the Germans consider any moral judgment flexible unless it becomes consecrated as duty.

In a chapter titled "Instead of intelligence, duty," in which he criticizes the eminent neo-Kantian philosopher Paul Natorp, Rivière declares that the Germans had lost the capacity to grasp ideas (*begreifen*) and had transformed culture into a demand or a task (*Forderung, Aufgabe*). He blames Kantian philosophy for weakening the conceptual virtues of the German mind, invading its most disinterested regions with practical reason, thereby establishing a dominance of duty over intelligence. The critical philosophy is held responsible for a contemporary pragmatism that blinds Germans to direct knowledge, dulls their insight, and distorts the fabric of intelligence from a perceptive to an imperative faculty. Rivière proceeds to describe contemporary Germans in more Faustian tones as mindless demons of activity. Despite a shared anti-Germanism, no programmatic politics could be based on an aesthetic division of tradition à la Maurras that pit *ancien régime* clarity against post-revolutionary turmoil. The future editor of the *NRF* recognized in captivity that the political consequences of intelligence were unforeseeable. Rather than attempt to produce a future that would reproduce the past, Rivière sought to preserve a space in language that could welcome the unforeseen.

Throughout his memoir, Rivière invents his identity as a French critic. Rather than repressing the violence of the war, the death of friends, and his own failure to participate in the action, *L'Allemand* reinforces his identity through defensive exercises of "isolation," identifying and delimiting the psychic traits he attributes to German alterity in order to secure his own sense of Frenchness. In prefaces added after the war, Rivière voiced doubts about his decision to publish the volume, as he considered it would inevitably contribute to the already immense hostility that existed towards the Germans in Europe. Although he hesitated to contribute rhetorically to the suffering and aggression he had witnessed, his book was a necessary step for freeing his psyche from the war and purging the hatred he felt for the Germans.[69] Reading his memoir, one is struck by the methodic, analytic procedure used to excise such a passionate attitude. Its failure is somewhat immaterial. The effect of Rivière's procedure was not only the invention of a postwar rhetoric of French critical neutrality, but also his practical willingness to foster the tentative renewal of Franco-German relations until his untimely death of typhoid fever in 1925. In his correspondence, he explores the possibility or the interest of reestablishing the *NRF*'s prewar agenda and realizes the literary organ will have to make room for politics. He was nonetheless increasingly convinced of the importance of his own "task," ironically borrowing the imperative language he attributed to his captors. He alone could prepare a future that was unbound by any institution other than art and literature. Such convictions allowed him to return from the war, and willfully negotiate an unlikely place as the sole editor of the review, which he restored to its prewar pacifist agenda, rather than deploying it to defend the martial primacy of French culture in Europe as expected.

Demobilizing Intelligence (June 1919)

In a talk given in Geneva in 1918, Rivière had occasion to reflect on the *NRF* and its role in the prewar literary moment. Describing the era as "formidably distant," because situated before the outbreak of the war, he added:

> You know as well as I do how everything that preceded the war is, now, difficult to recapture. Even when it comes to our own thoughts, our own actions from then, we feel somewhat at a loss to find their origins and motives. Our prewar being is almost like a foreigner, whose gestures we manage to glean only through mental effort and concentration.[70]

The continuum of chronological time was broken and neither cultural memory nor critical tradition alone could overcome the gap.

The *NRF*'s silence during the war was shattered in 1919 when a flurry of manifestos from the left and the right sought to control the meaning of the French "victory" and the memory of those who had made "sacrifices."[71] The intense anxiety behind these debates concerned the correct intellectual attitude to emerge from the war, one able to vigilantly prepare for a future where war, especially against Germany, would be impossible, or at least impossible to lose. The demands of the Versailles Treaty and what Keynes called "the economic consequences of the peace," had already determined much of the coming conflict. No single intellectual position could ever satisfy a need to delimit the future. The desire or the refusal of "cultural demobilization," alongside a "will to remobilize for or against the war," made it difficult to measure the passage from war to peace using purely economic, military or chronological markers.[72] Indeed these competing positions disrupt linear histories, since some figures chose to demobilize well before the end of the war, while others refused to do so after the end of the hostilities, if at all. The process of demobilization, which should have secured the transition into peace, instead became the impasse defining the postwar period. The war had largely interrupted dissent within French letters. The armistice brought what Julien Benda dubbed the time of partisans.

As noted earlier in the case of Gide, a generation of writers unable to participate in the war had instead mobilized their minds.[73] The end of the war thus raised the question of whether it was possible to demobilize or disarm the French intelligentsia—to return to a fantasy of a demilitarized, prewar impartiality—or whether this heightened political consciousness should promote French hegemony over Europe, as the Maurrasians proposed.[74] Although Rivière momentarily considered the possibility of accounting for the war by making the *NRF* more intellectual than literary, by including theoretical contributions, social and political philosophy, he finally decided that the best preparation for the future was to establish a review of literature and criticism where creation could be "ingenuous, naïve, useless." "It is necessary at a time when the most beautiful French qualities seem to reawaken, that we rediscover the secret of transcendence and the taste for analysis." Rivière was proposing nothing less than a return to "intelligence in literature" through its demobilization. As Compagnon notes, Rivière relaunched the *NRF* by calling for the "demobilization of intelligence and the independence of literature in relation to patriotism and nationalism, to morals and politics."[75] The editorial introducing the June 1919 volume should be read as a triple ethical, aesthetic, and civic charter declaring the review a speculative one, forming a new literary canon, and exposing it to political discourse.[76] Nevertheless, there was to be an almost Pascalian "separation of orders" dividing "writers without politics" from "citizens without literature."

Despite the wartime silence—which Rivière described as valuable insofar as it allowed for an "examination of conscience"—the review now returned to its disinterested orientation: "The *NRF* [. . .] ought to be above all a territory conducive to creation, that a critical intelligence would keep constantly furnished."[77] The task of critical intelligence was to hold at bay extraneous preoccupations of a "utilitarian, theoretical or moral order that could deform the spontaneous vegetation of genius or talent."[78] In short, it had to be able to demarcate an independent literary space once again.[79] Yet, despite all appearances, this was not simply a return to mantras of *l'art pour l'art*. Rather, Rivière and the critics of the *NRF* were carefully reconceptualizing the relation of politics and aesthetics in terms of critical neutrality, which soon became one of the touchstones of twentieth-century French literature. After the Second World War, the debate would be recast in terms of engaged and disengaged literature.[80]

One might justly ask how such a demarcation could be accomplished after the devastation of the war. Rivière addressed the problem explicitly:

> The war came, the war is over. It profoundly upset everything, particularly our minds. It put each of us in the crucible and recomposed a truly new soul for many of us. More than one of us will dare to remain

grateful to it for having thus started us on a new and more perfect model. Yet despite this moral and psychological recasting [...] we return more deliberately if possible than before, to our first design. We want to remake a disinterested review, a review in which we continue to judge and create in total freedom of mind, not as if "nothing had happened," but by continuing to only obey specific principles in each order.[81]

The specific principles of "critical intelligence" and "creative gratuity" rely on a tautology. Rivière writes: "The war may have changed many things but not this, that literature is literature, art is art."[82] In its simplest sense, tautology is a form of a proposition or a judgment of identity. Instead of defining literature as a particular kind of discourse or linguistic activity, Rivière identifies it with itself. Literature is no more or less than itself.[83] The unwillingness to develop these terms further, or to define criticism except in terms of its own activities, constitutes an attempt to protect a sphere of aesthetic autonomy against the demands of postwar engagement. Commenting on the "least naïve" tautology of criticism, "literature is literature," Francesco Orlando writes: "most times this procedure will have to be accepted as being pertinent and shrewd, and on rare occasions it might lend itself to the suspicion of being shrewd as part of an evasive tactic inasmuch as the homogeneity that is not guaranteed between literature and reality is guaranteed between literature and other, previous literature."[84] The tautology functions, whether reliant on a synchronic or diachronic canon, as a way of eliding relations to contemporary sociopolitical demands.

The war may have diminished the relative importance of art and literature for some, Rivière writes, but it was unable to "modify its essence."[85] The task of an *NRF* critic is thus to read literary works without erasing their place in a larger tradition. Yet nothing can step in lieu of literature, especially not politics, as Maurras would have liked. In this sense, the revived review continued the project of the *NRF* critics before the war. "Intelligent criticism" preserved a space for creation through its disinterested separation of spheres. Rivière was particularly drawn to the notion of a "critical intelligence" capable of cataloguing the richness of romanticism and the refinement of symbolism into an archive of clear ideas.

Rivière's definition of creation, too, although not perfectly tautological, is certainly autotelic: "Today as yesterday, despite mounds of ruins, it remains true that artistic creation is an original act, that creating is perhaps above all to feel nothing, to want nothing other than what one does."[86] While this refusal of the demands of history may seem like the will to dissociate the aesthetic and the political in the name of "pure" art, Rivière's gesture emphasizes that literature offers its own formal modalities, which must be preserved from the calculated imposition of ideological content. The critical potential of literature would reside in its formal dimension, or it would simply not exist. Rivière's *NRF* thus welcomes "the claim of intelligence" in contemporary literature: "We will welcome the claim of intelligence that clearly seeks to regain its rights in art; not to supplant feeling, but to probe it, to analyze and reign over it."[87] Rather than supplanting sentiment, the new analytic moment in French letters would make the affective intelligible. Perhaps this left room for an ideological unconscious but one that, by definition, could hardly serve as a point of departure.

Rivière went so far as to declare that the great misdeed of the war had been to occupy mental space.[88] All ideas were turned towards the fate of the country, a univocal ideological vector that he identified as being strictly "monarchical." Intellectual liberation after the war was the true civic priority: "Our intention is to work as far as possible to stop the constraint that the war still exerts over intelligences and which they have so much difficulty in ridding themselves on their own."[89] After the war, "demobilizing intelligence" was the only way to honor and defend the reign of French intelligence, which Rivière celebrates in an astonishing passage, one he could not have written before the war:

> For it is true that French intelligence is incomparable; there isn't one stronger, sharper, or more profound. Even if I were to be accused of insolence, I would pursue my thinking to the end; French intelligence is the only one left in the world. We alone have been able to keep an intellectual tradition; we alone have been able to save ourselves, more or less, from pragmatist dumbing down; we alone have continued to believe in the principle of identity. We alone in the world, I repeat coldly, still know how to think. In philosophical, literary, and artistic matters, only what we say will count.[90]

Despite such grand nationalistic rhetoric, Rivière's program for aesthetic autonomy caused a wave of hostile reactions for not being committed enough to nationalism, even before it was published. For Arnauld, Ghéon, and Schlumberger, demobilizing intelligence was tantamount to national suicide. Within the *NRF*, Drouin insisted that forgetting the war was a redundant cause, since habit and time would do as much. The review should have met the challenge of reflecting on the war, scrutinizing the latent structures of events that led to it, and call for testimony before institutionalization destroyed memory. Ghéon, who had been transformed by the war, claimed the hour had come to place politics first.

These internal dissensions were echoed outside the debates of the editorial collective. After the Russian Revolution, the *Clarté* group, created during the war by combatant intellectuals, began asking how European reconstruction would proceed on the ruins of Europe. In response, it soon published a journal that billed itself as a "review of revolutionary culture" (*revue de culture révolutionnaire*). Reducing intellectual life to a defense of national interest and the "sacred laws of the city," the group argued, was a form of debasement. In France, Henri Barbusse popularized its ideas in a manifesto published in *L'Humanité* on May 10, 1919. On June 16, 1919, Romain Rolland published the "Déclaration de l'indépendance de l'esprit" in *L'Humanité*, calling for French intellectuals to break with state interests and work instead for the good of humanity. This was followed by "Un appel: Fière déclaration d'intellectuels," also published in *L'Humanité* ten days later.[91] Whereas Rivière had sought to overcome the conflict, shed the weight of the war, and raise the tenor of intellectual discourse to prewar liberal neutrality, Rolland, who had spent most of the war in Switzerland, tried to mobilize international intellectuals for peace. Despite claims to intellectual independence, Rolland's position was paradoxically marked in its very French assertion of a universal "intelligence" predicated on particular values. Rolland saw his break with nationalism as reparation for "the near total abdication of intelligence and its willful subjugation to unfettered forces" during the war.[92] The arguments of competing factions hinged upon notions of "intelligence," suggesting the overdetermined and contradictory hopes invested in the term.

These debates sought to wrest intelligence away from Maurras's program and its corrosive consequences. Under Maurras's influence, Henri Massis aimed to rally French intellectuals to defend national greatness against the "Bolshevism of thinking" represented by Rolland and *Clarté*. Three days after Rolland's text was published, Massis, an influential polemicist known under the pseudonym Agathon, launched the "Manifeste du parti de l'intelligence," signed by leading Maurrasian and conservative Catholic intellectuals in *Le Figaro*.[93] It zeroed in on the impossibility of thinking in the postwar period outside of a system of values and emphasized the necessity of narrowly linking intelligence to a political cause: "a national intelligence (or intelligentsia) at the service of the national" was its first principle.[94] Such mobilization was meant to defend the future of civilization, ensure spiritual salvation, offer an organizing principle for life, but above all to defend society, nation, family and the individual from the destructive forces of a certain kind of thinking: "There is a thinking that arrests thinking, an art that is the end of art, a politics that destroys politics; these are the only ones we seek to proscribe."⁹⁵ The goal of the party, which claimed to know clearly what they "wanted and did not want" from the future, was to oppose both international humanitarianism and liberal disorder with a hierarchical, classificatory method allowing for understanding and action. Its monotheologico-political guarantor was the Catholic "unity of faith," "unity of thinking" and "unity of obedience to an explicit and fundamental law." Its programmatic statement declared:

> Reflection of the public spirit in France by the royal road of intelligence and classic methods, the intellectual federation of Europe and the world under the aegis of victorious France, the guardian of all civilization, this is our double design that derives from a higher unity.⁹⁶

The hegemonic defense of French intelligence was anchored to nothing less than the future of civilization as a whole: "We believe—and the world believes with us—that it is the destination of our race to defend the spiritual interests of humanity. Victorious France wants to regain its sovereign position in the spiritual order, which is the only one by which legitimate domination can be exercised."⁹⁷ A superior position in the order of mind and spirit would ground "legitimate domination" over the world.

Reactions at the *NRF* were once again divided. Cosmopolitanism was easier to ignore than the pathos of intelligence. During the war Gide himself had declared *Action française* "the only movement capable of organizing the intellectual defense of the nation."⁹⁸ When Schlumberger wrote that he would have signed the manifesto if he had been Catholic, Gallimard added sarcastically that doing so would be a mark of his freedom of thought and absence of intelligence. Henri Ghéon, a former ally, signed the *Figaro* manifesto, and attacked many of Rivière's positions. His most interesting objection pointed to Rivière's taste for analysis that supposedly reduced intelligence to the faculty of distinction rather than synthesis. For Ghéon, this meant that Rivière was perpetually preparing to think, rather than thinking.⁹⁹ With Thibaudet's exceptional support, Rivière alone in his critical note, "Le parti de l'intelligence," called for the demobilization of intelligence, attacking the fallacies of the manifesto:

> Intelligence is decidedly fashionable. There is no one who does not lay claim to its favor; no manifesto appears in which it is not prescribed as the paramount virtue. And now we have a Party of Intelligence to

which many distinguished minds already belong. [. . .] To judge it only as a whole, it seems to me marked by a certain confusion, which is a bit astonishing coming from people whose avowed concern is to honor the logical faculty.[100]

Putting intelligence at the service of the nation was a desertion of intelligence. Protecting French intelligence, Rivière argued, meant "protecting, preserving, and demarcating it from the ensemble of properties that comprise France [. . .] freeing reflection from preconceived finality."[101] Once again the goal was immanent analysis, not the advancement of an external end: "We must not reach anything other than what we will find; we must allow French intelligence to see what it sees and to say it, whatever the result may be."[102] Returning to Du Bellay's formula, Rivière situated the task of the postwar intellectual on the side of illustration rather than the defense of intelligence: "Let us illustrate it through the supreme work, that no one other than us is capable of: the analysis, the description, the translation into exact formulas of the immense chaos that the war created."[103] Charged with the translation of chaos into order, the role of intelligence was no anodyne matter.

Rivière saw partisans of intelligence reducing it to a linking tool, a coordinating apparatus meant to synthesize and control the nation, to recreate monarchy, even as writers from Proust to Bataille used the anachronistic character of the aristocracy to explore the material contradictions of an overdetermined modernity.[104] For the critic, intelligence was not a centralizing agency. Instead, he defined it as "the faculty of recognizing difference as difference, to perceive two ideas, two objects where those who are less gifted only perceive one; its first movement is discrimination and analysis. If we do not allow it to accomplish itself freely, composedly, and all alone so to speak, all the rest of its operation is purged."[105] In a text that defended Rivière's turn away from Maurras, despite paying calculated homage to the latter, Thibaudet struck an ironically mediating tone: "French intelligence in this state of permanent mobilization will soon run the risk of being neither intelligent, nor French."[106]

It is difficult to overestimate how acutely the critical turn of the war informed the literary return of the *NRF*. The prewar stance of political neutrality and aesthetic liberality had now sharpened itself into Rivière's intractable tautology: not *l'art pour l'art*, but *l'art est l'art*.[107] Intelligence rejected the task Maurras had set it, refusing to anchor itself to an institution or a cause. The future of intelligence remained torn between a promise and a menace that could not be overcome. In the meantime, the

NRF transformed the literary field in France. As Auguste Anglès, the most influential historian of the journal, notes:

> Such widespread victories erase the traces of the battle and transform those who had been formidable adversaries at first into the anonymous vanquished: the names of many of those whom the *NRF* disqualified would no longer mean much to today's readers. Yet the primary task of this criticism of summary executions was to reverse the scale of literary values.[108]

While the editors and critics of the *NRF* were shaping the literary canon, demoting and promoting authors, and disputing the values attached to intelligence, a solitary figure had been working to free literature from dominant intellectual strictures and renew the novel while doing so.[109] Proust dissected the polemics in the press around the *Parti de l'intelligence*. In a 1919 letter to Daniel Halévy, who had signed the manifesto, he rejected its rhetoric, as well as the reaction in the press:

> One would weep with joy to learn that France had been appointed custodian of world literature, but it's a little shocking to see us assume that role for ourselves. This "hegemony," born of "Victory," is an unconscious reminder of "Deutschland über alles" and, for that reason, rather distasteful. To know how to temper such pride with modesty used to be one of the characteristics of our "race" (can it be proper French, to speak of a "French race"?).[110]

Proust's doubts about the existence of a "French race," and his skepticism about "victory" and "hegemony," suggest that the triumphant outcome of the war was more akin to defeat. To Rivière, he was even more direct:

> Speaking of Flaubert, do you remember the "Intelligence Club" in *A Sentimental Education*. What a "prediction" of the ridiculous "Intelligence Party," what dangerous nonsense the postwar is breeding.[111]

The allusion to Flaubert here is surely significant beyond its prescience. If Flaubert imagined that *L'Éducation sentimentale* foresaw the events of 1871, Proust hurried to inscribe life during wartime within the folds of his novel. As Edward Hughes rightly notes, "the myriad calls emanating from the public arena—from the forces of nationalism, Germanophobia, laicity, and social progressivism, among others—prompt Proust to ask how these interpellations are to be answered by writers committed to their art."[112] While a literary work's national character lent it universal appeal, institutionalizing this particularity could render it illegible beyond national borders.[113] Proust's solution was axiomatic: "there is only one way to write for all which is to write without thinking about anyone."[114] Writing for no one would soon prove increasingly risky as literary style became even more intensely identified as the battleground of politics.

A little over a decade after Proust's death, the stakes were raised for the French literary intelligentsia from the Surrealists to Gide at the 1935 *Congrès international des écrivains pour la défense de la culture* (International Writers' Congress for the Defense of Culture) organized by the Comintern in Paris.[115] The gathering of anti-Fascist writers was meant to seal the cultural pendant of the recent Franco-Soviet pact between Laval and Stalin. Bringing together Aldous Huxley, E. M. Forster, Robert Musil, Max Brod, Bertold Brecht, Boris Pasternak and Isaac Babel alongside their French counterparts, the congress fulfilled the Soviet mission by ushering in the era of popular, allied fronts against Nazism. It also led to the definitive break between Surrealism and the French Communist Party—largely due to the fight for the release of Russian revolutionary writer Victor Serge—momentarily drawing them closer to Georges Bataille and the milieu of Contre-Attaque instead. These fraught moments raised analogous questions to those discussed in this chapter: what is the political and aesthetic task of literature within the national (and international) community? In the meantime, one of Proust's closest readers and translators, Benjamin, was generalizing these demands by improbably reconfiguring literary technique as the site of radical politics.

As this chapter has shown, literary polemics around World War I transformed intelligence into a political category. Maurras's vision for the future of intelligence, and its reactivation by Massis and other adherents of the *Parti de l'intelligence*, led the *NRF* to take a stance concerning the possibility of directing literary production to defend cultural and national values. Instead of placing literature and criticism under the aegis of a nationalist agenda, Rivière led the *NRF* critics toward a neutral and tautological understanding of literature as an end in itself. He defined intelligence as the capacity of recognizing difference as difference, lending it a crucial role in the act of critical discernment. The increasing economic instability of the interwar years led to a heightened call for an engaged intelligentsia, one whose political significance was once more laid open to conflict.

CHAPTER FIVE

Situating Intelligence

WALTER BENJAMIN AND POLITICAL TECHNIQUE

THE CATEGORY OF intelligence is marginal to German thought and criticism, which tends to relegate it to a foreign tendency of thinking. Terms like *Geist*, *Kunde*, and *Besinnung* (roughly, spirit, knowledge, and mindfulness) had mapped much of the philosophical territory in competing ways, while German scientific and laboratory culture in the late nineteenth century was primarily interested in thought processes (*Denkprozesse*) and Gestalt psychology, rather than individual differences as in France.[1] The literary historian Ann Jefferson, for instance, suggests that the conceptual histories of the term "genius" may have been more varied in France than Germany because France has no single dominant intellectual framework to provide a consistent context comparable to the German "literary–philosophical" tradition.[2] The chapters above confirm this view of French thought vis-à-vis intelligence. Yet, post-Kantian and post-Idealist thought has a more fractured relation to the notion of intelligence than such a distinction implies.

The core of this chapter, as its title suggests, is centered on Benjamin's notion of political technique, developed in the interstices of his essays on the social situation of the French writer. Intelligence is endowed with a literary–political role through the invention and dissemination of literary forms. Writing here becomes a medium for distributing techniques capable of dislocating the intellectual, and possibly economic, ground of private property. First, a tension is introduced between Heidegger's culturally reactionary discussions of *Intelligenz* as a kind of decadence of the spirit and Benjamin's attunement to and radicalization of the situation, style, and technique of French writing. Very schematically put, two conceptions of literature emerge: *Dichtung*, which is supposed to redeem the metaphysical dangers brought about by the instrumentalization of technology (of which *Intelligenz* is both an offshoot and symptom) and Benjamin's conception of writing, capable of harnessing and sharing the resources of technique (which Heidegger would likely dismiss as *Schriftstellertum*). At the risk of overstating the point, it is when Benjamin turns to his French contemporaries from Apollinaire to the Surrealists that his notion of political style as a device for gauging and betraying the capacities and class interests of the intelligentsia comes to the fore. The term intelligence in this chapter consequently refers largely to the problems posed by a free-floating intelligentsia whose tactical conceptions of thinking are susceptible to ideological capture.

Dissecting Intelligenz

French translators of German thinkers are often obliged to use multiple words for identical German terms. Such translations have both the benefit of rendering the dynamic contextual meaning of a single word and the drawback of fetishizing isolated terms in the original. Conversely, various German terms can be rendered by the same French word. An exemplary instance is *intelligence*, which translates *Klugheit, Verstand, Einsicht*, or *Intelligenz*.[3] While much could be said about the shades of meaning here, the following pages contend that *Intelligenz* carries a specific significance among the host of terms that are commonly translated back into the same French word. Its Latinate character sets it apart in the German philosophical idiom, where it comes to denote something calculating, free-floating, and disreputable, pit against the historically grounded resources of German thought.[4]

Adorno had an intriguing theory about why Valéry lacked an audience in Germany, which succintly differentiates between the two philosophical traditions after the Enlightenment. Beyond the usual qualifications about the difficulties of translating poetic language, he considers that the most significant obstacle to reception consists in the different "rationalist and irrationalist motifs" in the history of French and German thought:

> The status of these motifs, however, is the opposite in France of what it is in Germany. In Germany, it is customary to class rationalism with progress, and irrationalism, as a legacy of Romanticism, with reaction. For Valéry, however, the traditional movement is identical to the Cartesian rationalist movement, and the irrationalist movement

is Cartesianism's self-criticism. The rational–conservative moment in Valéry is the dictatorial civilizing moment, the autonomous ego's avowed power to control the unconscious.[5]

The two traditions of thinking are not merely incommensurate in this view. Rather, they represent inverted intellectual genealogies in relation to the values ascribed to rationalism and the ego's struggle to control the unconscious. Significant for the present study is Adorno's location of both Valéry's reaction and radicalism within aspects of Cartesian thought. By traversing doubt in quest of certitude, Descartes posits self-consciousness as the cornerstone of philosophical modernity. The gap separating *res cogitans* from *res extensa*, as well as the technical mastery of nature such a separation enables, becomes a central target for German thinkers of mediation from Hegel onward. Ontological critiques focus on the neglect of "being" in favor of thought, while phenomenologists contest the impoverished transposition of abstract thought onto material reality. The very thinkers who perceived an unjustifiable opposition between thought and being in Cartesianism also attacked the supposedly universally shared faculty of intelligence for its disembodied character.

In the *Genealogy of Morals*, Nietzsche contends that concepts can only be defined if they do not have a history, whereas semantically complex notions require a genealogy. In countless fragments, he uncovers the cognitive element in the passions, thereby showing that while a unified subject has intelligent desires, only a shattered subject's desires truly supersede intelligence. In Nietzsche's trans-valuation of all value, the lack of objective measures to gauge intelligence proves revelatory of reason's unfounded claim to universality. A striking passage from the *Nachlass* reads as follows:

> There are likely many kinds of intelligence, but each has its own regularity, which makes it impossible according to another regularity. Since we cannot have any *empirical* control over the different kinds of intelligence, every way of insight into the origin of intelligence is sealed off. The *general* phenomenon of intelligence is unknown to us; we only have *special cases*, and *cannot generalize*. Here we are all Slaves, even if we would like to be visionaries! On the other hand, each kind of intelligence must bear an *understanding of the world*—but I believe, it is merely the adaptation suited to the rules of each kind of intelligence—it gets by on its own everywhere. All intelligence believes in itself."[6]

Without venturing into discussions of slave morality, one can glean the anti-universalist impulse of this passage. Just as for Valéry intelligence reveals itself as a form of personal belief, for Nietzsche the faculty is a thinly veiled form of adaptation and self-assertion, if not will-to-power. Each form of intelligence is a belief that tries to impose its subjective standards upon others and the world. The illusion of objectivity results merely from a momentary imbalance of power. In this view, we lack any empirical standards to study, let alone measure, the variation of intelligence. Its very particularity forecloses the possibility of generalization. There is nothing intelligent to be said about intelligence, other than underscoring the stupidity of the fantasy that one could somehow isolate its source once and for all.

How the Nietzschean genealogy of consciousness—born out of servility to a "superior" body—relates to the relativity of intelligence, which threatens to make "slaves" of us all, is a question that exceeds the bounds of the present discussion. We can however suggest that, for Nietzsche, the keenest psychological insights into different forms of intelligence should be sought in and as fiction. An unparalled connoisseur of French tradition, from the moralists to Flaubert, Nietzsche took note of the efforts made by novelists to catalogue and expose "bourgeois stupidity" in literature. In *Beyond Good and Evil*, he proposes that contemporary literature shift its attention from *bêtise bourgeoise* to unconscious cunning and instinctive intelligence which would offer "drama enough for the gods."

> The French psychologists—and where else are there still psychologists today?—have never grown tired of their bitter and manifold delight in the *bêtise bourgeoise* [. . .] this reveals something about them. For instance, Flaubert, the good citizen of Rouen, ultimately stopped seeing, hearing, or tasting anything else: this was his brand of self-torture.[7]

The realist novelist's obsession with describing the stupidity of his fellow citizens became monomaniacal. As an antidote, Nietzsche prescribes that novelists turn their gaze upon creatures closer, if not identical, to themselves:

> Now—because this is getting boring—I recommend another source of amusement for a change: the unconscious cunning that all good, fat, well-behaved, mediocre spirits have shown towards higher spirits and their tasks, that subtle, intricate Jesuitical cunning that is a thousand times more subtle than any taste or understanding evinced by the middle class in its best moments—it is even more subtle than its victims' understanding (which is on-going proof that "instinct" is the most intelligent type of intelligence discovered so far). In short, you psychologists should study the philosophy of the "rule" in its struggle

against the "exception" [...]. Or, to be even more up date, vivisect the "good man," the *"homo bonae voluntatis"* ... *yourselves*.[8]

The "man of goodwill" whom Nietzsche wants to dissect is a distant heir to the Cartesian figure of the generous man, one who masters his passions through reason. The instinctive intelligence used against such figures provides insight into the unspoken norms that govern popular morality, allowing a portrait of the exceptional figure to emerge in contradistinction. That he considered French literature fertile ground for self-analysis signals Nietzsche's antipathy towards more systematic forms of philosophical discourse. An emergent moment in the Germanic novel from Robert Musil and Franz Kafka to Hermann Broch and Thomas Mann would take up that mantle in his wake.

Overcoming Intelligence

Nietzsche's provocations against philosophers were hardly limited to their intellectualism. The "highest" philosophical concepts of tradition were not immune to the philologist's destructive gaze. He asks, for instance, whether the category of "being" itself is not an insubstantial word, one of the "last wisps of smoke from the evaporating end of reality."[9] In *Introduction to Metaphysics*, Heidegger takes up Nietzsche's challenge concerning the insubstantiality of being: "Is Being a mere word and its meaning a vapor, or does what is named with the word 'Being' hold within it the spiritual fate of the West?"[10] For Heidegger, philosophy is neither a foundation for culture nor does it provide a worldview. Rather, within the limits of its own capacity, philosophy seeks to restore the "historical Dasein of human beings [...] back to the power of Being that is to be opened up originally."[11] The "fundamental question" his 1935 lecture course poses is "why are there beings rather than nothing?" The very possibility of addressing such a question requires an investigation into the historical conditions that make it difficult to articulate. Such unfamiliar questions dissolve when placed "in the cheap acid of merely logical cleverness." Alongside the dominance of scientism and rationalism, Heidegger identifies the central obstacles to thinking about "being" as intellectualism:

> Thinking is called *intelligere* in Latin. It is the business of the *intellectus*. If we are struggling against intellectualism, then in order to actually struggle against it, we must know our opponent: that is, we should know that intellectualism is just the impoverished contemporary offshoot and derivative of a preeminent position of thinking that was

long prepared and was build up by means of Western metaphysics. It is important to prune the outgrowths of contemporary intellectualism.[12]

How does the *Introduction to Metaphysics* propose to respond to the fundamental question it sets itself without falling prey to the intellectualism that is so ingrained in the history of Western metaphysics?[13] This question, once more, exceeds the bounds of the present discussion. We can, however, note some of the ways that Heidegger "prunes the outgrowths of contemporary intellectualism." To craft a philosophical language that can speak about nothing, he confronts the risk of sounding "unscientific." Yet, he emphasizes that the belief that "scientific thinking alone is authentic, rigorous thinking" is "a great misfortune." Significantly, we are told that philosophy and *Dichtung* occupy a privileged position to address the question of being: "Philosophy stands in a completely different domain and rank of spiritual Dasein. Only *Dichtung* is of the same order as philosophical thinking, although thinking and poetry are not identical."[14] An "essential superiority of the spirit holds sway in poetry" that allows the poet to speak "as if beings were expressed and addressed for the first time." In poetic speech, everyday things lose their "indifference and familiarity."[15]

If poetic speech makes the familiar foreign or uncanny, it is because "talk of Nothing always remains unfamiliar." Intelligence, on the contrary, "arms us against the possibility that beings are *not*." It forecloses the possibility of thinking about being. Moreoever, intelligence disrupts or degrades spirit (*Geist*), from which Heidegger is careful to separate it in his analysis, which he quotes from his 1935 Rectoral Address at the University of Freiburg: "Spirit is neither empty acuity, nor the noncommittal play of wit, nor the understanding's boundless pursuit of analysis, nor even world reason, but rather spirit is originally attuned, knowing resolution to the essence of Being."[16] One of the key forces in the near incomprehensibility of the question of Being, we are told, is the "collapse of German Idealism" prepared by nineteenth-century Europe. The contemporary "darkening of the world"—comprising the flight of the gods, the destruction of the earth, and the reduction of human beings to a mass—contains within its center "a *disempowering of the spirit*, its dissolution, suppression, and misinterpretation." Heidegger's complex analysis of this movement would require a sustained reading. For now, consider the primary feature of this disempowering, namely the reinterpretation of *Geist* as *Intelligenz*:

> One decisive aspect is the reinterpretation of the spirit [*Geist*] as *intelligence* [*Intelligenz*], and this as mere astuteness in the

examination, calculation and observation of given things, their possible modification, and their additional elaboration. This astuteness is a matter of mere talent and practice and mass distribution. This astuteness is itself subject to the possibility of organization, none of which ever applies to the spirit. The whole phenomenon of literati and aesthetes is just a late consequence and mutation of the spirit falsified as intelligence. *Mere* ingenuity is the semblance of spirit and veils its absence.[17]

Just as *Geist* is devalued into free-floating *Intelligenz*, *Dichtung*, too, appears to devolve into the mere talent of the rootless literati and the free-floating intelligentsia.

The political implications of this "mutation of the spirit" are manifold. Germany finds itself stuck between America and Soviet Russia, which are both deemed metaphysically identical in their devaluation of spirit. The tool-like character of intelligence can be just as easily placed at the service of Marxism ("the regulation and mastery of the material relations of production") as it can be made to serve capitalist positivism ("the clever ordering and clarification of everything that lies before us and is already posited"). In short, "the spirit as intelligence" becomes the "powerless superstructure to something else, which, because it is spirit-less or even hostile to spirit, counts as authentic reality."[18] No longer capable of acting as the basis of history, spirit becomes a formal ornament that can be used to prop up any ideology in power. The malleability of spirit is the foremost sign of its degeneration.

The instrumental misinterpretation of *Geist* as *Intelligenz* makes every aspect of human activity fall under the purview of consciousness, thereby perpetuating instrumentalization. "Poetry and fine arts, statecraft and religion" shift from being "powers of spiritual happening" to being "*consciously* cultivated and planned."[19] Individuals seek fulfillment through the creation and conservation of culture, while the self becomes the ultimate measure of validity in an atomized world.

> Cultural values secure meaning for themselves in the whole of a culture only by restricting themselves to their self-validity: poetry for poetry's sake, art for art's sake, science of science's sake [. . .]. The spirit as intelligence in the service of goals and the spirit as culture [*Der Geist als zweckdienliche Intelligenz und der Geist als Kultur*] finally become showpieces and spectacles that one takes into account along with many others, that one publicly trots out and exhibits as proof that one does *not* want to deny culture in favor of barbarism.[20]

Cultural artifacts accrue value through their exposition and their supposedly talismanic capacity to hold "barbarism" at bay. One could hardly imagine an attitude more opposed to Benjamin's dictum that "there is no document of civilization which is not at the same time a document of barbarism." Benjamin's *Kulturkritik*, to be sure, belongs to a significantly different context; yet in passages such as the one above one can glean Heidegger's own susceptibility to the rhetoric of "barbarism."

In Heidegger's explications of Hölderlin, where one could conceivably look for what he took to be an authentic response to the "darkening of the world," one finds a surprising allusion to Valéry. The philosopher recalls the poet's essay on the crisis of intelligence, asking his readers whether Europe has not already become a "mere cap" placed at the services of "technical-industrial planetary-interstellar calculation." He appends a third question, after citing Valéry's original two, by turning to Europe's origin rather than its future:

> "Perhaps Europe has already become what it is: a mere cap, yet as such, also the brain of the entire terrestrial body, the brain that manages the technological-industrial, planetary-interstellar calculation." Because this is so, and because what is in such a manner cannot remain, we may perhaps let a third question follow both of Paul Valéry's questions. Our question does not pass over and beyond Europe, but back into its beginning. It could read thus: Must Europe, as this cap and brain, first become a land of an evening from which another morning of world-destiny prepares its rise?[21]

The language of the question Heidegger poses about the "morning of world-destiny" suggests how far his own thought attempts to divest European modernity of its *Intelligenz*. The systematic rejection of *Intelligenz* in his thinking is a powerful sign that the concept, which had enjoyed such great fortune in the French tradition, reached its limit in a certain radicalized strain of German thinking.

Benjamin, who could not have been writing in more different circumstances in 1935, had also reflected intensely on Paul Valéry's essays, not to mention most of the key figures of French modernity since Baudelaire. It is illuminating to contrast Heidegger's ontologically destructive view with the mobility of Benjamin's Parisian essays. His writings on Proust, Valéry, Gide, and the contemporary social situation of the French writer, while usually read as practical criticism, contain a series of provocative remarks about the French attitude toward intelligence and the precarious class of the intelligentsia. As a critic and translator of French literature, especially

Proust, Benjamin remains attuned to the political potential of a term that was increasingly associated with rootlessness, abstraction, and neutrality in the sociology of knowledge during the Weimar Republic.

In his essay on Surrealism, a movement he characterized as "the last snapshot of the European intelligentsia" (*die letzte Momentaufnahme der europäischen Intelligenz*), Benjamin uses a striking image to situate his relation to the French literary and intellectual tradition as a German critic:

> Intellectual currents [*Geistige Strömungen*] can generate a sufficient head of water for the critic to install his power station on them. The necessary gradient, in the case of Surrealism, is produced by the difference in intellectual level [*Niveauunterschied*] between France and Germany.[22]

Here, the very difference between languages and intellectual movements that Adorno describes as an obstacle becomes a possibility for criticism to exploit. Throughout his essays on French literature, from Baudelaire to the Surrealists, Benjamin tracks the loss of the aura of the artwork, and the crisis of artistic reproducibility, which are symptomatic of a larger crisis in perception itself.

While attuned to intelligence in the Marxist sense of "the regulation and mastery of the material relations of production," to which Heidegger alludes, Benjamin was equally interested in *Intelligenz* as a faculty and a class. In his notes for *Krise und Kritik*, a periodical he had planned with Brecht, Benjamin proposed a range of topics dealing with the term: "'Research on the Intelligence of Apes,' to be undertaken by a scholar"; "a detailed essay on 'Measuring Human Intelligence'"; "On intelligence's suitability to lead"; "Censorship of Intelligence"; and reflections on the use-value of intelligence: "Is intelligence useful? The subject is not immaterial, and what we object about such writers is not that they occupy themselves with intelligence but do so in the wrong way."[23] Although not a single issue of *Krise und Kritik* appeared, Benjamin's published essays enter into dialogue with contemporary French critics, especially Albert Thibaudet, Julien Benda, and Emmanuel Berl, concerning the nature of intellectual responsibility, class allegiance, and the extent to which it was being betrayed. In his attempts to offer an overview of the French literary field, he does not classify the activities of the literati according to any preexisting political or aesthetic labels, let alone answer the proposed questions of *Krise und Kritik*. Instead, he identifies a writer's political potential as the ability to transform and redistribute a productive device. Developing an idea shared by Brecht and Valéry, Benjamin approaches texts in this period as technical "apparatuses" that could be redistributed to the reading public, thereby interrupting, and possibly altering the existing conditions of production.[24] Such a highly mediated form of intervention was the only political potential of literature, in an era where the survival of tradition was increasingly under threat.

Benjamin and Political Style

Benjamin expressed the ambition to become the greatest German critic of his generation. A more strategic albeit equally elusive goal, once an academic career proved impossible, was to be the leading authority on contemporary French literature in the German press.[25] His essays on Gide, Proust, Valéry, and the Surrealists contributed to this reputation, before *The Arcades Project* absorbed his attention entirely. Although scholars have mined these texts for their remarkable insights into now canonical French authors, Benjamin's claims about the social and political challenges facing writers in the interwar years have received less sustained attention. Here I turn to "The Present Social Situation of the French Writer" ("Zum gegenwärtigen gesellschaftlichen Standort des französischen Schriftstellers"), to offer a reconstruction of its theory of "political style."[26] While the 1934 essay is routinely described as a montage of passages from previous texts on French literature, its unusual form allows Benjamin to transcend familiar oppositions of form and content. Instead, it relates political tendency to literary form through an unspoken notion of "political style," which lends a new role to the literary intelligentsia.

Key aspects of Benjamin's argument remain implicit in this survey of French writers and critics. Drawing on hypotheses developed in the contemporaneous "The Author as Producer" essay (1934) and the related correspondence with Adorno, Scholem, and Brecht, I argue that, according to Benjamin, the political potential of interwar French literature resides precisely in its inability to escape the economizing effects of capitalism.[27] The fault lines of a crisis, in which the social and historical function of the intellectual—collectively referred to as *Intelligenz*—is no longer guaranteed, become particularly visible in narrative fiction. Benjamin's survey of French writers, from Apollinaire to Benda, constitutes one of the most generative points of contact between politics and literature in modern criticism, since it does not conceptualize literary practice as lying beyond the pale of economic life. Rather, it exploits the Franco-German disjunct invoked above, around which intellectual and literary production invariably foundered.

Benjamin urges us to gauge the political potential of literature not by its themes, but by the intensity with which a writer produces and disseminates "technical" advances that reveal the larger forces of production shaping society. Advances in technique not only reveal concrete conditions, and thus connect and expose readers to material reality—as opposed to promoting idealism or nihilism—but also make literary and aesthetic works available to those not usually counted as experts, artists, or even audiences. Such redistribution, which undoes the opposition between authors and public, is the watermark of "political style."

The difficulty of reading "The Present Social Situation of the French Writer" can be attributed to its halting form. As with much of Benjamin's writing, this form deserves as much scrutiny as the propositional content it presents. Framed by a fictive prophecy about the imminent massacre of all poets taken from Apollinaire's *Poète assassiné* (1916), Benjamin's essay offers a telegraphic overview of contemporary French literary production.[28] Written shortly before the First World War, Apollinaire's novella foreshadows the book burnings and mass persecutions of intellectuals in the following decades.[29] Rather than classifying authors he considers according to their preferred themes or political beliefs, Benjamin locates the limits of themes and politics within one another. His survey focuses largely on the essay and the novel, using the latter as a lens to introduce something "resembling an ordered point of view into the chaos of production."[30]

Benjamin presents the shift in the novelistic form, from Zola's Naturalism to the interwar *roman populaire*, as a declining ability to describe social conditions within fiction. Such a shift is often mistakenly attributed to a turn away from the technique of omniscient narration.[31] Zola was only able to portray French society "omnisciently" in the 1860s because he rejected its terms, whereas his successors mostly failed in exposing their situation because of their tendency to accept it "at face value." This shift in the novel's critical powers parallels the militant posture of the intelligentsia: "whereas between 1789 and 1848 they occupied a leading position as part of the bourgeois offensive, now their role is defensive. The less rewarding such a stance frequently is, the more urgent is the demand that intellectuals demonstrate their class reliability."[32] Since novels offer an image of authors "in the process of adapting to society," the study chooses them as its finely calibrated instrument for measuring class reliability and class treason. The demand for writers to align themselves with class interests implies a politics transparently and unequivocally committed to the depiction and defense of certain values, which overly literary or aesthetic concerns seem to undermine.

A distinct typology of literary–political attitudes emerges in these pages.[33] Writers like Paul Morand defend bourgeois attitudes, the philosopher Alain's followers espouse radical socialism, while figures from Charles Péguy to Julien Benda question the political role of intellectuals altogether. Proust, Julien Green, Francis Carco, and Louis-Ferdinand Céline forge divergent paths for the novel, whereas Valéry, Gide, and the Surrealists prove to be "antagonists" to existing models of politics.[34] While this typology is intriguing, as it moves beyond the usual martial metaphors of *avant-garde* and *arrière-garde* writers, its suggestiveness resides more in its underlying equation of politics and technique within literary style than in verdicts on the works of individual writers.[35]

Benjamin's judgments do not merely divide writers into revolutionaries and reactionaries along party lines. Rather, they locate their politics within literary form. Maurice Barrès's *Les déracinés* depends upon a "romantic and ultimately political apparatus" in which enthusiasm is preferable to truth, and wealth is the precondition of independence. At the opposite end, we find his former teacher Jules Lagneau's categorical refusal of inheritance in the quest to fight falsity. The binary of rootedness and rootlessness does not present intellectuals with an actual choice to which they can adhere. "Decisive" political action forgets this impasse, sliding into what the essay calls, the "sectarian and the romantic." Péguy's mystic nationalism and Benda's polemic provide ideological proof of the slippery nature of the social substructure. Attempts by authors like Céline and Green to displace the protagonist toward marginal narrative spaces founder politically on their stylistic inability to identify with the masses they describe, or to take the fundamentally ambivalent nature of personal identity and memory into account.

In contrast, for Benjamin, Proust and Valéry are "great technicians" because their works constantly question their own principles of construction. In Valéry, writing is "primarily a matter of technique."[36] Progress is possible not in ideas but in techniques, not in creation, but in analytic construction.[37] Despite the fact that *Monsieur Teste* seems to embody the perfect "technician," Valéry remains unwilling to extend his ideas of "planning" from works of art to forms of community. Benjamin emphasizes Valéry's technical constructivism, which instead attends to the ways that art is impacted by technique. Rather than relying on mock-romantic variants of genius or vestiges of Renaissance humanism, his emphasis on classical artifice outstrips these sources of reassurance. If Valéry and Teste both place art and thinking on the side of the inhuman and the technical, their solipsistic Cartesianism also proves to be the source of a failed political intersubjectivity.[38]

Proust's physiology of society proves his unparalleled eye as a social critic. His narrative style counts as a major technical breakthrough since "the writer is everywhere present, taking a stance, giving an account of himself and constantly placing himself at the reader's disposition."[39] His genre-crossing narratives—fusing fiction and commentary, poetry and prose, focalization and montage—constitute a great "achievement for freedom." Rather than finding this freedom in thematic depictions of social class, homosexuality, or Jewish life, Benjamin locates it in Proust's portrayal of a world of consumption, which rigorously "excludes everything that is involved in production."[40] Proust and Valéry prove surprisingly pertinent politically since they expose the reader to the role of technique and consumption, rather than occluding these forces through humanist or aesthetic ideologies.

Benjamin specifies that only revolutionary writers turned "militant politicians" can "interpret the dark prophecy of Apollinaire"—which pits the survival of the world against the persistence of literature—because they "know from experience [*Erfahrung*] why literature—the only literature they still think worthy of the name—is dangerous." The revolutionary writers being alluded to are the Surrealists who reposition the "intellectual as a technician." They treat literature as the "key to psychoses," opening the possibility of a non-didactic revolutionary literature. Their startling avatar is Gide's Lafcadio, who rejects writing, only to throw a fellow passenger off a train in an impulsive act (*acte gratuit*) meant to clarify his own contradictory position. Surrealism wagers that poetic language possesses the ability to transform social relations over time. Yet the essay should not be read teleologically. Benjamin's final reference to Aragon's call for class betrayal makes it easy to misinterpret his larger argument as a conclusion (especially considering Aragon's eventual turn away from Surrealism to doctrinaire Communism). At stake in class betrayal, for Benjamin, is the possible survival of the writer in a time of economic attrition; a problem that has existed since antiquity.

While Plato questions the poet's right to exist in an ideal republic, the interwar period questions literary autonomy in imperfect political communities. Rather than mourning an impossible ideal of intellectual independence, Benjamin argues the present writer's most urgent task is to "recognize how poor he is and how poor he has to be in order to begin again from the beginning."[41] As Patrick Greaney notes, poverty must first be recognized and realized, before appearing as a means to begin again.[42] The writer's realization of poverty leads to a renunciation of the illusory freedom to write whatever. The Soviet state does not banish its poets, in

Benjamin's wishful thinking, but assigns them tasks that "do not permit them to display in new masterpieces the long-since counterfeit wealth of creative personality."[43] An "impoverished" writer's work is not creative or expressive. It is never merely "work on products but always, at the same time, work on the means of production."[44] While his position lacks historical accuracy in hindsight, what matters here is the marginalization of the "creative or expressive." The intelligence of writers is to be located in the degree to which it can expose their own conditions and means of production.

Considering the author as a producer of "means for producers," and the word as an act unto itself, as Benjamin does, questions the economic futility ascribed to the "creative" writer. Many French critics, as the previous chapter showed, argued that the precarious socio-historic situation forced the intelligentsia to put their work at the service of sectarian interests. Benjamin insists that the proper writerly response to economic pressure does not involve espousing extant political programs. Only poetic language can have political effects. The redistribution of "technique" remains an uncertain procedure, since Benjamin does not fully develop his insight, let alone signal how it might function concretely. Yet, his recourse to the literary means of production and a transformed apparatus redresses a tendency to "constrict the relationship between politics and art," as Stanley Mitchell notes.[45] It opens this relation to a conflict of interpretation. Such openness lends his essay a greater theoretical freedom than Benjamin found in Idealism or orthodox Marxism. His understanding of language had long opposed him to conventional critiques of cultural production. The following section argues that the concept of technique—central to understanding how the different aspects of Benjamin's argument about French writers hang together—depends on a notion of "highly political style" developed in his earliest writings.

On the Techniques of "Political Style"

In a July 1916 letter, Benjamin declined Martin Buber's invitation to contribute to *Der Jude* due to his disagreement with the journal's prowar stance, as well as his own attitude toward "politically effective literature."[46] Benjamin described his conception of "highly political style" as the "power to awaken what was denied to the word." Everyday language is commonly understood as an expressive means, providing and communicating motives for action. Yet such an attitude treats language as an instrument and vitiates the deed that it is supposed to motivate, by placing its source outside itself. Here language is neither a mode of communication, nor a means to realize an external end, nor even an end, writes Samuel Weber, "unless 'end' is understood not as *goal* but as *interruption*."[47] Benjamin takes language to be the purest medium of communication that "communicates itself *in* itself." "Mediation [*Das Mediale*], which is the immediacy of all mental communication, is the fundamental problem of linguistic theory and if one chooses to call this immediacy magic, then the primary problem of language is its magic."[48] This early attention to the problematic, magical immediacy of thought in language provides an unspoken model for relating material bases to cultural superstructures without relying on dialectical strategies common to Marxist theory, which delimit the writer's role. This is another instance in which the abstract rationality intelligence is expected to produce becomes complicated by its linguistic basis and mediation, whose effects are likened to magic.

The letter to Buber selects "poetry and prophecy" (*Dichtung und Prophetie*) as "effective forms" of political writing since they refuse to treat language as a means to affect reality.[49] They instead posit a relation of "magical" immediacy between language and events. As exceptional forms that "effectively" relate language to worldly events, they attempt to eliminate the ineffable, while acknowledging the speechless core of speech:

> My concept of objective and, at the same time, highly political style and writing is this [*sachlichen und zugleich hochpolitischen Stils und Schreibens ist*]: to awaken interest in what was denied to the word; only where this magic sphere of speechlessness reveals its unutterably pure power can the magic spark leap between the word and the motivating deed, where the unity of the two equally real entities resides.[50]

"Highly political style and writing" produces a relation between speech and action other than the syntactic equation of motive, meaning, and action. Rather, it directs attention to the intensive core of language in order to make legible the relation between the unsayable and the said.[51] The triad of poetry, prophecy, and "highly political style" suggests why Benjamin begins and ends his essay on the French writer by alluding to Apollinaire's prophecy about the imminent assassination of poets. By choosing a poet's vision, rather than historical events, as his point of departure, Benjamin confirms the significance of locating political content within literary form. His essay begins by likening Apollinaire to Bellachini, a renowned nineteenth-century conjurer. Apollinaire is said to have pulled fully formed "theories and slogans," which have ripened in his "style of writing and being," as a "magician pulls objects out a hat."[52] His enchanting ability to unveil and proclaim new movements—Futurism, Dada, Surrealism—makes him a clairvoyant figure, equally attuned to literary styles and coming conflicts.

Benjamin does not expect poetic technique, however magical, to function exactly like intellectual or technical knowledge, which promises control over material means of production or capital. Yet the political effects of having control over perceptive and interpretive modes hardly seems a negligible kind of intelligence. Benjamin credits Apollinaire with discovering the "trick" of how to master the "world of things" by substituting "a political point of view for a historical one."[53] Apollinaire argues poetry can prefigure ways in which technology will transform social relations.[54] His poets appeal to Plato in supplication: if the philosopher banishes them from his republic, at least he should give them an audience. Rather than rejecting science as mere positivism, they harness the forces of mimesis to imagine inventions for the "good of collectivity to which they belong." Yet their efforts remain unacknowledged. Standing halfway between enchantment and productivity, Apollinaire foresees that poets have forfeited their "right to exist" today. The "present social situation" entails a lost "right," which must be recuperated by the right to produce, and redistribute means of production, in writing.

During Benjamin's exchanges with Brecht, his early notion of "political style," understood as a relation of "magical" equivalence between language and event, developed into one of "writerly technique." His thinking moves from questioning the relation between the word and the deed to examining the space linguistic practices occupy as well as the role they play in the production of a social situation.[55] Here it bears recalling the principal axiom introduced in "The Author as Producer": "A literary work can be politically correct only if it is also literarily correct."[56] Political and literary correctness are linked, that lecture argues, because "technical progress is for the author as producer the foundation of his political progress."

Benjamin counters the Fascist call for "spiritual renewal" with an appeal to "technical innovation."[57] His essay proceeds by drawing attention to the ongoing recasting of intellectual and literary production in relation to transformations in mass media, especially in journalism. In Russia, these changes tend toward socialization, while in Western Europe, they highlight the tension between the collective potential of technology and its private exploitation.[58]

Platforms like the newspaper collapse the distinction between reader and writer, scholar and popularizer, criticism and literary production, poetry and prose. In response, Benjamin's inquiry brushes away rigid designations such as books and genres altogether, choosing instead to "examine the function a work has within the literary relations of its time." The question does not concern the attitude a literary work takes *toward* contemporary relations of production, but rather "its position *in* them" (*wie steht sie* in *ihnen*).[59] Politically effective forms of writing do not tell readers what to think, but expose the greater social situation in which readers, writer, and works are caught. Literary techniques enable writers to situate themselves within these conditions.

Benjamin calls the "writerly *technique* of works" (*die schriftstellerische Technik der Werke*) the concept that makes "literary products accessible to an immediately social, and therefore materialist, analysis." He adds:

> The concept of technique provides the dialectical starting point from which the unfruitful antithesis of form and content can be surpassed. And furthermore, this concept of technique [*Begriff der Technik*] contains an indication of the correct determination of the relation between tendency and quality [...] the correct political tendency of a work includes its literary quality, because it includes its literary tendency [...] [which] can consist either in progress or in regression of literary technique.[60]

The difficulty of interpreting this passage can be ascribed to the undefined concept of *Technik*, which not only designates technics, technology, and artistic techniques, but also the mediating element between contradictory forces and relations of production.[61] Much depends on how charitably one reads this lack of determination, which can be viewed as an absence of political realism, or a promising space of transformation. Benjamin's writings consciously play upon this overdetermination in the "Critique of Violence," for instance, where *Unterredung* or "discussion" is called a *Technik* of civil agreement.[62] *Technik* names the domain in which untested social relations are configured and prefigured. Even if we grant that form and content are surpassed in technique, it remains to be shown how and why a work's political tendency comprises its literary quality. Furthermore, this passage does not offer any examples of what is meant by a "literary technique."

What constitutes "progress" in technique for a thinker as averse to progressive narratives as Benjamin? An allusion to Sergei Tretiakov, the Russian constructivist writer and factographer, provides a clue by invoking Tretiakov's distinction between the "informing" and the "operating" writer.[63] The latter does not aim to "report but to struggle; not to play the spectator but to intervene actively." Before it was corralled into Socialist

Realism, Soviet art experimented with forms including film, newspapers, radio, posters, but also writers' workshops and popular theatre.[64] Benjamin admits that the incongruence of the Soviet example "does not prove a great deal in this context." Yet, it is precisely its discordance in Western Europe, where literature is still distinguished from journalism and propaganda, based on largely nostalgic criteria, that such a jarring example can reveal how extensively literary genres must be rethought "in view of the technical factors affecting our present situation if we are to identify the forms of expression that can channel the literary energies of the present."[65]

The technical factors affecting the "present" consist not only in the revolutions in media and the sciences, but also the economic upheaval of interwar Europe. On a philosophical level, the search for new expressive forms relates to Benjamin's attempts to discover techniques amenable to historical materialism.[66] The entirety of *The Arcades Project* can be described as an attempt to harness the "power of awakening" encrypted in material remnants of nineteenth-century France.[67] To do so, it mobilizes Baudelaire's allegorical poetry to reveal "correspondences" that protect experience from the crisis of shock, just as it borrows techniques of remembrance from Proust's *Recherche*, and urban geography from Aragon's *Paysan de Paris*. Benjamin compares his own method to Proust's, writing, "what follows here is an experiment in the technique of awakening" (*Technik der Erwachens*).[68] The revolutionary artist responds to shock critically through "heightened attention."[69] The "technique of awakening" the reader or the spectator, here and elsewhere, announces political style. The potential of political style is an unspoken force animating Benjamin's critical engagement with French writers. It proposes an alternative to the rhetoric of intelligence that structures the literary field in the interwar years, even as it takes the intelligence of writers seriously rather than relegating it to bourgeois cunning or the degradation of spirit, as Nietzsche and Heidegger seem to do.

As we have seen, Benjamin does not locate political attitudes in spiritual affirmations or literary themes, but in technical innovations. Formal conservatism, it posits, undoubtedly marks literary production in difficult economic times. Nothing bars a conventional writer from choosing a political theme. However, writing that is not willing to transform its devices merely treats political struggle as a consumer artifact. The fitting response is not Socialist Realism, but a form of production that incites others to produce by placing the means of production at their disposal. Since existing forms are "means *against* producers," since they betray producers, the writer as producer must not hesitate to betray established forms in order to invent "means *for* producers."[70] Here Benjamin cites the Brechtian concept of "refunctioning" or *Umfunktioniering*, the capacity of an apparatus to interrupt and signal its own processes, not to stimulate its audience, but to compel it to take a stance, to situate itself. Benjamin calls this capacity of epic theatre to "expose the present" its "great and venerable chance."[71] As Maria Gough notes, the practice of refunctioning becomes the "specific responsibility of the contemporary intellectual and specialist."[72]

Up to a point, "The Present Social Situation of the French Writer" tries to "expose the present." It does so by situating contemporary authors along a continuum: from those like Barrès who allow readers to identify with a reified discourse of inheritance to those like Apollinaire and Gide, who constantly incite readers to take a stance.[73] Such reading meets the single demand Benjamin makes of the author as producer: "the demand to think, to consider his position in the process of production." This consideration leads writers who count, "(that is, for the best technicians in their field), to observations that provide the most factual foundation for solidarity with the proletariat."[74] Benjamin calls for criticism to transform its productive tropes and devices, to acknowledge its embattled economic situation. Instead of a credo, we are faced with a text that attends to its situation as a critical overview, allowing readers to become critics, and discover their own situation (*Standort*) in turn. This inversion is the process Benjamin, following Brecht, refers to as the "literarization of living conditions."[75] Benjamin's thinking at this juncture led to some of the most intense critiques that his work would encounter, especially from his closest allies. At stake in the debate was nothing less that the proper use of the critical intelligence, although not discussed explicitly in these terms. Just as the *NRF* and the Maurrasians fought over the future of intelligence, the Marxist tenor of Benjamin's argument exposed him to accusations of reducing the ambit and freedom of writing to a narrowly ideological sphere.

"The Literarization of Living Conditions"

Although the essay on the French writer constitutes one of Benjamin's most "uncompromising experiments in Marxist-sociological literary analysis," Adorno and Scholem considered it to be an instance of Benjamin's vulgar materialism.[76] Most accusations of vulgar materialism target the causal relations between base and superstructure. The policing party identifies an aberrant causality relating the economic infrastructure—relations of production (classes) and forces of production (technology, ecology, and population)—to the superstructure—culture, ideology, law, politics, and the state—which it then condemns as "vulgar."[77] In a properly dialectical view, the relation between base and superstructure always requires mediation. Benjamin rejects both the illness of mechanistic determinism and the palliative of dialectical mediation, opting instead for a paradoxical relation of immediacy, which recalls the immediate communication of mental content in language discussed above. His own critique of vulgar Marxism diverges from the dialectics of the Frankfurt school toward what Margaret Cohen calls "Surrealist Marxism," which supplements historical materialism with a psychoanalytic attentiveness to dreams, awakening, and threshold states of (un)consciousness.[78] If *The Arcades Project* imagines the relation of base and superstructure as a kind of overdetermination, akin to the relation between the unconscious and the dream world, then the earlier essay on the French writer attempts to do so through the language of magic and prophecy.

Benjamin's essays invoke the right to alter relations of production through the act of writing itself. This right, as Peter Fenves notes, should be understood as an extralegal rather than a positive political right.[79] The social crisis in the function of intellectuals certainly has economic roots to be located in the conflict between relations and forces of production. Yet writing, as a cultural form, is not determined, but saturated by its economic base. Both the economic roots and fruits of writing remain invisible to conventional criticism. Benjamin's critique sets out to make these invisible connections recognizable. Rather than limiting literature to its "proper" place in the cultural superstructure, the writer as producer attempts to intervene in the base itself. Writing becomes a force of production that can have disruptive effects in the cultural, legal, ideological, and political realm. In this sense, Benjamin's account sets economic determinism on its head by allowing the superstructure to alter the base and enabling the base to overdetermine the superstructure. Despite all appearances, this transversal impulse does not constitute a dialectic. Rather it cancels the separation between base and superstructure, positing a relation of immediacy instead. Since his materialism does not rely on a deterministic or a dialectical thesis, but a speculative one, base *is* superstructure for Benjamin.[80]

"The Present Social Situation of the French Writer" shares its premises with Marx's "Preface to the *Critique of Political Economy*." The Preface held a special place among Benjamin's milieu, especially for Karl Korsch, who deemed it the "most complete, lucid, and forceful expression of the bases and consequences of Marx's theory."[81] The Preface insists that the social consciousness of a period must be explained from the "existing conflict between social productive forces and the relations of production." The critique of the Hegelian philosophy of right led to the recognition that "legal relations as well as forms of state are to be grasped neither from themselves, nor from the so-called general development of the human mind [*Entwicklung des menschlichen Geistes*], but rather have their roots in the material conditions of life."[82] Consequently, the anatomy of civil society is located in political economy: "It is not the consciousness of men that determines their being, but, on the contrary, their social being that determines their consciousness," declares Marx.[83] Social revolutions stem from the moment when relations of production become "fetters," rather than support structures, for forces of production.[84]

Benjamin's essay does not argue that a writer's poetics are determined by socio-economic factors. Writerly technique, and thus political tendency, is co-determined by the degree to which writers register their social situation and alter their style as a result. Rather than hastening the advent of social revolution, the literary techniques of the author as producer loosen the fetters, momentarily freeing up space for another form of life, which recalls the possibility of more than mere survival. Such transformations in technique open the "body and image space" concealed in any present social situation.[85]

Capitalism conventionally divides artworks into popular forms for the people, on the one hand, and rarified pieces for connoisseurs, on the other. Benjamin addresses this dilemma in a diary entry concerning "Marxism and art" (1931).[86] He argues that every form of art that rejects popularity finds itself consigned to the "luxury segment of the market," while popular forms cease to have productive force. Yet a social situation that spells the "demise of literature" can prepare the way for "its reinstatement when conditions change." The transformed public dimensions of writing—its newfound breadth (as journalism) and its loss of depth (as literature)—entail a change within the economy of writing. This change is dubbed the "literarization of living conditions." In subsequent texts, such as the versions of the essay on the work of art, literarization is crossed out and replaced with politicization. Quoting himself as an anonymous "left-wing author," he glosses this phrase in "The Author as Producer":

> For the reader is at all times ready to become a writer—that is to say, a describer, or even a prescriber [...]. Literary competence is no longer founded on specialized training but is now based on polytechnical

education, and thus becomes public property. It is, in a word, the literarization of living conditions [*die Literarisierung der Lebensverhältnisse*], that masters the otherwise insoluble antinomies.[87]

Only by abandoning a specialized, hierarchical position can an author work through the antinomies that dominate art. This turn puts him in "solidarity with certain other producers who earlier seemed scarcely to concern him." Literary work no longer simply creates a public that consumes it. Rather, it inscribes and extends its means of production. "*An author who teaches writers nothing teaches no one.*"[88] Textual forms situate their authors and readers within the web of economic life, suspending an otherwise tautological process of consumption and production.[89] At stake is the potential collapse of the separation between intellectual and other forms of labor.

The "literarization of living conditions" condenses "the complex idea that modern life is susceptible to analysis and finally to change only as it is rendered in very specific textual forms," as Howard Eiland and Michael Jennings note.[90] Neither of the two essays in question, "The Present Social Situation of the French Writer" nor "The Author as Producer," can be read as a cryptic handbook meant to train authors to "politicize" literature. Rather these investigations allow us to pull away from persistent misreadings of the later and much more famous essay on "The Work of Art in the Age of its Technological Reproducibility" that pit the conclusive politicizing of art by Communism against the Fascist aestheticization of politics. In the second version of his famous essay, Benjamin develops a distinction between "first" and "second" *Technik*. The conflict between Fascism and Communism is thus presented as a struggle for the control of *Technik*, which can be used in its first guise, to master nature, or in its second one, to enable the "interplay between nature and humanity." Fascist technique only finds release as total mobilization, seeking a "magical turning point" in the next war. The "Marxist trick" locates this crisis in the everyday, thus "transforming this war into civil war."[91] Nor can the politicization of art be considered the "answer" to the aestheticization of politics. Instead, Benjamin's ongoing inquiry into the decline of aura, and the independence of political from legal criteria, should lead to the acknowledgment that although criticism has no "solutions," its task depends on the possibility of altering relations of authority, production, consumption, and circulation.[92] No single critic can accomplish this task, yet criticism *as a whole* cannot renounce it—even as it betrays larger narratives of political progress.

Techniques of Treason

Despite accusations of vulgar materialism, Benjamin does not espouse a deterministic view linking the economic base and the cultural superstructure. Rather, the intellectual and cultural sphere is determined by technical factors, especially the unresolved tension between forces and modes of production. A progressive writer's political task does not consist in mere class betrayal, but entails treason understood as the distribution of a transformed *Apparat* (variously translated as "apparatus," "device," or "machine").[93] How could such a seemingly apolitical activity—akin to honing and sharing one's craft—constitute a form of treason? Between the wars, French criticism offered competing narratives castigating intellectuals and writers for betraying politically progressive causes.[94] Benjamin's essay debates Thibaudet, Benda, and Berl, three leading interwar critics, on the nature of intellectual responsibility and the extent to which it was being betrayed. Thibaudet argued that the revolutionary impulse had receded into literature, as political forces increasingly became invisible. Benda denounced the turn of intellectuals from the defense of universal values to partisan politics. Benjamin faults Benda for failing to recognize the economic and scientific roots of the political and cultural crises he identifies. He counters Benda's humanism with Berl's insights into the politics of fear and the impossibility of becoming revolutionary. Even Aragon's call to class treason falls short. Benjamin provides a technical alternative to treason understood as sectarianism, subservience, and a break with class origin. The writer's "treason" consists instead in the ability to transform and redistribute a productive apparatus.

In *The Republic of Professors*, Thibaudet, the foremost critic of the *Nouvelle Revue Française*, describes interwar France as a "republic of the intellect," one whose topography had been transformed since the defeat of the 1871 Commune as its revolutionary impulses retreated from politics into literature. The dominant intellectual mood was directed against the "mysticism of heritage," a genealogy that Thibaudet tracks from Plotinus to Barrès. He opposes the figure of the inheritor, exemplified by Barrès, to the scholarship recipient, personified by Jules Lagneau, Barrès' influential philosophy teacher. The Barrès–Lagneau opposition marks the two extremes from which young provincials approach Paris. Benjamin makes it his own essay's point of entry into contemporary France to distinguish between the rooted and the uprooted.

Republicanism lends itself to the dominance of orators and secret societies, in Thibaudet's analysis, thus occluding the true socio-political forces of the Third Republic. Thibaudet considers these structures by examining economic clichés.[95] The right is obsessed with production, while the left emphasizes consumption as the fundamental economic term, attacking inheritance and private fortunes through taxation. He adds nuance to this stark picture. While the right may align itself with production, the left is committed to redistribution, rather than consumption alone. He thus confirms Benjamin's views on this point, allowing him to conceive of the author as a redistributor of language. The promise of such language lies in remaining inconsumable for a well-established class of readers unless they allow themselves to be transformed.

The unprecedented relevance of politics for the writer was part of Benda's conundrum in *La trahison des clercs*. Benda "is shocked by the slogans of an intelligentsia that defends the causes of nations against that of mankind, of parties against justice, and of power against the mind."[96] Benjamin charges Benda with mistaking economic turmoil for the intellectual abandonment of universal values: "The author understands as little of the economic basis of their crisis as he does of their crisis in the sciences—the undermining of the dogma of an objective research free from preconceptions."[97] Benda's outlook remains thoroughly "romantic" and leads him to assert a "dual morality," which prescribes "force for states and people" and "Christian humanism for intellectuals." In his *Discours à la nation européenne*, he envisions a "unified world whose economic forms have survived unaltered." This future Europe is built on a renunciation of literature and art in favor of objectivity. Benda's Europe will be "scientific rather than literary, intellectual rather than artistic, philosophical rather than picturesque." Benjamin excoriates this future as an "oversized monk's cell, to which the intellectuals—'the spiritual'—retreat in order to weave the text of a sermon, undaunted by the thought that it will be delivered to rows of empty seats, if indeed it is delivered at all."[98]

Benjamin shares his skepticism with Emmanuel Berl, referring throughout to *Mort de la pensée bourgeoise* and *Mort de la morale bourgeoise*, at times without attribution. Berl's two "roughhewn pamphlets" against liberal values, observes Denis Hollier, launched the "self-designated anti-conformist trend that dominated the committed literature" of the next two decades.[99] Other than a "depreciatory" materialism, Berl does not articulate his own method, proposing instead to take a haphazard voyage through contemporary political affects. Like Benjamin, his method is detour. Yet his inquiry remains guided by the possible meanings of the word "revolution." Berl argues that writers take refuge in artistic and political conformism because they are afraid of the possibility of revolution. Reversing the roles of the Dreyfus affair, interwar intellectuals seek authority figures to counter democratic anomie, while the bourgeois put their faith in the freedom of conscience. Aesthetes seek a pure aesthetic because they fear the alienation of "modern man," while liberals cling to dead values, even as the machine of progress crushes them.

Though Berl considers revolution to be the condition of possibility of thinking, he admits that it remains a murky concept. A revolution only becomes definable if one knows which class it will benefit. Lenin's definition, for instance, is only clear because it hands all the power to the Bolsheviks. A revolutionary political program is much harder to articulate in the absence of the event or the class interest that justifies it.[100] In 1929, contemporary thought is "terrified by the feeling that it is not ineffective." Unlike Benda, Berl does not attribute the "treason" of the intelligentsia to a politicized betrayal of humanism in favor of partisan interests. He provides a crucial corrective by specifying that a "particular attitude becomes treason only when it is dictated by fear or indolence. The treason of intellectuals lies in their willingness to submit to prevailing moods and prejudices."[101] It is not particularity, but susceptibility to their surroundings, that makes writers politically reprehensible.

Benjamin approvingly invokes Berl's view that revolutionary art that does not transform its mode of production remains a fashion accessory for the *haute bourgeoisie*. Literary practice can lessen the stricture of prevailing moods, or intensify it, through a varying use of indolent forms. The contemporary writer is not hindered by an obsession with politics. Berl writes: "If politics hinders the intellectual's gait today, it cannot be because he thinks about it too much, but because he thinks about it badly."[102] His attention to moods provides an alternative to Benda's polemic. The treason of intellectuals does not consist in the rise of ideology, but in the manner in which ideas are formed, received, and deployed: "Even a distorted, harmful idea does not constitute treason. It must be in a certain relation with the person who utters it."[103] Arguably, the gap between the idea and its utterance constitutes the site of literary politics.

Berl describes the French writer as caught in a double bind: it is impossible to withstand the "stench of death" coming from "capitalist tyranny" or to adhere to the "stupid" inefficient demands of Communism.[104] Either the writer becomes a "traitor to the revolution, without which his thinking falls apart" or he betrays the revolutionary party, to which he can only adhere with great "mental reservations."[105] The contemporary drama consists in the impossibility of becoming revolutionary. While the Surrealists do not deny being bourgeois, "dialectical movement" opposes them to this very origin. "Revolutionary writers, if they are of bourgeois stock," Aragon holds, "are essentially and crucially traitors to the class of their origins."[106] Variants of this claim appear at the end of "The Present Social Situation of the French writer" and "The Author as Producer." Aragon declares that any writers outside of the Communist Party can only be the "disguised servants" of the bourgeoisie. Benjamin's understanding of literary treason is, however, more complex than Aragon's slogan. If anything, class betrayal becomes a collateral effect rather than the goal of writing. In the writer's case:

> Treason [*Verrat*] consists in conduct that transforms him from a supplier of the productive apparatus [*Produktionsapparates*] into an engineer who sees it as his task to adapt this device to revolutionary proletarian purposes.[107]

No uniquely political conviction motivates a writer's treason, which arises through the tension between literary and political economies. Rather, the shift entails a disruption willing to reappropriate technique to other ends, while trying to collapse the difference between intellectual and nonintellectual labor.

Treason shares a root with tradition: both acts consist in a "handing down" or a "handing over." We are far from the figure of the "enemy of the state" accused of treason (*Staatsverräter*) as many political militants, including Benjamin's brother, were during this period. Benjamin's critique of violence rejects higher authorities that issue such decrees as "mythical" forces. The writer as traitor (*Verräter*) is not guilty of betraying national secrets, but of giving misleading, potentially destructive advice (*ver-raten*). He resembles the duplicitous figure of the courtly plotter that Benjamin analyzes in his *Ursprung des deutschen Trauerspiels* as torn between fidelity and betrayal, and the storyteller, who appears in the eponymous essay armed with a dubious tale for every occasion. Confronted by the declining "communicability of experience," counsel (*Rat*) does not answer questions as much as it comes up with a trick to continue a still unfolding story.

Honing this ability becomes the writer's lot, whether the story being told involves the unforeseeable fate of an individual, or the collective historical fate of the intelligentsia as a social class. The perplexed reader is left at a loss to face the world without advice (*ratlos*). Any moral gleaned between the lines is incomplete, bereft of experience, and finally misleading. It only leads to other stories. Such leading astray is also the chance of storytelling, which can dislocate individuals from the security of stable, logically structured selfhood toward fragmentary and inconsistent narratives. Benjamin's essays on French writers break from the rhetoric of scholarly objectivity and the moods of subjectivity to exploit the lack of theoretical and practical ground. They replace a historical point of view with a literary–political one, to reveal the structure of the French intellectual and literary landscape from the Catholic right to the Surrealist left.

Between Pure Bluff and Magic

For many contemporary readers "The Present Social Situation of the French Writer" seems to run the gamut of modern French literature dismissing most authors for their "bogus social and political pretensions," only to bestow favor on Proust, Valéry, Gide, and, above all, the Surrealists.[108] While it frustrates any desire for progressive narratives, such expectations themselves fail to distinguish Benjamin's critical practice from commonplace Marxism. One is tempted to consign it to a minor key, since it is "too cautious, too conscious of its publishing venue, and to ready to toe a line." Yet "as a carefully angled survey of the state of French letters at a moment of crisis, it far surpasses Benjamin's own estimate of it."[109] One cannot, however, account for its acuity, without attending to this self-conscious position, especially toward "its publishing venue." The article was intentionally modeled after Adorno's first piece for the journal of the Institute of Social Research, the *Zeitschrift für Sozialforschung*.[110] In the meantime, Benjamin's economic situation had worsened as his writings became the object of a boycott in Germany, which could not have been better organized had he been, as he put it, "a small Jewish cloth merchant in Neu-Stettin."[111]

The details of Benjamin's situation—the *Standort* to which his title refers—throw his estimate of the published work into sharp relief. Although he conducted preliminary research in Paris, the essay was written in exile in Ibiza, with few primary sources at hand, other than the volumes in Felix Noegerrath's library.[112] Benjamin explained to Scholem:

> The very fact that I have to write this essay, which in any case constitutes pure bluff [*reine Hochstapelei*] virtually without any source material [*fast ohne alle Literatur*], gives it a certain magical face [*magisches Gesicht*] that will be displayed boldly in Geneva but hidden from you [. . .]. I believe, however, that readers nevertheless will derive from this an insight into connections that have never before been made so clearly recognizable.[113]

A *Hochstapler* is a confidence man who claims to have fallen on hard times in order to trick others.[114] Yet the word also literally suggests an inflationary movement, a "piling high," which does not simply aim to deceive or delude but comes closer to a bluffing tactic used by the weak to negotiate a differential of power. The essays's "pure bluff" is reflected in a certain voluntarism, no doubt necessary for it to be written at all, but which also spills over, as we have seen, in its tendency to equate forms of linguistic, intellectual, and economic production.

These interpretive challenges explain the essay's status as a critical stumbling block. Yet the avoidance of commentators continues to hide its "magical face," as well as the unseen connections it makes recognizable. Since Marx's critique of commodity fetishism, magic has been aligned with the fraudulent workings of capitalism, rather than critique. Benjamin attempts to demystify the conditions from which literature, art, and criticism emerge. He rejects tropes of creation and conjuration in favor of techniques and modes of production. Rather than choosing between bluff and magic, one ought to collapse these two poles, focusing instead on the critical insights they afford to Benjamin's essay. The essay shifts focus from Leninist aesthetics to the very disappearance of class ties, which writing must make legible.[115]

We may wonder how Benjamin could write an overview of French literature with almost no literature at hand, unless we count it among one of the marvels of modern criticism, alongside the allegedly virgin birth of Auerbach's *Mimesis* in Istanbul. The sparse conditions are reflected in the essay's unusual form: it leaps from one author's work to the next, rarely quotes from their writings, and identifies the core of their poetic projects in a few terse passages, breaking off at the point where literary limits reveal political failings. Its jolting effect is exemplary of an editorial policy of "deletions and distortions" that Benjamin likened to the "advance of fascism in Europe."[116] The reorganization of passages from other essays functions as a tactical exercise allowing Benjamin to revisit his views of French writers. Uwe Steiner identifies two consequential changes in the notion of authorship in the essay: not only a step toward the "self-reflection of technique, but also toward a social and political commitment" shared with Aragon, Berl, and Gide.[117] Unlike his French interlocutors, however, Benjamin considers the dissemination of new techniques to be a politically performative act, even before it enables or interrupts forms of social commitment.

Although Horkheimer approved of the essay, both Adorno and Scholem contested its merits, because they felt it was written under the deleterious influence of Brecht. While the essay tracked the social freefall of intellectuals, Adorno and Scholem attacked what they considered its vulgar Marxist stance. "The whole difficult problem is connected to the figure of Brecht," wrote Adorno, "and the credence you are willing to give him."[118]

He urged Benjamin to resume *The Arcades Project*, a work in which the "aesthetic" dimension promised to intervene in "an incomparably more profound and revolutionary manner than a class theory conceived of as a *deus ex machina*." A theatrical device, the *deus ex machina* produces magically reparative effects. Adorno's metaphor implies that Benjamin's essay on the French writer offers a similarly mechanistic resolution, which he cannot accept.

Scholem asked openly whether Benjamin's efforts were to be understood as a "communist credo." Benjamin responded to the provocation with unusual vehemence:

> Among all the possible forms and means of expression, a credo is the last thing my communism resorts to: that—even at the cost of its orthodoxy—my communism is absolutely nothing other than the expression of certain experiences I have undergone in my thinking and in my existence; that is a drastic, not infertile expression of the fact that the present intellectual industry and the present economic system find it impossible to give my thinking and my life any space; that it represents the obvious reasoned attempt on the part of a man who is completely, or almost completely deprived of any means of production to proclaim the right to have them, both in his thinking and in his life. [...] Is it really necessary to say all this to you?[119]

This passage should not be read merely as a *cri de coeur*. Rather, it offers two clarifications about Benjamin's "communism." First, it is a form of expression, not belief. It tracks material deprivation, rather than espousing dogmatic views. Second, his criticism concerning the French writer instantiates a "reasoned attempt" to respond to this "intellectual industry and [...] economic system" by proclaiming a right to have and alter the means of production.

Social demotion constitutes the primary problem of the essay, which studies how French writers react to the diminishing material resources of production available since the First World War. Economic attrition made it harder to maintain attitudes of aesthetic autonomy, which many writers willingly abandoned in favor of ideological commitments: inheritance (Maurice Barrès), abstract truth (Jules Lagneau), Christian humanism (Julien Benda), the soil (Charles Péguy), to name but a few options. Benjamin shows how these specious alternatives obscure the actual relation between "literary technique" and "political tendency."[120] Unsurprisingly, Brecht praised this effort, declaring the article "reads splendidly and says more than a four-hundred-page book on the subject, a decent one at that."[121]

Benjamin's account of the French intelligentsia is not a failed exercise in Frankfurt school critical theory, let alone a Communist credo, but a repurposing of the journal article—a work he had no material to produce, but also one whose objective ideal of production he could not fail to criticize. Any insight into the undermined moral and economic ground of the writer's position in society is "predicated in radical changes in society itself." These changes—a renewed spiritual nationalism, a crisis in parliamentarianism, and internationalism—cannot simply be perceived from an apolitical, theoretical standpoint. They only become perceptible once the observer admits to being inscribed within relations of production, questioning these relations, rather than shielding them behind inherited notions of humanism, universalism, or democracy. Consequently, any response to the crisis cannot take the form of a credo, or the expression of political belief in the first-person singular.

"Is there a genuine revolutionary literature [*Schrifttum*] without didacticism?" the essay asks. For Benjamin, only those writers who understand their practice as productive and redistributive, rather than merely "creative," come to acknowledge their solidarity with the masses. The political potential of literature consists in a writer's ability to arrest and alter the technical means of production, by inventing literary devices, and making them available to the proletariat. If we read the essay on the French writer considering Benjamin's larger arguments concerning political style and writerly techniques, its political insights come to light.

Later in the decade, Adorno objected to Benjamin's "ascetic" tendency to omit "the conclusive theoretical answers to questions," even making the questions "apparent only to initiates."[122] As a result, his writings stood at the "crossroads of magic and positivism." Rather than producing the pure abstraction expected from intelligence, the "magical" immediacy of language introduces a kind of literarity that derails its logic. Only more theory—dialectic rather than immediacy—could break the spell. Here, too, Benjamin does not provide "conclusive answers" concerning the relation of political tendency to literary innovation.

What is lost by the privileged of immanence over discursive sequence? More crucially, in the context of this book, what are the implications of this reading of Benjamin for the concept of intelligence? Benjamin's attention to the French literary landscape allows him to specify how the *Intelligenz* (intelligentsia) must articulate its political technique within its practice of writing. While his complicated attraction to Soviet and Surrealist instances have been studied often, his peripheral survey of the entire field of contemporary French production risks taking the politics of literature—and the politicization of criticism—seriously. What emerges is an alternative both to a tradition of German thinking, from Nietzsche to Heidegger, that casts *Intelligenz* as a superficial form of analysis particular to a free-floating class, and a turn away from doctrinaire Marxism to a historical materialism that leaves room for overdetermination, awakening, prophecy, and magic—forms ordinarily excluded from its realm.

In an essay on Benjamin's Marxism, T. J. Clark casts him in the role of "Fabrice del Dongo at Marxism's Waterloo."[123] He views the "very flimsiness" of Benjamin's materialism as an asset, in opposition to doctrinaire currents of "high Stalinism" and the more methodological Marxism of the Frankfurt School. It is even more striking that Benjamin was charged with espousing a "communist credo" in this seemingly derivative survey of French letters. Such reactions may be attributed to his refusal to take "a position, through discourse, on the *subject of* society" or to affirm revolutionary theses, as Derrida notes, without "transforming the very structure of the device, without twisting it, betraying it, drawing it outside its element."[124]

Benjamin's first essay for the Institute of Social Research proves no exception in this sense. It does not mimic the present social situation of the French writer, but narrows in on it, with no guarantee of ever locating, appropriating, or visualizing it. It questions the use-value of terms like "social situation" for criticism, while declaring it impossible to understand "great" writers without defining the role their works have in society. Analyzing the essay allows us to unravel how Benjamin's partial and singular engagement with Marxism affected his understanding of poetics and politics in the early thirties, before the Moscow trials, the Stalinist work camps, and the Spanish civil war excluded many theoretical and practical sources of hope in the struggle against Fascism. To condemn this period of Benjamin's thought for confusing the languages of the political, the economic, and the literary would amount to repressing its "magical" face. This aspect of the essay imagines a political style capable of betraying capitalist modes of production through a disruption and redistribution of techniques. In a passing gloss, Benjamin contends that the effect of time on Apollinaire's prophecy has been to "transform a whim, an exuberant improvisation, and to lay bare the truth it contained."[125] Benjamin's essay undergoes a similar transformation, turning a "pure bluff" into an incisive theory of literary politics.

This chapter has argued that intelligence was marginalized in modern German thought. This marginalization can be broadly ascribed to the anti-Cartesian philosophical tradition; the Nietzschean view that one cannot generalize about intelligence, whose myriad strains tend to impose competing world views; and the Heideggerean conviction that it is a rootless, degraded form of *Geist* that remains complicit in the forgetting of being. Benjamin's reflections on the French tradition, on the contrary, enable a sustained argument about the function and limits of the writer as a producer and distributor of intellectual techniques. By judging contemporary writers on the extent of their abilities to spur readers to become writers in turn, Benjamin interrupts the barriers between intellectual consumers and producers, while also questioning extant theories of cultural and linguistic mediation. Modern French poetics and criticism thus become the site to exploit the gradient between German and French thought.

In reconstructing the complex conceptual history of intelligence, one of the arguments of the book has been that the disputes about the term in late nineteenth-century psychology and philosophy prove central to the evolution and reception of modern French literature, thought, and criticism. Throughout this book, my intention has been to underscore the ways in which the omnipresence and plasticity of the term give it a surprising centrality. As I discussed in the introduction, these works necessarily vary in their views of intelligence, even as the concerns they expressed about the value and limits accorded to conscious rationality (especially in the creation and reception of literary works) remained constant. Many of the texts examined fought with the difficulty of language to grasp and reveal the conscious and marginal workings of mind, to recognize error and rectify it. The belated temporalities of such recognition, that dilate and inverse the logical relation of cause and effect, intuition and intelligence, become legible in literary styles and architectures. Whether or not such poetics can bolster a national agenda or betray class interest became a politically divisive question. Obliged to yield to and coexist with other forces, to test its mettle and measure its worth, intelligence remained an embattled concept. The writers and critics studied here laid out its analytic excess and cultural overdetermination rather than considering intelligence to be an ideologically neutral or conceptually stable basis for understanding the operations of mind and matter, self and other, tradition and rupture. In differing ways, Bergson, Proust, Valéry, the *NRF* critics, and Benjamin suspended then reconfigured the role and limits of intelligence. Moving the emphasis from the anxious intelligence of subjectivity to the disarming intelligence of a certain conception of literature, these writers and critics implied that "intelligence" was at once less advantageous a faculty than it was usually taken to be and one that was increasingly difficult to negotiate.

EPILOGUE

Crises of Intelligence

It happens that someone has been asked whether there is a crisis in intelligence, whether the world is becoming stupid, whether there is a distaste for culture, whether the liberal professions are suffering, perhaps dying—their strength declining, their ranks thinning, their prestige gradually diminishing, their existence more and more thankless, precarious near its end.[1]

With these words, Valéry begins his 1925 "Remarks on intelligence" ("Propos sur l'intelligence"). Suddenly, he halts this imaginary scenario, and tries to clarify the situation by commenting on the terms he has just used.

> A crisis is the passage from one mode of functioning to another; a passage made perceptible by signs or symptoms. During a crisis, time seems to change its nature, duration no longer gives the same impression as in the normal state of things. Instead of measuring permanence it measures change. Every crisis involves the intervention of new "causes" that disturb the existing equilibrium, whether mobile or immobile.[2]

What does the crisis in intelligence signal? Turning to his second term, Valéry observes, "intelligence is one of those notions that derive all their value from the other terms coupled with them, by affinity or contrast in some discourse."[3] After running it through the field of semantic associations we discussed earlier—from sensation and memory to instinct and stupidity—he concludes that intelligence has undergone a series of crises, from a "crisis in one's faculties, to a crisis in *values*, to a *class* crisis."[4]

A somewhat more contemporary discussion of crisis, no less prescient, would be Deleuze's "Postscript on the Societies of Control," which takes up

Foucault's account of the transformation of societies of sovereignty into disciplinary societies in the eighteenth and nineteenth century. Since the Second World War, writes Deleuze, "we are in a generalized crisis in relation to all environments of enclosure—prison, hospital, factory, school, family."[5] Instead of decaying institutions, societies of control require perpetual training, -dividuals (rather than individuals), banks (rather than masses), and computers enabling speculative, coded capitalism. "Man is no longer enclosed but man is in debt."[6] The acceleration of societies of control is made easier today thanks to facial recognition, profiling, and large-scale automated cross-analysis. A large part of contemporary machine learning thus becomes reciprocal, fed by data provided by individual consent to optimize experience, while at the same time enabling the possibility of control and manipulation. Deleuze imagines cities controlled by card access, open prisons that track and trace, schools that replace research with corporate logic at all levels, and hospitals that dispense with both doctors and patients. Most of these prognostics have now been realized. The point, however, is not to face these prognostics with fear or hope, "but only to look for new weapons."[7]

{⁂⁂⁂}

This epilogue shifts from the corpus studied in this book to a (decidedly non-expert) discussion of the ways in which "artificial intelligence" not only reveals the artificiality of naturalized, literary, and polemical notions of the term, but also intensifies the complexities and depredations of its historical uses. In what way might the literary–critical debates about "intelligence" discussed in this book resonate in contemporary scientific and medical idioms? In the second half of the twentieth century, intelligence ceases to be intellectual. Current permutations of machine learning, that exploit associations with intelligence, are no longer a matter of mental processes accessible to the thinking subject. Intelligence in its various guises—biological, social, artificial—challenges the history of ideas as it seems at once resistant to definition and influential in its imperceptible effects and enduring outcomes. As Stephen Cave observes, "the concept of intelligence is highly value-laden in ways that impact on the field of AI and debates about its risks and opportunities. This value-ladenness stems from the historical use of the concept [. . .] in the legitimation of dominance hierarchies."[8] Although many specialists of AI would object to its being aligned with the biological and the social, the semantic persistence of intelligence is hardly anodyne.

Between 1870 and 1930, the rise of evolutionary biology and psychometric studies of mind suggested intelligence unified mental and material aspects of knowledge, culminating in intelligence testing. As we saw, for Binet, intelligence consisted in a combination of comprehension, inventiveness, direction, and criticism. The test would soon be adapted, transformed, and applied beyond recognition through the invention of the intellectual quotient and the measure of general intelligence hypothesized by Charles Spearman: IQ and g. The early interest coming from psychophysics was brought to bear on measuring intelligence. An instance within the longer history of the naturalization and reification of reason in modernity, to borrow a formulation by Lorraine Daston invoked in the introduction to this study, intelligence became general, measurable, biological, morally neutral, innate, and unequal. At the same time, it went from enjoying limited to expansive cultural significance, as intellectual historians such as John Carson, Martin Staum, and Sander Gilman have shown.

The contemporary French philosopher Catherine Malabou writes about intelligence as part of her larger investigation into neural plasticity and genetic transformation. The constellation I have just described corresponds to the first metamorphosis of intelligence in Malabou's *Morphing Intelligence: From IQ Measurement to Artificial Brains*: "The first metamorphosis is the characterization of intelligence as a measurable factor that can be assessed with tests and is associated with the g factor or IQ."[9] Bringing together Galton's eugenics, the translation and commodification of the Binet-Simon scale, and the quest for the identification of a gene for intelligence, the first metamorphosis of intelligence is roughly genetic fatalism or biological determinism.

The second metamorphosis, the most widely developed in Malabou's own thinking, is the one that:

> occurs with the shift from the genetic to the epigenetic paradigm in early twentieth-century biology. This change allowed for a reconsidering of the idea of blind genetic determinism and opened the possibility of a new examination of the action of the environment on the constitution of the phenotype. Brain development is largely epigenetic, meaning that habit, experience, and education play a determining role in the formation and life of neuronal connections.[10]

To recall Gould, this suggests that in the so-called battle between innate nature and transformative environments of care and nurture, the latter plays as much, if not a greater role in determining one's intelligence.

Drawing on the insights of the Human Genome project, studies by Jean-Pierre Changeux, Bourdieu's habitus, and Piaget's genetic epistemology, epigenesis, for Malabou, amounts to a change in the "relation between biology and history," effectively extracting "the concept of intelligence [...] from the innatist, preformationist, or genetic ore in which it lies."[11] Intelligence becomes plastic, capable of giving, receiving, and exploding forms.

The third metamorphosis is the ongoing development of machine learning, synaptic and quantum computing, and the potential of artificial general intelligence or superintelligence. For most AI researchers, until now, neural networks do not mimic the behavior of neurons and artificial neural networks have little in common with a biological brain. Yet Malabou suggests that "natural intelligence and 'synaptic' machines somehow have the same structure."[12] "While the metaphor of the computer-brain has been obsolete for some time now, the idea of a machine that becomes a brain, a machine that is just as evolving and adaptive as neuronal architecture to the point of being able to simulate it perfectly," she writes, "also reveals the essential nature of [biology's] complicity with technological simulation."[13] Malabou's interest in genetics, epigenetics, and narrow and general AI—in "intelligence" *tout court*—make her something of an outlier in French philosophy. Continental philosophers, from Bergson and Canguilhem to Foucault and Agamben, have constructed a defensive formation against the questions raised by psychologists, biologists, and computer scientists, which she likens to the *testudo* formation of Roman armies which enabled soldiers to advance through hostile territory while protecting themselves.

Beginning with Bergson's critique of quantification, deemed unable to capture the quality of intensities in numbers, philosophy proceeds to reduce psychology's interest in intelligence to the police, biopolitics, surveillance, and the ambivalence of techno-science. From their inception such techniques of power and control have ranged from metropole to the colonies in a bio-hermeneutic imperial paradigm that Baidik Bhattacharyra calls "somapolitics."[14] Given philosophy's suspicion of, repulsion to, and protection from the very category of intelligence, what can be said about the metamorphosis of intelligence into artificial intelligence? The terms of this question elicit resistance for, even as neural networks and deep learning have remarkable applications, they remain unable—for now—to emulate the context specificity or quick-witted flexibility of "human" intelligence.

One way of connecting the two forms of intelligence is to think about the shared aspects of language, number, and code. French philologist, historian, and archeologist Clarisse Herrenschmidt traces the emergence of written language, numbers, and code across vast arrays of time and territories, spurred by economics and war.[15] Dating the emergence of writing with letters to a period ranging from 3300 to 750 BCE, of numbers written as digits and consolidated through the making and circulation of "monetary arithmetic writing" or currency from 620 BCE to the collapse of the gold standard in 1971, and of code as the machine transformation of letters and numbers, sounds and images, into binary, bits, and electric signals to 1939 onward, Herrenschmidt notes that of the three only written language is reflexive. "Language, number, and code do not bring about the same semiotic universe [. . .]. Languages are reflexive, in the sense that using its words and rules, it remains possible to say in a given language what this language is and what a language is: languages explain themselves (to one another)." Numbers designate mathematical operations and geometric forms, while modern states use them demographically to "record persons according to their gender, assign them Social Security numbers, addresses, birth and death certificates and denote cerebral activity or even their IQ." Code can be understood as:

> an arbitrary, technical language, consciously calculated and written by specialists for the work of machines in industrial, military, financial and social industrial contexts. Historically, code derives from the generalized use of numbers and the figures that they represent for recording, measuring beings, things, and their relations, so that the procedure of knowledge becomes criticizable and transformable. In practice, this represents an extension of the cipher and secret coding long used in military and diplomatic intelligence to avoid enemy interception.[16]

Such codes, too, are not yet reflexive for Herrenschmidt insofar as no one writes in code independently of a machine. Yet the most recent iterations of AI—from OpenAI to ChatGPT—do generate new software code at a high level. If code became fully reflexive, concludes Herrenschmidt, one would witness a catastrophe for the way machines work that would signal the end of human exceptionalism, begging the question whether such an eclipse has not already occured.

In the mid-1930s, a mathematics student at Cambridge, Alan Turing, set out to solve the problem David Hilbert had set in 1928. "The Entscheidungsproblem asked whether there are mathematical questions that cannot be answered by simply following a recipe [...]. Decision problems are mathematical questions that have a yes/no answer."[17] Does 2 + 2 = 4, or is 7919 a prime number? Both are decidable questions according to the precise application recipes or rules, what we today call algorithms, the application of which requires no intelligence. To establish that there were mathematical decision problems that were undecidable, for which there is no recipe for finding the answer no matter the time or computing power at one's disposition, Turing invented a mathematical problem-solving machine. "To settle Hilbert's problem all Turing had to do was show that there was some decision problem that could not be answered by any Turing machine," Michael Wooldridge writes, "and he did so by asking questions about other Turing machines, namely whether a given Turing machine and an associated input would eventually halt with an answer, or could it go on doing its work forever?"[18] If a given machine did solve the problem a contradiction ensues, as there is still no recipe for checking whether a Turing machine would halt, and thus the question, "Does a Turing machine halt?" becomes an undecidable problem. "It is one of the great ironies of scientific history," Wooldridge adds, "that Turing invented computers in order to show that there are things that computers are fundamentally incapable of doing—that some problems are inherently undecidable."[19]

As Konrad Zuse designed the Z3 for the Reich Air Ministry, John von Neumann established the fundamental architecture of conventional computers during the war, and the Manchester group, including Turing, produced the first commercial computer in 1948. It was in 1950 that Turing turned from the *undecidable* to the *indistinguishable*. Responding to public debates set off in part by Norbert Wiener's *Cybernetics*—which drew parallels between machines, animal brains, and nervous systems—Turing clarified much of the confused polemic about whether machines could think by reimagining a version of the Victorian-era parlor game called the Imitation game, in which players tried to guess the gender of an unseen player based on their responses to questions.[20] Turing's update had

> human interrogators interact via a computer keyboard and screen with something that is either a person or a computer program—the interrogator does not know in advance whether it is a person or a program. The interaction is purely in the form of textual questions and answers: the interrogator types a question, and a response is displayed. The task of the interrogator is to determine whether the thing being interrogated is a person or a computer program.[21]

If, after a reasonable period of interaction, the interrogator cannot decide whether they are interacting with a program or a person, then Turing argued, you should concede that the program has passed the test, thus being said to think. He predicted that "at the end of the century the use of words and general educated opinion will have altered so much that one will be able to speak of machines thinking without expecting to be contradicted."[22] Turing evades the question of whether the machine is really intelligent (or conscious, or self-aware). The question is not "can machines 'really' think?" because passing the test renders the simulation of thinking *indistinguishable from the real thing*. Turing's "Computing Machinery and Intelligence," published in *Mind* in 1950, is considered the origin of AI research and continues to cut through much of the noise that lay interest in the field generates among non-programmers.

Turing pointed out that "if a machine is expected to be infallible, it cannot also be intelligent [. . .]. The machine must be allowed to have contact with human beings so that it may adapt itself to their standards." Elsewhere, he adds, "intelligence consists in a departure from the completely disciplined behavior involved in computation."[23] For twentieth-century neurologists, as David Bates notes, "intelligence was in a sense considered to be a consequence of a certain disorganization and unpredictability, and potentially even pathological disorder might explain leaps of a genius intelligence."[24] The problem thus became how to free machine intelligence from automaticity by exposing it to error and disruption within and beyond itself in order to approximate the neuro-physical phenomenon of brain plasticity.

Shane Legg and Marcus Hutter of DeepMind, an AI research laboratory and subsidiary of Google, propose the following aggregate definition of intelligence: "intelligence measures an agent's ability to achieve goals in a wide range of environments."[25] While it is broadly agreed that artificial intelligence designates the ability of computers to execute specific tasks at or above the level of a human actor, Wooldridge argues that the term AI itself is something of a misnomer, since it designates processes that are neither artificial (ersatz as opposed to genuine), nor intelligent (as many of these tasks do not require intellect for human actors). If arithmetic and simple board games have been easy for computers to handle since the later 1950s, interpreting works of art, translation, and writing fiction "at a human level" remain nowhere near solved today.[26]

Early AI researchers, from John McCarthy and Marvin Minsky to Allen Newell and Herbert A. Simon, proceeded with the premise that computers could simulate "intelligent processes" to replicate logical thinking. While "electronic brains" could do useful work that was extremely challenging for humans, the ability to accurately follow precise lists of "if / then" instructions did not constitute intelligence, insofar as they could only make decisions when told how to do so. Before machine learning, algorithms could be followed and understood step by step, and programmers "knew" how the machine was reaching a decision. With deep learning the algorithm "self-generates" by the training of the neural network and in most cases, programmers can no longer understand or explain how the machine reaches decisions. Weak AI usually denotes the simulation of understanding language, whereas strong AI implies the program understands the dialogue in much the same sense as a human. Artificial General Intelligence (AGI) would entail the ability to converse in natural language, solve problems, reason, perceive its environment, and so on, at or above a human level (whatever that might be).

A spectrum of approaches developed from the early capabilities model, which sought to achieve AGI by dividing and conquering, to its opposite in the "Singularity," a notion popularized by Ray Kurzweil. Mathematicians use the term to "denote a value that transcends any finite limitation," the point where an asymptote appears to approach infinity, while physicists use it to designate "a point of zero size with infinite density of mass and therefore infinite gravity" (a point that does not actually exist because of quantum uncertainty).[27] Adapting the notion, Kurzweil contends that the Singularity in AI would follow and outstrip Moore's Law of the exponential growth of computing, leading to the unforeseen moment when machines surpass human intelligence. While Kurzweil is in a vocal minority when it comes to the Singularity, its proponents point to milestones of ANI (Artificial Narrow Intelligence), including Deep Blue's victory over Gary Kasparov and DeepMind beating Lee Sedol, the South Korean Go champion. The path to AGI is premised on improvements in computing power to allow for vast, complex tasks, while reducing the time and energy required using software modeled on synaptic or neural plasticity that could teach computers to learn. Early Heideggerean critics like Hubert Dreyfus maintained that there is simply no path that leads from classical symbolic AI and computational intelligence to AGI, let alone superintelligence.[28] While Dreyfus is correct that intuition cannot be reduced to a recipe, his objection does not fully acknowledge that such intuition or vital improvisation is itself gathered through experience over time, evolution, and genetic coding across generations, which computers have yet to undergo.

Still purely speculative, superintelligence is defined by Nick Bostrom as:

> an intellect that is much smarter than the best human brains in practically every field, including scientific creativity, general wisdom, and social skills. This definition leaves open how the superintelligence is implemented: it could be a digital computer, an ensemble of networked computers, or cultured cortical tissues or what have you. It also leaves open whether the superintelligence is conscious and has subjective experiences.[29]

Types of superintelligence include the Oracle, a question-answering robot that might interpret complex questions that humans cannot comprehend, a Genie understood as a machine that can execute any high-level task, or a Sovereign, a machine on an open-ended pursuit. Moreover, Artificial Superintelligence would be durable and smaller than humans, inviting the prospect of immortality or human extinction.

AI has gone through its own crises from the golden age of symbolic AI, problem-solving and search-based AI, to knowledge-based models, ontological engineering and "behaviorist" ones that use subsumption architecture; from computing brains to cognitive computing; from reactive and proactive to interactive machine intelligence; from weak AI to the dream of Artificial General Intelligence and Superintelligence. If a "crisis," to recall Valéry, is "the passage from mode of functioning to another," AI was enabled by a crisis of "conditions" and ways of functioning: the sudden abundance of data thanks to the internet, the drastic decrease in data storage and handling costs, and the sharp increase in computation power due to parallel processing.

Most cinematic representations of the rise of the machines often take the form of species-wide termination, travels through simulacra, matrices, and metaverses, or gendered scenarios that sheepishly wonder whether beautiful women are robots or vice versa. The more immediate dangers of AI are already present in its use in deep learning systems used in finance capitalism (as algorithmic trading and actuarial assistance), criminal justice, data mining and endangered privacy, military drones which reverse Clausewitzian definitions of war as duels into a paradigm of hunter and prey, facial recognition, and fake news, data mining and brokering, intensifying allocative and representative harm, and confirmation biases. Fake AI digital assistants, such as Apple's Siri and Google's Alexa, undertake a massive harvesting of metadata, down to the most granular level imaginable, as Anna Wiener writes in *Uncanny Valley* (according to "age, gender, political affiliation, hair color, dietary restrictions, kinks, proclivities") leading to the imposed homogeneity of "optimized, prioritized, monetized and controlled" algorithmic life.[30] As Malabou formulates it, the present conundrum is how to oppose the power of automatism to these automatisms of power.

While much is being written about the possibility of artificial intelligence and its relation to and departure from human variants, less is said about what life will look like when full-fledged AI and human intelligence must coexist. Here, it is tempting to retreat to the defenses constructed by philosophers. In a 1967 lecture in Athens, "On the Provenance of Art and the Destiny of Thinking," Heidegger observes:

> The fundamental characteristic of the world, in its cybernetic blueprint, is this feedback control system. The capacity for self-regulation, the automation of a system of motion, depend on such a system. The world as represented in cybernetic terms abolishes the difference between automatic machines and living beings. It is neutralized in this indiscriminate processing of information [...] [that] makes possible a completely homogenous—and in this sense universal—calculability, that is, the absolute controllability of both the animate and inanimate world. Humanity also has its place assigned to it within the uniformity of the cybernetic world [...]. Biochemistry has discovered the scheme of life in the genes of the germ cell. This scheme, inscribed and stored as prescription inside the genes, is the program of evolution. Science already knows the alphabet of this prescription. We speak of an "archive of genetic information." On its knowledge is founded the firm expectation that one day we shall be able to master the scientific-technological production and breeding of the human being.[31]

In the present age of Crispr and gene editing, there would be much to say about the prescient insights and strategic blindness of this passage. The "alphabet of prescription" referring to the genetic archive and the cybernetic blueprint draws together the first and third metamorphosis of intelligence, binding genetic determinism to artificial intelligence, while avoiding the epigenetic. Perhaps this can be attributed to Heidegger's view of natural and technical language, a distinction which reflects the danger of reducing *technē* to an anthropological conception of instrumental technology and language to binary forms of encoded information.[32]

In the "Conquest of Ubiquity," technical breakthroughs lead Valéry to imagine the coming world of clouds and streams in which all art, music, and sensory reality would be instantly available, further transforming one's relation to space and time. His essays on the interconnected "military, economic and spiritual" crises of mind and intelligence speculate on the rule of the machine, describing not the breeding of humans, but their training:

> The machine rules. Human life is rigorously controlled by it, dominated by the terribly precise will of mechanisms. These creatures of man are exacting. They are now reacting on their creators, making them like themselves. They want well-trained humans; they are gradually wiping out the difference between men, fitting them into their own orderly functioning, into the uniformity of their own regimes. They are thus shaping humanity for their own use, almost in their own guise. There is almost a sort of pact between the machine and ourselves, like the terrible contract between the nervous systems and the subtle demon of drugs. The more useful the machine seems to us, the more it becomes so; and the more it becomes so, the more *incomplete* we are, the more incapable of doing without it. There is such a thing as the *reciprocal* of the useful.[33]

Valéry underscores that transformation of the human habit and the sensorium by interaction, noting that reciprocal use leads to a zone of indistinction between subject and object, man and machine. It is likely that any notion of intelligence will be further transformed by the continued entanglement of the natural and the artificial, which will eventually become indistinguishable as instrumental forms continue to reify, commodify, and disappropriate the self.

This epilogue may seem to bring us far from the concerns of modern writers and critics studied in this book. Yet any contemporary discussion of intelligence cannot afford to ignore the ways in which the notion is being transformed by its artificial afterlives. While late nineteenth-century philosophers fought over the extent to which the mind was mechanical, quantifiable, and measurable, twentieth-century writers saw in it an impetus and obstacle to literary invention, one that needed to be disarmed to rectify its errors and yield its affordances. The outbreak of the First World War made intelligence a flashpoint among factions that sought to make cultural life subservient to political programs and critics who were determined to locate politics within aesthetic and literary forms. What role, if any, will remain for literature and critical thought under the new regimes of machine intelligence, and the positivisms they intensify and exploit is one of the questions that will determine coming interpretive conflicts. Knowing the intricacies of the multiple discourses and problematics of intelligence in the texts studied in this book could make such discussions less acrimonious, if only by recalling that the definitions and uses of intelligence are always value-laden and thus the object of real disagreement.

ACKNOWLEDGMENTS

THIS BOOK WAS fostered by many engaging and ongoing conversations. Daniel Heller-Roazen directed the dissertation in which these pages began. My research has benefited enormously from his seminars, scholarship, and insights. Michael Wood, Peter Brooks, and Ann Smock were marvelous advisers. I feel deeply grateful to have studied with them. Jean-Michel Rabaté, whom I was lucky to meet during my studies in Paris, has been very generous with his expertise over time. My interest in comparative modernism and critical theory was sparked by my undergraduate teachers, especially Maud Ellmann, Peter Fenves, and Rainer Rumold. Samuel Weber has been my first source of guidance and encouragement since then.

The Department of Comparative Literature at New York University has been a wonderfully stimulating and sustaining environment. My sincere gratitude to the staff, students, and all my colleagues who have made the past years transformative ones. Emily Apter, who was chair of the department when I was hired, has been exceptionally generous and supportive of my research and teaching. Mark Sanders, as the current chair, continues to make the department a fertile place to think, teach, and work. Thanks also to the departments of English and French Thought, Literature, and Culture for welcoming me as an associate faculty member.

Since I have been at NYU, Peter Nicholls has consistently commented on my work with skeptical generosity. I thank him for reading and discussing this manuscript more than once. Denis Hollier disclosed French intellectual and editorial history in and outside the seminar room. Special thanks to them, as well as Emily Apter, Suzanne Guerlac, and Françoise Meltzer for participating in my book manuscript workshop. Their challenging questions and comments were crucial as I revised the project. Thanks to Hannah Freed-Thall, Benjamin Lewis Robinson, and Dora Zhang for reading chapters of this book and offering their invaluable comments. Atsuo Morimoto and William Marx guided me through the material dealing with Valéry. More than a word of thanks to Athanassia Williamson, Daniella Gitlin, and Simon Leser for their editorial assistance. Many more interlocutors than I can name here have discussed this material with me at various stages, for which they have my gratitude.

My sincere thanks to Anne Savarese for her constant support while this manuscript took shape. Thanks to Tash Siddiqui for her precise copyediting. It has been a real pleasure to work with them, Jill Harris, James Collier, and the production team at Princeton University Press. Three anonymous reviewers offered exacting responses that helped improve my manuscript. Sections of this project were completed with the assistance of a Graduate Research Initative Fellowship at NYU Florence and the Prix André Gide-Jean Schlumberger from the Fondation des Treilles. Sections of chapters 1, 2, and 4 were published in special issues of *l'esprit créateur* and *The Germanic Review: Literature, Culture, Theory*. I thank the journals and editors for the permission to reproduce them here.

Warm thanks to my friends for their reliable wit and vigilance in trying times: Alexandra Lukes, Alicia Mireles Christoff, Cornelius Reiber, Dora Zhang, Joseph Gelfand, Lila Walsh, Matthew Davies, Nathaniel Young, Rachel Galvin, Sarah Wasserman, Scott Branson, and Torrey Shanks.

My greatest gratitude goes to my parents—Shahnaz and Shahid Paul—for their support, generosity, and love across continents. They have kept me afloat in more ways than one. My brother and sister-in-law—Aamir and Mariam Paul—have been wonderfully generous and lighthearted at once. Merci de tout cœur aux Rousselière de m'avoir accueilli toutes ces années. Geneviève Rousselière read and discussed this book with her brilliance and insight, while treating its author with patience and love. Adam brings laughter, curiosity, music, and joy to our days.

NOTES

Wherever possible, published translations from the French and German are quoted. As necessary, these translations have been silently modified. The endnotes contain the original French and German in most, but not all, instances.

Introduction

1. Gérard Genette argues that at the very moment that rhetoric was no longer taught as an academic subject in France, it reemerged, from Mallarmé to Blanchot, as a kind of self-reflexive literature that incorporated its own critical and poetic function. Genette, *Figures II*, 41. The third chapter on Valéry revisits the topic of reflexivity in detail.

2. Brooks, *Balzac's Lives*, 33.

3. Nizan, *Les chiens de garde*, 151.

4. Weber, *Peasants into Frenchmen*; Sowerwine, *France Since 1870*; Gildea, *Children of the Revolution*; Jennings, *Revolution and Republic*; Mitchell, *The German Influence in France after 1870*; Nicholls, *Revolutionary Thought after the Paris Commune*; Clark, *The Sleepwalkers*.

5. Finn, *Figures of the Pre-Freudian Unconscious*, 159.

6. Cited in Winock, *Le siècle des intellectuels*, 29–30.

7. Barrès, *Scènes et doctrines du nationalisme*, vol. 1, 76; 96. See also Winock, *Le siècle des intellectuels*, 45; Apter, *Continental Drift: From National Characters to Virtual Subjects*, 25–37.

8. Lalande, *Vocabulaire technique et critique de la philosophie*, 523–4. For an overview of the cultural history and representations of the intellectual, see Sirinelli, *Intellectuels et passions françaises*; Winock, *Le siècle des intellectuels*; and Said, *Representations of the Intellectual*.

9. Foucault, "La fonction politique de l'intellectuel"; "The political function of the intellectual."

10. "Ceux qui ont vécu pendant la guerre de 1870, par exemple, disent que l'idée de la guerre avait fini par leur sembler naturelle, non pas parce qu'ils ne pensaient pas assez à la guerre, mais y pensaient toujours. Et pour comprendre combien c'est un fait étrange et considérable que la guerre, il fallait, quelque chose les arrachant à leur obsession permanente, qu'ils oubliassent un instant que la guerre régnait, se retrouvassent pareils à ce qu'ils étaient quand on était en paix, jusqu'à ce que tout à coup sur ce blanc momentané se détachât, enfin distincte, la réalité monstrueuse que depuis longtemps ils avaient cessé de voir, ne voyant pas autre chose qu'elle." Proust, *À la recherche*, vol. 4, 115; *In Search*, vol. 5, 720–21.

11. Benjamin, "Experience and Poverty" (1933), *Selected Writings*, vol. 2, 731–2.

12. Sapiro, *La responsabilité de l'écrivain*; Compagnon, *La Troisième République des lettres*.

13. "À l'égard des objets de l'intelligence, on peut se comporter de deux manières. Tout esprit est plus ou moins armé, en présence des idées, du bouclier ou miroir de la réflexion, et du glaive de l'invention, de l'action pénétrante et remuante: réfléchir et oser. Le génie consiste dans l'alliance proportionnée des deux moyens, avec la prédominance d'oser." Sainte-Beuve, "M. Jouffroy," *Nouveaux portraits et critiques littéraires*, vol. 1, 199.

14. For a comparative overview, see Ball et al., eds., *Cultures of Intelligence*.

15. See Sternberg, *Metaphor of Mind*; Danziger, *Naming the Mind*.

16. I borrow the term "societies of profiling" from Huneman, *Les sociétés du profilage*.

17. A recent exception is Lyons, *Assessing Intelligence: The Bildungsroman and the Politics of Human Potential in England*.

18. David, *Le procès de l'intelligence*. See also Citti, *La mésintelligence*; Buchet, *Écrivains intelligents du XXème siècle*; Archambault, ed., *Le procès de l'intelligence*.

19. Daston, "The Naturalized Female Intellect," 211.

20. Bourdieu, *Questions of Sociology*, 177–79.

21. Carson, *The Measure of Merit*, 78.

22. Littré, *Dictionnaire de la langue française*. Edmond Goblot provided a more succint definition: "La faculté des faits intellectuels—s'oppose à *sensibilité*, faculté des faits affectifs. L'intelligence peut aussi s'opposer à *l'instinct*." Goblot, *Le vocabulaire philosophique*, 306.

23. Carson, "Intelligence," in *A Companion to American Thought*, 342–3.

24. Carson, "The Culture of Intelligence," in *The Cambridge History of Science*, vol. 7, 635–48.

25. Foucault, *Les mots et les choses*.

26. "Le moment vint, au XIXème siècle, où l'intelligence de l'homme, porté à son haut degré d'acuité, cessa de se tenir pour le centre et l'achèvement du monde. Au sentiment d'une dignité infinie succédait celui de la détresse et de l'abandon. L'ironie sapait la dignité, la faim et la passion la rendaient haïssable." Bataille, "De l'existentialisme au primat de l'économie," 518.

27. Étienne Balibar, "Soul," in Cassin et al., eds., *Dictionary of Untranslatables. A Philosophical Lexicon*, 1009–22.

28. As Christian Sommer notes, this *legere* might equally be understood as a kind of *audire* or listening, considering antique traditions of dictation and oral transmission. Sommer, *Heidegger, Aristote, Luther*, 203. The Latin verb *intellego* is the common source for *intelligentia* and *intellectus*. On the complex connections between *intelligere*, the polysemic medieval term *intellectus*, and the Greek *nous*, see Alain de Libera, "Intellectus," in Cassin et al., eds., *Dictionary of Untranslatables*, 492–500; see also the preceding entry by Emmanuel Faye, "Intellect, Intelliger," 490–92.

29. Blanchot, *The Blanchot Reader*, 208.

30. Taine's historical coinages suggest how *esprit* designates collective mentality: *esprit gaulois* (in his study of La Fontaine), *esprit révolutionnaire*, *esprit scientifique*, *esprit classique* (in *Origines de la France contemporaine*), and *esprit français*, which he claimed was given to abstraction, extrapolation, and simplification.

31. For a graph showing the upsurge in the use of the term in French, see "Dictionnaire vivant de la langue française": http://dvlf.uchicago.edu/mot/intelligence.

32. Broca, Ferrier, and Charcot refined the pathological method by associating patients' intellectual failures with damage to brain tissue. It was this clinical approach to pathology that Bergson and his milieu had in mind. In contrast, Binet and Simon used statistical methods to arrive at ideals of the normal and pathological through population averages. While the French pioneered clinical approaches, they trailed German psychologists when it came to experimental psychology. This is one reason Bergson had already published three books by the time Binet's intelligence test hit the market. I thank Larry McGrath for pointing out these nuances to me.

33. The drive to measure intelligence, from Galton to Herrnstein and Murray's *The Bell Curve*, is best captured and criticized in Gould, *The Mismeasure of Man*.

34. On the French "science of difference," see Carson, *The Measure of Merit*, 113–58.

35. Naturalization here names "ways of fortifying various social cultural, political, or economic conventions by presenting them as part of the natural order." Daston, "The Naturalized Female Intellect," 209. More recently, Daston has offered an account of the main forms of "natural order" in the Western philosophical tradition—specific natures, local natures, and universal natural laws. Daston, *Against Nature*.

36. Daston, "The Naturalized Female Intellect," 226.

37. In addition to Gould, *The Mismeasure of Man*, see Staum, *Nature and Nurture in the French Social Sciences*; Conklin, *In the Museum of Man*; Conklin, *A Mission to Civilize*; Rabinow, *French Modern*; Jones, *The Racial Discourses of Life Philosophy*. For comparative histories see Sussman, *The Myth of Race*; Schuller, *The Biopolitics of Feeling*.

38. "Qu'entendent-ils par *intelligence*? Beaucoup semblent la confondre avec la raison, ou avec la logique, ou avec ces deux outils de l'intelligence. Ou bien s'agit-il de cette lucidité d'esprit, celle qui manque à certains inspirés, et aux idiots? Ou bien cette faculté qui 'comprend' le jeu des antécédents et des conséquences; qui vous éduque à anticiper, à disposer lucidement des causes pour en obtenir des effets prévus à inventer? Certes une bonne intelligence claire comprend fort bien que son pouvoir est limité; elle sait qu'elle a besoin d'autres facultés, comme l'intelligence intuitive, pour devenir intelligence globale." Amédée Ozenfant to Jean David, February 16, 1952, in David, *Le procès de l'intelligence*, 284.

39. Sabin, *The Dialect of the Tribe*, 46.

40. Sabin, *The Dialect of the Tribe*, 43.

41. Kahler, *Die Verinnerung des Erzählens*; *The Inward Turn of Narrative*.

42. Jenny, *La fin de l'intériorité*.

43. Bowie, *Freud, Proust and Lacan*, 173. The original context of Bowie's phrase is psychoanalysis.

44. "L'intelligence fut considérée comme explosive, et celui qui vivait de son intelligence en apparût l'ennemi né de l'ordre réel." Maurras, *L'avenir de l'intelligence*, 48.

45. This may be an allusion to Kant, despite Maurras's Thomism. Kant considers intelligence to be comprised by understanding, judgment and reason in the *Critique of Pure Reason*, adding a distinction between genius and the spirit of imitation. It is noteworthy that the conceptual history of "intelligence" is distinct from "genius" in French thought. See Jefferson, *Genius in France: An Idea and its Uses*.

46. Wood, *Literature and the Taste of Knowledge*, 5.

47. See Streuver, *Rhetoric, Modality, Modernity*, 190–230.

48. "Nous apprenant à n'être pas dupes de la langue, la littérature nous rend plus intelligents, ou autrement intelligents. Le dilemme de l'art social ou l'art pour l'art devient caduc face à un art qui convoite une intelligence du monde libérée des contraintes de la langue." Compagnon, *La littérature, pour quoi faire?*

49. "Philologie, wo sie es wirklich ist, beantwortet die Fragen, Provokationen und Attacken, die von der Literatur organisiert werden, nicht, wenn sie das technische Instrumentarium dazu parat hat, sondern wenn sie, entwaffnet, nach anderen Antworten als den paraten suchen muß." Werner Hamacher, *Für—die Philologie*, 55; *Minima Philologica*, 139.

50. Hamacher, *On the Brink*, 40.

51. Eliot, "The Perfect Critic," in *The Sacred Wood*, 10. For Eliot's comparison of the Arnoldian tradition with French criticism, especially Julien Benda and Rémy de Gourmont, see "The French Intelligence," in *The Sacred Wood*, 39–41. See also Eliot, "From Poe to Valéry." For a reading of Eliot's critical stance in relation to literary theory, see Kermode, "Intelligent theory."

52. I borrow the expression "relational modes" from Leo Bersani's reception of Foucault. Bersani writes, "Foucault summoned us to seek both new relational modes and new pleasures of the body. It is unlikely that such discoveries will be made through rational reflection. We must be shocked into otherwise inconceivable states of availability." Art and literature thus become crucial sources for the discovery of modes unavailable to rationality. See Bersani, *Thoughts and Things*, 93.

53. Gourgouris, *Does Literature Think?*, 2.

54. On the idea of the "idea" in relation to literary history, see Walter Benjamin's "Erkenntniskritische Vorrede," in *Ursprung des deutschen Trauerspiels*, 207–37; "Epistemo-critical Prologue," in *The Origin of the German Mourning Play*, 1–39.

55. *Mētis* is "a type of intelligence and of thought, a way of knowing; it implies a complex but very coherent body of mental attitudes and intellectual behavior which combine flair, wisdom, forethought, various skills, and experience acquired over the years. It is applied to situations which are transient, shifting, disconcerting and ambiguous, situations which do not lend themselves to precise measurement, exact calculation, or rigorous logic." Detienne and Vernant, *Les ruses de l'intelligence*, 10; *Cunning Intelligence in Greek Culture and Society*, 3–4.

56. Aristotle was an exception in his treatment of intelligence among ancient philosophers, according to Detienne and Vernant, *Les ruses de l'intelligence*, 10.

57. Erskine, *The Moral Obligation to be Intelligent and Other Essays*.

58. Ball, *Zur Kritik der deutschen Intelligenz*; *Critique of the German Intelligentsia*. See also Rabinbach, "The Inverted Nationalism of Hugo Ball's *Critique of the German Intelligentsia*," in *In the Shadow of Catastrophe*, 66–94.

59. Carson, *The Measure of Merit*.

60. See Debaene, *Far Afield*, 25–50.

61. Foucault, *Les mots et les choses*; Aarsleff, *From Locke to Saussure*; Derrida, *L'archéologie du frivole*.

62. Proust, *Contre Sainte-Beuve*, in *Essais*, 696; *Proust on Art and Literature*, 19. Sabin, *The Dialect of the Tribe*, 43, suggests that with this phrase, Proust almost poses a greater challenge to the tradition of Anglophone criticism and its configuration of values that cling to the "provincial banner" of intelligence, from Matthew Arnold and

Henry James to F. R. Leavis, than it does to French criticism. As the culmination, or the reification, of this tradition, Leavis distinguishes "intelligence" from "intellectual analysis." He praises Lawrence as expressing the former and dismisses Proust for being mired in the latter.

63. Healey does proceed to present a model of French literary modernism focused on "a dynamic that exists within the text rather than on an enumeration of key characteristics." Healey, "French Literary Modernism," 801. For more evaluations of the French context, see Ellison, "Modernism"; Rabaté's two essays, "French Modernism: Gide, Proust, and Larbaud" and "Modernism and the French Novel: A Genealogy (1888–1913)"; Rentzou and Benhaïm, eds., *1913: The Year of French Modernism*; Hollister, "Missing Modernism (Gide)."

64. The case is somewhat different when it comes to the visual arts and architecture. See Clark, *Farewell to an Idea*; Cone, *French Modernisms*; Kwinter, *Architectures of Time*.

65. This tendency is reflected by critics from Wilson in *Axel's Castle* to Friedman, who describes the novel from Huysmans to Malraux as "the symbolist novel."

66. Compagnon, *Proust entre deux siècles*.

67. Descombes, "Le régime moderne de l'art," in *Proust: Philosophie du roman*, 119–54.

68. Descombes, *Proust: Philosophie du roman*, 120.

69. The prefatory letter to Arsène Houssaye (1869) before *Le Spleen de Paris* describes Baudelaire's ambition as "to apply to the description of modern life, or rather of *one* modern and more abstract life, the process [. . .] applied in the depicting of ancient life, so strangely picturesque." Baudelaire, "Lettre à Arsène Houssaye," *Œuvres complètes*, vol. 1, 276.

70. Descombes, *Proust: Philosophie du roman*, 153. As Wood writes, "by the time we have moved from Ruskin to Proust only unregistered experience counts as real." *Unregistered Experience*, 36.

71. Rabaté, *La penultième est morte*, 18. Rabaté notes that mentions of "modernisme" in Proust's novel are limited to Charlus's mockery, while Morel lauds Rachel's "diction moderniste," whose specious elevation over La Berma's delivery is itself a sign of decadence. To these instances, we might add Saint Loup who is described as a devotee of "manifestations modernistes de la littérature et de l'art" and spends hours studying Nietzsche and Proudhon.

72. "Cette fois du reste, le public qui avait résisté aux modernistes de la littérature et de l'art suit ceux de la guerre, parce que c'est une mode adoptée de penser ainsi et puis que les petits esprits sont écrasés, non par la beauté, mais par l'énormité de l'action." Proust, *À la recherche*, vol. 4, 358; *In Search*, vol. 6, 130.

73. Huyssen, "Introduction: Modernism after Postmodernity," 1.

74. Rogers, "Death by Prefix?"

75. Jameson, *A Singular Modernity*, 104.

76. Sherry, *Modernism and the Reinvention of Decadence*; Hutchinson, *Lateness and Modern European Literature*.

77. Jameson notes that this use stretches back to Pope Gelasius I and Cassiodorus in Fifth Century AD, suggesting that the "disenchantment of the world" may have begun earlier than anyone cares to recall. *A Singular Modernity*, 17.

78. De Man, *Blindness and Insight*, 144.

79. Albright, *Putting Modernism Together*.

80. For a wide-ranging comparative overview, see Nicholls, *Modernisms*. For a historian's account of the period, see Gay, *Modernism: The Lure of Heresy*.

81. Hamacher, *Premises*, 294.

82. Valéry, "Existence du symbolisme," *Œuvres*, vol. 1, 686–706.

83. "Eh bien! l'Europe de 1914 était peut-être arrivée à la limite de ce modernisme. Chaque cerveau d'un certain rang était un carrefour pour toutes les races de l'opinion; tout penseur, une exposition universelle de pensées [. . .]. Dans tel livre de cette époque—et non des plus médiocres—on trouve, sans aucun effort:—une influence des ballets russes,—un peu du style sombre de Pascal,—beaucoup d'impressions du type Goncourt, quelque chose de Nietzsche,—quelque chose de Rimbaud,—certains effets dus à la fréquentation des peintres, et parfois le ton des publications scientifiques,—le tout parfumé d'un je ne sais quoi de britannique difficile à doser!" Valéry, "La Crise de l'esprit," *Œuvres*, vol. 1, 988. "The Crisis of the Mind," *Collected Works*, vol. 10, 28, my italics. In "Le triomphe de Manet," Valéry suggests that an era feels "modern" when it equally permits the coexistence of a multiplicity of doctrines, tendencies, and "truths" within the same individuals. See *Œuvres*, vol. 2, 1327.

84. Jarrety, "Valéry: Du classique sans classicisme."

85. Thibaudet, "Discussion sur le moderne," *Réflexions sur la littérature*, 428; "A Discussion of the 'Modern' in Literature," *N.R.F. Essays from the Nouvelle Revue Française*, 18–19.

86. Rentzou and Benhaïm, eds., *1913: The Year of French Modernism*; Rabaté, *1913: The Cradle of Modernism*.

87. On modernity and anti-modernity, see Compagnon, *Les cinq paradoxes de la modernité* and *Les antimodernes: de Joseph de Maistre à Roland Barthes*.

88. Milne, *"La Nouvelle Revue Française* in the Age of Modernism," 3.

89. Eliot writes that Proust stands, "as a point of demarcation for whom the dissolution of value had in itself a positive value, and the generation for which the recognition of value is of utmost importance, a generation which is beginning to turn its attention to an athleticism, a training, of the soul, as severe and ascetic as the training of the body of a runner." Eliot, "Books of the Quarter," 752–3. On Valéry and American poetry, see Goldfarb, *Unexpected Affinities*.

90. Cronan, *Against Affective Formalism: Matisse, Bergson, Modernism*.

91. Freed-Thall, *Spoiled Distinctions*, 12.

92. Forster, *Aspects of the Novel*, 26; 146–8.

93. Compagnon, *Les cinq paradoxes de la modernité*, 11.

94. Maurice Samuels, "France," *Cambridge Companion to European Modernism*, 14.

95. As Christopher Bush notes, "the global turn puts conflicting methodological pressures on modernist studies' desire for context" between historical context and aesthetic autonomy. Building on this contradiction, modern French literature only seems modernist to those willing to sacrifice the singularity claimed by and as Frenchness, while modernism only appears significant if such a status of exception is put into question. While some of the interest *for* French modernism comes from French studies itself, in a bid to find comparative relevance and interlocutors beyond the field, this does not overcome the problematic status of context and concept at play. See Bush, "Context," 75.

96. Benjamin, *Gesammelte Schriften*, vol. 3, 119. "Sainte-Beuve hat an einer berühmten Stelle die *intelligence-miroir* und die *intelligence-glaive* einander gegenübergestellt. Das Schwert ist diesem Jüngling manchmal entfallen. Aber er hielt stand, gepanzert. In dieser Rüstung spiegelt sich die Welt, verzerrt und golden: *intelligence-cuirasse.*"

Chapter One: Gathering Intelligence

1. Carson, *The Measure of Merit*, 78.
2. Carson, *The Measure of Merit*, 78.
3. Gutting, *French Philosophy in the Twentieth Century*; McGrath, *Making Spirit Matter*; Janicaud, *Ravaisson et la métaphysique*.
4. "Réaction de l'intelligence contre le génie [...] obligée à un effort critique général contre ses prédécesseurs, il semble qu'elle ait placé tous les courants de la production sous le contrôle de la critique." Thibaudet, *L'histoire*, 326.
5. Giuseppe Bianco, "What was 'Serious Philosophy' for the Young Bergson?," in Lefebvre and Schott, eds., *Interpreting Bergson*, 33.
6. Gutting, *French Philosophy in the Twentieth Century*, 9–10.
7. Thibaudet, *L'histoire*, 373.
8. Renan, *L'avenir de la science*, 46.
9. "Taine a pour la première fois accompagné la notion d'intelligence d'un soutènement scientifique et social. Thibaudet, tout en trouvant en 1923 que le livre *De l'intelligence* était désuet, a déclaré que Taine en transformant le monde de choses en monde de signes avait posé le problème [...]. Les pièces d'ordre philosophique qui seront versées au dossier ressortiront plutôt à Taine. Celles d'ordre politique, littéraire, ou social, à Renan." David, *Le procès de l'intelligence*, 12. See also Thibaudet, "Renan et Taine."
10. Nias, *The Artificial Self: The Psychology of Hippolyte Taine*.
11. Finn, *Figures of the Pre-Freudian Unconscious*, 11–42.
12. Bergson, "À propos de 'l'évolution de l'intelligence géometrique,'" 32.
13. Walsh, *French Literature and the Philosophy of Consciousness*, 127.
14. See Leonard Lawlor, "Bergson on the True Intellect," in Lefebvre and Schott, eds., *Interpreting Bergson*, 67–86.
15. Aarsleff, *From Locke to Saussure*, 356.
16. Sabin, "The Community of Intelligence."
17. Fechner, *Elements of Psychophysics*, 55–6.
18. Taine, *Histoire de la littérature anglaise*, vol. 4, 421.
19. For Bergson, "Fechner's psychometrics threatens to reduce the person to the body, construed mechanistically along the lines of Descartes' human machine." Guerlac, *Thinking in Time*, 25.
20. Staum, *Nature and Nurture in the French Social Sciences*, 85.
21. Ribot, "De l'intelligence," 583–4. See also Ribot, *Les maladies de la personnalité*, 33.
22. Staum, *Nature and Nurture in the French Social Sciences*, 106.
23. Staum, *Nature and Nurture in the French Social Sciences*, 106.
24. Finn, *Figures of the Pre-Freudian Unconscious*, 35.
25. Staum, *Nature and Nurture in the French Social Sciences*, 140.

26. Binet, *Le fétichisme dans l'amour*. Wolf, "A New Perspective on Alfred Binet."

27. Binet and Simon, "Sur la nécessité d'établir un diagnostic scientifique des états inférieurs de l'intelligence," 163.

28. Staum, *Nature and Nurture in the French Social Sciences*, 131; see also Jefferson, *Genius in France: An Idea and its Uses*, 173–82.

29. "L'intelligence, considérée indépendamment des phénomènes de sensibilité, d'émotion et de volonté, est avant tout une faculté de connaissance, qui est dirigée vers le monde extérieur, et qui travaille à le reconstruire en entier, au moyen des petits fragments qui nous en sont donnés." Binet, *Les idées modernes sur les enfants*, 117.

30. For a provocative reading of Valéry's apprenticeship under the anthropologist and craniometer Georges Vacher de Lapouge, see Mehlman, "Craniometry and Criticism."

31. Piaget, *Psychology of Intelligence*, 21–2.

32. Binet and Simon, "Méthodes nouvelles pour le diagnostic," 196.

33. Gould, *The Mismeasure of Man*, 180.

34. Binet, *Les idées modernes sur les enfants*, 141.

35. Binet and Simon, "Méthodes nouvelles pour le diagnostic," 196–7; *The Development of Intelligence in Children*, 42–3.

36. "Il est vraiment trop facile de découvrir les signes d'arriération chez un individu quand on est prévenu. Autant opérer comme ces graphologues qui du temps où l'on croyait Dreyfus coupable découvraient dans son écriture les signes d'un traître et d'un espion." Binet, "Application des méthodes nouvelles au diagnostic du niveau intellectuel chez des enfants normaux et anormaux d'hospice et d'école primaire," 325.

37. Staum, *Nature and Nurture in the French Social Sciences*, 140.

38. Binet, *Les idées modernes sur les enfants*, 288.

39. Carson, *The Measure of Merit*, 139–47.

40. For an account of the "dismantling of Binet's intentions in America" that focuses on Goddard, L. M. Terman, and R. M. Yerkes, see Gould, "The Hereditarian Theory of IQ," in *The Mismeasure of Man*, 176–263.

41. For a discussion of Jacques Rancière's reworking of egalitarian intelligence via Joseph Jacotot, see Paul, "Intellectual Equality."

42. Guerlac notes the gendered reception of positivism and spiritualism. While positivism was associated with rationalism and the virile power of quantifiable nature, spiritualism was associated with instinct and considered feminine. Guerlac, *Thinking in Time*, 22.

43. "D'*inter* et de *legere*, lire entre. Faculté de voir, de saisir les choses telles qu'elles sont, voir *Bon sens*. De là on a donné ce nom à la substance qui voit. Dieu est la suprême *intelligence*, il y a eu des philosophes qui ont répandu des *intelligences* partout." Quoted in Labarrière, "L'intelligence," 436–7.

44. "Le bon sens et l'intelligence ne sont que concevoir ou imaginer et ne diffèrent que par la nature de l'objet dont on s'occupe. Comprendre, par exemple, que deux et deux font quatre, ou comprendre tout un cours de mathématiques, c'est également concevoir; mais avec cette différence que l'un s'appelle bon sens, et l'autre l'intelligence." Condillac, *L'essai sur l'origine des connaissances humaines*, § 98, 106; *Essay on the Origin of Human Knowledge*, 65.

45. "L'objet du bon sens ne paraît donc se recentrer que dans ce qui est facile et ordinaire, et c'est à l'intelligence à faire concevoir ou imaginer des choses

plus composées et plus neuves." Condillac, *L'essai sur l'origine des connaissances humaines*, § 98, 106; *Essay on the Origin of Human Knowledge*, 65.

46. Nordmann, "Taine et le positivisme," 21–33. See also Nordmann, *Taine et la critique scientifique*; Richard, *Hippolyte Taine*.

47. Vatan, "La 'puissance de l'image' Bouvard et Pécuchet, disciples de Taine?," 112–13.

48. Taine, *Hippolyte Taine, sa vie et correspondance*, vol. 1, 120.

49. Taine, *Philosophie de l'art*, 20.

50. "L'etat général d'esprit," Taine, *Philosophie de l'art*, 13.

51. Wilson, *To the Finland Station*, 47–9.

52. "La vie politique nous est interdite [...] le seul chemin est la science pure ou la pure littérature." Taine, *Hippolyte Taine, sa vie et correspondance*, vol. 1, 205.

53. He specifies that he owes the thesis that all general ideas can be reduced to signs to Condillac, the theory of induction to Mill, and the account of spatial perception to Bain. Taine, *De l'intelligence*, vol. 1, 5; *On Intelligence*, vol. 1, ix.

54. "Notre esprit touche juste en visant mal." Taine, *De l'intelligence*, vol. 2, 190; *On Intelligence*, vol. 2, 92.

55. Taine, *De l'intelligence*, vol. 1, 96; *On Intelligence*, vol. 1, 51.

56. "Ainsi notre perception extérieure est un rêve du dedans qui se trouve en harmonie avec les choses du dehors et au lieu de dire que l'hallucination est une perception extérieure fausse, il faut dire que la perception extérieure est une hallucination vraie." Taine, *De l'intelligence*, vol 2, 12–13; *On Intelligence*, vol. 1, 226.

57. Watt, "The Naive Realism of Henri Bergson," in *The Bergsonian Mind*, 164–5.

58. "En général, tout état singulier de l'intelligence doit être le sujet d'une monographie; car il faut voir l'horloge dérangée pour distinguer les contrepoids et les rouages que nous ne remarquons pas dans l'horloge qui va bien." Taine, *De l'intelligence*, vol. 1, 17; my translation.

59. Taine, *Histoire de la littérature anglaise*, vol. 2, 157–9.

60. See the theory of "réducteurs antagonistes" that repress hallucinatory images, in Taine, *De l'intelligence*, vol. 1, 77–128; *On Intelligence*, vol. 1, 35–74.

61. Marquer, *Naissance du fantastique clinique*.

62. Taine, *De l'intelligence*, vol. 1, 13–14. For an account of how Flaubert pastiches Taine, see Vatan, "La 'puissance de l'image' Bouvard et Pécuchet, disciples de Taine?," 121–37.

63. "un psychologue qui naturellement et involontairement met la psychologie en action [...] Il aime à se représenter des sentiments, à sentir leurs attaches, leurs précédents, leurs suites." Taine, *Histoire de la littérature anglaise*, vol. 5, 117.

64. "Ce qui nous intéresse dans un être réel, et ce que nous prions l'artiste d'extraire et de rendre, c'est sa logique [...] sa structure, sa composition et son agencement." Taine, *Philosophie de l'art*, 45; *Philosophy of Art*, 61.

65. See Gaulin, "La théorie du signe d'Hippolyte Taine."

66. "Éxpérience présente qui nous suggère l'idée d'une expérience possible." Taine, *De l'intelligence*, vol. 1, 26; *On Intelligence*, vol. 1, 2. This translation is complicated by the fact that "expérience" also means "experiment."

67. Nordmann, *Taine et la critique scientifique*, 67–8.

68. Taine, *De l'intelligence*, vol. 1, 32; *On Intelligence*, vol. 1, 6.

69. James, "A World of Pure Experience," 1169.

70. Tortonese, "Taine: Art et Hallucination."

71. Mill underscores the "analytic" and "synthetic" in aspects of Taine's treatise: Mill, "Taine's *De l'intelligence*," 444–5.

72. Nias, *The Artificial Self: The Psychology of Hippolyte Taine*, 44.

73. "Il n'y a rien de réel dans le moi, sauf la file de ses événements; que ces événements, divers d'aspect, sont les mêmes en nature et se ramènent tous à la sensation; que la sensation elle-même [. . .] se réduit à un groupe de mouvements moléculaires." Taine, "Préface," *De l'intelligence*, vol. 1, 7.

74. Taine, *De l'intelligence*, vol. 1, 313.

75. Taine, *De l'intelligence*, vol. 1, 314.

76. "Sensation non-présente." Taine, *De l'intelligence*, vol. 2, 52.

77. Perrin, "Taine et la mémoire involontaire."

78. "La nouveauté de mon livre est d'être entièrement composé de petits faits, cas significatifs, observations individuelles, descriptions de fonctions psychologiques, atrophiées ou hypertrophiées." Taine, *Hippolyte Taine, sa vie et correspondance*, vol. 3, 253. Carson, *The Measure of Merit*, 117.

79. "Un flux et un faisceau de sensations et d'impulsions, qui, vus par une autre face, sont aussi un flux et un faisceau de vibrations nerveuses, voilà l'esprit." Taine, *De l'intelligence*, vol. 1, 7. Labarrière places Taine's treatise at the forefront of articulating the biological function of intelligence against analyses of *esprit* generated by separating action, sensation, and intelligence: "L'intelligence," 458–9.

80. Taine, *De l'intelligence*, vol. 1, 16–17.

81. "Le cerveau humain est alors un théâtre où se jouent à la fois plusieurs pièces différentes, sur plusieurs plans dont un seul est en lumière." Taine, *De l'intelligence*, vol. 1, 16.

82. David, *Le procès de l'intelligence*, 60.

83. Nias, *The Artificial Self: The Psychology of Hippolyte Taine*, 186.

84. Valéry, *Cahiers*, ed. Robinson, vol. 2, 1187.

85. For an important discussion of Taine and Saussure, see Aarsleff, *From Locke to Saussure*, 356–71.

86. See Marx, *Naissance de la critique moderne*, 28. On Valéry's relation to Bergson, see Blanchot, "Bergson et le symbolism," in *Faux pas*, 132–5, and de Man, "Modern Poetics in France and Germany," in *Critical Writings*, 153–4. See also Valéry, "Discours sur Bergson," in "Variété," *Œuvres*, vol. 1, 883–5.

87. "The object of art is to put to sleep the active or resistant powers of our personality and thus to bring us in a state of perfect responsiveness in which we realize the idea that is suggested to us and sympathize with the feeling that is expressed." *Les données immédiates de la conscience*, 11; *Time and Free Will*, 14.

88. Marx, *Naissance de la critique moderne*, 57.

89. Valéry, "Fragments des mémoires d'un poème," in *Œuvres*, vol. 1, 1487.

90. "Ses intuitions, Valéry ne pourrait peut-être pas les organiser en philosophe, faute de technique, car cette anti-technique qu'est, pour M. Bergson, la philosophie pure, ne peut venir au jour de l'intelligence que par une technique d'autant plus serrée qu'on va chercher plus loin, aux antipodes de la technique, une philosophie plus pure. Mais surtout il [Valéry] ne *veut* pas les organiser en philosophe." Thibaudet, *Paul Valéry*, 30.

91. "A quoi vise l'art, sinon à nous montrer, dans la nature et dans l'esprit, hors de nous et en nous, des choses qui ne frappaient pas explicitement nos sens et notre conscience?" Bergson, *La pensée et le mouvant*, 149; *The Creative Mind*, 112. Bergson remained inherently suspicious of literature; his art of choice was music.

92. Pflug, *Henri Bergson. Quellen und Konsequenzen einer induktiven Metaphysik*, 139.

93. "Instinct devenu désintéressé, conscient de lui-même, capable de réflechir sur son objet et de l'élargir indéfiniment." *Evolution créatrice*, 178; *Creative Evolution*, 159.

94. Guerlac, *Thinking in Time*, 21.

95. The same essay contests the basic claim of psychophysics postulating "differences of quantity between purely internal states." Differences of intensity in sensation, unlike numbers, simply cannot be ranked on a scale. As Catherine Malabou notes, "the question of quantifying intensity remained a point of profound disagreement between Bergson and Binet, as shown by [. . .] a meeting of the Société Française de Philosophie on December 2, 1904 [. . .]. Binet offered a severe critique of Bergson's arguments in *Matière et mémoire* [. . .] while Bergson countered that experimental study and the rigorous measuring of the higher forms of intellectual activity were impossible." *Essai sur les données immédiates de la conscience*, 1, 172; *Time and Free Will: An Essay on the Immediate Data of Consciousness*, 1, 229; *Morphing Intelligence*, 42.

96. Malabou, *Morphing Intelligence*, 42.

97. Nias, *The Artificial Self: The Psychology of Hippolyte Taine*, 203.

98. Taine, *De l'intelligence*, vol. 1, 124; *On Intelligence*, vol. 1, 71.

99. Bergson, *Matière et mémoire*, 6; *Matter and Memory*, 14.

100. Guerlac, *Thinking in Time*, 120.

101. Bergson, *Pensée et le mouvant*, 220; *The Creative Mind*, 165.

102. Worms, "L'intelligence gagnée par l'intuition."

103. Bergson, "De l'intelligence."

104. Bergson, "De l'intelligence," 275–6.

105. "C'est une adaptation exacte de l'esprit à son objet, un ajustement parfait de l'attention, une certain tension intérieure, qui nous donne au moment voulu la force nécessaire pour saisir promptement, étreindre vigoureusement, retenir durablement." Bergson, "De l'intelligence," 276. Bergson proceeds to argue that while there is no such thing as a universally intelligent person, there are "mysterious laws of analogy" that secretly link domains of intelligence between themselves. Here one might think of the "miracle of analogy" discovered by the Proustian narrator toward the end of *À la recherche*.

106. Canguilhem, *Études d'histoire et de philosophie des sciences concernant les vivants et la vie*, 348.

107. Guerlac, *Thinking in Time*, 7.

108. Bergson, *L'Évolution créatrice*, 192; *Creative Evolution*, 171–2.

109. "De cet océan de vie, où nous sommes immergés, nous aspirons sans cesse quelque chose, et nous sentons que notre être ou du moins notre intelligence qui le guide, s'y est formé par une espèce de solidification locale. La philosophie ne peut être qu'un effort pour se fondre à nouveau dans le tout. L'intelligence se résorbant

dans son principe, revivra à rebours sa propre genèse. Mais l'entreprise ne pourra plus s'achever tout d'un coup; elle sera nécessairement collective et progressive. Elle consistera dans un échange d'impressions qui, se corrigeant entre elles et se superposant aussi les unes aux autres, finiront par dilater en nous l'humanité et par obtenir qu'elle se transcende elle-même." Bergson, *L'Évolution créatrice*, 192–3; *Creative Evolution*, 172.

110. "Nous ne sommes aisés que dans le discontinu, dans l'immobile, dans la mort. *L'intelligence est caractérisée par une incomprehension naturelle de la vie.*" Bergson, *L'Évolution créatrice*, 166; *Creative Evolution*, 149. Italics in the original.

111. "Notre pensée, sous sa forme purement logique, est incapable de se représenter la vraie nature, la signification profonde du mouvement évolutif." Bergson, *L'Évolution créatrice*, vi; *Creative Evolution*, 2.

112. "Seule l'émotion diffère en nature à la fois de l'intelligence et de l'instinct, à la fois de l'égoïsme individuel intelligent et de la pression sociale quasi-instinctive," Deleuze, *Le bergsonisme*, 116; *Bergsonism*, 110.

113. "Il n'y a pas d'intelligence où on ne découvre des traces d'instinct, pas d'instinct surtout qui ne soit entouré d'une frange d'intelligence." Bergson, *L'Évolution créatrice*, 136–7; *Creative Evolution*, 125.

114. "La fonction essentielle de l'intelligence sera donc de démêler, dans les circonstances quelconques, le moyen de se tirer d'affaire." Bergson, *L'Évolution créatrice*, 151; *Creative Evolution*, 137.

115. "L'intelligence est caractérisée *par la puissance indéfinie de décomposer selon n'importe quelle loi et de recomposer en n'importe quel système*." Bergson, *L'Évolution créatrice*, 158; *Creative Evolution*, 142. Italics in the original.

116. "*Il y a des choses que l'intelligence seule est capable de chercher, mais que, par elle même, elle ne trouve jamais. Ces choses, l'instinct seul les trouverait; mais il ne les cherchera jamais.*" Bergson, *L'Évolution créatrice*, 152; *Creative Evolution*, 138. Italics in the original.

117. Bergson, *La pensée et le mouvant*, 95; *The Creative Mind*, 70.

118. Bergson, *L'Évolution créatrice*, 156; *Creative Evolution*, 141.

119. "Vous pourrez spéculer aussi intelligemment que vous voudrez sur le mécanisme de l'intelligence, vous n'arriverez jamais, par cette méthode, à le dépasser. Vous obtiendrez du plus compliqué, mais non pas du supérieur ou même simplement du différent. Il faut brusquer les choses, et, par un acte de volonté, pousser l'intelligence hors de chez elle." Bergson, *L'Évolution créatrice*, 195; *Creative Evolution*, 173–4.

120. Nias, *The Artificial Self: The Psychology of Hippolyte Taine*, 204.

121. "Sans arrière-pensée d'utilisation pratique, en se dégageant des formes et des habitudes proprement intellectuelles." Bergson, *L'Évolution créatrice*, 197; *Creative Evolution*, 175–6.

122. "Plus le sentiment est profond et la coïncidence complète, plus la vie où ils nous replacent absorbe l'intellectualité en la dépassant. Car l'intelligence a pour fonction essentielle de lier le même au même, et il n'y a d'entièrement adaptable au cadre de l'intelligence que les faits qui se répètent. Or, sur le moment réel de la durée l'intelligence trouve sans doute prise après coup, en reconstituant le nouvel état avec une série de vues prises du dehors sur lui et qui ressemblent autant que possible au déjà connu: en ce sens, l'état contient de l'intellectualité 'en puissance' pour ainsi dire." Bergson, *L'Évolution créatrice*, 201; *Creative Evolution*, 179.

123. "Ni l'espace n'est aussi étranger à notre nature que nous nous le figurons, ni la matière n'est aussi complètement étendue dans l'espace que notre intelligence et nos sens se la représentent." Bergson, *L'Évolution créatrice*, 204; *Creative Evolution*, 181.

124. "Ce qui me déplaît dans la doctrine de Bergson, c'est tout ce que je pense déjà sans qu'il le dise, et tout ce qu'elle a de flatteur, de caressant même, pour l'esprit. Plus tard, on croira découvrir partout son influence sur notre époque, simplement que lui-même est de son époque et qu'il cède sans cesse au movement. D'où son importance représentative." Gide, *Journal*, vol. 1: 1887-1925, 1246; translated as Gide, *The Journals of André Gide*, vol. 2, 348.

125. In the chapters that follow, accounts of sources that these writers might have read have been largely elided because, barring a few exceptions, their familiarity with them rarely exceeded the most passing knowledge. Their responses were thus closer to reactions to a contemporary critical idiom than scholary interventions.

Chapter Two: Abdicating Intelligence

1. Proust, *À la recherche*, vol. 1, 256; *In Search*, vol. 1, 369.

2. "L'intelligence, le sens moral"; "la douceur, le naturel, l'intelligence": Proust, "Confidence du 4 Septembre 1887, sur l'album d'Antoinette Faure," *Essais*, 54.

3. Finn, *Figures of the Pre-Freudian Unconscious*, 155.

4. Proust, "Contre l'obscurité," *Essais*, 130-35.

5. For Proust, deadening habit founds most of what is considered "innate," "natural" or "characteristic" about individuals. In fact, these contingent qualities could just as easily be dissociated from self over time. "If Habit," writes Proust, "is a second nature, it keeps us in ignorance of the first, and is free of its cruelties and enchantments." In Beckett's gloss on this phrase, "Habit has laid its veto on this [primary] form of perception, its action being precisely to hide the essence—the Idea—of the object in the haze of conception—preconception." See Beckett, *The Grove Centenary Edition*, vol. 4, 517.

6. See Prendergast, *The Classic*, 4. Much of the charge in *Contre Sainte-Beuve* is directed against Hippolyte Taine, and the subordinate relation of literature to philosophy. Proust questions whether art bears a heteronomous or autonomous relation to philosophy, whether art needs philosophy to interpret and supplement its figural truth. On this point, see Quaranta, "L'autonomie de l'art: critique de l'intelligence, intériorisation du génie et parodie," in *Le Génie de Proust*, 183-201.

7. Prendergast, *The Classic*, 295.

8. The existence and nature of the unconscious—and *cérébration inconsciente*—was the object of a heated debated between Charcot, Janet, Ribot, Binet, and Bergson, well before the arrival of Freud. See Finn, "Before Freud: The Quarrel of the Unconscious in Late Ninteenth-Century France," in *Figures of the Pre-Freudian Unconscious*, 11-42.

9. Deleuze, *Proust et les signes*, 9-10; *Proust and Signs*, 3-4.

10. Barthes, "Une idée de recherche," *Œuvres complètes*, vol. 3, 918; *The Rustle of Language*, 272-3.

11. Barthes, "Une idée de recherche," *Œuvres complètes*, vol. 3, 920.

12. Many critics have noted Proust's hesitation, around 1909, in choosing a form for his critique of Sainte-Beuve and intelligence, vacillating between writing a novel

and an essay. Barthes suggests that he chose a third form—literature as research—that would change the future of writing. See Barthes, "Longtemps, je me suis couché de bonne heure," *Œuvres complètes*, vol. 5, 463.

13. Empson, *Seven Types of Ambiguity*, 249.

14. Watt, "État Présent: Marcel Proust."

15. Proust to Rivière (February 6, 1914), "Enfin je trouve un lecteur qui *devine* que mon livre est un ouvrage dogmatique et une construction! Et quel bonheur pour moi que ce lecteur, ce soit vous!" Kolb, ed., *Marcel Proust-Jacques Rivière: Correspondance, 1914-1922*, 7. See also Rivière, *Quelques progrès en l'étude du cœur humain*.

16. On Proust and psychoanalysis, see Tadié, *Le lac inconnu: Entre Proust et Freud*.

17. When the French word is not translated into English by its homonym, the various attempts are: "intellect," "mind," "understanding," "agreement," "secret understanding," "signs of complicity," and "to be on good or bad terms with someone."

18. Proust, *Essais*, 133.

19. "Les mots ne sont pas de purs signes pour le poète." Proust, *Essais*, 133.

20. Descombes, *Proust: Philosophie du roman*, 87. Descombes points out that in "Proust's day philosophy was generally accepted as meaning the construction of a *world-system* more satisfying than the one constructed by *common sense*." It is because systems were supposed to be more logically coherent, and free of the contradictory observations of average men and common language, that they invariably appeared "obscure."

21. Barthes, "Une idée de recherche," in *Œuvres complètes*, vol. 3, 917–21. A similar claim could be made about the massive library of criticism on Proust. Christie McDonald divides this archive into three large phases: the phenomenological approach of the mid-1960s focused on consciousness, the object, and time; the semiological and structuralist analyses of the 1960s and 1970s, which drew attention to linguistic and rhetorical patterns; and the genetic criticism which studied manuscripts from the 1980s onward. Descombes proposes a distinction between historical, aesthetic, and philosophical readings, which rely on facts, interpretations, and concepts accordingly. See McDonald, *The Proustian Fabric* and Descombes, *Proust: Philosophie du Roman*; *Proust: Philosophy of the Novel*. Influential early readings of Proust that do not quite fit within these categories for criticism are those by Walter Benjamin (1929), Samuel Beckett (1930), Georges Bataille (1943; 1957) and Maurice Blanchot (1959).

22. Barthes, "Proust et les noms" (1972), in *Œuvres complètes*, vol. 4, 66–77.

23. Wood, "Enemies: Proust's Intelligence."

24. One would be hard pressed to argue that Proust's novel owes its philosophical or structural fabric to nineteenth-century psychologists, as Edward Bizub proposes in *Proust et le moi divisé*. Joshua Landy shows the limits of such an argument in "Proust Among the Psychologists."

25. "Mais le XVIIe siècle français avait une manière très simple de dire des choses profondes. Quand j'essaye dans mes romans de me mettre à son école, des philosophes me reprochent d'employer dans le sens courant le mot 'intelligence,' etc." Proust, "A propos du 'style' de Flaubert," *Essais*, 1220. On more about the polemic over Flaubert's style, see Philippe, *Sujet, verbe, complément*, 47–66. Like Virginia Woolf's claim about human character changing "on or around December 1910," the historical dimension of Proust's remark should not be taken too literally.

26. Compagnon, "Joseph Reinach et l'éloquence française."
27. "Je sais bien que Descartes avait commencé avec son 'bon sens' qui n'est pas autre chose que les principes rationnels. On apprenait cela autrefois en classe. Comment M. Reinach qui, différent au moins en cela des Émigrés, a tout appris et n'a rien oublié, ne le sait-il pas et peut-il croire que Descartes a fait preuve d'une 'ironie délicieuse,' en disant que le bon sens est la chose du monde la mieux partagée? Cela signifie dans Descartes que l'homme le plus bête use malgré soi du principe de causalité, etc." Proust, *Essais*, 1220.
28. Finn, *Figures of the Pre-Freudian Unconscious*, 60–61.
29. "L'intelligence [...] cherche à se faire trépidation d'un bateau à vapeur, couleur des mousses, îlot dans une baie [...]. Cette ondulation-là, c'est de l'intelligence transformée, qui s'est incorporée à la matière. Elle arrive aussi à pénétrer les bruyères, les hêtres, le silence et la lumière des sous-bois," Proust, *Essais*, 1213–14.
30. Kristeva, *Le temps sensible*; Descombes, *Proust: Philosophie du roman*; Landy, *Philosophy as Fiction*; De Beistegui, *Proust as Philosopher*.
31. Fraisse, *L'éclectisme philosophique de Marcel Proust*, 73–174.
32. White, *Marcel Proust*, 34–5.
33. Galeteria, "Contre Taine: Sur une source théorique de la *Recherche*."
34. "Conception intellectualiste de la réalité [qui] ne laissait de vérité que dans la science." Proust, *Essais*, 703.
35. Schopenhauer, *The World as Will and Representation*, cited in Quaranta, *Le Génie de Proust*, 184.
36. "Les puissantes intuitions de mon esprit, même un soir d'épuisement ou de mort. Principes de renouvellement qu'est la vérité. Comme homme spirituel on se fige comme les autres." Proust, *Le Carnet de 1908*, 59.
37. Quaranta, *Le Génie de Proust*, 190.
38. See Freed-Thall, "Prestige of a Momentary Diamond."
39. "Chaque jour j'attache moins de prix à l'intelligence. Chaque jour je me rends mieux compte que ce n'est qu'en dehors d'elle que l'écrivain peut ressaisir quelque chose de nos impressions passées, c'est-à-dire atteindre quelque chose de lui-même et la seule matière de l'art. Ce que l'intelligence nous rend sous le nom de passé n'est pas lui. En réalité, comme il arrive pour les âmes des trépasssés dans certaines légendes populaires, chaque heure de notre vie aussitôt morte s'incarne et se cache en quelque objet materiel. Elle y reste captive, à jamais captive, à moins que nous ne rencontrions l'objet. À travers lui nous la reconnaissons, nous l'appelons, et elle est délivrée. L'objet où elle se cache—ou la sensation, puisque tout objet par rapport à nous est sensation—, nous pouvons très bien ne le rencontrer jamais. Et c'est ainsi qu'il y a des heures de notre vie qui ne ressusciteront jamais." Proust, *Essais*, 695–96. Published translations of this text bury much of the issue by translating *l'intelligence* as "intellect." See *Proust on Art and Literature*, 19.
40. The italics are in the text. Deleuze, *Proust et les signes*, 40; *Proust and Signs*, 29.
41. Wood, "Enemies: Proust's Intelligence."
42. "Une œuvre où il y a des théories est comme un objet sur lequel on laisse la marque du prix." Proust, *À la recherche*, vol. 4, 461; *In Search*, vol. 6, 278.
43. As Leo Spitzer notes, Proust's critical method consisted of stylistic textual analysis: "the critic reads, disturbed at first by the strangeness of the style, stops on a 'somewhat transparent sentence' allowing one to appreciate the character of the

artist, in pursuing his reading finds a second, then a third sentence of the same time, and ends by intuiting a 'law.'" *Études de style*, 397–8.

44. See Barthes, *The Rustle of Language*, 279.

45. "Or 'l'intelligence' (mot proustien) [...] si l'on suit la tradition romantique, est une puissance qui blesse ou assèche l'affect; Novalis présentait la poésie comme 'ce qui guérit les blessures de l'entendement'; le Roman aussi peut le faire, mais pas n'importe lequel: un roman qui ne soit pas fait selon les idées de Sainte-Beuve." Barthes, "Longtemps je me suis couché de bonne heure." *Œuvres complètes*, vol. 5, 461.

46. Unless this is meant to be read as an "autobiographical" reading: Barthes's own mother had recently died when he wrote these lines, an event that would inform his later projects, from the lecture course on the *Neutre* to the *Préparation du roman*, both of which attempt to theorize a science of the singular, modeled upon the act of mourning. See Rushworth, "Mourning and Intermittence between Proust and Barthes."

47. "Bien que chaque jour j'attache moins de prix à la critique et même, s'il faut le dire, à l'intelligence, car de plus en plus je la crois impuissante à cette recréation de la réalité qui est tout l'art, c'est à l'intelligence que je me fie aujourd'hui pour écrire un essai tout critique. Sainte-Beuve." Proust, *Essais*, 695.

48. "Et cette infériorité de l'intelligence c'est tout de même à l'intelligence que qu'il faut demander de l'établir. Car si l'intelligence ne mérite pas la couronne suprême, c'est elle seule qui est capable de la décerner. Et si elle n'a dans la hiérarchie des vertus que la seconde place, il n'y a qu'elle qui soit capable de proclamer que l'instinct doit occuper la première." Proust, *Essais*, 700; *Proust on Art and Literature*, 25–6.

49. Bouveresse, *La connaissance de l'écrivain*, 206.

50. Proust, *À la recherche*, vol. 4, 458; *In Search*, vol. 4, 275.

51. Indeed, as Valéry argues, "pure intelligence" is a matter of superficial forms and surfaces that leave no room for the pathos of humane profundities. The following chapter on Valéry discusses this point in further detail.

52. "Car l'instinct dicte le devoir et l'intelligence fournit les prétextes pour l'éluder"; "Là où la vie emmure, l'intelligence perce une issue [...]. L'intelligence ne connaît pas ces situations fermées de la vie sans issue." *À la recherche*, vol. 4, 458, 484; *In Search*, vol. 4, 275, 313. Cocking, *Proust: Collected Essays*, 165.

53. Cocking, *Proust: Collected Essays*, 174.

54. One of the more original readings of these episodes is Anne Carson's poetic litany, *The Albertine Workout*.

55. "Les êtres les plus bêtes, par leur gestes, leurs propos, leurs sentiments involontairement exprimés manifestant des lois qu'ils ne perçoivent pas, mais que l'artiste surprend en eux." Proust, *À la recherche*, vol. 4, 480; *In Search*, vol. 6, 307. Here it seems that Proust partakes of a French literary tradition going back to Flaubert for which a particular kind of stupidity, *bêtise*, rather than intellectuality, becomes the most fecund source of literary creation. For Cocteau, "la magnifique intelligence de Proust s'est surtout plu à peindre la bêtise: ce qui fatigue à la longue." *Le passé défini*, vol. 1, 298.

56. Proust, *À la recherche*, vol. 2, 192; *In Search*, vol. 2, 566–7.

57. Here it is helpful to recall how the Verdurins manage the public reputations of the luminaries of the *petit clan*, influencing the market value of Elstir's painting,

Bergotte's prose, Vinteuil's music, Cottard's medical practice, and Brichot's success as an academic and a pamphleteer.

58. Bal, *Mottled Screen: Reading Proust Visually*.
59. This account of "creative intelligence" draws on Leonard, "Intelligence."
60. Ruskin, *Modern Painters*, in *The Works of John Ruskin*, vol. 6, 38.
61. Ruskin, *The Elements of Drawing*, in *The Works of John Ruskin*, vol. 15, 27–8; Leonard, "Intelligence," 512.
62. "L'effort qu'Elstir faisait pour se dépouiller en présence de la réalité de toutes les notions de son intelligence était d'autant plus admirable que cette homme qui avant de peindre se faisait ignorant, oubliait tout par probité (car ce qu'on sait n'est pas à soi), avait justement une intelligence exceptionellement cultivée." Proust, *À la recherche*, vol. 2, 196; *In Search*, vol. 2, 572–3.
63. Proust, *À la recherche*, vol. 3, 692; *In Search*, vol. 5, 244.
64. This is hardly the task the Proustian novel sets for art. It remains deeply unclear, *pace* Bersani, how Proust's aesthetic, or his narrator's, could be inscribed into a "culture of redemption." As Benjamin points out, any aesthetic redemption there is in Proust remains enclosed in the work, and no reader can hope to find shelter within it: "there is nothing more ingenious or more loyal than the way [Proust] nonchalantly and constantly strives to make the reader aware that 'redemption is my own private show'" (*die Erlösung ist meine private Veranstaltung*). See "Über einige Motive bei Baudelaire," in *Gesammelte Schriften*, vol. 1.2, 643.
65. "Il est arrivé que Mme de Sévigné, comme Elstir, comme Dostoïevski, au lieu de présenter les choses dans l'ordre logique, c'est-à-dire en commençant par la cause, nous montre d'abord l'effet, l'illusion qui nous frappe. C'est ainsi que Dostoïesvki présente ses personnages. Leurs actions nous apparaissent aussi trompeuses que ces effets d'Elstir où la mer a l'air d'être dans le ciel. Nous sommes tout étonnés d'apprendre que cet homme sournois est au fond excellent, ou le contraire." *À la recherche*, vol. 3, 880; *In Search*, vol. 5, 510.
66. "Noble, inintelligible et précis." *À la recherche*, vol. 1, 207; *In Search*, vol. 1, 296.
67. *À la recherche*, vol. 1, 343; *In Search*, vol. 1, 496.
68. "Aussi débarrassée des formes analytiques du raisonnement que si elle s'était exercée dans le monde des anges." *À la recherche*, vol. 3, 760; *In Search*, vol. 5, 341.
69. Leibniz, "Leibniz à Goldbach, le 17 d'avril 1712."
70. Beckett, *Proust* in *The Grove Centenary Edition*, vol. 4, 553.
71. Nattiez, *Proust Musicien*, 83–4.
72. "Elle choisissait des morceaux ou tout nouveaux ou qu'elle ne m'avait encore joués qu'une fois ou deux car, commençant à me connaître, elle savait que je n'aimais proposer à mon attention que ce qui m'était encore obscur, et pouvoir, au cours de ces exécutions successives, rejoindre les unes aux autres, grâce à la lumière croissante, mais hélas! dénaturante et étrangère de mon intelligence, les lignes fragmentaires et interrompues de la construction, d'abord presque ensevelie dans la brume [. . .]. Elle devinait qu'à la troisième ou quatrième exécution, mon intelligence en ayant atteint, par conséquent mis à la même distance, toutes les parties, et n'ayant plus d'activité à déployer à leur égard, les avait réciproquement étendues et immobilisées sur un plan uniforme. Elle ne passait pas cependant encore à un nouveau morceau, car sans peut-être bien se rendre compte du travail qui se faisait en moi, elle savait qu'au moment

où le travail de mon intelligence était arrivé à dissiper le mystère d'une oeuvre, il était bien rare qu'elle n'eût pas, au cours de sa tâche néfaste, attrapé par compensation telle ou telle réflexion profitable." *À la recherche*, vol. 3, 874; *In Search*, vol. 5, 501–2.

73. Leonard, "Intelligence," 513.

74. See Deleuze, "Boulez, Proust and Time: 'Occupying without Counting.'"

75. "Ce travail de l'artiste, de chercher à apercevoir sous de la matière, sous de l'expérience, sous des mots quelque chose de différent, c'est exactement le travail inverse de celui que, à chaque minute, quand nous vivons détourné de nous-même, l'amour-propre, la passion, l'intelligence, et l'habitude aussi accomplissent en nous, quand elles amassent au-dessus de nos impressions vraies, pour nous les cacher entièrement, les nomenclatures, les buts pratiques que nous appelons faussement la vie." *À la recherche*, vol. 4, 474–5; *In Search*, vol. 6, 299–300.

76. "Or la recréation par la mémoire d'impressions qu'il fallait ensuite approfondir, éclairer, transformer en équivalents d'intelligence, n'était-elle pas une des conditions, presque l'essence même de l'oeuvre d'art?" *À la recherche*, vol. 4, 621; *In Search*, vol. 6, 525.

77. "La vraie vie, la vie enfin découverte et éclaircie, la seule vie par conséquent pleinement vécue, c'est la littérature. Cette vie qui, en un sens, habite à chaque instant chez tous les hommes aussi bien que chez l'artiste. Mais il ne la voient pas, parce qu'ils ne cherchent pas à l'éclaircir. Et ainsi leur passé est encombré d'innombrables clichés qui restent inutiles parce que l'intelligence ne les a pas 'développés.' Notre vie; et aussi la vie des autres; car le style pour l'écrivain aussi bien que la couleur pour le peintre est une question non de technique mais de vision. Il est révélation, qui serait impossible par des moyens directs et conscients, de la différence qualitative qu'il y a dans la façon dont nous apparaît le monde, différence qui, s'il n'y avait pas l'art, resterait le secret éternel de chacun." *À la recherche*, vol. 4, 474; *In Search*, vol. 4, 298–9.

78. Focusing on the verbal incommunicability of the *moi profond*, Sabin argues that, "within the French tradition [...] the investigation of cliché in Flaubert's *Dictionnaire* is extended by Proust in the direction of an even more profound rejection of common speech." On the different semiotic implications of "cliché" and "stéréotype" vs. "idiom," see Sabin, *The Dialect of the Tribe*, 110–42.

79. "Mais [...] l'intelligence n'est pas l'instrument le plus subtil, le plus puissant, le plus approprié pour saisir le vrai, ce n'est qu'une raison de plus pour commencer par l'intelligence et non par un intuitivisme de l'inconscient, par une foi aux pressentiments toute faite. C'est la vie qui, peu à peu, cas par cas, nous permet de remarquer que ce qui est le plus important pour notre coeur, ou pour notre esprit, ne nous est pas appris par le raisonnement mais par des puissances autres. Et alors, c'est l'intelligence elle-même qui se rendant compte de leur supériorité, abdique par raisonnement devant elles, et accepte de devenir leur collaboratrice et leur servante. Foi expérimentale." *À la recherche*, vol. 4, 7; *In Search*, vol. 5, 569.

80. Wood, *Literature and the Taste of Knowledge*, 120.

81. Proust, *Cahier 57, fo. 32v*. Quoted in Hughes, *Marcel Proust*, 177.

82. "Un philosophe qui n'était pas assez moderne pour elle, Leibniz, a dit que le trajet est long de l'intelligence au coeur." *À la recherche*, vol. 3, 315; *In Search*, vol. 4, 437–8.

83. Leibniz, *Essais de théodicée*, vol. 3, § 311.

84. Interview with Elie-Joseph Bois, "A la recherche du temps perdu," November 13, 1913, in *Le Temps*, in Proust, *Contre Sainte-Beuve*, 559. See also Maya, "L'anti-intellectualisme de Proust," 90.

85. "Un petit coup au carreau, comme si quelque chose l'avait heurté suivi d'une ample chute légère comme des grains de sable qu'on eût laissés tomber d'une fenêtre au-dessus, puis la chute s'étendant, réglant, adoptant un rythme, devenant fluide, sonore, musicale, innombrable, universelle: c'était la pluie." *À la recherche*, vol. 1, 100; *In Search*, vol. 1, 140–41. Shklovsky discusses the effect of "defamiliarization" in "Art as Device," and Watt the effect of "delayed decoding" in *Conrad in the Nineteenth Century*, 270–285.

86. See Samuels, "Jews and the Construction of French Identity from Balzac to Proust."

87. Proust, *À la recherche*, vol. 2, 97; *In Search*, vol. 2, 433.

88. Samuels, *Inventing the Israelite: Jewish Fiction in Nineteenth-Century France*, 252.

89. On the divide between the maternal and the paternal attitudes toward the narrator's stance on the Dreyfus affair, see McDonald, *The Proustian Fabric*, 67 and passim. For a wide-ranging reading of Proust in relation to Dreyfus, see Rose, *Proust among the Nations*.

90. Deleuze, *Proust et les signes*, 123; *Proust and Signs*, 101.

91. Benda, *La France byzantine*, 290–91. Benda nonetheless recognized Proust as being free from the twin evils of nationalism and class-based politics that constituted *la trahison des clercs* or the betrayal of France by its intellectuals. See Hughes, *Proust, Class, Nation*, 253–7.

92. "L'impression est pour l'écrivain ce qu'est l'expérimentation pour le savant, avec cette différence que chez le savant le travail de l'intelligence précède et chez l'écrivain vient après." Proust, *À la recherche*, vol. 4, 459; *In Search*, vol. 6, 276.

93. Wais, *Die Gegenwartsdichtung der europäischen Völker*, 214–15. Upon reading excerpts from *À l'ombre des jeunes filles en fleurs*, Pierre Janet had already reduced Proust's narrator to an example of "maladies of reverie" prone to the "loss of happiness in the real world." See Finn, *Figures of the Pre-Freudian Unconscious*, 188–9.

94. For classic discussions of Proust and homosexuality, see Sedgwick, *Epistemology of the Closet* and Ladenson, *Proust's Lesbianism*.

95. Arendt, *Reflections on Literature and Culture*, 156–66.

96. Étiemble, "Proust et la crise de l'intelligence," 166. My thanks to Michael Wood for pointing me to this study.

97. Proust, *À la recherche*, vol. 4, 468; *In Search*, vol. 6, 924–5.

98. Wais is wrong not only about Proust's genre, but also in terms of technique. As Jean-Yves Tadié points out, Proust strategically preferred interrogation to monologue. He perfected this method for interrogating laws that lay beyond language very early. Tadié argues that all the unlikely passages on military intelligence at the garrisons of Doncières and during the First World War are important precisely because they interrogate covert, non-verbal forms of intelligence, which take on their fully coded significance in the garrison and on the battlefield. Significantly, Charlus criticizes those who form nationalist opinions on such military action through the distorted lens of the mass media of newspaper journalism rather than insider knowledge. See

Tadié, *Marcel Proust*, 130. For an analysis of the intelligence and wartime in Proust, see Mahuzier, "Proust, War, Intelligence, and Idiocy."

99. "While Balzac's creatures, for instance, are easily reducible to the power relations of the society of which they are, so to speak, the algebraic expressions, a character of Proust materializes into the opacity of a particular language, and it is reality at this level that his whole historical situation—his profession, his class, his wealth, his heredity, his bodily frame—is integrated and ordered. In this way, Literature begins to know society as a Nature, the phenomena of which it might perhaps be able to reproduce." Barthes, *Œuvres complètes*, vol. 1, 219; *Writing Degree Zero*, 80.

100. Dupee notes a shift in the "relations of the one and the many" between the nineteenth-century French novelists and Proust: "Persons of marked imaginative powers were the exceptions in Balzac, Stendhal, and Flaubert [. . .]. The exceptional souls have taken over society in Proust's conception of it." "The Imagination of Duchesses," 110.

101. *À la recherche*, vol. 2, 702; vol. 2, 798; vol. 2, 749; vol. 2, 482; vol. 3, 428–9; vol. 4, 394; vol. 1, 247; vol. 2, 835, respectively.

102. Lucey, "Proust and Bourdieu: Distinction and Form," *What Proust Heard*, 185–219.

103. Descombes, "Suis-je invite?" *Proust: Philosophie du roman*, 194–210.

104. "Puis, il apartenait à cette catégorie d'hommes intelligents qui ont vécu dans l'oisiveté et qui cherchent une consolation et peut-être une excuse dans l'idée que cette oisiveté offre à leur intelligence des objets aussi dignes d'intérêt que pourrait faire l'art ou l'étude, que la 'Vie' contient des situations plus intéressantes, plus romanesques que tous les romans." *À la recherche*, vol. 1, 190; *In Search*, vol. 1, 272.

105. "Nos amis m'ont dit que vous étiez souffrant. Je vous plains beaucoup. Et puis malgré cela je ne vous plains pas trop, parce que je vois bien que vous devez avoir les plaisirs de l'intelligence." *À la recherche*, vol. 1, 559; *In Search*, vol. 2, 196.

106. "Mon père avait pour mon genre d'intelligence un mépris suffisamment corrigé par la tendresse pour qu'au total, son sentiment sur tout ce que je faisais fût une indulgence aveugle." *À la recherche*, vol. 1, 447; *In Search*, vol. 2, 35.

107. "Quant aux 'joies de l'intelligence,' pouvais-je appeler ainsi ces froides constatations que mon œil clairvoyant ou mon raisonnement juste relevaient sans aucun plaisir et qui restaient infécondes?" *À la recherche*, vol. 4, 444; *In Search*, vol. 6, 254.

108. "Car mon intelligence devait être une, et peut-être même n'en existe-t-il qu'une seule dont tout le monde est co-locataire, une intelligence sur laquelle chacun, du fond de son corps particulier, porte ses regards, comme au théâtre où si chacun a sa place, en revanche, il n'y a qu'une seule scène." *À la recherche*, vol. 1, 558; *In Search*, vol. 2, 194–5.

109. Wood, "Enemies: Proust's Intelligence."

110. Benjamin, "The Image of Proust," 206. For a close reading of this essay, see Jacobs, "Walter Benjamin: Image of Proust," *In the Language of Walter Benjamin*, 39–58.

111. Benjamin, "The Image of Proust" (trans. modified), 212.

112. *À la recherche*, vol. 1, 1527.

113. "—Tout dépend de ce que vous appelez intelligence, dit Forcheville qui voulait briller à son tour. Voyons, Swann, qu'entendez-vous par intelligence? Voilà! s'écria Odette, voilà les grandes choses dont je lui demande de me parler, mais il ne veut

jamais.—Mais si... protesta Swann.—Cette blague! dit Odette.—Blague à tabac? demanda le docteur.—Pour vous, reprit Forcheville, l'intelligence, est-ce le bagout du monde, les personnes qui savent s'insinuer?" *À la recherche*, vol. 1, 256; *In Search*, vol. 1, 369. Here I have modified the Montcrieff–Kilmartin translation by consulting Davis's choices in her edition of *Swann's Way*.

114. "—Il y a, dit Brichot en martelant les syllabes, une définition bien curieuse de l'intelligence dans ce doux anarchiste de Fénelon... —Écoutez! dit à Forcheville et au docteur Mme Verdurin, il va nous dire la définition de l'intelligence par Fénelon, c'est intéressant, on n'a pas toujours l'occasion d'apprendre cela. Mais Brichot attendait que Swann eût donné la sienne. Celui-ci ne répondit pas et en se dérobant fit manquer la brillante joute que Mme Verdurin se réjouissait d'offrir à Forcheville." *À la recherche*, vol. 1, 256; *In Search*, vol. 1, 370–71.

115. The marriage first appears in *Albertine disparue*, but there is a further twist of irony in *Temps retrouvé*, when after his death Odette describes Forcheville as a mediocre man, adding that she only ever loved intelligent people: "c'était un médiocre et je n'ai jamais pu aimer véritablement que des gens *intelligents*." *À la recherche*, vol. 4, 598, my emphasis.

116. Fraisse, *L'éclectisme philosophique de Marcel Proust*, 130.

117. Devillairs, "Fénelon et le Dieu de la Première Méditation de Descartes."

118. Fénelon, *Œuvres complètes*, vol. 2, 192. Davis also cites this passage in her translator's notes in *Swann's Way*, 455, n. 60.

119. Proust, *Essais*, 1272.

120. "Pour dire un dernier mot du roman dit d'analyse, ce ne doit être nullement un roman d'intelligence pure, selon moi. Il s'agit de tirer hors de l'inconscient, pour le faire entrer dans le domaine de l'intelligence, mais en tâchant de lui garder sa vie, de ne pas la mutiler, de lui faire subir le moins de déperdition possible, une réalité que la seule lumière de l'intelligence suffirait à détruire, semble-t-il. Pour réussir ce travail de sauvetage, toutes les forces de l'esprit, et même du corps, ne sont pas de trop." Proust, "Une enquête littéraire," *Essais*, 1267.

121. Cocking, *Proust: Collected Essays*, 10.

122. Shattuck, *Proust's Way*, 221.

Chapter Three: Testing Intelligence

1. Among many other writers, Blanche also painted a portrait of Proust in 1892. See Proust's essay on Blanche, in *Essais*, 1193–2107.

2. Major studies in English of Valéry's work include volumes by Christine Crow, Paul Gifford, Geoffrey Hartman, Jean Hytier, W. N. Ince, James Lawler, Suzanne Nash, Judith Robinson, and Norman Suckling. The literature in French is too vast to survey in a note. From Gide and Paulhan to Michel Jarrety and William Marx, Valéry remains a constant object of critical inquiry. One of the most interesting documents in this massive archive is Maurice Merleau-Ponty's recently transcribed 1953 Collège de France lecture course on the literary uses of language. Merleau-Ponty approaches the vexed question anew through the experience of two writers he considers representative of the classic and the modern: Stendhal and Valéry. See Merleau-Ponty, *Recherches sur l'usage littéraire du langage*.

3. The four quatrains on the façade are meant to allegorize peace and culture.

4. For a compelling version of this argument, see the concluding chapter in Cronan, *Against Affective Formalism: Bergson, Matisse, Modernism*, 221–51.

5. Oster, *Monsieur Valéry*, 51–6; 104–13.

6. Guerlac, *Thinking in Time*, 14–41.

7. Valéry, *Œuvres*, vol. 1, 1314–39; "Poetry and Abstract Thought," *Collected Works*, vol. 7, 52–81.

8. Adorno, "Valérys Abweichungen," in *Noten zur Literatur*, 165; "Valéry's Deviations," *Notes to Literature*, vol. 1, 143.

9. Such an operation extends to images. In the epistemic context of the period, the image forms a distinct problematic, as demonstrated by Bergson's *Matter and Memory*. The *Cahiers* show us Valéry's version of this concern.

10. *Intelligence-Trouvaille* also contains an element of both chance and composition—in the shared root with the poet as *trouvère* or *trouveur*.

11. The following account of Proust-Valéry relations draws on Mauriac Dyer, "Paul Valéry" entry in *Dictionnaire Marcel Proust*, 1019–20.

12. Proust, *Correspondance*, vol. 18, 252.

13. "À Monsieur Paul Valéry qui dans le Cimetière Marin a fixé l'abstrait dans un concret mouvant comme personne ne l'avait fait jusque-là." Mauriac Dyer, "Paul Valéry," 1019.

14. Ils "créent tout ce dont une lignée de mille artistes seulement bien portants n'auraient pu faire un alinéa." Proust, "À propos de Baudelaire," *Essais*, 1237.

15. "Je ne me suis pas encore excusé de mon silence auquel devant un si grand poète j'eusse préféré substituer une voix louangeuse." Proust, *Correspondance*, vol. 21, 384.

16. "Quoique je connaisse à peine un seul tome de la grande oeuvre de Marcel Proust, et que l'art même du romancier me soit un art presque inconcevable, je sais bien toutefois, par ce peu de la *Recherche du Temps perdu* que j'ai eu le loisir de lire, quelle perte exceptionnelle les Lettres viennent de faire; et non seulement les Lettres, mais d'avantage cette secrète société que composent, à chaque époque, ceux qui lui donnent sa véritable valeur." Valéry, *Œuvres*, vol. 1, 769–70; "Homage to Marcel Proust," *Collected Works*, vol. 9, 295.

17. "L'intérêt de ses ouvrages réside dans chaque fragment. On peut ouvrir le livre où l'on veut; sa vitalité ne dépend point de ce qui précède, et en quelque sorte de l'*illusion acquise*; elle tient à ce qu'on pourrait nommer l'*activité propre* du tissu même de son texte." Valéry, *Œuvres*, vol. 1, 772; *Collected Works*, vol. 9, 298.

18. "Quant à ses moyens, ils se rattachent sans conteste à notre tradition la plus admirable. On trouve quelquefois que ses ouvrages ne sont pas d'une lecture bien aisée. Mais je ne cesse de répondre qu'il faut bénir les auteurs difficiles de notre temps. S'ils se forment quelques lecteurs, ce n'est pas seulement pour leur usage. Ils les rendent du même coup à Montaigne, à Descartes, à Bossuet." Valéry, *Œuvres*, vol. 1, 774; *Collected Works*, vol. 9, 300–301.

19. "Tous ces grands hommes parlent abstraitement; ils raisonnent; ils approfondissent; ils dessinent d'une seule phrase tout le corps d'une pensée achevée. Ils ne craignent pas le lecteur, ils ne mesurent pas leur peine, ni la sienne. Encore un peu de temps, et nous ne les comprendrons plus." Valéry, *Œuvres*, vol. 1, 774; *Collected Works*, vol. 9, 301.

20. "Le fait Proust montre que ce n'est pas là une condition littéraire—." Valéry, *Cahiers*, vol. 1, 143.

21. "Je suppose que Proust avait une excellente mémoire, et se plaisait à en raviver les détails les plus fins, comme on colore, pour le microscope, les chevelures des neurones. J'ai mauvaise mémoire. J'oublie les événements en tant qu'ils auraient pu être ceux d'un autre individu. Je n'ai pas de souvenir d'enfance. En somme, le passé est pour moi aboli dans sa structure chronologique et narrable. J'ai le sentiment invincible que ce serait perdre mon temps que de retrouver le temps perdu." Valéry, *Œuvres*, vol. 1, 1788. In his notes for an auto-analysis ("Propos me concernant") we find a variant of this resistance to Proust, coupled with an attack addressed to Freud: "Non, non! Je n'aime pas du tout me retrouver en esprit sur les voies anciennes de ma vie. Ce n'est pas moi qui rechercherais le Temps perdu! Encore moins approuverais-je ces absurdes analyses qui inculquent aux gens les rébus les plus obscènes, qu'ils auraient déjà composés dès le sein de leur mère." *Œuvres*, vol. 2, 1508.

22. Letter to Aimé Lafont, September 1922: "Figurez-vous que l'on s'éveille au milieu de la nuit, et que toute sa vie se revive, et se parle à soi même [. . .]. Sensualité, souvenirs, paysages, émotions, sentiments de son corps, profondeur de la mémoire." Valéry, *Lettres à quelques-uns*, 144; *Œuvres*, vol. 1, 1626.

23. Curtius, *Französischer Geist im zwanzigen Jahrhundert*. Merleau-Ponty brings together the two figures to elaborate his notion of "flesh" and the body in "Entrelacs—le chiasme" at the end of *Le visible et l'invisible*.

24. Benjamin, "Über einige Motive bei Baudelaire," *Gesammelte Schriften*, vol. 1.2, 639; "On Some Motifs in Baudelaire," *Selected Writings*, vol. 4, n. 163, 352–3.

25. Thematically, "Valéry–Proust Museum" in *Prisms* is one of Adorno's most Benjaminian essays, influenced as it is by the latter's readings of Proust and Valéry, as well as the notion of the critical *Nach- und Fortleben* ("afterlife," "living on," "survival") of works of art.

26. Blanchot makes a similar point in his two texts on museums ("The Museum, Art, and Time," and "Museum Sickness") in *Friendship*, 12–49.

27. Adorno, *Prisms*, 176–7.

28. This view adapts and extends Stendhal's definition of beauty as "a promise of happiness."

29. Adorno, *Prisms*, 180–81.

30. Adorno, *Prisms*, 181.

31. "Leur mère est morte, leur mère Architecture. Tant qu'elle vivait, elle leur donnait leur place, leur emploi, leurs contraintes. La liberté d'errer leur était refusée. Ils avaient leur espace, leur lumière bien définie, leurs sujets, leurs alliances. . . . Tant qu'elle vivait, ils savaient ce qu'ils voulaient . . .—Adieu, me dit cette pensée, je n'irai pas plus loin." Valéry, *Œuvres*, vol. 2, 1293; *Collected Works*, vol. 12, 206.

32. "On raisonne, c'est-à-dire on vagabonde, chaque fois qu'on n'a pas la force de s'astreindre à faire passer une impression par tous les états successifs qui aboutiront à sa fixation, à l'expression." Proust, *À la recherche*, vol. 4, 461; *In Search*, vol. 6, 279.

33. Rancière, *La parole muette*, 167; *Mute Speech*, 167.

34. "Le grand intérêt de l'art classique est peut-être dans les suites de transformations qu'il demande pour exprimer les choses en respectant les conditions *sine qua non* imposées." Valéry, *Œuvres*, vol. 2, 636; *Collected Works*, vol. 14, 210.

35. Rancière, *La parole muette*, 168; *Mute Speech*, 168.

36. "Longtemps, longtemps, la *voix humaine* fut base et condition de la *littérature*. La présence de la voix explique la littérature première, d'où le classique prit forme et cet admirable *tempérament*. Tout le corps humain présent *sous la voix*, et support, condition d'équilibre de l'*idée* . . .

Un jour vint où l'on sut lire des yeux sans épeler, sans entendre, et la littérature en fut tout altérée.

Évolution de l'articulé, à l'effleuré, —du rythmé et enchaîné à l'instantané, —de ce que supporte et exige un auditoire à ce que supporte et emporte un œil rapide, avide, libre sur une page."

Valéry, *Œuvres*, vol. 2, 549; *Collected Works*, vol. 14, 99.

37. Rancière, *La parole muette*, 171; *Mute Speech*, 170–71.

38. Bowie, "Dream and the Unconscious," 262.

39. Benjamin, *Gesammelte Schriften*, vol. 1.1, 100–101.

40. Valéry insists that any theory of language must proceed from the recognition that "inner language creates an *Other* within the *Same*," *Cahiers 1894–1914*, ed. Robinson-Valéry and Celeyrette-Pietri, vol. 24, 31. See Lechantre, "Valéry Bouchoreille"; Crow, *Paul Valéry and the Poetry of Voice*.

41. Here, as elsewhere, Benjamin opposes the *Schriftsteller* to the *Dichter*.

42. Thibaudet, *Paul Valéry*, 13.

43. For a recent collection of his poetry and prose in translation, see Rudavsky-Brody, *The Idea of Perfection: The Poetry and Prose of Paul Valéry*.

44. Many of Valéry's previously unanthologized poems were published in the 1922 collection *Charmes*.

45. Merleau-Ponty, *Recherches sur l'usage littéraire du langage*, 64, n. 5.

46. Merleau-Ponty, *Recherches sur l'usage littéraire du langage*, 110.

47. Thibaudet, *Paul Valéry*, 78–9.

48. Hartman, "Valéry," 100.

49. Sarraute, *Paul Valéry ou L'Enfant de l'éléphant*, 9–57.

50. Adorno, "Valéry's Deviations," *Notes to Literature*, vol. 1, 147.

51. Oster locates key concerns of postwar thought from Althusser ("Idéologie et appareil idéologique d'Etat") and Sartre (the "pratico-inerte") to Bourdieu (the management of subjects by symbolic orders) and Foucault in Valéry's critique of idols and doxa. See *Monsieur Valéry*, 97.

52. "Un homme d'intelligence profonde et impitoyable pourrait-il s'intéresser à la littérature? Sous quel rapport? Où la placerait-il dans son esprit?" Valéry, *Œuvres*, vol. 2, 570; *Collected Writings*, vol. 14, 125.

53. "J'appelle ainsi toutes croyances qui ont de commun l'oubli de la condition verbale de la littérature. Ainsi existence et *psychologie des personnages*, ces vivants *sans entrailles*." Valéry, *Œuvres*, vol. 2, 569; *Collected Writings*, vol. 14, 125.

54. "LITTÉRATURE: Ce qui est la 'forme' pour quiconque est le 'fond' pour moi." Valéry, *Œuvres*, vol. 1, 1456.

55. Hartman, "Valéry," 171.

56. For a discussion of Valéry's critique of realism in the novel, see Genette, "La littérature comme telle." For a novelist's critique of Valéry's ideas on the novel, see Gracq, *En lisant, en écrivant*, 115–16, 124–7.

57. "Une conséquence plaisante de cet état de choses, en littérature par exemple, est l'abondance des romans. Chacun y va de sa petite 'observation.' Par besoin

d'épuration, M. Paul Valéry proposait dernièrement de réunir en anthologie un aussi grand nombre que possible de débuts de romans, de l'insanité desquels il attendait beaucoup. Les auteurs les plus fameux seraient mis à contribution. Une telle idée fait encore honneur à Paul Valéry qui, naguère, à propos des romans, m'assurait qu'en ce qui le concerne, il se refuserait toujours à écrire: *La marquise sortit à cinq heures.* Mais a-t-il tenu parole?" Breton, *Manifestes du surréalisme*, 16–17; *Manifestoes of Surrealism*, 6–7. For wider context, see Josipovici, "The Marquise went out at Five."

58. Valéry does mention variants in the *Cahiers*: "La comtesse prit le train à 8 heures"; "La marquise prit le train de 9 heures," *Cahiers*, ed. Robinson, vol. 2, 1162.

59. Aragon satirizes Valéry's style as syntactic obscurantism concealing false depth: "*Je me voyais me voir* cette formule qui résume assez le Père Ed. Teste et sa soeur la petite Parque, ce jeu de miroirs, qui cache un peu partout des fantômes de profondeur." See Aragon, *Traité du style*, 155. The accusation largely misses the mark, as Valéry was adamantly a thinker of surfaces, rather than depths. In an aphorism, Valéry insists, "le plus profond, c'est la peau."

60. The attack is not exclusively directed against the minor novelist. Breton takes aim at everyone from Dostoevsky to Proust and Barrès.

61. "Toute oeuvre littéraire est à chaque instant exposée à l'*initiative* du lecteur. A chaque instant, celui-ci peut réagir à sa lecture en effectuant des substitutions qui affectent ou le détail de l'ouvrage ou son évolution. Le décor, le récit, le ton peuvent être plus ou moins altérés, avec conservation plus ou moins sensible de l'ensemble. Presque tout l'art consiste à faire oublier à ce lecteur son pouvoir personnel d'intervention, à devancer sa réaction par tous moyens, ou à les rendre très difficile par la rigueur et les perfections de la forme. Tout roman peut recevoir un ou plusieurs dénouements tout autres que celui qu'il offre; mais il est plus malaisé de modifier comme l'on veut un poème bien exécuté." *Œuvres*, vol. 2, 407–8; *Collected Works*, vol. 2, 87–88.

62. This is also the sentence that Barthes invokes in his discussion of the historian's use of the preterite. See "L'écriture du Roman," *Le degré zéro de l'écriture, Œuvres completes*, vol. 1, 190.

63. Ironically, the marquise enjoyed a legendary afterlife through the initiatives of a few intrepid readers. She lent the title to a novel by Claude Mauriac, became a refrain in Donoso's *Casa de Campo*, was analyzed by John Barth, and became the object of a detective novel, Gilles Heuré's *L'homme de cinq heures*—in which the seemingly random time of her outing is revealed to be the overdetermined hour at which Trotsky was assassinated and Benjamin ended his life. While these connections prove intriguing, one risks losing sight of the objection underlying the sentence.

64. Valéry, *Œuvres*, vol. 2, 38; *Collected Works*, vol. 6, 36–7.

65. Gide referred to some of his brief narratives as "soties."

66. "Valéry ne voit dans les moyens et les effets de l'art que l'arbitraire, conventions et c'est parce qu'il nie la valeur réelle de la forme qu'il en affirme et observe les exigences: il n'est parfait écrivain que parce que la perfection n'a pour lui aucune vérité." Blanchot, *La part du feu*, 212; *The Work of Fire*, 216.

67. Paulhan, "Carnet du spectateur."

68. Blanchot, *La part du feu*, 213; *The Work of Fire*, 217.

69. "En somme, le sens qui est la tendance à une substitution mentale uniforme, unique, résolutoire, est l'objet, la loi, la limite d'existence de la prose pure." Valéry, *Œuvres*, vol. 1, 1510; *Collected Works*, vol. 7, 156.

70. "Est prose l'écrit qui a un but exprimable par un autre écrit." Valéry, Œuvres, vol. 1, 555; Collected Works, vol. 14, 106.

71. "Il ne s'agit point du tout en poésie de transmettre à quelqu'un ce qui se passe d'intelligible dans un autre. Il s'agit de créer dans le premier un état dont l'expression soit précisément et singulièrement celle qui le lui communique [. . .] il en résulte que le lecteur jouit d'une très grande liberté quant aux idées, liberté analogue à celle que l'on reconnaît à l'auditeur de musique." Valéry, Œuvres, vol. 1, 1511; Collected Works, vol. 7, 157.

72. "On pourrait illustrer cette opposition [prose et vers] des extrêmes en l'exagérant quelque peu: on dirait que le langage a pour limites la *musique*, d'un côté, *l'algèbre*, de l'autre." See "Propos sur la poésie," Œuvres, vol. 1, 1370. Elsewhere, Valéry, following Mallarmé, compared the mystery of verse to "algebra cultivated for its own ends."

73. Valéry was finely attuned to choreography and dance, as evinced by "Philosophie de la danse" and other essays. Œuvres, vol. 1, 1390–1404.

74. For a discussion of Valéry's remark in terms of a larger history of literary physiology, see Dames, *The Physiology of the Novel*, 26–32.

75. Jarrety, *Valéry devant la littérature: Mesure de la limite*, 295–6.

76. "Pourquoi un 'roman' ne serait-il pas le journal d'une journée de quelqu'un? Ce serait cet enchaînement incohérent et pourtant enchainement de substitutions de moments et phrases bien différents qui constitue—mais pour un *certain regard*—*de temps à autre*—une journée de nous—qu'il faudrait *d'abord* étudier abstraitement." *Cahiers*, ed. Robinson, vol. 2, 1355.

77. Davis, "Valéry and the Truth of Poetry and Prose," 261.

78. "Quant à moi, j'ai passé ma vie à chercher des énoncés et non des solutions." *Cahiers 1894–1914*, ed. Robinson-Valéry and Celeyrette-Pietri, vol. 13, 663. For a consideration of Valéry as an "antiphilosopher," see Bouveresse, "Philosophy from an Antiphilosopher: Paul Valéry."

79. *Gesammelte Schriften*, vol. 2.1, 388; Benjamin, *Selected Writings*, vol. 2, 532–3.

80. Valéry, Œuvres, vol. 2, 11; Collected Works, vol. 6, 3.

81. Agamben's reading of *Monsieur Teste* relates the first-person pronoun "I" to the seeing "eye" and the voice via Descartes and Wittgenstein. See Agamben, "L'io, l'occhio, la voce," 98.

82. Oster, *Monsieur Valéry*, 79.

83. For readings that deal with Teste and possibility, see Deppman, "Re-Presenting Paul Valéry's *Monsieur Teste*"; Mairesse, "Return to Teste? Or 'What is a Man Capable of?': Valéry, Anthropologist of Modernity."

84. "Il n'y a pas d'image certaine de Teste." Œuvres, vol. 2, 63; Collected Works, vol. 6, 67.

85. Mehlman, "Craniometry and Criticism," 89.

86. The epigraph to the cycle, taken from a letter by the Dutch Cartesian Johannes de Raey to the theologian Philipp Van Limborch, announces *vita cartesii res est simplicissima*. For a Cartesian reading of Teste, see Goldmann, "Valéry: Monsieur Teste."

87. Roland Barthes, *Le Neutre*, 133. See also "Roland Barthes," in Joqueviel-Bourjea, ed., *Faut-il oublier Valéry?*, 65–8.

88. Charney, "*Monsieur Teste* and *Der Mann ohne Eigenschaften*: Homo possibilis in Fiction."

89. Kaufmann, "1925, December. I cannot abide stupidity," 878.
90. On the vagaries of this translation, see Derrida, *The Beast and the Sovereign*, vol. 1, 187–206.
91. Valéry, *Œuvres*, vol. 2, 18; *Collected Works*, vol. 6, 12.
92. "L'art délicat de la durée, le temps, sa distribution et son régime [. . .] était une des grandes recherches de M. Teste [. . .]. Il était l'être absorbé dans sa variation, celui [. . .] qui se livre tout entier à la discipline effrayante de l'esprit libre." *Œuvres*, vol. 2, 17–18; *Collected Works*, vol. 6, 11. For the Bergsonian subtext of this passage, see Guerlac, *Literary Polemics*, 114–15.
93. "l'histoire d'un bonhomme qui pense," letter to Gide, May 18, 1896; cited in Oster, *Monsieur Valéry*, 79.
94. "Apôtre intime de la consciousness" and "un mystique et un physicien de la Self-conscience—pure et appliquée" [*sic*], *Cahiers*, ed. Robinson, vol. 1, 262–3.
95. "Chaque esprit qu'on trouve puissant commence par la faute qui le fait connaître. En échange du pourboire public, il donne le temps qu'il faut pour se rendre perceptible." *Œuvres*, vol. 2, 16; *Collected Works*, vol. 6, 9.
96. "On est *beau*, on est extraordinaire que pour les autres! *Ils* sont mangés par les autres!" *Œuvres*, vol. 2, 20; *Collected Works*, vol. 6, 15.
97. Marion, *God without Being: Hors-Texte*, 112–13. Marion invokes Teste in a discussion of attitudes of phenomenological "suspension."
98. See Valéry, "Essai sur le mortel" (1892), *Cahiers 1894–1914*, ed. Robinson-Valéry and Celeyrette-Pietri, vol. 3, 559–70, and *Œuvres*, vol. 2, 1395.
99. "Tout ce que je fais et pense n'est que Specimen de mon possible. L'homme est plus général que sa vie et ses actes. Il est comme *prévu* pour plus d'éventualités qu'il n'en peut connaître. M. Teste dit: Mon possible ne m'abandonne jamais." *Œuvres*, vol. 2, 73; *Collected Works*, vol. 6, 78.
100. "Je n'ai jamais eu plus fortement l'impression du *quelconque*. C'était un logis quelconque, analogue au point quelconque des théorèmes—et peut-être aussi utile. Mon hôte existait dans l'intérieur le plus général." *Œuvres*, vol. 2, 23; *Collected Works*, vol. 6, 18.
101. "Ce n'est pas vivre que vivre sans objections, sans cette résistance vivante, cette proie, cette autre personne, adversaire, reste individué du monde, obstacle et ombre du moi—autre moi—intelligence rivale, irrépressible—ennemi, le meilleur ami, hostilité divine, fatale—intime." *Œuvres*, vol. 2, 45; *Collected Works*, vol. 6, 45.
102. Here a comparison suggests itself with the opening scene of the *Recherche*, in which the body becomes the repository of non-integrated memories.
103. Starobinski, "Monsieur Teste face à la douleur," 93–120. For Valéry's resistance to Freud, see Derrida, *Marges*, 356–63.
104. Oster notes that Valéry's objection to psychic automatism separated him from the Surrealists: "prétendre exprimer par un 'automatisme psychique' [. . .] le fonctionnement réel de la pensée (*self-variance* et *self-consciousness*) lui interdisait précisément d'accorder le moindre crédit à la réduction surréaliste à l'illimité et au mythe." Oster, *Monsieur Valéry*, 134.
105. "La vie d'intelligence constitue un univers lyrique incomparable, un drame complet, où ne manquent ni l'aventure, ni les passions, ni la douleur (qui s'y trouve d'une essence toute particulière), ni le comique, ni rien d'humain." *Œuvres*, vol. 1, 796; *Collected Works*, vol. 9, 18.

106. "Les choses du monde ne m'intéressent que sous le rapport de l'intellect; tout par rapport à l'intellect." *Œuvres*, vol. 1, 994; *Collected Works*, vol. 10, 30–31. For Thibaudet, Valéry's thought tends toward "relation" rather than "substance": "Le monde dans lequel vit la pensée de Valéry est moins un monde de choses qu'un monde de rapports. Là où la pente de l'intelligence mène à penser substance, il appartient à la famille de ceux qui pensent relation." Thibaudet, *Paul Valéry*, 42.

107. "Ce point de vue [de l'intellecte] est *faux*, puisqu'il sépare l'esprit de tout le reste des activités; mais cette operation abstraite et cette falsification sont inévitables: tout point de vue est faux." *Œuvres*, vol. 1, 995; *Collected Works*, vol. 10, 31.

108. "Elles montent, originales; dans un ordre insensé; mystérieusement mues jusque vers le midi admirable de ma présence, où brûle, telle qu'elle est, la seule chose qui existe, l'une quelconque." Valéry, "Agathe," *Œuvres*, vol. 2, 1393; *Collected Works*, vol. 2, 212.

109. Thibaudet, *Paul Valéry*, 24.

110. On this point, see Morimoto, *Paul Valéry*, 279.

111. "Je ne sais pourquoi [. . .] on loue un auteur d'être humain quand tout ce qui agrandit l'homme est l'inhumain ou surhumain et que d'ailleurs on ne peut approfondir quoi que ce soit sans perdre bientôt ce commerce impur, cette vue mêlée des choses qu'on appelle humanité." *Cahiers 1894–1914*, ed. Robinson-Valéry and Celeyrette-Pietri, vol. 18, 20.

112. Geoffrey Hartman suggests that the aesthetic in Valéry is not affective or human but a "withholding from view of all human, that is to say, all immediately moral, emotional, or sensual attributes, and it is precisely this kind of retardation which is often termed aesthetic." See Hartman, "Valéry," 104.

113. "'Intelligence'?—Sensibilité articulée—à plusieurs dim[ensions]—toutefois *intelligenti pauca?*—ce peu, c'est une hypersensibilité—un rien donne tout. Donc attente, donc organisation cachée." Valéry, *Cahiers 1894–1914*, ed. Robinson-Valéry and Celeyrette-Pietri, vol. 18, 281.

114. For a rare attempt to approach the entirety of the 29-volume edition of the *Cahiers 1894–1914*, ed. Robinson-Valéry and Celeyrette-Pietri, see de la Rochefoucauld, *En lisant les "Cahiers" de Paul Valéry*.

115. Tadié, *Marcel Proust*, 108.

116. Proust writes, "Quand je lis par exemple un poème de Leconte de Lisle, tandis que j'y goûte les voluptés infinies d'autrefois, l'autre *moi* me considère, s'amuse à considérer les causes de mon plaisir, les voit dans un certain rapport entre moi et l'oeuvre, par là détruit la certitude de la beauté *propre* de l'oeuvre, surtout immédiatement des conditions de beauté opposées, tue enfin presque tout mon plaisir." Letter to his philosophy professor, Alphonse Darlu, October 2, 1888. *Correspondance*, vol. 1, 121–2.

117. Tadié, *Marcel Proust*, 108–9; *Marcel Proust: A Life*, 80.

118. Adorno, "Valérys Abweichungen," in *Noten zur Literatur*, 158–202; "Valéry's Deviations," *Notes to Literature*, vol. 1, 137–73.

119. Adorno, "Valéry's Deviations," *Notes to Literature*, vol. 1, 137.

120. "Teste: L'intelligence, l'esprit, ces mythes inévitables, chacun se les définit—se les donnent, se les refusent à telle occasion—L'idée que j'en ai ce matin—je l'exprime ainsi: l'intelligence est le pouvoir des substitutions (en tant que plus adaptées). Son problème serait: À un ensemble proposé de choses, circonstances, en substituer un autre tel que . . . etc.—et ainsi ce qui n'était possible, le devient. Le rôle des langages

dans l'intelligence paraît alors très clair. C'est une substitution typique fondamentale. Substitutions de mots et subst[itutions] de choses. Comprendre est opérer une substitution—traduction." Valéry, *Cahiers*, ed. Robinson, vol. 1, 952; *Cahiers/Notebooks*, ed. Stimpson, vol. 3, 107.

121. Kay, Cave, and Bowie, eds., *A Short History of French Literature*, 262.

122. On the tension between theme and problem, source and origin in Valéry, see Derrida's "Qual Quelle: Les sources de Valéry," in *Marges*, 333-8.

123. "Tu te vois obéir avec un retard. Compare avec ce qui se passe quand tu cherches un mot, un nom 'oublié' . . . Ce retard, c'est toute la psychologie, que l'on pourrait qualifier paradoxalement: ce qui se passe entre quelque chose [. . .] et elle-même!" Letter to Pierre Louÿs, November 13, 1915, *Œuvres*, vol. 2, 1483.

124. "l'idée du fonctionnement m'a dominé. J'ai pensé que le type Acte-Réflexe était le fait fondamental." *Cahiers 1894-1914*, ed. Robinson-Valéry and Celeyrette-Pietri, vol. 27, 312.

125. See Gauchet, "Un réflexologue inconnu: Valéry," in *L'inconscient cérébral*, 153-70.

126. See Morimoto, "Le Réflexe, le mouvement, et l'inconscient," *Paul Valéry*, 181-237.

127. "La substance de celle-ci [de la vie psychique] est *fonctionnement* et ce que nous observons—le voile." *Cahiers*, ed. Robinson, vol. 1, 1057.

128. "L'état naissant du réfléchi est réflexe." *Cahiers*, ed. Robinson, vol. 2, 244.

129. Hartman, "Valéry," 111.

130. The implexe, Derrida comments, is "that which cannot be simplex. It marks the limit of every analytic reduction to the simple element of the point. An implication-complication, a complication of the same and the other which never permits itself to be undone, it divides or equally multiplies infinitely the simplicity of every source, every origin, every presence." *Marges*, 360; *Margins*, 302. For a monograph devoted to the implexe, see Crescimanno, *Implexe, fare, vedere. L'estetica nei Cahiers di Paul Valéry*.

131. "J'entends par l'*Implexe*, ce en quoi nous sommes éventuels." *Œuvres*, vol. 2, 236; *Collected Works*, vol. 5, 57-8.

132. Zaccarello, "Pour une littérature pensée," 36.

133. Morimoto, "L'implexe chez Valéry: une notion de potentialité et la théorie motrice de la psychologie à l'époque de Valéry," in *L'intelligence de la complexité*, 390.

134. "Ils [les psychologues, etc.] entendent par eux [l'Inconscient et le Subconscient] je ne sais quels ressorts cachés, —et parfois, des petits personnages plus malins que nous, très grands artistes, très forts en devinettes, qui lisent l'avenir, voient à travers les murs, travaillent à merveille dans nos caves [. . .] Non, l'*implexe* n'est pas *activité*, tout le contraire. Il est *capacité*. Notre capacité de sentir, de réagir, de faire, de comprendre—individuelle, variable, plus ou moins perçue par nous—, et toujours imparfaitement, et sous des formes indirectes (comme la sensation de fatigue),—et souvent trompeuses." Valéry, *Œuvres*, vol. 2, 234; *Collected Works*, vol. 5, 55-6.

135. Phillipon, *Implexe* in *Le vocabulaire de Valéry*, 45.

136. See "Qual Quelle: Les sources de Valéry," in *Marges*, 346-51; *Margins*, 291-5. Merleau-Ponty too considers Valéry as a model for a more inventive form of philosophy that would acknowledge its written character, namely as an operation on language and sensibility. See *Recherches sur l'usage littéraire de la langue*, 27-8.

137. "Mais la littérature jusqu'ici a peu considéré, que je sache, ce trésor immense de sujets et de situations [. . .]. Que faire de ces termes que l'on ne peut préciser sans les recréer? *Pensée*, *esprit* lui-même, *raison, intelligence, compréhension, intuition* ou *inspiration*? . . . Chacun de ces noms est tour à tour un moyen et une fin, un problème et un résolvant, un état et une idée; et chacun d'eux, dans chacun de nous, est suffisant ou insuffisant, selon la function que lui donne la circonstance." Valéry, *Œuvres*, vol. 1, 797; *Collected Works*, vol. 9, 19.

138. "La mesure de 'l'intelligence' est la promptitude des *réponses* heureuses, inédites, et non réfléchies—Que signifie *heureuses*? (Il arrive que celui-là même qui vient d'émettre une de ces réponses soit bien embarrassé de la justifier—(cf. l'inspiration banale)). Du moins ceci est une des apparences qui font employer le mot 'intelligence.'" Valéry, *Cahiers*, ed. Robinson, vol. 2, 1051; *Cahiers/Notebooks*, ed. Stimpson, vol. 2, 154.

139. This notion recalls the function of metaphor in Proust, that which reveals the essential commonality linking two different objets in "the necessary rings of a beautiful style." Proust, *À la recherche*, vol. 4, 468; *In Search*, vol. 3, 924–5.

140. "Mon mouvement le plus désespéré, le plus certain fut celui qu'exprimaient pour moi seul et sans autre rigueur, ces mots: Tout par l'intelligence, tout remplacé, combattu, attaqué, défendu par l'intelligence. Ce nom, quel sens s'y attachait?—

Il est certain que j'appelai d'abord ainsi le pouvoir de changer l'eau en vin, de remplir l'ennui, de couper les racines de la douleur, l'analyse et l'imagination mêlées—La volonté de supprimer, soit par substitution, soit par observation, soit par le grossissement qui les défigure sans le toucher,—les pensées ou les heures ou les difficultés ou les fantômes—quand ces formations étaient contre moi.

Au lieu d'un plaisir qu'on ne peut pas avoir ou qu'on ne peut avoir qu'impur, mêlé de craintes—se plaçait l'idée—le succédané.

Je tendais simultanément à composer le réel et l'imaginaire et à ne jamais confondre l'idée et la sensation, le signe et la chose. Je voulais tout reconstruire avec ce respect de distinction, à l'*état pur*—et net, même l'informe et le vague dont j'ai fait une catégorie,—et je désirais la richesse de nouvelles combinaisons qui résulte de la bonne division des composants, des opérations, des forces . . .

Il y a quelque chose d'une religion dans ce propos.

Mon pouvoir séparatif et distinctif." *Cahiers*, ed. Robinson, vol. 1, 71.

141. This linguistic operation explains part of Valéry's appeal for the *Tel Quel* group and thinkers associated with Structuralism.

142. "Chose très remarquable. Mes moyens étaient au-dessous de ces ambitions. Je le savais. J'en étais souvent désespéré. Parfois je me disais que cette insuffisance était au contraire favorable à ma clarté. Mon intelligence, pour se mieux saisir, *devait* être pour une bonne part, simulée, voulue, et donc ressentie plus nettement par moi [. . .] D'ailleurs j'ai toujours joué la difficulté, puisque la facilité est automatisme—Se fait sans y penser.

L'intelligence a pour département tout ce que l'automatisme ne règle ou ne résout pas. Elle n'est pas définie (pour moi) par le *trouver*, mais bien par le *chercher*. Parvenue à l'état habituel (elle-même!) elle dédaigne ce qu'elle trouve et ce qu'elle a trouvé. Elle est fidèle au *quid agendum* et au *nihil reputans actum*.—Il arrive que cette disposition ou éducation réagisse sur ses pouvoirs, lui fasse trouver des difficultés insurmontables dans les facilités d'hier, la paralyse devant un rien." Valéry, *Cahiers*, ed. Robinson, vol. 1, 72.

143. This situation is akin to observing intelligence, rather than possessing it, as the narrator of *La soirée avec Monsieur Teste* realizes.

144. *Cahiers*, ed. Robinson, vol. 1, 1026.

145. "Il y a une Intelligence-Recherche,—et une Intelligence-Trouvaille, une des demandes et une des réponses. Les uns ont l'esprit toujours éveillé et d'un éveil interrogeant. Ils trouvent des résistances, des arrêts excitants de toutes parts où les autres ne s'inquiètent pas. Les seconds,—qui ne sont pas toujours les mêmes—produisent des productions parfois sans cause et non attendues d'eux-mêmes. Ils inventent sans cesse. Parfois, ils ne trouvent qu'après, la question dont la réponse leur est venue." *Cahiers*, ed. Robinson, vol. 1, 1026.

146. Brooks, *Realist Vision*, 12.

147. Jameson, *The Antinomies of Realism*, 4–5.

148. "Faîtes moi un roman cérébral et sensuel et je vous couvrirai d'or." Cited in Gifford and Stimpson, eds., *Reading Paul Valéry: Universe in Mind*, 144.

149. "Quant au roman sensuel et cérébral, rien que la pensée d'écrire matériellement un volume me rend vache et fou." Cited in Jarrety, *Paul Valéry*, 542.

150. "Quant au roman 'cérébral et sensuel'—diable!—je crois bien que je suis l'homme le moins fait pour bâtir un roman. Toutefois, je vous confesse que je suis en train d'essayer le montage d'un conte fantaisiste ou féerique. Je voudrais obtenir un système de composition très étrange à la vérité, et aussi éloigné que vous voudrez l'imaginer de la fabrication ordinaire, mais adapté à mon genre d'esprit qui me paraît de travailler selon mes manies et mes forces à un ouvrage d'*apparence* 'roman.'" Cited in Jarrety, *Paul Valéry*, 542.

151. In his correspondence with Pierre Louÿs in June 1917, Valéry admits that he thought (in vain) that he had in fact discovered the secret of prose. Valéry to Louÿs, June 6, 1917, in Gide, Valéry, Louÿs, *Correspondances à trois voix*, 1261.

152. "Robinson, au milieu de ses biens, redevenait un homme—c'est-à-dire un animal indécis, un être qui ne peut se définir par les circonstances toutes seules." *Œuvres*, vol. 2, 412; *Collected Works*, vol. 2, 93.

153. "Robinson reconstitue sans livre, sans écrit, sa vie intellectuelle [. . .]. Ce Robinson doit voir et traiter 'sub specie intellectus'—les choses humaines." *Œuvres*, vol. 2, 416; *Collected Works*, vol. 2, 97–8.

154. "Robinson finit par avoir fait son île." *Œuvres*, vol. 2, 417; *Collected Works*, vol. 2, 100.

155. "La mémoire n'est que mensonges, et les récits ne conviennent qu'aux enfants. Ceux qui écoutent les histoires sont plus simples que ces reptiles que le charmeur induit à suivre la flûte qui les ensorcelle, ils obéissent à la parole, ils subissent tous les prestiges, ils ont froid, ils ont chaud, ils tremblent, et ils s'exaltent, et ils ressentent sans défense les puissances du langage. Pour eux, les mots sont des êtres, et les phrases des événements!" *Œuvres*, vol. 2, 423; *Collected Works*, vol. 2, 105.

156. "Je chanterai les sens, les sens. Mais les sens sont vérité, et les sens sont pureté. Car ce qui est réel n'a aucune signification et ne vise point autre chose. Ni souvenir, ni interprétation, ni raisonnement, mais les sens et les sensations présentes et les choses immédiates, voilà ce qui est profond." *Œuvres*, vol. 2, 426; *Collected Works*, vol. 2, 108.

157. *Œuvres*, vol. 2, 439; *Collected Works*, vol. 2, 122.

158. *Œuvres*, vol. 2, 442; *Collected Works*, vol. 2, 126.

159. "Mais la réalité est ce qu'elle est, c'est-à-dire qu'elle se refuse ou se dérobe à toute expression; on ne sait ni où elle commence ni où elle finit, et prétendre la représenter est aussi vain que la tentative du peintre, qui prête aux choses et aux visages des traits, cependant que la nature les ignore, n'est ni faite de lignes ni de surfaces . . ." *Œuvres*, vol. 2, 453; *Collected Works*, vol. 2, 137–8.

160. Stimpson, in Gifford and Stimpson, eds., *Reading Paul Valéry: Universe in Mind*, 145.

161. "Le passage d'un certain régime de fonctionnement à quelque autre; passage que des signes ou des symptômes rendent sensible. Pendant une crise, le temps semble changer de nature, la durée n'est plus perçue comme dans l'état ordinaire des choses: au lieu de mesurer la permanence, elle mesure la variation." Valéry, *Œuvres*, vol. 1, 1041; *Collected Works*, vol. 10, 72.

162. "Depuis quelques années, ce mot, déjà embarrassé de plusieurs idées assez différentes, a contracté, par une contagion très fréquente dans les langues, une valeur nouvelle et tout étrangère." Valéry, *Œuvres*, vol. 1, 1042; *Collected Works*, vol. 10, 74.

163. "*Crise d'intelligence* peut donc être entendue comme altération d'une certaine faculté dans tous les hommes; ou bien seulement chez ceux d'entre eux qui en seraient les plus doués, ou *devraient l'être*; ou bien comme crise de l'ensemble des facultés de l'esprit moyen; ou encore crise de la *valeur* et du prix de cette vertu dans la société actuelle ou prochaine. Enfin on peut y voir aussi, en tenant compte du nouveau sens venu des Russes, une crise affectant une classe de personnes qui se trouverait atteinte dans la qualité, ou le nombre, ou les conditions d'existence de ses membres." Valéry, *Œuvres*, vol. 1, 1042–3; *Collected Works*, vol. 10, 74.

164. Valéry, *Œuvres*, vol. 1, 1044; *Collected Works*, vol. 10, 75. In these passages, Valéry comments on the disappearance of leisure, and the increasingly exacting measurements of time itself required by new technology.

165. "On assiste à la disparition de l'*homme qui pouvait être complet*, comme de l'homme qui pouvait matériellement se suffire." Valéry, *Œuvres*, vol. 1, 1045; *Collected Works*, vol. 10, 77.

166. "Ces machines ne laissent point de mortel qu'elles ne l'absorbent dans leurs structures et n'en fassent un sujet de leurs opérations, un élément quelconque de leurs cycles [. . .]. Comme telles, nous ne sommes plus que des objets de spéculations, de véritables *choses*." Valéry, *Œuvres*, vol. 1, 1046–7; *Collected Works*, 10, 78. For Valéry's classic essay on technology, which influenced Benjamin's thinking on technological reproducibility, see Valéry, "La conquête de l'ubiquité," *Œuvres*, vol. 2, 1284–7.

167. "Des intelligences vivantes, les unes se dépensent à servir la machine, les autres à la construire, les autres à prévoir ou à préparer une plus puissante; enfin une dernière catégorie d'esprits se consume à essayer d'échapper à la domination de la machine. Ces intelligences rebelles sentent avec horreur se substituer à ce tout complet et autonome qu'était l'âme des anciens hommes je ne sais quel *daîmon* inférieur qui ne veut que collaborer, s'agglomérer, trouver son apaisement dans la dépendance, son bonheur dans un système fermé qui se fermera d'autant mieux sur soi-même qu'il sera plus exactement créé par l'homme pour l'homme. Mais *c'est une définition nouvelle de l'homme*." Valéry, *Œuvres*, vol. 1, 1050; *Collected Works*, vol. 10, 79–80.

168. Valéry anticipated and inspired a host of postwar thinkers of technology, the self, and the *dispositif*, from Simondon, Deleuze, and Foucault to Kittler and Stiegler.

169. "*Elle ne peut admettre que personne demeure, de qui le rôle et les conditions d'existence ne soient précisément définis.* Elle tend a éliminer les individus imprécis à son point de vue." Valéry, *Œuvres*, vol. 1, 1051; *Collected Works*, vol. 10, 81, italics in the original.

170. "Nous autres, civilisations, nous savons maintenant que nous sommes mortelles." *Œuvres*, vol. 1, 988; *Collected Works*, vol. 10, 23. In *L'autre cap*, Derrida turns to Valéry as a privileged interlocutor to think about the "géographie spirituelle" of Europe, trying to steer between the double bind of eurocentrism and anti-eurocentrism. These pages, written after the fall of the Communist bloc, take on a renewed relevance today during the rise of populist xenophobic nationalism and closed borders. Derrida, *L'autre cap*; see also Weber's reading of these texts in "Mind the Cap: A Singular Approach to Europe," *Singularity*, 209–42.

171. "Le plus intense pouvoir émissif uni au plus intense pouvoir absorbant." Valéry, *Œuvres*, vol. 1, 995; *Collected Works*, vol. 10, 31.

172. "L'Europe deviendra-t-elle *ce qu'elle est en réalité*, c'est-à-dire: un petit cap du continent asiatique? Ou bien l'Europe restera-t-elle *ce qu'elle paraît*, c'est-à-dire: la partie précieuse de l'univers terrestre, la perle de la sphère, le cerveau d'un vaste corps?" Valéry, *Œuvres*, vol. 1, 995; *Collected Works*, vol. 10, 31.

173. "Le phénomène de la mise en exploitation du globe, le phénomène de l'égalisation des techniques et le phénomène démocratique, qui font prévoir une *diminutio capitis* de l'Europe, doivent-ils être pris comme des décisions absolues du destin?" Valéry, *Œuvres*, vol. 1, 1000; *Collected Works*, vol. 10, 36.

174. Heller-Roazen, *Absentees*, 77–82.

175. See especially Husserl, *The Crisis of European Sciences and Transcendental Phenomenology*, 3–18.

176. Derrida, *Heidegger et la question*, 77–9.

177. Valéry, *Œuvres*, vol. 2, 926; *Collected Works*, vol. 10, 18.

178. For a discussion of relativity in relation to Bergsonism, see Canales, *The Physicist and the Philosopher*.

179. "La crise singulière des sciences, qui semblent désespérer maintenant de conserver leur antique idéal d'unification, d'explication de l'univers. L'univers se décompose, perd tout espoir d'une image unique. Le monde de l'extrême petitesse semble étrangement différent de celui qu'il compose par son agglomération. Même l'identité des corps s'y perd, et je ne parlerai pas non plus de la crise du déterminisme, c'est-à-dire de la causalité." Valéry, *Œuvres*, vol. 1, 1036–7; *Collected Works*, vol. 10, 109.

180. Adorno, *Notes to Literature*, 152–3.

181. "Comme des causes naturelles produisent la grêle, le typhon, les épidémies, ainsi les causes intelligentes agissent sur des millions d'hommes, dont l'immense majorité les subit comme des caprices du ciel, de la mer, de l'écorce terrestre. L'intelligence et la volonté affectant les masses en tant que causes physiques et aveugles—*ce qu'on nomme politique*." Valéry, *Œuvres*, vol. 2, 932; *Collected Works*, vol. 10, 229.

182. "La politique fut d'abord l'art d'empêcher les gens de se mêler de ce qui les regarde. À une époque suivante, on y adjoignit l'art de contraindre les gens à décider sur ce qu'ils n'entendent pas." Valéry, *Œuvres*, vol. 2, 947.

183. Valéry, *Œuvres*, vol. 1, 996.

184. "L'inégalité si longtemps observée au profit de l'Europe devait *par ses propres effets* se changer progressivement en inégalité du sens contraire." Valéry, *Œuvres*, vol. 1, 997; *Collected Works*, vol. 10, 34.

185. Valéry, *Œuvres*, vol. 2, 1016–21. A detailed textual history can be found in Yeschua, "Le Yalou: Enigmes, formes, signification." For a compelling reading of *La jeune parque* that takes historico-political insights of "Le Yalou" as its point of departure, see Hamacher, "History, Teary: Some Remarks on *La Jeune Parque*."

186. "L'intelligence, pour vous, n'est pas une chose comme les autres. Elle n'est ni prévue, ni amortie, ni protégée, ni réprimée, ni dirigée; vous l'adorez comme une bête prépondérante. Chaque jour elle dévore ce qui existe. Elle aimerait à terminer chaque soir à un nouvel état de société." Valéry, *Œuvres*, vol. 2, 1018; *Collected Works*, vol. 10, 373.

187. "Un particulier qu'elle enivre, compare sa pensée aux décisions des lois, aux faits eux-mêmes, nés de la foule et de la durée: il confond le rapide changement de son cœur avec la variation imperceptible des formes réelles et des Êtres durables." Valéry, *Œuvres*, vol. 2, 1018; *Collected Works*, vol. 10, 373.

188. "Mais notre écriture est trop difficile. Elle est politique. Elle renferme les idées [...]. Tous les pouvoirs contenus dans l'intelligence restent donc aux lettrés, et un ordre inébranlable se fonde sur la difficulté de l'esprit." Valéry, *Œuvres*, vol. 2, 1020; *Collected Works*, vol. 10, 375–6. See Bush, *Ideographic Modernism: China, Writing, Media*, 122–49. Such passages are hardly free of orientalist tropes: see Said, *Orientalism*, 250–52.

189. Bush, *Ideographic Modernism: China, Writing, Media*, 133.

190. "Car vos idées sont terribles et vos cœurs faibles. Vos pitiés, vos cruautés sont absurdes, sans calme, comme irrésistibles. Enfin vous craignez le sang de plus en plus. Vous craignez le sang et le temps." Valéry, *Œuvres*, vol. 2, 1018; *Collected Works*, vol. 10, 373. Cormac McCarthy uses these words as an epigraph to his *Blood Meridian*: see Cronan, "Paul Valéry's Blood Meridian or How the Reader became a Writer."

191. "L'individu alors sent profondément sa liaison avec ce qui se passe sous ses yeux, l'eau." Valéry, *Œuvres*, vol. 2, 1021; *Collected Works*, vol. 10, 378.

192. "Qui sait si toute notre culture n'est pas une hypertrophie, un écart, un développement insoutenable, qu'une ou deux centaines de siècles auront suffit à produire et à épuiser." Valéry, *Œuvres*, vol. 1, 1066; *Collected Works*, vol. 10, 139. As Bush points out, "Le Yalou" anticipates Foucault's description of the "dissolution of Man" in *Les mots et les choses*, as the traces of Teste and the sage dissolve on the beach. Bush, *Ideographic Modernism*, 138.

193. See Lloyd, "Valéry on Value: The Political Economy of Poetics."

194. Calvino, *Six Memos for the Next Millenium*, 118.

195. Valéry, *Œuvres*, vol. 1, 1043; *Collected Works*, vol. 10, 74.

Chapter Four: Mobilizing Intelligence

1. For an anthology of war writing from the period, see Compagnon, ed., *La grande guerre des écrivains*. Historical accounts that focus on the relations of French intellectuals to the war include Wohl, *The Generation of 1914*; Prochasson and Rasmussen, eds., *Vrai et faux dans la Grande Guerre*; Rasmussen, *Au nom de la patrie*; Codazzi, *André Gide et la Grande Guerre*.

2. Philippe, "Du 'Style NRF,'" in *La Nouvelle Revue Française: Les colloques du centenaire*, 194–207. In the same volume, see also Hunkeler, "Comment défendre l'intelligence française?," 130-143.

3. Macé, *Le temps de l'essai*, 54.

4. For an overview of the period, see Hanna, *The Mobilization of Intellect: French Scholars and Writers during the Great War*, 1–25; Sirinelli, *Intellectuels et passions françaises*, 29–181; Jennings, "France, Intellectuals, and Engagement," *Revolution and the Republic*, 440–506.

5. Koffeman, "La naissance d'un mythe," 17.

6. Michel Puy, "Les revues" (1911); quoted in Koffeman, "La naissance d'un mythe," 18.

7. Koffeman, "La naissance d'un mythe," analyzes the *NRF* in terms of "champ littéraire" and "capital symbolique."

8. An essential reference on the *NRF* is the three-volume study by Anglès, *André Gide et le premier groupe de la Nouvelle Revue Française*. See also Dagan, *La NRF entre guerre et paix*; Koffeman, *Entre classicisme et modernité: La Nouvelle Revue Française*; Brisset, *La "NRF" de Paulhan*; Cerisier, *Une histoire de "La NRF"*; Cerisier et al., eds., *La Nouvelle Revue Française: Les colloques du centenaire*; Kopp, ed., *La place de "La NRF" dans la vie littéraire du XXème siècle*. Special issues of *L'esprit créateur*, "The Critics of the *Nouvelle Revue Française*" (vol. 13, 1974) and *Romanic Review*, "*La Nouvelle Revue Française* in the Age of Modernism" (vol. 99, 2008), deal with the journal in English.

9. Anglès describes the group of writers as constituting a "circuit."

10. Bowie in Kay, Cave, and Bowie, eds., *A Short History of French Literature*, 258–9.

11. Gide, *Journal*, vol. 1: 1887–1925, 846; *The Journals of André Gide*, vol. 2, 68.

12. The full archives of the review from 1908 to 1943 have been available online since its centenary. A significant anthology of the documents discussed here can be found in Hebey, ed., *L'esprit NRF*. For a contextual analysis, see David, *Le procès de l'intelligence*; Richard, "Jacques Rivière et l'orientation idéologique de la *Nouvelle Revue Française*."

13. Rodic, "Lyricism, Aesthetic Tradition, and the Debates on Nationalism in *La Nouvelle Revue Française*," 806.

14. See, for instance, Hanna, *The Mobilization of Intellect: French Scholars and Writers during the Great War*, 44-49.

15. For an overview of Maurras's milieu, see Sutton, *Nationalism, Positivism, and Catholicism: The Politics of Charles Maurras and French Catholics 1890-1914*; Nguyen, *Aux origines de l'Action française: intelligence et politique vers 1900*; Rubenstein. *What's Left? The Ecole Normale Supérieure and the Right*.

16. Thibaudet, "L'Esthétique des trois traditions," 359.

17. Guerlac, "La politique de l'esprit et les usages du classicisme à l'époque moderne," 404–5.

18. "Être stupide comme un conservateur ou naïf comme un démocrate." Maurras, *L'avenir de l'intelligence*, 12.

19. "La notion d'un certain jeu supérieur de l'esprit est donc perdue complètement." Maurras, *L'avenir de l'intelligence*, 8.

20. Maurras infamously declares the Jewish reader, however learned or erudite, incapable of appreciating the simple nobility of Racine's "lieux charmants où mon

coeur vous avait adoré" (*Bérénice*, Act 1). See Compagnon, *Connaissez-vous Brunetière? Enquête sur un antidreyfusard et ses amis*.

21. "Mais qu'importe [. . .] les barbares sont les barbares, et nos amis sont nos amis!" Maurras, *L'avenir de l'intelligence*, 9.

22. Berthelier, *Le style réactionnaire: De Maurras à Houllebecq*, 37.

23. Compagnon, *Les Antimodernes: de Joseph de Maistre à Roland Barthes*, 301.

24. The church and state were formally separated in 1905, following an initiative led largely by Aristide Briand.

25. "La souveraineté de la force brutale est en voie de disparaître et [. . .] nous nous acheminons, non sans heurts, vers la souveraineté de l'intelligence." Maurras, *L'avenir de l'intelligence*, 23.

26. "La règne de l'esprit sur les multitudes"; "La question morale redevient question sociale, point de mœurs sans institutions." Maurras, *L'avenir de l'intelligence*, 17, 22.

27. For a comprehensive overview of the "responsibility of the writer" in this period, see Sapiro, *La responsabilité de l'écrivain*.

28. Maurras, *L'avenir de l'intelligence*, 27.

29. "Le successeur des Bourbons, c'est l'homme de lettres [. . .]. L'époque révolutionnaire marque le plus haut point de la dictature littéraire." Maurras, *L'avenir de l'intelligence*, 30–32.

30. "Le courant naturel de la littérature continue les divagations naturelles de l'âge précédent; mais la suite des faits militaires, économiques et politiques contredit ces divagations une à une." Maurras, *L'avenir de l'intelligence*, 36.

31. Maurras, *L'avenir de l'intelligence*, 38, 46–7.

32. "Plus soucieuse d'*intelligence* (c'était le mot dont on usait) que de jugement, la critique servait et favorisait ce penchant; de sorte que, au lieu de se corriger en se rapprochant de meilleurs modèles de sa race et sa tradition, devenait de plus en plus Gautier et abondait fatalement dans son péché, qui était la manie de la description sans mesure; un Balzac, un Hugo ne s'efforçait que de se ressembler à eux-mêmes, c'est à dire de se distinguer par les caractères d'une excentricité qui leur fut personnelle. L'intervalle devait s'accroître entre le public moyen, bien élevé, lettré, et les écrivains que lui accordait le siècle. Ils commencèrent presque tous par être non méconnus, mais déclarés bizarres et incompréhensibles." Maurras, *L'Avenir de l'intelligence*, 46.

33. At the time, some French journalists colluded with the enemy during the Italian unification and the Austro-Prussian War, accepting funds to promote their causes in the press without considering French national interest.

34. "L'intelligence fut considérée comme explosive, et celui qui vivait de son intelligence en apparût l'ennemi né de l'ordre réel." *L'avenir de l'intelligence*, 48. It suffices to think of the bomb-making anarchist art-critic Félix Fénéon (1861–1944) to see that Maurras's analysis was not far off the mark in this case. That Fénéon had an impeccable flair for recognizing important writers and artists amongst his contemporaries and was simultaneously an expert administrator at the *ministère de la guerre* only complicates the issue of merging literary and administrative authority. See McGuinness, *Poetry and Radical Politics in Fin de Siècle France: From Anarchism to Action Française*, 125–81.

35. "L'avenir, c'est de la crainte ou de l'espérance. Mais on peut craindre à juste titre et espérer à contresens. Où n'atteint pas la précision de la science, l'appréciation

délicate du jugement et de la raison, un mélange d'intuition et de calcul peuvent entrevoir et saisir ce que vaut promesse ou menace." Maurras, L'avenir de l'intelligence, 11.

36. "La représentation de la Force sans la signature du Fort"; "La patrie libre, telle que la peut seule maintenir l'héréditaire vertu du Sang." Maurras, L'avenir de l'intelligence, 15.

37. "C'est dans la critique littéraire que cette pensée, elle aussi, a fait sa rhétorique, et comme autrefois, sa logique. C'est dans le commerce des formes et normes esthétiques qu'elle a puisé et les problèmes qu'elle se pose et l'esprit des solutions qu'elle leur donne [. . .]. Ayant dégagé clairement l'idée littéraire de tradition et d'ordre, elle a porté son analyse, employé son instrument sur la tradition et l'ordre religieux, politique." Thibaudet, "L'Esthétique des trois traditions," 10-11.

38. For a wider history of reviews in the Belle Epoque, see Leroy and Bertrand-Sabiani, "Les revues: traditions et innovations."

39. Rivière, "La *Nouvelle Revue Française*," 239.

40. "Tout épris de doute, de 'disponibilité,' d'inquiétude, fervent de pensée précieuse, de logique sybilline, d´ésotérisme verbal, méprisant de l'affirmé, du net, du rectiligne." Benda, *Exercice d'un enterré vif*, 314.

41. "Il y a, en art, des problèmes de circonstances et des problèmes essentiels. Les premiers se renouvellent tous les quinze ans, tous les trente ans ou tous les demi-siècles, selon qu'ils sont affaire de mode, de goût ou de mœurs. Plus ils sont éphémères et plus ils absorbent l'attention. Quant aux problèmes essentiels, ils ne sont jamais à l'ordre du jour. Chaque artiste les affronte, seul, dans les moments les plus décisifs de sa vie. Mais il connaît l'inquiétude de l'isolement; il doute de la vitalité de son œuvre; il interroge anxieusement les anciens et les maîtres, ce qui est remonter aux principes mêmes, aux matrices premières de toute création artistique." Schlumberger, "Considérations," 11.

42. An example of this shared style, the seed of *l'esprit NRF*, was Copeau's battle against ephemeral drama with the foundation of the *Théâtre du Vieux-Colombier* and Schlumberger's own rejection of traditionalism.

43. Schlumberger, "Considérations," 13-14.

44. Gide, "Les limites de l'Art," in *Essais critiques*, 422.

45. "Il avait en effet cette double et merveilleuse propriété premièrement de ne rien exclure à priori, de ne lancer anathème sur aucun genre, sur aucune forme d'art, et deuxièmement de marquer tout de même une direction, d'encourager de nouvelles tendances. [. . .] Entrer à la *Nouvelle Revue Française*, ce fut tout de suite recevoir un brevet non pas de perfection, mais de vie; quiconque était accepté dans ses pages recevait par là la preuve que son effort était de ceux qui avaient un sens et qu'il avait su enfiler la direction de l'avenir." Rivière, "Histoire abrégée de *La Nouvelle Revue Française*," 87-8.

46. Thibaudet, "De la critique gidienne," 236. See also Rivière, "Le roman d'aventure."

47. Koffeman, "La naissance d'un mythe," 27.

48. Koffeman, "La naissance d'un mythe," 25.

49. Rodic convincingly suggests that, from 1909 to 1914, *le classicisme moderne* focused on the relation between "lyric voice and poetic form," while attempting to revive the spoken qualities of language. "Lyricism, Aesthetic Tradition, and the Debates on Nationalism in *La Nouvelle Revue Française*," 817. Yet, one might also

argue that the analytic of the passions Rivière would later discover in Proust was equally representative of the critical character of the *NRF*.

50. "Une force consciente qui discerne, hiérarchise, discipline." Thibaudet, "L'Esthétique des trois traditions," 22.

51. "La notion et le goût du classique, fructueux comme régulateurs de notre intelligence, comme moyens de notre critique, comme principes de notre jugements, peuvent-ils nous fournir aujourd'hui en outre, les éléments d'une fondation positive? Peuvent-ils féconder et gouverner un art vivant? Peuvent-ils redevenir 'institution' esthétique?" Thibaudet, "L'Esthétique des trois traditions," 42.

52. Dagan, *NRF entre la guerre et la paix*, 39.

53. Winock, *Le siècle des intellectuels*, 145.

54. Benjamin, "The Storyteller," *Selected Writings*, vol. 3, 143–4.

55. "Conversations humanitaires, patriotiques, internationalistes et métaphysiques"; "Plus de style, avais-je entendu dire alors, plus de littérature, de la vie." Proust, *À la recherche*, vol. 4, 461; *In Search*, vol. 6, 279. On Proust's belated decision to include the war in his novel, see Rancière, "Proust: la guerre, la vérité, le livre," in *La chair des mots*, 137–55.

56. *Correspondance Jacques Rivière et Alain Fournier*, vol. 2, 118, 256; Rivière, "Notes sur un événement politique," Hebey, ed., *L'esprit NRF*, 316.

57. Jackson, *La Grande Illusion*. For a study of mutual Franco-German hostility, see Michael E. Nolan, *The Inverted Mirror: Mythologizing the Enemy in France and Germany*.

58. Rivière, *L'Allemand*, 167. He had also compiled notes for a companion volume, *Le Français*, which was published posthumously in 1928.

59. Rivière, *L'Allemand*, 24. Many of these oppositions are, again, at play in *La grande illusion*.

60. For Gide's reaction to *L'Allemand*, see "Réflexions sur L'Allemagne."

61. Agamben, *Potentialities*, 77.

62. Agamben, *Potentialities*, 77.

63. Offering a critical account of national "sensibility and intelligence" through literature remained a priority for Rivière after the war.

64. "Tenir compte de toutes les conséquences de ce que je dis, notais-je. Me représenter toujours à l'avance le poids en efforts et en souffrances de chaque phrase qu'il me vient l'envie de prononcer. Traduire mentalement chacune des impulsions de mon esprit en termes de réalité." Rivière, *L'Allemand*, 9.

65. Rivière was likely the first critic to recognize the analytic insights shared by Proust and Freud in *Quelques progrès dans l'étude du coeur* (1925).

66. "Et j'en venais à cette idée qu'en temps de guerre toute pensée est soumise à une sorte de gravitation. Les passions de chaque individu, plus profondément encore sa race, sa naissance forment un centre, forment un astre, autour duquel sa réflexion tourne, retenue par une invisible influence, ne peut rien faire de mieux que de tourner. En réalité on ne pense plus [...] on happe au passage tout ce qui peut vous encourager dans votre système; et le reste, on ne le voit pas; il glisse sous votre nez, sans qu'un soupçon vous effleure du désordre qu'il pourrait porter dans vos représentations." Rivière, *L'Allemand*, 11–12.

67. "Ils ne sont rien, ils ne désirent rien, n'attendent, ne prétendent rien." Rivière, *L'Allemand*, 23.

68. "Une si grave inertie de la sensibilité ne peut manquer d'avoir ses répercussions sur l'intelligence. L'indifférence du cœur entraîne chez l'Allemand une inaptitude à saisir les différences entre les idées, un affaiblissement de ses valeurs." Rivière, L'Allemand, 53.

69. Rivière supported German reconstruction efforts by writing a series of columns on the topic in the Luxemburger Zeitung at the behest of Aline and Émile Mayrisch. For German reactions to L'Allemand, see Bock, "La querelle de L'Allemand: les réactions allemandes à la publication du livre de Rivière."

70. "Vous savez comme moi combien tout ce qui a précédé la guerre est, en ce moment, difficile à ressaisir. Même quand il s'agit de nos propres pensées, de nos propres actions d'alors, nous sentons un certain embarras à en retrouver les origines et les motifs. Notre être antérieur à la guerre est presque comme un étranger, dont nous ne réussissons à comprendre les gestes et la conduite que par un effort et une application de tout notre esprit." "La NRF et son role dans le mouvement littéraire d'avant guerre," 1918, 32 ff., consulted at the Fondation des Treilles.

71. For the *NRF* the essential documents are as follows: Arnauld, "Explication," July 1919; Rivière, "Le parti d'intelligence," September 1919; Schlumberger, "Sur le parti de l'intelligence," October 1919; Ghéon, "Réflexions sur le rôle actuel de l'intelligence française," November 1919; followed by a reply by Rivière, "Catholicisme et nationalisme," November 1919, supported by Thibaudet, "Sur la démobilisation de l'intelligence," January 1920. Massis's manifesto can be found in Sirinelli, *Intellectuels et passions françaises*, 62-4.

72. See Horne, "Remobilizing for 'total war': France and Great Britain 1917-1918."

73. For a discussion of Gide viz. Maurras, see Fauré, "Huguenots ou Barbares . . . ces adversaires sont les mêmes: Charles Maurras, André Gide, et l'esthétique comme résistance à la race."

74. The phrase "demobilizing intelligence" alludes to Thibaudet's crucial article, "Sur la démobilisation de l'intelligence."

75. "Rivière venait d'inaugurer la nouvelle série de la *NRF* par un éditorial réclamant la démobilisation de l'intelligence et l'indépendance de la littérature par rapport au patriotisme et au nationalisme, à la morale et à la politique." Compagnon, *Les Antimodernes: de Joseph de Maistre à Roland Barthes*, 306.

76. Dagan, *NRF entre la guerre et la paix*, argues that the literary "direction" of the *NRF* can be equated with anything that could spur a "classical, profound, and interior renaissance."

77. "La *Nouvelle Revue Française*, dans leur esprit, devait être surtout un terrain propice à la création, qu'une critique intelligente maintiendrait constamment ameubli." Rivière, *NRF*, June 1, 1919, 1-2.

78. Rivière, *NRF*, June 1, 1919, 2.

79. Rivière uses the metaphor of spontaneous generation to discuss creativity. Its vegetal register is surely an allusion to Proust's *À l'ombre des jeunes filles en fleurs*, which won the Prix Goncourt in 1919.

80. See Just, *Literature, Ethics, and Decolonization in Postwar France*, 1-23.

81. "La guerre est venue, la guerre a passé. Elle a profondément bouleversé toute chose, et en particulier nos esprits. Elle a remis chacun de nous au creuset et a recomposé à plusieurs d'entre nous une âme véritablement nouvelle. Plus d'un osera lui rester à jamais reconnaissant de l'avoir ainsi comme recommencé sur un nouveau et plus

parfait modèle. Et pourtant malgré cette refonte morale et psychologique [...] nous revenons, plus délibérément si c'est possible qu'autrefois, à notre premier dessein. Nous voulons refaire une revue désintéressée, une revue où l'on continuera de juger et de créer en toute liberté d'esprit, non pas comme si 'rien ne s'était passé,' mais en continuant de n'obéir, dans chaque ordre, qu'à des principes spécifiques." Rivière, *NRF*, June 1, 1919, 2.

82. "C'est que la guerre a pu changer bien des choses, mais pas celle-ci, que la littérature est la littérature, que l'art est l'art," Rivière, *NRF*, June 1, 1919, 3.

83. Here one might think of a romantic tradition of "tautegorical" criticism—stretching back to Coleridge and Schelling—which deals with infinitely differentiated ideality, or the same subject with a difference.

84. Orlando, *Obsolete Objects in the Literary Imagination*, 53.

85. It is noteworthy that this essence, like Rivière's notion of "literary color," remains undefined. It may very well be empty, fulfilled only by the singular performance of each literary work.

86. "Aujourd'hui comme hier, et malgré des monceaux de ruines, il reste vrai que la création artistique est un acte original, que créer c'est peut-être avant tout ne rien sentir, ne rien vouloir d'autre que ce qu'on fait." Rivière, *NRF*, June 1, 1919, 3.

87. "Nous accueillerons la revendication de l'intelligence qui cherche visiblement aujourd'hui à reprendre ses droits en art; non pas pour supplanter entièrement la sensibilité, mais pour la pénétrer, pour l'analyser et pour régner sur elle." Rivière, *NRF*, June 1, 1919, 8.

88. This notion of "preoccupation" recalls Freud's military and theatrical understanding of occupation or cathexis (*Besetzung*). For Rivière and Freud the wartime triggered the projection and investment of psychic energy in misdirected ways.

89. "Notre dessein est de travailler dans la mesure de nos moyens à faire cesser cette contrainte que la guerre exerce encore sur les intelligences, et dont elles ont tant de mal à se débarrasser toutes seules." Rivière, *NRF*, June 1, 1919, 4.

90. "Car c'est vrai que l'intelligence française est incomparable; il n'en existe pas de plus puissante, de plus aiguë, de plus profonde. Dût-on m'accuser d'effronterie, j'irai jusqu'au bout de ma pensée: c'est la seule aujourd'hui qu'il y ait au monde. Nous seuls avons su conserver une tradition intellectuelle; nous seuls avons su nous préserver à peu près de l'abêtissement pragmatiste; nous seuls avons continué de croire au principe d'identité; il n'y a que nous dans le monde, je le répète froidement, qui sachions encore penser. Il n'y aura, en matière philosophique, littéraire et artistique, que ce que nous dirons qui comptera." Rivière, "Le parti de l'intelligence," 615.

91. Rolland, "Un appel: Fière déclaration d'intellectuels," *L'Humanité*, June 26, 1919, 1. Its signatories included Georges Duhamel, Henri Barbusse, Bertrand Russell, Albert Einstein, Stefan Zweig, Hermann Hesse, and Benedetto Croce.

92. Rolland, " Un appel: Fière declaration d'intellectuels," 1.

93. Massis, "Manifeste pour un parti de l'intelligence," *Figaro littéraire*, July 19, 1919, 1. The signatories included Charles Maurras, Henri Massis, Jacques Maritain, Jacques Bainville, Gaëtan Bernoville, Pierre Champion, Henri Longnon, Maurice Denis, Francis Jammes, Edmond Jaloux, Louis Le Cardonnel, and Pierre Lalo. In a 1952 letter to Jean David, Massis evokes the way his fellow Maurrasians and signatories of the *Parti de l'intelligence* manifesto understood "intelligence": "We understood the word intelligence in the sense used by Maurras, but also in the sense used by Maritain. Aristotle, St Thomas, and Bossuet met in this way. For us Catholics, *fides*

quaerens intellectum [faith seeks understanding] defines our intellectualist position [. . .]. It was to this metaphysical restoration that we were associated." David, *Le procès de l'intelligence*, 276.

94. "Intelligence nationale au service de l'intérêt national." Massis, "Manifeste pour un parti de l'intelligence," 1.

95. "Il existe une pensée qui arrête la pensée, un art qui est la fin de l'art, une politique qui détruit la politique, ce sont les seuls que nous soyons décidés de proscrire." Massis, "Manifeste pour un parti de l'intelligence," 1.

96. "Réflection de l'esprit public en France par les voies royales de l'intelligence et des méthodes classiques, fédération intellectuelle de l'Europe et du monde sous l'égide de la France victorieuse, gardienne de toute civilisation, tel est notre double dessein qui procède d'une unité supérieure." Massis, "Manifeste pour un parti de l'intelligence," 1.

97. "Nous croyons—et le monde croit avec nous—qu'il est dans la destination de notre race de défendre les intérêts spirituels de l'humanité. La France victorieuse veut reprendre sa place souveraine dans l'ordre de l'esprit, qui est le seul ordre par lequel s'exerce une domination légitime." Massis, "Manifeste pour un parti de l'intelligence," 1.

98. That he had done so out of his unrepentant Germanophilia—combined with an erotic attraction to order, the semblance of force, violence, and vitality—was typical of his ambivalent politics. See Lucey, *Gide's Bent*.

99. Ghéon, "Réflexions sur le rôle actuel de l'intelligence française." See David, *Le procès de l'intelligence*, 92.

100. "L'intelligence est décidément à la mode. Il n'est plus personne qui ne se réclame de ses faveurs; il ne paraît plus de manifeste où elle ne soit préconisée comme la première des vertus. Et voici même que se forme un Parti de l'Intelligence auquel adhèrent d'emblée plusieurs esprits distingués. [. . .] À ne la juger que d'ensemble, elle me paraît empreinte d'une certain confusion, qui étonne un peu de la part de gens dont le souci avoué est de rendre la place d'honneur à la faculté logique," Rivière, "Le parti de L'intelligence," 612.

101. Rivière, "Le parti de l'intelligence," 613.

102. Rivière, "Le parti de l'intelligence," 613.

103. Rivière, "Le parti de l'intelligence," 615.

104. For a sustained analysis of the "anachronism of aristocracy" in interwar film and literature, especially Renoir, Proust, and Bataille, see Amaral, "Act Six: Aristocracy and History in Interwar French Literature and Film."

105. Rivière, "Le parti de l'intelligence," 617.

106. "L'intelligence française dans cet état de mobilisation permanente risquerait bientôt non seulement de ne plus être intelligence, mais de ne plus être française." Thibaudet, "Sur la démobilisation de l'intelligence," 132-3.

107. Rivière, in Hebey, ed., *L'esprit NRF*, 240.

108. "Ces victoires trop complètes effacent les traces du combat et transforment en vaincus anonymes ceux qui avaient commencé par être des adversaires redoutables: les noms de beaucoup de ceux que la *NRF* a déclassés ne diraient plus rien aux lecteurs d'aujourd'hui. La première tâche de cette critique d'exécutions sommaires fut pourtant de renverser le barème des valeurs littéraires." Anglès, "*NRF*," in *Circumnavigations*, 260.

109. See Lewis, "Citizen of the Plain: Proust and the Discourse of the Novel," in *Modernism, Nationalism, and the Novel*, 126–74.

110. "Que la France doive veiller sur les littératures du monde entier, c'est un mandat qu'on pleurerait de joie d'apprendre qu'on nous a confié, mais qu'il est un peu choquant de nous voir assumer de nous-même. Cette 'hégémonie,' cette 'victoire' fait involontairement penser à 'Deutschland über alles' et à cause de cela est légèrement désagréable. Le caractère de notre 'race' (est-il d'un bien bon français, de parler de 'race française'?) était de savoir allier à autant de fierté plus de modestie." Proust, *Correspondance*, vol. 18, 335.

111. "À propos de Flaubert, vous rappelez-vous dans *L'Éducation sentimentale* le 'Club de l'Intelligence.' Quelle 'anticipation' du ridicule 'Parti de l'intelligence.' Que de dangereuses niaiseries fait éclore l'après-guerre," Proust to Rivière, December 2–3, 1919. Kolb, ed., *Marcel Proust–Jacques Rivière: Correspondance, 1914–1922*, 68.

112. Hughes, *Proust, Class, Nation*, 19.

113. Hughes, *Proust, Class, Nation*, 19.

114. "Il n'y a qu'une manière d'écrire pour tous, c'est d'écrire sans penser à personne." Proust, *Essais*, 1102.

115. Winock, "Le congrès des écrivains de 1935," in *Le siècle des intellectuels*, 312–22.

Chapter Five: Situating Intelligence

1. Ash, *Gestalt Psychology in German Culture*.

2. Jefferson, *Genius in France: An Idea and its Uses*, 6.

3. Lefebvre, "Allemand," 63. Schlegel discusses the ambiguous uses of *Klugheit* in Athenaeum Fragment 362, in Schlegel, *Kritische Schriften und Fragmente 1798–1801*, 142. On *Intelligenz* and Hegel's semiotics in the *Encyclopedia*, see Derrida, "Le puits et la pyramide," in *Marges*, 79–127.

4. Only recently, given the rise of cognitive science and artificial intelligence, has German returned to using *Intelligenz* in a more Anglicized sense.

5. Adorno, *Notes to Literature*, vol. 1, 151–2. Pace Adorno, Guerlac notes that "we have lost track of the Bergsonian code in Valéry and exaggerated the importance of the Cartesian one." Guerlac, *Literary Polemics*, 201.

6. "Es giebt wahrscheinlich viele Arten von Intelligenz, aber jede hat *ihre Gesetzmäßigkeit*, welche ihr die *Vorstellung* einer *anderen* Gesetzmäßigkeit *unmöglich* macht. Weil wir also keine *Empirie* über die verschiedenen Intelligenzen haben *können*, ist auch jeder Weg zur Einsicht in den *Ursprung* der Intelligenz verschlossen. Das *allgemeine* Phänomen der Intelligenz ist uns unbekannt, wir haben nur den *Spezialfall*, und *können nicht verallgemeinern*. Hier allein sind wir ganz Sklaven, selbst wenn wir Phantasten sein wollten! Anderseits wird es von *jeder* Art Intelligenz aus ein *Verständniß der Welt* geben müssen—aber ich glaube, es ist nur die zu Ende geführte Anpassung der Gesetzmäßigkeit der einzelnen Art Intelligenz—sie führt sich selber überall durch. Jede Intelligenz glaubt an sich." Nietzsche, *Nachlass*, Fall 1881, 11 [291], in *Kritische Studienausgabe*, vol. 9, 553.

7. Nietzsche, *Kritische Studienausgabe*, vol. 5, 153; *Beyond Good and Evil*, part 7, § 218, 110–11.

8. Nietzsche, *Kritische Studienausgabe*, vol. 5, 153; *Beyond Good and Evil*, 111.
9. Nietzsche, *The Anti-Christ, Ecce Homo, Twilight of the Idols, And Other Writings*, 168.
10. Heidegger, *Einführung in die Metaphysik*, 32–3; *Introduction to Metaphysics*, 45.
11. Heidegger, *Einführung in die Metaphysik*, 45; *Introduction to Metaphysics*, 44.
12. Heidegger, *Einführung in die Metaphysik*, 130; *Introduction to Metaphysics*, 129.
13. As a complement to this question, one might consider the many passages in *Being and Time* that critique "freischwebenden Spekulation" and the various attitudes of free-floating subjectivity, which echo debates in the sociology of knowledge beginning with Alfred Weber, later adopted by Karl Mannheim. See Hoeges, *Kontroverse am Abgrund. Ernst Robert Curtius und Karl Mannheim*.
14. Heidegger, *Einführung in die Metaphysik*, 28; *Introduction to Metaphysics*, 28.
15. Heidegger, *Einführung in die Metaphysik*, 29; *Introduction to Metaphysics*, 28.
16. Heidegger, *Einführung in die Metaphysik*, 53; *Introduction to Metaphysics*, 52.
17. Heidegger, *Einführung in die Metaphysik*, 50; *Introduction to Metaphysics*, 49.
18. Heidegger, *Einführung in die Metaphysik*, 51; *Introduction to Metaphysics*, 49.
19. Heidegger, *Einführung in die Metaphysik*, 51; *Introduction to Metaphysics*, 50.
20. Heidegger, *Einführung in die Metaphysik*, 51–3; *Introduction to Metaphysics*, 50–52.
21. "'Vielleicht ist Europa schon geworden, was es ist: ein bloßes Kap, als dieses jedoch zugleich das Gehirn des ganzen Erdkörpers, jenes Gehirn, das die technish-industrielle, planetarisch-interstellare Rechnung bewerkstelligt.' Weil dem so ist und weil, was auf solche Weise ist, nicht bleiben kann, dürfen wir den beiden Fragen Paul Valérys vielleicht eine dritte folgen lassen. Sie frägt nicht über Europa hinweg, sondern in seinen Anfang zurück. Sie könnte so lauten: Muß Europa als dieses Kap und Gehirn erst zum Land eines Abends werden, aus dem ein anderer Morgen des Weltgeschicks seinen Aufgang vorbereitet?" Heidegger, *Erläuterungen zu Hölderlins Dichtung*, 176–7; *Elucidations of Hölderlin's Poetry*, 201.
22. Benjamin, *Gesammelte Schriften*, vol. 2.1, 295; *Selected Writings*, vol. 2, 207.
23. "Krise und Kritik," in Wizisla, *Walter Benjamin and Bertold Brecht*, 192–3.
24. In a commentary on the "Cimetière marin," Valéry writes: "Whatever the author may have *wanted to say*, he has written what he has written. Once published the text is like an apparatus that anyone may use as he will and according to his ability: it is not certain that the one who has constructed it can use it better than another." *Collected Works*, vol. 7, 152.
25. For a synthetic overview and bibliography of Benjamin's "French" writings, see Bernardi, "Zur französischen Literatur und Kultur," 332–42. On the somewhat mythic character of Benjamin's retrospective reputation as a critic of French literature, see 335.
26. Benjamin, "Zum gegenwärtigen gesellschaftlichen Standort des französischen Schriftstellers," *Gesammelte Schriften*, vol. 2.2, 776–803; "The Present Social Situation of the French Writer," *Selected Writings*, vol. 2, 744–67.
27. "Der Autor als Produzent," *Gesammelte Schriften*, vol. 2.2, 683–701; "The Author as Producer," *Selected Writings*, vol. 2, 768–82.

28. The fictive purge is led by Horace Tograth, a brilliant German engineer, with almost miraculous technical abilities, who bears no affinity for poets despite his lyrical first name. Tograth's polemic against poets sets off a series of book burnings and massacres across the globe. See Apollinaire, *Œuvres complètes en prose*, vol. 1, 290–91; quoted in Benjamin, "The Present Social Situation of the French Writer," *Selected Writings*, vol. 2, 744–5.

29. As Einfalt, in "L'engagement intellectuel des écrivain français" notes, the date of the publication of Benjamin's essay coincides almost perfectly with the first large Fascist rally in Paris on February 6, 1934.

30. Benjamin, "The Present Social Situation of the French Writer," *Selected Writings*, vol. 2, 753.

31. For an exploration of how naturalism anticipates cinematic techniques, see Blood, "The Precinematic Novel."

32. Benjamin, "Zum gegenwärtigen gesellschaftlichen Standort des französischen Schriftstellers," *Gesammelte Schriften*, vol. 2.2, 788; "The Present Social Situation of the French Writer," *Selected Writings*, vol. 2, 753.

33. It is noteworthy, as Einfalt points out, that Benjamin does not mention Henri Barbusse or Romain Rolland, two literary figures sanctioned by the French Communist Party.

34. Palmier, *Walter Benjamin*, 295–6.

35. For an overview, see Marx, ed., *Les arrière-gardes au XXe siècle*.

36. *Gesammelte Schriften*, vol. 2.2, 792; *Selected Writings*, vol. 2, 756.

37. *Gesammelte Schriften*, vol. 2.2, 792; *Selected Writings*, vol. 2, 756.

38. As mentioned in chapter 3 above, Benjamin considers Teste's "inoperativity" or "inactivity" (*Untätigkeit*) to be the most radical immanent critique of Valéry's work. *Gesammelte Schriften*, vol. 2.1, 1145.

39. *Gesammelte Schriften*, vol. 2.2, 792; *Selected Writings*, vol. 2, 755 (trans. modified).

40. *Gesammelte Schriften*, vol. 2.2, 792; *Selected Writings*, vol. 2, 755.

41. *Gesammelte Schriften*, vol. 2.2, 695; *Selected Writings*, vol. 2, 776.

42. Greaney, *Untimely Beggar: Poverty and Power from Baudelaire to Benjamin*, 143.

43. *Gesammelte Schriften*, vol. 2.2, 695; *Selected Writings*, vol. 2, 777.

44. *Gesammelte Schriften*, vol. 2.2, 696; *Selected Writings*, vol. 2, 777.

45. Mitchell, *Understanding Brecht*, xv.

46. Benjamin, *Correspondence*, 80. For a close reading of the letter to Buber in terms of a politics of refusal and silence, see Weber, "Der Brief an Buber vom 17.7.1916." For a discussion of Benjamin's style, see Weber, *Benjamin's -abilities*, esp. 115–21.

47. Weber, *Benjamin's -abilities*, 118.

48. "On Language as Such and on the Language of Man," *Selected Writings*, vol. 1, 64. The main reference on the relation between language and magic in Benjamin is Menninghaus, *Walter Benjamins Theorie der Sprachmagie*.

49. For Ian Balfour, prophecy in Benjamin's writings "emerges as a model and not a special case for the historian, and the critic, because every text, every event that is cited attains, if only retroactively, a prophetic aura." See Balfour, *The Rhetoric of Romantic Prophecy*, 18.

50. Benjamin, *Correspondence*, 80.
51. See Weber, "Der Brief an Buber vom 17.7.1916," 606.
52. *Gesammelte Schriften*, vol. 2.2, 776; *Selected Writings*, vol. 2, 744.
53. "Der Sürrealismus. Die letzte Momentaufnahme der europäischen Intelligenz," *Gesammelte Schriften*, vol. 2.1, 300; "Surrealism: The Last Snapshot of the European Intelligentsia," *Selected Writings*, vol. 2, 210.
54. Apollinaire theorizes the relation of poetics to technical innovation in his 1918 manifesto, "L'esprit nouveau et les poètes."
55. Margel, "Langage et politique: Le pouvoir critique des mots, de Brecht à Benjamin," 44.
56. *Gesammelte Schriften*, vol. 2.2, 684–5; *Selected Writings*, vol. 2, 769.
57. *Gesammelte Schriften*, vol. 2.2, 691; *Selected Writings*, vol. 2, 774. Here it is enlightening to juxtapose Benjamin's essay on the "The Work of Art in the Age of its Technological Reproducibility" (1935) to Heidegger's contemporaneous essays on "The Origin of the Work of Art" (1935 and 1937), if only to schematically underscore the differences between the "conservatism" of the latter and the critique of ongoing transformations in media ecologies and conditions of intelligence in the former.
58. For a thorough analysis of the Soviet case in relation to "The Author as Producer," see Gough, "Paris, Capital of the Soviet Avant-Garde." Drawing on Benjamin, Hal Foster argues that the committed contemporary artist struggles "in the name of the cultural or ethnic other" rather than the working class. Foster analyzes the critical significance of this shift from "economic relation" to "cultural identity" in "The Artist as Ethnographer."
59. *Gesammelte Schriften*, vol. 2.2, 686; *Selected Writings*, vol. 2, 770.
60. *Gesammelte Schriften*, vol. 2.2, 686; *Selected Writings*, vol. 2, 770.
61. The concept of art as technique or device also occurs in Viktor Shklovsky, where it is connected to the effect of "defamiliarization" (*ostranenie*). See "Art as Device."
62. *Gesammelte Schriften*, vol. 2.1, 192; *Selected Writings*, vol. 1, 244; see also Leslie, *Walter Benjamin: Overpowering Conformism*.
63. On this point, see Fore, "The Operative Word in Soviet Factography."
64. *Gesammelte Schriften*, vol. 2.2, 686–7; *Selected Writings*, vol. 2, 770.
65. *Gesammelte Schriften*, vol. 2.2, 687; *Selected Writings*, vol. 2, 771.
66. See Fenves, *Arresting Language*, 225–6.
67. Benjamin's distance due to his outsider status in France combined with the marked historical and topographic differences between French and German culture made the *Schwebezustand* of the French intellectual and literary figures susceptible to historical materialist inquiry. *Gesammelte Schriften*, vol. 4, 486.
68. Benjamin, *The Arcades Project*, 388.
69. *Gesammelte Schriften*, vol. 1.1, 503; *Selected Writings*, vol. 4, 267.
70. *Gesammelte Schriften*, vol. 2.2, 696; *Selected Writings*, vol. 2, 777.
71. As Weber argues, Brecht's epic theatre brings "a certain history to a standstill," thereby paradoxically preserving the possibility of a still unforeseeable future within the now. See *Benjamin's -abilities*, 105. *Gesammelte Schriften*, vol. 2.1, 698; *Selected Writings*, vol. 2, 779.
72. Gough, "Paris, Capital of the Soviet Avant-Garde," 60.

73. According to Einfalt, "L'engagement intellectuel des écrivain français," Benjamin's interest in Gide as a leading intellectual figure may have been rekindled by the pro-Communist speech the latter delivered during an anti-Nazi demonstration in Paris on March 21, 1933.

74. *Gesammelte Schriften*, vol. 2.2, 699; *Selected Writings*, vol. 2, 779.

75. *Gesammelte Schriften*, vol. 2.2, 688; *Selected Writings*, vol. 2, 772.

76. Nägele, "Vexierbild einer kritischen Konstellation," 350.

77. Jameson, *The Political Unconscious*, 17.

78. Cohen, *Profane Illumination*, 30.

79. Fenves, "Is there an Answer to the Aestheticizing of the Political?," 62.

80. Agamben, *Infancy and History*, 123.

81. Korsch, "Introduction to the *Critique of the Gotha Program*," *Marxism and Philosophy*, 145.

82. *Karl Marx: Selected Writings*, 425.

83. *Karl Marx: Selected Writings*, 425.

84. *Karl Marx: Selected Writings*, 425.

85. I borrow this expression from the conclusion to the 1929 essay on Surrealism.

86. Benjamin, "Diary from August 7, 1931, to the Day of my Death," *Selected Writings*, vol. 2, 501–6.

87. Benjamin, *Gesammelte Schriften*, vol. 2.2, 688; *Selected Writings*, vol. 2, 771–72.

88. *Gesammelte Schriften*, vol. 2.2, 696; *Selected Writings*, vol. 2, 777, italics in the original.

89. Benjamin remains skeptical about the possibility of an emancipatory socialism developing out of capitalist modes of production as prognosticated by Marx. If it arrived, socialism would be the mere perpetuation of the "debt history of capital." See Hamacher, "Guilt History: Benjamin's Sketch 'Capitalism as Religion.'"

90. Eiland and Jennings, *Walter Benjamin*, 440.

91. Benjamin, *Gesammelte Schriften*, vol. 3, 250; *Selected Writings*, vol. 2, 321.

92. Benjamin's declaration is made *pace* Marx, who declares in the "Preface to the *Critique of Political Economy*" that humanity poses no problems for itself that it cannot resolve. Fenves points to Benjamin's greater proximity to the Kantian notion that there are indeed problems that impose themselves on human reason, yet whose solutions are beyond these very human faculties. "Is there an Answer to the Aestheticizing of the Political?," 61.

93. By occasionally translating *Apparat* as "device," I am drawing attention to a continuum between the literary and the technical. It is nonetheless important to keep the collective and institutional connotations of the German word in mind. For instance, in his Wyneken-inspired critiques of instrumentalized education, Benjamin refers to the university system as an "apparatus."

94. A useful comparative analysis can be found in Gipper, *Der Intellektuelle: Konzeption und Selbstverständnis schriftstellerischer Intelligenz in Frankreich und Italien*. For the reading of "treason" in Alain and Benda, see "Die Theorie des Verrats," 142–68.

95. Thibaudet, *La république des professeurs*, 173–6.

96. Benjamin, *Gesammelte Schriften*, vol. 2.2, 782; *Selected Writings*, vol. 2, 748.

97. The scientific developments referred to here are likely those of quantum physics, which Benjamin followed via Emile Meyerson and Arthur Stanley Eddington.

98. Benjamin, *Gesammelte Schriften*, vol. 2.2, 784; *Selected Writings*, vol. 2, 749.

99. Hollier, *Absent Without Leave: French Literature under the Threat of War*, 162.

100. Berl, *Mort de la pensée bourgeoise*, 19–20.

101. Benjamin, *Gesammelte Schriften*, vol. 2.2, 784; *Selected Writings*, vol. 2, 750.

102. Berl, *Mort de la pensée bourgeoise*, 27.

103. Berl, *Mort de la pensée bourgeoise*, 47.

104. Berl, *Mort de la pensée bourgeoise*, 136.

105. Berl, *Mort de la pensée bourgeoise*, 136.

106. Benjamin, *Gesammelte Schriften*, vol. 2.2, 802; *Selected Writings*, vol. 2, 763. See Aragon, "Le surréalisme et le devenir révolutionnaire," 5.

107. *Gesammelte Schriften*, vol. 2.2, 700; *Selected Writings*, vol. 2, 780.

108. Andrew and Ungar, *Popular Front Paris and the Poetics of Culture*, 368. In his edition of Benjamin's *Écrits français*, Monnoyer suggests that the violent demystification of the French writer is the reason the essay was prudently not translated into French. *Écrits français*, 49.

109. Eiland and Jennings, *Walter Benjamin*, 406.

110. Adorno, "Zur gesellschaftlichen Lage der Musik," *Zeitschrift für Sozialforschung*, vol. 1 (1932).

111. Benjamin, *Gesammelte Schriften*, vol. 2.3, 1509.

112. For a memoir of Benjamin's time in Ibiza, see Jean Selz, "Walter Benjamin à Ibiza" in Benjamin, *Ecrits français*, 469–86.

113. Geneva was the interim seat of the Institute of Social Research. Scholem, *Walter Benjamin: Story of a Friendship*, 247–8.

114. The term *reine Hochstapelei*, usually translated as "pure fraud," could equally be translated as "sheer fakery" or a "pure con."

115. Martin Jay reads the essay as "taking distance from the Leninist strain in Marxist aesthetics" whereas Rita Copeland likens Benjamin to Gramsci for his realization that intellectual class ties have become invisible. See Jay, *The Dialectical Imagination*, 339; Copeland, *Pedagogy, Intellectuals, and Dissent*, 27.

116. Leslie, *Walter Benjamin: Overpowering Conformism*, 131.

117. Steiner, *Walter Benjamin: An Introduction to his Work and Thought*, 108.

118. Adorno and Benjamin, *The Complete Correspondence*, 53.

119. Benjamin, *Correspondence of Walter Benjamin and Gershom Scholem*, 110.

120. In his correspondence, Benjamin insists on the "rejection of *every* contemporary political tendency" when elaborating his own theory of politics. See Eiland and Jennings, *Walter Benjamin*, 127.

121. *Gesammelte Schriften*, vol. 2.3, 1515; Adorno and Benjamin, *The Complete Correspondence*, 53; Brecht, *Briefe*, vol. 1, 554.

122. Adorno and Benjamin, *The Complete Correspondence*, 281.

123. Clark, "Should Benjamin Have Read Marx?," 41.

124. Derrida, *La vérité en peinture*, 171–2.

125. *Gesammelte Schriften*, vol. 2.2, 803; *Selected Writings*, vol. 2, 745. Elsewhere, Benjamin remarks that throughout Apollinaire's work a "prophet and a charlatan" struggle for control over his poetic voice.

Epilogue

1. "Il arrive que l'on demande à quelqu'un s'il y a une *Crise de l'Intelligence*, si le monde s'abêtit, s'il y a un dégoût de la culture,—si les *professions libérales* pâtissent, songent à la mort, sentent leurs forces décroître, leurs rangs s'éclaircir, leur prestige devenir de plus en plus mince, leur existence de plus en plus ingrate, précaire, mesurée . . ." Valéry, *Œuvres*, vol. 1, 1040; *Collected Works*, vol. 10, 72.

2. "Une crise est le passage d'un certain régime de fonctionnement à quelque autre; passage que des signes ou des symptoms rendent sensible. Pendent une crise, le temps semble changer de nature, la durée n'est plus perçue comme dans l'état ordinaire des choses: au lieu de mesurer la permanence, elle mesure la variation. Toute crise implique l'intervention de 'causes' nouvelles qui troublent un équilibre mobile ou immobile qui existait." Valéry, *Œuvres*, vol. 1, 1041; *Collected Works*, vol. 10, 72.

3. "*L'Intelligence* est l'une de ces notions qui ne prennent leur valeur que des autres terms auxquels elles sont jointes dans quelque discours qui les compose ou les oppose." Valéry, *Œuvres*, vol. 1, 1042; *Collected Works*, vol. 10, 74.

4. "Crise d'une *faculté*, crise d'une *valeur*, crise d'une *classe*." Valéry, *Œuvres*, vol. 1, 1043; *Collected Works*, vol. 10, 75.

5. Deleuze, "Postscript on the Societies of Control," 3–4.

6. Deleuze, "Postscript on the Societies of Control," 6.

7. Deleuze, "Postscript on the Societies of Control," 4.

8. Cave, "The Problem with Intelligence: Its Value-Laden History and the Future of AI."

9. Malabou, *Morphing Intelligence*, 14.

10. Malabou, *Morphing Intelligence*, 14–15. A parallel could be drawn with the training of a neural network which is mostly "epigenetic" by construction.

11. Malabou, *Morphing Intelligence*, 15.

12. Malabou, *Morphing Intelligence*, 15.

13. Malabou, *Morphing Intelligence*, 16.

14. See Bhattachrya, "Somapolitics."

15. Herrenschmidt, *Les trois écritures: Langue, nombre, code*; "Á propos de l'ouvrage 'Les trois écritures.' Langue, nombre, code."

16. Herrenschmidt, "Á propos de l'ouvrage 'Les trois écritures.' Langue, nombre, code."

17. Wooldridge, *A Brief History of Artificial Intelligence*, 11. See also Canales, "Computer Daemons," in *Bedeviled: A Shadow History of Demons in Science*, 185–245.

18. Wooldridge, *A Brief History of Artificial Intelligence*, 14.

19. Wooldridge, *A Brief History of Artificial Intelligence*, 57. On undecidability, see Bates, "Crisis Between the Wars: Derrida and the Origins of Undecidability."

20. On the response in post-war France, see Johnson, "'French' Cybernetics."

21. Wooldridge, *A Brief History of Artifical Intelligence*, 24.

22. Turing, *The Essential Turing*, 449.

23. Turing, *The Essential Turing*, 394, 463.

24. Bates, "Automaticity, Plasticity, and the Deviant Origins of Artificial Intelligence," 202.

25. Legg and Hutter, "Universal Intelligence: A Definition of Machine Intelligence."

26. Wooldridge, *A Brief History of Artificial Intelligence*, 19.
27. Kurzweil, *The Singularity is Near: When Humans Transcend Biology*, 486.
28. Dreyfus, *What Computers Still Can't Do: A Critique of Artificial Reason*.
29. Bostrom, "How Long Before Superintelligence?," 11.
30. Wiener, *Uncanny Valley*, 43.
31. Heidegger, "The Provenance of Art and the Destination of Thought"; "Die Herkunft der Kunst und die Bestimmung des Denkens."
32. On Heidegger's distinction between traditional and technical language, see "Überlieferte Sprache und Technische Sprache"; "Traditional Language and Technological Language." Thanks to Tobias Keiling for bringing this text to my attention.
33. Valéry, *Œuvres*, vol. 1, 1045–46; *Collected Works*, vol. 10, 77–8.

BIBLIOGRAPHY

Aarsleff, Hans. *From Locke to Saussure: Essays in the Study of Language and Intellectual History.* Minneapolis: University of Minnesota Press, 1982.
Adorno, Theodor. "Zur gesellschaftlichen Lage der Musik." *Zeitschrift für Sozialforschung* 1 (1932), 103–24, 356–78.
———. *Noten zur Literatur.* Frankfurt am Main: Suhrkamp, 1981. *Notes to Literature,* vol. 1. Translated by Shierry Weber Nicholsen. New York: Columbia University Press, 1991.
———. *Prisms.* Translated by Shierry Weber Nicholsen and Samuel Weber. Cambridge, MA: MIT Press, 1983.
Adorno, Theodor, and Walter Benjamin. *The Complete Correspondence 1928–1940.* Edited by Henri Lonitz and translated by Nicholas Walker. Cambridge, MA: Harvard University Press, 2001.
Agamben, Giorgio. "L'io, l'occhio, la voce." *La potenza del pensiero: Saggi e conferenze.* Vicenza: Neri Pozza Editore, 2005, 91–106.
———. *Infancy and History: On the Destruction of Experience.* Translated by Liz Herson. London: Verso Books, 2007.
———. *Potentialities: Collected Essays in Philosophy.* Edited, translated, and with an introduction by Daniel Heller-Roazen. Stanford: Stanford University Press, 1999.
Albright, Daniel. *Putting Modernism Together: Literature, Music, and Painting, 1872–1927.* Baltimore: Johns Hopkins University Press, 2015.
Amaral, Genevieve. "Act Six: Aristocracy and History in Interwar French Literature and Film." Ph.D. Dissertation, Northwestern University, 2017.
Andrew, Dudley, and Steven Ungar. *Popular Front Paris and the Poetics of Culture.* Cambridge, MA: Harvard University Press, 2005.
Anglès, Auguste. *André Gide et le premier groupe de la Nouvelle Revue Française.* Paris: Gallimard, 1978.
———. *"NRF." Circumnavigations: littérature, voyages, politique 1942–1983.* Lyon: Presses Universitaires de Lyon, 1986.
Apollinaire, Guillaume. "L'esprit nouveau et les poètes." *Mercure de France* 491 (December 1, 1918), 385–96.
———. *Œuvres en prose complètes,* vol. 1. Edited by Michel Décaudin. Paris: Gallimard, 1977.
Apter, Emily. *Continental Drift: From National Characters to Virtual Subjects.* Chicago: University of Chicago Press, 1999.
Aragon, Louis. *Traité du style.* Paris: Gallimard, 1928, 2011.
———. "Le surréalisme et le devenir révolutionnaire." *Le surréalisme au service de la révolution* 3 (December 1931).
Archambault, Paul, ed. *Le procès de l'intelligence.* Paris: Bloud et Gay, Éditeurs, 1922.
Arendt, Hannah. *Reflections on Literature and Culture.* Edited by Susannah Young-ah Gottlieb. Stanford: Stanford University Press, 2007.

Arnauld, Michel. "Explication." *Nouvelle Revue Française* 70 (July 1919), 204-11.
Ash, Mitchell. *Gestalt Psychology in German Culture 1890-1967: Holism and the Quest for Objectivity*. Cambridge: Cambridge University Press, 1998.
Bal, Mieke. *Mottled Screen: Reading Proust Visually*. Stanford: Stanford University Press, 1997.
Balfour, Ian. *The Rhetoric of Romantic Prophecy*. Stanford: Stanford University Press, 2002.
Ball, Hugo. *Zur Kritik der deutschen Intelligenz*. Bern: Der Freie Verlag, 1919. *Critique of the German Intelligentsia*. Translated by Brian L. Harris. New York: Columbia University Press, 1993.
Ball, Simon et al., eds. *Cultures of Intelligence in the Era of the World Wars*. Oxford: Oxford University Press, 2020.
Barrès, Maurice. *Pour la haute intelligence française*. Paris: Plon, 1925.
———. *Scènes et doctrines du nationalisme*. Paris: Plon, 1925.
Barthes, Roland. *The Rustle of Language*. Translated by Richard Howard. New York: Farrar, Strauss and Giroux, 1986.
———. *Le Neutre: Cours au Collège de France 1977-78*. Paris: Seuil, 2002.
———. *Œuvres complètes*. 5 vols. Edited by Éric Marty. Paris: Seuil, 2002.
———. *La préparation du roman: Note de cours et de séminaires au Collège de France, 1978-1980*. Edited by Nathalie Léger. Paris: Seuil, 2003.
———. *Writing Degree Zero*. Translated by Annette Lavers and Colin Smith. New York: Hill and Wang, 2012.
Bataille, Georges. *L'expérience intérieure*. Paris: Gallimard, 1943, 1954.
———. "De l'existentialisme au primat de l'économie." *Critique* 21 (1947), 515-26.
———. *La littérature et le mal*. Paris: Gallimard, 1957, 1967.
Bates, David. "Crisis Between the Wars: Derrida and the Origins of Undecidability." *Representations* 90 (2005), 1-27.
———"Automaticity, Plasticity, and the Deviant Origins of Artificial Intelligence." *Plasticity and Pathology: On the Formation of the Neural Subject*. Edited by David Bates and Nima Bassiri. New York: Fordham University Press, 2016, 194-218.
Baudelaire, Charles. *Œuvres complètes*. Paris: Gallimard, Bibliothèque de la Pléiade, 1961.
Beckett, Samuel. *The Grove Centenary Edition*. New York: Grove Press, 2006.
Benda, Julien. *La trahison des clercs*. Paris: Grasset, 1927, 2003.
———. *Exercise d'un enterré vif: juin 1940-août 1944*. Genève, Paris: Éditions des trois collines, 1944.
———. *La France byzantine ou le triomphe de la littérature pure*. Paris: Gallimard, 1945.
Benjamin, Walter. *Ursprung des deutschen Trauerspiels*. Frankfurt am Main: Suhrkamp, 1963; *The Origin of the German Mourning Play*. Translated by Howard Eiland. Cambridge, MA: Harvard University Press, 2019.
———. "The Image of Proust." *Illuminations*. Translated by Harry Zohn. New York: Schocken Books, 1968.
———. *Gesammelte Schriften*. Edited by Rolf Tiedemann and Hermann Schweppenhäuser. 7 vols. Frankfurt am Main: Suhrkamp, 1972-91.
———. *The Correspondence of Walter Benjamin, 1910-1940*. Chicago: University of Chicago Press, 1994.
———. *Selected Writings of Walter Benjamin*. 4 vols. Edited by Howard Eiland and Michael W. Jennings. Cambridge, MA: Harvard University Press, 1996-2003.

———. *The Arcades Project*. Translated by Howard Eiland and Kevin McLaughlin. Cambridge, MA: Harvard University Press, 2002.
———. *Écrits français*. Edited by Jean-Maurice Monnoyer. Paris: Gallimard, 2003.
Benjamin, Walter and Gershom Scholem. *The Correspondence of Walter Benjamin and Gershom Scholem, 1932-1942*. Translated by Gary Smith and Andre Lefevere. Cambridge, MA: Harvard University Press, 1996.
Bergson, Henri. *L'énergie spirituelle: essais et conférences*. Paris: PUF, 1919, 1996.
———. *La pensée et le mouvant*. Paris: PUF, 1938, 1993. *The Creative Mind*. Translated by Mabelle L. Andison. Minnesota, New York: Dover Publications, 1946.
———. *Matière et Mémoire*. Edited by Frédéric Worms. Paris: PUF, 1939, 2008. *Matter and Memory*. Translated by N. Margaret Paul and W. Scott Palmer. New York: Zone Books, 1998.
———. *L'Évolution créatrice*. Edited by Frédéric Worms. Paris: PUF, 1941, 1991, 2009. *Creative Evolution*. Translated by Donald A. Landes. London: Routledge, 2023.
———. *Essai sur les données immédiates de la conscience*. Paris: PUF, 2001. *Time and Free Will: An Essay on the Immediate Data of Consciousness*. Translated by F. L. Pogson. London: Dover Publications, 2001.
———. "De l'intelligence." *Écrits philosophiques*. Edited by Frédéric Worms. Paris: PUF, 2011, 272-8.
———. "À propos de 'L'évolution de l'intelligence géometrique.'" *Revue de métaphysique et de morale* 16 (1908), 28-33.
Berl, Emmanuel. *Mort de la pensée bourgeoise*. Paris: Grasset, 1929.
———. *Mort de la morale bourgeoise*. Paris: Éditions de la Nouvelle Revue Française, 1930.
Bernardi, Laure. "Zur französischen Literatur und Kultur." *Benjamin Handbuch: Leben—Werk—Wirkung*. Edited by Burkhardt Lindner. Stuttgart: J.B. Metzler, 2006, 332-42.
Bersani, Leo. *Marcel Proust: Fictions of Life and Art*. New York: Oxford University Press, 1965.
———. *The Culture of Redemption*. Cambridge, MA: Harvard University Press, 1990.
———. *Thoughts and Things*. Chicago: University of Chicago Press, 2015.
Berthelier, Vincent. *Le style réactionnaire: De Maurras à Houllebecq*. Paris: Amsterdam éditions, 2022.
Bhattacharya, Baidik. "Somapolitics: A Biohermeneutic Paradigm in the Era of Empire." *boundary 2* 45, 4 (November 2018), 127-59.
Binet, Alfred. "Application des méthodes nouvelles au diagnostic du niveau intellectuel chez des enfants normaux et anormaux d'hospice et d'école primaire." *L'année psychologique* 11 (1904), 245-336.
———. *Les idées modernes sur les enfants*. Paris: Flammarion, 1909.
———. *Le fétichisme dans l'amour*. Paris: Payot, 1887, 2001.
Binet, Alfred and Théodore Simon, "Méthodes nouvelles pour le diagnostic du niveau intellectuel des anormaux." *L'année psychologique* 11 (1904), 191-244.
———. "Sur la nécessité d'établir un diagnostic scientifique des états inférieurs de l'intelligence." *L'année psychologique* 11 (1904), 163-90.
———. *The Development of Intelligence in Children (The Binet-Simon Scale)*. Translated from articles in *L'Année psychologique* by Elizabeth Kite. Baltimore: Williams and Wilkins, 1916, 1973.

Bizub, Edward. *Proust et le moi divisé: 'La Recherche,' creuset de la psychologie expérimentale (1874-1914)*. Paris: Droz, 2006.

Blanchot, Maurice. *Faux pas*. Paris: Gallimard, 1943, 1987. *Faux pas*. Translated by Charlotte Mandell. Stanford: Stanford University Press, 2001.

———. *La part du feu*. Paris: Gallimard, 1949. *The Work of Fire*. Translated by Charlotte Mandell. Stanford: Stanford University Press, 1995.

———. *L'espace littéraire*. Paris: Gallimard, 1955. *The Space of Literature*. Translated by Ann Smock. Lincoln: University of Nebraska Press, 1982, 1989.

———. *The Blanchot Reader*. Translated and edited by Michael Holland. Oxford: Blackwell Publishers, 1995.

———. *L'Amitié*. Paris: Gallimard, 1971. *Friendship*. Translated Elizabeth Rottenberg. Stanford: Stanford University Press, 1997.

Blood, Susan. "The Precinematic Novel: Zola's *La Bête humaine*." *Representations* 93 (2006), 49-75.

Bock, Hans-Manfred. "La querelle de *L'Allemand*: les réactions allemandes à la publication du livre de Rivière." *Jacques Rivière l'Européen, Actes du colloque international, ARJAF* 87-88 (1998), 25-36.

Bostrom, Nick. "How Long Before Superintelligence?" *Linguistic and Philosophical Investigations* 5, 1 (2006), 11-30.

Bourdieu, Pierre. *Questions of Sociology*. London: Sage, 1984.

Bouveresse, Jacques. "Philosophy from an Antiphilosopher: Paul Valéry." Translated by Christian Fournier and Sandra Laugier. *Critical Inquiry* 21, 2 (Winter 1995), 354-81.

———. *La connaissance de l'écrivain: Sur la littérature, la vérité et la vie*. Marseille: Agone, 2008.

Bowie, Malcolm. *Freud, Proust and Lacan: Theory as Fiction*. Cambridge: Cambridge University Press, 1987.

———. "Dream and the Unconscious." *Reading Paul Valéry: Universe in Mind*. Edited by Paul Gifford and Brian Stimpson. Cambridge: Cambridge University Press, 1998, 262-79.

———. *Proust Among the Stars*. New York: Columbia University Press, 1998.

Brecht, Bertolt. *Briefe*, vol. 1. Berlin: Aufbau Verlag, 1998.

Breton, André. *Manifestes du surréalisme*. Paris: Gallimard, 1985, 1996. *Manifestoes of Surrealism*. Translated by Richard Seaver and Helen R. Lane. Ann Arbor: University of Michigan Press, 1969.

Brisset, Laurence. *La "NRF" de Paulhan*. Paris: Gallimard, 2003.

Brooks, Peter. *Realist Vision*. Princeton: Princeton University Press, 2005.

———. *Balzac's Lives*. New York: NYRB Books, 2020.

Buchet, Edmond. *Écrivains intelligents du XXème siècle*. Paris: Éditions Corrêa et Cie, 1945.

Bush, Christopher. *Ideographic Modernism: China, Writing, Media*. Oxford: Oxford University Press, 2010.

———. "Context." *A New Vocabulary for Global Modernism*. Edited by Eric Hayot and Rebecca Walkowitz. New York: Columbia University Press, 2016, 75-95.

Calvino, Italo. *Six Memos for the Next Millenium*. Translated by Patrick Creagh. New York: Vintage, 1989.

Canales, Jimena. *The Physicist and the Philosopher: Einstein, Bergson, and the Debate That Changed Our Understanding of Time*. Princeton: Princeton University Press, 2016.

———. *Bedeviled: A Shadow History of Demons in Science*. Princeton: Princeton University Press, 2020.

Canguilhem, Georges, *Études d'histoire et de philosophie des sciences concernant les vivants et la vie*, Paris: Vrin, 1994.

Carson, Anne. *The Albertine Workout*. New York: New Directions Poetry Pamphlet, 2015.

Carson, John. "Intelligence." *A Companion to American Thought*. Edited by Richard Fox and James Kloppenberg. Cambridge: Blackwell Publishers, 1995, 342–3.

———. "The Culture of Intelligence." *The Cambridge History of Science*, vol. 7, *Modern Social Sciences*. Edited by Theodore M. Porter and Dorothy Ross. New York: Cambridge University Press, 2003, 635–48.

———. *The Measure of Merit: Talents, Intelligence, and Inequality in the French and American Republics, 1750–1940*. Princeton: Princeton University Press, 2007.

Cassin, Barbara et al., eds. *Vocabulaire européen des philosophes: Dictionnaire des intraduisibles*. Edited by Barbara Cassin et al. Paris: Seuil, Le Robert, 2004. *Dictionary of Untranslatables: A Philosophical Lexicon*. Princeton: Princeton University Press, 2014.

Cave, Stephen. "The Problem with Intelligence. Its Value-Laden History and the Future of AI." *AIES'20: AAAI/ACM Conference on AI, Ethics, and Society Proceedings*, February 7–8, New York.

Cerisier, Alban. *Une histoire de "La NRF."* Paris: Gallimard, 2009.

Cerisier, Alban et al., eds., *La Nouvelle Revue Française: Les colloques du centenaire, Paris, Bourges, Caen*. Paris: Gallimard, 2013.

Charney, Hanna. "*Monsieur Teste* and *Der Mann Ohne Eigenschaften*: Homo possibilis in Fiction." *Comparative Literature*, 27 1 (Winter 1975), 1–7.

Citti, Pierre. *La mésintelligence: essais d'histoire de l'intelligence francaise du symbolisme à 1914*. Saint Etienne: Éditions des Cahiers intempestifs, 2000.

Clark, Christopher. *The Sleepwalkers: How Europe Went to War in 1914*. New York: Harper Collins, 2013.

Clark, T. J. *Farewell to an Idea: Episodes from a History of Modernism*. New Haven: Yale University Press, 1999, 2014.

———. Should Benjamin Have Read Marx?" *boundary 2* 30, 1 (2003).

Cocking, J. M. *Proust: Collected Essays on the Writer and his Art*. Cambridge: Cambridge University Press, 1982.

Cocteau, Jean. *Le passé défini*, vol. 1. Paris: Gallimard, 1983.

Codazzi, Paola. *André Gide et la Grande Guerre: L'émergence d'un esprit européen*. Genève: Droz, 2021.

Cohen, Margaret. *Profane Illumination: Walter Benjamin and the Paris of the Surrealist Revolution*. Berkeley: University of California Press, 1993.

Compagnon, Antoine. *La Troisième République des lettres entre Flaubert et Proust*. Paris: Gallimard, 1983.

———. *Proust entre deux siècles*. Paris: Seuil, 1989.

———. *Les cinq paradoxes de la modernité*. Paris: Seuil, 1990.

———. *Connaissez-vous Brunetière? Enquête sur un antidreyfusard et ses amis*. Paris: Seuil, 1997.

———. "Taine: philosophie de l'art ou philosophie du musée." *Relire Taine*. Paris: École Nationale Supérieure des Beaux-Arts, 2001, 11–50.

———. *Les Antimodernes: de Joseph de Maistre à Roland Barthes*. Paris: Seuil, 2005.

———. "Joseph Reinach et l'éloquence française." *Comptes rendus des séances de l'Académie des Inscriptions et Belles-Lettres* 151, 2 (2007).

———. *La littérature, pour quoi faire?* Paris: Collège de France / Fayard, 2007.

Compagnon, Antoine, ed. *La grande guerre des écrivains: De Apollinaire à Zweig*. Paris: Folio, 2014.

Condillac, Étienne Bonnot de. *L'essai sur l'origine des connaissances humaines: ouvrage où l'on réduit à un seul principe tout ce qui concerne l'entendement humain* in *Oeuvres completes de Condillac*, vol. 1. Paris: Baudouin Éditeurs, 1746, 1827. *Essay on the Origin of Human Knowledge*. Translated and edited by Hans Aarsleff. Cambridge: Cambridge University Press, 2001.

Cone, Michèle C. *French Modernisms: Perspectives on Art Before, During, and After Vichy*. Cambridge: Cambridge University Press, 2001.

Conklin, Alice L. *A Mission to Civilize: The Republican Idea of Empire in France and West Africa 1895–1930*. Stanford: Stanford University Press, 1997.

———. *In the Museum of Man: Race, Anthropology, and Empire in France, 1850–1950*. Ithaca: Cornell University Press, 2013.

Copeland, Rita. *Pedagogy, Intellectuals, and Dissent in the Later Middle Ages*. Cambridge: Cambridge University Press, 2001.

Crescimanno, Emanuele. *Implexe, fare, vedere: L'estetica nei Cahiers di Paul Valéry*. Palermo: Aesthetica Preprint, "Supplementa," 2006.

Cronan, Todd. "Paul Valéry's Blood Meridian or How the Reader became a Writer." *Nonsite* Issue 1 (2011).

———. *Against Affective Formalism: Matisse, Bergson, Modernism*. Minneapolis: University of Minnesota Press, 2013.

Crow, Christine. *Paul Valéry and the Poetry of Voice*. Cambridge: Cambridge University Press, 1982.

Curtius, Ernst-Robert. *Französischer Geist im zwanzigsten Jahrhundert*. Bern: Francke Verlag, 1952.

Dagan, Yaël. *La NRF entre guerre et paix 1914–1925*. Paris: Tallandier, 2008.

Dames, Nicholas. *The Physiology of the Novel: Reading, Neural Science, and the Form of Victorian Fiction*. Oxford: Oxford University Press, 2007.

Danziger, Kurt. *Naming the Mind: How Psychology Found Its Language*. London: Sage, 1997.

Daston, Lorraine. "The Naturalized Female Intellect." *Science in Context* 5 (1992), 209–35.

———. *Against Nature*. Cambridge, MA: MIT Press, 2019.

Daston, Lorraine, et al., "The Social Intelligence Hypothesis." *Human by Nature: Between Biology and the Social Sciences*. Edited by Peter Weingart et al. London: Routledge, 1997.

David, Jean. *Le procès de l'intelligence dans les lettres françaises au seuil de l'entre-deux-guerres 1917–1927*. Paris: Nizet, 1966.

Davis, Colin. "Valéry and the Truth of Poetry and Prose." *Orbis Litterarum* 43 (1988), 1–10.
Debaene, Vincent. *Far Afield: French Anthropology between Science and Literature.* Translated by Justin Izzo. Chicago: University of Chicago Press, 2014.
De Beistegui, Miguel. *Proust as Philosopher: The Art of Metaphor.* London: Routledge, 2013.
de la Rochefoucauld, Edmée. *En lisant les "Cahiers" de Paul Valéry.* 3 vols. Paris: Éditions Universitaires, 1964–67.
Deleuze, Gilles. *Le bergsonisme.* Paris: PUF, 1966, 2008. *Bergsonism.* Translated by Hugh Tomlinson and Barbara Habberjam. New York: Zone Books, 1991.
———. *Proust et les signes.* Paris: PUF, 1976, 2006. *Proust and Signs: The Complete Text.* Translated by Richard Howard. Minneapolis: University of Minnesota Press, 2014.
———. "Postscript on the Societies of Control." Translated by Michael Joughin. *October* 59 (Winter 1992).
———. "Boulez, Proust, and Time: 'Occupying without Counting.'" Translated by Timothy S. Murphy. *Angelaki: Journal of Theoretical Humanities,* 3, 2 (1998), 69–74.
de Man, Paul. *Blindness and Insight: Essays in the Rhetoric of Contemporary Criticism.* Minneapolis: Minnesota University Press, 1971.
———. *Critical Writings 1953–1978.* Edited by Lindsay Waters. Minneapolis: University of Minnesota Press, 1989.
Deppman, Jed. "Re-Presenting Paul Valéry's *Monsieur Teste*." *symplokē* 11, 1–2 (2003), 197–211.
Derrida, Jacques. *La voix et le phénomène.* Paris: PUF, 1967.
———. *Marges de la philosophie.* Paris: Éditions de Minuit, 1972. *Margins of Philosophy.* Translated by Alan Bass. Chicago: University of Chicago Press, 1984.
———. *La vérité en peinture.* Paris: Flammarion, 1978.
———. *Heidegger et la question: De l'esprit et autres essais.* Paris: Flammarion, 1987, 1990.
———. *L'archéologie du frivole.* Paris: Galilée, 1990.
———. *L'autre cap.* Paris: Éditions de Minuit, 1991.
———. *La bête et le souverain*, vol. 1. Paris: Galilée, 2008. *The Beast and the Sovereign,* vol. 1. Translated by Geoffrey Bennington. Chicago: University of Chicago Press, 2009.
Descombes, Vincent. *Proust: Philosophie du Roman.* Paris: Éditions de Minuit, 1987. *Proust: Philosophy of the Novel.* Translated by Catherine Chance Macksey. Stanford: Stanford University Press, 1992.
Detienne, Marcel, and Jean-Pierre Vernant. *Les ruses de l'intelligence: La mètis des Grecs.* Paris: Flammarion, 1974. *Cunning Intelligence in Greek Culture and Society.* Translated by Janet Lloyd. Chicago: University of Chicago Press, 1978.
Devillairs, Laurence. "Fénelon et le Dieu de la Première Méditation de Descartes." *Revue philosophique de la France et de l'étranger* 128, 2 (2003), 173–90.
Dreyfus, Hubert. *What Computers Still Can't Do: A Critique of Artificial Reason.* Cambridge, MA: MIT Press, 1972, 1992.
Dupee, F. W. "The Imagination of Duchesses." *The King of Cats, and Other Remarks on Writers and Writing.* New York: Noonday Press, 1945, 1965, 108–16.
Eiland, Howard, and Michael Jennings. *Walter Benjamin: A Critical Life.* Cambridge, MA: Harvard University Press, 2014.

Einfalt, Michael. "L'engagement intellectuel des écrivains français de l'entre-deux-guerres sous le regard de Walter Benjamin." *Agone: Philosophie, Critique & Littérature* 20 (1998), 91–105.

Eliot, T. S. *The Sacred Wood: Essays on Poetry and Criticism*. New York: Alfred A. Knopf, 1921.

———. "Books of the Quarter." *The New Criterion* 4 (October 1926), 751–7.

———. "From Poe to Valéry." *The Hudson Review* 2 (Autumn 1949), 327–42.

Ellison, David. "Modernism." *Marcel Proust in Context*. Edited by Adam Watt. Cambridge: Cambridge University Press, 2013, 214–20.

Empson, William. *Seven Types of Ambiguity*. New York: New Directions Books, 1930, 1947.

Erskine, John. *The Moral Obligation to be Intelligent and Other Essays*. New York: Duffield and Company, 1915, 1921.

Étiemble, René, "Proust et la crise de l'intelligence." *C'est le Bouquet!*, vol. 5. Paris: Gallimard, 1967, 150–212.

Fauré, Clémentine. "Huguenots ou Barbares... ces adversaires sont les mêmes: Charles Maurras, André Gide, et l'esthétique comme résistance à la race." *Esprit créateur* 59, 2, (2019), 150–64.

Fechner, Gustav. *Elements of Psychophysics*. Translated by Helmut Adler. New York: Holt, Reibhart and Winston, 1966.

Fénelon, François de Salignac de La Mothe-, *Œuvres complètes*. Vol. 2. Paris: Briand, 1810.

Fenves, Peter. *Arresting Language: From Leibniz to Benjamin*. Stanford: Stanford University Press, 2001.

———. "Is there an Answer to the Aestheticizing of the Political?" *Walter Benjamin and Art*. Edited by Andrew Benjamin. London: Continuum, 2005, 60-72.

Finn, Michael R. *Figures of the Pre-Freudian Unconscious from Flaubert to Proust*. Cambridge: Cambridge University Press, 2017.

Fore, Devin. "The Operative Word in Soviet Factography." *October* 118 (Fall 2006), 95–131.

Forster, E. M. *Aspects of the Novel*. London: Penguin, 1927, 2005.

Foster, Hal. "The Artist as Ethnographer." *The Return of the Real: The Avant-Garde at the End of the Century*. Cambridge: MIT Press, 1996, 171–204.

Foucault, Michel. *Les mots et les choses: Une archéologie des sciences humaines*. Paris: Gallimard, 1966.

———. "La fonction politique de l'intellectuel." *Dits et écrits*, vol 2: 1976-1988. Edited by Daniel Lefebvre and François Ewald. Paris: Gallimard, 2001, 109–14.

Fraisse, Luc. *L'éclectisme philosophique de Marcel Proust*. Paris: Presses Universitaires-Paris Sorbonne, 2013.

Freed-Thall, Hannah. "Prestige of a Momentary Diamond: Economies of Distinction in Proust." *New Literary History* 43, 1 (2012), 159–78.

———. *Spoiled Distinctions: Aesthetics and the Ordinary in French Modernism*. Oxford: Oxford University Press, 2015.

Friedman, Melvin J. "The Symbolist Novel: Huysmans to Malraux." *Modernism: A Guide to European Literature 1890–1930*. Edited by Malcolm Bradbury and James McFarlane. New York: Penguin, 1976, 1991, 453–67.

Galeteria, Daria, "Contre Taine: Sur une source théorique de la *Recherche*." *Bulletin d'information proustiennes* 29–30 (1998–99), 31–9.

Gauchet, Marcel. *L'inconscient cérébral*. Paris: Seuil, 1992.
Gaulin, Morgan. "La théorie du signe d'Hippolyte Taine." *Nineteenth-Century French Studies* 35 (Winter 2007), 384-92.
Gay, Peter. *Modernism: The Lure of Heresy from Baudelaire to Beckett and Beyond*. New York: W. W. Norton, 2008.
Genette, Gérard. "La littérature comme telle." *Figures I*. Paris: Seuil, 1966, 253-65.
———. *Figures II*. Paris: Seuil, 1969.
Ghéon, Henri. "Réflexions sur le rôle actuel de l'intelligence française." *Nouvelle Revue Française*, 74 (November 1919), 953-64.
Gide, André. "Réflexions sur L'Allemagne." *Nouvelle Revue Française* 69 (June 1919), 35-46.
———. *Journal*, vol. 1: 1887-1925. Edited by Éric Marty. Paris: Gallimard, Bibliothèque de la Pléiade, 1996.
———. *The Journals of André Gide*. Translated by J. O'Brien. New York: Knopf, 1948.
———. *Paul Valéry*. Paris: Domat, 1947.
———. *Essais critiques*. Edited by Pierre Masson, Paris: Gallimard, 1999.
Gide, André, Paul Valéry and Pierre Louÿs. *Correspondances à trois voix (1888-1920)*. Paris: Gallimard, 2004.
Gifford, Paul and Brian Stimpson, eds. *Reading Paul Valéry: Universe in Mind*. Cambridge: Cambridge University Press, 1998.
Gildea, Robert. *Children of the Revolution: The French, 1799-1914*. Cambridge, MA: Harvard University Press, 2008.
Gilman, Sander L. *Smart Jews: The Construction of the Image of Jewish Superior Intelligence*. Lincoln: University of Nebraska Press, 1997.
Gipper, Andreas. *Der Intellektuelle: Konzeption und Selbstverständnis schriftstellerischer Intelligenz in Frankreich und Italien 1918-1930*. Stuttgart: M&P Verlag für Wissenschaft und Forschung, 1992.
Goblot, Edmond. *Le vocabulaire philosophique*. Paris: Armand Collin, 1901.
Goldfarb, Lisa. *Unexpected Affinities: Modern American Poetry and Symbolist Poetics*. Eastbourne: Sussex Academic Press, 2018.
Goldmann, Lucien. "Valéry: Monsieur Teste." *Structures mentales et création culturelle*. Paris: Éditions Anthropos, 1970, 171-78.
Gough, Maria. "Paris, Capital of the Soviet Avant-Garde." *October* 101 (2002), 53-83.
Gould, Stephen Jay. *The Mismeasure of Man (Revised and Expanded)*. New York: W. W. Norton, 2006.
Gourgouris, Stathis. *Does Literature Think?* Stanford: Stanford University Press, 2003.
Gracq, Julien. *En lisant, en écrivant*. Paris: José Corti, 1980.
Greaney, Patrick. *Untimely Beggar: Poverty and Power from Baudelaire to Benjamin*. Minneapolis: University of Minnesota Press, 2008.
Guerlac, Suzanne. *Literary Polemics: Bataille, Sartre, Valéry, Breton*. Stanford: Stanford University Press, 1997.
———. *Thinking in Time: An Introduction to Henri Bergson*. Ithaca: Cornell University Press, 2006.
———. "La politique de l'esprit et les usages du classicisme à l'époque moderne." *Revue d'histoire littéraire de la France* 107, 2 (2007), 401-12.

———. "Valéry—Modernist Myths and (Anti)Modernist States of Mind." *The Romanic Review* 99 (2008).
———. "Derrida after Valéry (after Derrida)." *Understanding Derrida, Understanding Modernism.* Edited by Jean-Michel Rabaté. New York: Bloomsbury Academic, 2019, 178–94.
Gutting, Gary. *French Philosophy in the Twentieth Century.* Cambridge: Cambridge University Press, 2001.
Hamacher, Werner. "History, Teary: Some remarks on *La Jeune Parque*." Translated by Michael Shae. *Yale French Studies* 74, Phantom Proxies: Symbolism and the Rhetoric of History (1988), 67–94.
———. *Premises.* Translated by Peter Fenves. Stanford: Stanford University Press, 1996.
———"Guilt History: Benjamin's Sketch 'Capitalism as Religion.'" *Diacritics* 32, 3–4 (2002).
———. *Für—die Philologie.* Solothurn: Urs Engeler Roughbooks 4, 2009. *Minima Philologica.* Translated by Catharine Diehl and Jason Groves. New York: Fordham University Press, 2015.
———. *On the Brink: Language, Time, History, and Politics.* Edited by Jan Plug. New York: Rowman & Littlefeld, 2020.
Hanna, Martha. *The Mobilization of Intellect: French Scholars and Writers during the Great War.* Cambridge, MA: Harvard University Press, 1996.
Hartman, Geoffrey. "Valéry." *The Unmediated Vision: An Interpretation of Wordsworth, Hopkins, Rilke, and Valéry.* New Haven: Yale University Press, 1954, 97–124.
Healey, Kimberly. "French Literary Modernism." *Modernism*, vol. 2. Edited by Astradur Eysteinsson and Vivian Liska. Philadelphia: John Benjamins Publishing Company, 2007, 801–16.
Hebey, Pierre, ed. *L'esprit NRF 1908–1940.* Paris: Gallimard, 1990.
Heidegger, Martin. *Einführung in die Metaphysik.* Tübingen: Max Niemeyer Verlag, 1953. *Introduction to Metaphysics.* Translated by Gregory Fried and Richard Polt. New Haven: Yale University Press, 2000.
———. *Erläuterungen zu Hölderlins Dichtung. Gesamtausgabe*, vol. 4. Frankfurt: Klostermann, 1981. *Elucidations of Hölderlin's Poetry.* Translated Keith Holler. Amherst: Humanity Books, 2000.
———. *The Fundamental Concepts of Metaphysics: World, Finitude, Solitude.* Bloomington: Indiana University Press, 1996.
———. "Die Herkunft der Kunst und die Bestimmung des Denkens." *Gesamtausgabe*, vol. 80.2. Frankfurt: Klostermann, 2020, 1309–11."The Provenance of Art and the Destination of Thought." *Journal of the British Society for Phenomenology* 44, 2 (January 2013), 119–28.
———. "Überlieferte Sprache und technische Sprache." *Gesamtausgabe*, vol. 80.2. Frankfurt: Klostermann, 2020. "Traditional Language and Technological Language." Translated by Wanda Torres Gregory. *Journal of Philosophical Research* 23 (1998), 129–145.
Heller-Roazen, Daniel. *Absentees: On Variously Missing Persons.* New York: Zone, 2021.
Henry, Anne. *Marcel Proust: Théories pour une esthétique.* Paris: Klincksieck, 1983.
Herrenschmidt, Clarisse. *Les trois écritures: Langue, nombre, code.* Paris: Éditions Gallimard, 2007.

———. "A propos de l'ouvrage 'Les trois écritures.' Langue, nombre, code." *REVUE Asylon(s)*, 7 (June 2009), http://www.reseau-terra.eu/article890.html.

Hoeges, Dirk. *Kontroverse am Abgrund. Ernst Robert Curtius und Karl Mannheim: Intellektuelle und "freischwebende Intelligenz" in der Weimarer Republik*. Frankfurt am Main: Fischer, 1994.

Hollier, Denis. *Absent Without Leave: French Literature under the Threat of War*. Translated by Catherine Porter. Cambridge: Harvard University Press, 1997.

Hollier, Denis, ed. *A New History of French Literature*. Cambridge, MA: Harvard University Press, 1994.

Hollister, Lucas. "Missing Modernism (Gide)." *Contemporary French and Francophone Studies* 24 (2019), 564–72.

Horne, John. "Remobilizing for 'Total War': France and Great Britain 1917–1918." *State, Society, and Mobilization in Europe during the First World War*. Edited by John Horne. Cambridge: Cambridge University Press, 1997, 195–211.

Hughes, Edward J. *Marcel Proust: A Study in the Quality of Awareness*. Cambridge: Cambridge University Press, 1983.

———. *Proust, Class, Nation*. Oxford: Oxford University Press, 2011.

Huneman, Philippe. *Les sociétés du profilage: Évaluer, optimiser, prédire*. Paris: Payot, 2023.

Hunkeler, Thomas. "Comment défendre l'intelligence française? La NRF et les revues avant-gardistes en 1919–1920." *La Nouvelle Revue Française: Les colloques du centenaire*. Edited by Alban Cerisier et al. Paris: Gallimard, 2013, 130–43.

Husserl, Edmund. *Die Krisis der europäischen Wissenschaften und die transzendentale Phänomenologie: Eine Einleitung in die phänomenologische Philosophie*. The Hague: Martinus Nijhoff, 1954; 1962. *The Crisis of European Sciences and Transcendental Phenomenology: An Introduction to Phenomenological Philosophy*. Translated by David Carr. Evanston: Northwestern University Press, 1970.

Hutchinson, Ben. *Lateness and Modern European Literature*. Oxford: Oxford University Press, 2016.

Huyssen, Andreas. "Introduction: Modernism after Postmodernity." *New German Critique* 99 (2006), 1–5.

Hytier, Jean. *La poétique de Valéry*. Paris: Armand Colin, 1953, 1970.

Ince, W. N. *The Poetic Theory of Paul Valéry: Inspiration and Technique*. Leicester: Leicester University Press, 1961.

Jackson, Julian. *La Grande Illusion*. London: Bloomsbury Publishing, 2019.

Jacobs, Carol. *In the Language of Walter Benjamin*. Baltimore: The Johns Hopkins University Press, 1999.

James, Tony. *Dreams, Creativity, and Madness in Nineteenth-Century France*. Oxford: Oxford University Press, 1995.

James, William. "A World of Pure Experience." *Writings 1902–1910*. New York: The Library of America, 1987, 1159–83.

———. "On Intelligence." *Essays, Comments, and Reviews*. Cambridge, MA: Harvard University Press, 1987, 256–61.

Jameson, Frederic. *A Singular Modernity*. London: Verso Books, 2002.

———. *The Political Unconscious: Narrative as a Socially Symbolic Act*. London: Routledge Classics, 2002.

———. *The Antinomies of Realism*. London: Verso Books, 2015.
Janicaud, Dominique. *Ravaisson et la métaphysique: Une généalogie du spiritisme français*. Paris: Vrin, 1998.
Jarrety, Michel. *Paul Valéry devant la littérature: Mesure de la limite*. Paris: PUF, 1991.
———. "Valéry: du classique sans classicisme." *Revue d'histoire littéraire de la France* 107, 2 (2007).
———. *Paul Valéry*. Paris: Fayard, 2008.
Jay, Martin. *The Dialectical Imagination: A History of the Frankfurt School and the Institute of Social Research, 1923–1950*. Berkeley: University of California Press, 1996.
Jefferson, Ann. *Genius in France: An Idea and Its Uses*. Princeton: Princeton University Press, 2014.
Jennings, Jeremy. *Revolution and the Republic: A History of Political Thought in France since the Eighteenth Century*. Oxford: Oxford University Press, 2011.
Jenny, Laurent. *La fin de l'intériorité: Théorie de l'expression et invention esthétique dans les avant-gardes françaises 1885–1935*. Paris: PUF, 2002.
Johnson, Christopher. "'French' Cybernetics." *French Studies* 69, 1 (January 2015), 60–78.
Jones, Donna V. *The Racial Discourses of Life Philosophy: Negritude, Vitalism, and Modernity*. New York: Columbia University Press, 2010.
Joqueviel-Bourjea, Marie, ed. *Faut-il oublier Valéry?* Paris: L'Harmattan, 2006.
Josipovici, Gabriel. "The Marquise went out at Five." *Whatever Happened to Modernism*. New Haven: Yale University Press, 2010, 78–91.
Just, Daniel. *Literature, Ethics, and Decolonization in Postwar France: The Politics of Disengagement*. Cambridge, Cambridge University Press, 2015.
Kahler, Erich. *Die Verinnerung des Erzählens*. Munich: Deutscher Taschenbuch Verlag, 1970. *The Inward Turn of Narrative*. Translated by Richard and Clara Winston. Princeton: Princeton University Press, 1973.
Karpeles, Eric. *Paintings in Proust*. London: Thames & Hudson, 2008.
Kaufmann, Vincent. *Le livre et ses adresses*. Paris: Méridiens-Klincksieck, 1986.
———. "1925, December. I cannot abide stupidity." *A New History of French literature*. Edited by Denis Hollier. Cambridge, MA: Harvard University Press, 1994, 876–81.
Kay, Sarah, Terence Cave, and Malcolm Bowie, eds. *A Short History of French Literature*. Oxford: Oxford University Press, 2006.
Kermode, Frank. "Intelligent Theory." *London Review of Books* 4, 18 (October 1982).
Koffeman, Maaike N. "La naissance d'un mythe: La Nouvelle Revue Française dans le champ littéraire de la Belle Epoque." *Etudes littéraires* 40, 1 (2009), 17–36.
———. *Entre Classicisme et Modernité: La Nouvelle Revue Française dans le champ littéraire de la Belle Epoque*. Leiden: Brill, 2003.
Korsch, Karl. "Introduction to the *Critique of the Gotha Program*." *Marxism and Philosophy*. Translated and introduced by Fred Halliday. London: Verso Books, 2012, 145–70.
Kosofsky Sedgwick, Eve. *Epistemology of the Closet*. Berkeley: University of California Press, 1990, 2008.
Kopp, Robert, ed. *La place de "La NRF" dans la vie littéraire du XXème siècle (1908–1943)*. Paris: Gallimard, 2009.

Krämer, Olav. *Denken erzählen: Repräsentationen des Intellekts bei Robert Musil und Paul Valéry*. Berlin: de Gruyter, 2009.
Kristeva, Julia. *Le temps sensible: Proust et l'expérience littéraire*. Paris: Gallimard, 1993.
Kurzweil, Ray. *The Singularity is Near: When Humans Transcend Biology*. London: Penguin, 2006.
Kwinter, Sanford. *Architectures of Time: Toward a Theory of the Event in Modernist Culture*. New York: Zone Books, 2002.
Labarrière, Jean-Louis. "L'intelligence." *Notions de philosophie*, vol. 1. Edited by Denis Kambouchner. Paris: Gallimard, 1995, 423–88.
Ladenson, Elisabeth. *Proust's Lesbianism*. Ithaca: Cornell University Press, 1999.
Lalande, André. *Vocabulaire technique et critique de la philosophie*. Paris: PUF, 1926, 1962.
Landy, Joshua. *Philosophy as Fiction: Self, Deception and Knowledge in Proust*. Oxford: Oxford University Press, 2004.
———. "Proust Among the Psychologists." *Philosophy and Literature*, 35 (2011), 375–87.
Le Blanc, Guillaume, "Les trois psychologies." *L'esprit des sciences humaines*. Paris: Vrin, 2005, 213–55.
Lechantre, Michel. "Valéry Bouchoreille." *Le langage et l'homme* 18 (1971–72), 49–53.
Lefebvre, Alexandre, and Nils F. Schott. *Interpreting Bergson: Critical Essays*. Cambridge: Cambridge University Press, 2019.
Lefebvre, Jean-Pierre. "Allemand." *Vocabulaire européen des philosophes: Dictionnaire des intraduisibles*. Edited by Barbara Cassin. Paris: Seuil, Le Robert, 2004, 53–64.
Legg, Shane, and Marcus Hutter. "Universal intelligence: A Definition of Machine Intelligence." *Minds and Machines* 17, 4, (2007), 391–444.
Leibniz, G. W. "Leibniz à Goldbach, le 17 d'avril 1712." *La correspondance de Leibniz avec Goldbach*. Edited by A.P. Juschkewitsch and Juri C. Kopelewitsch. *Studia Leibnitiana*, vol. 20.2. Wiesbaden: F. Steiner Verlag, 1988, 181–3.
———. *Essais de théodicée*. Paris: Flammarion, 1999.
Leonard, Diane. "Intelligence." *Dictionnaire Marcel Proust*. Edited by Annik Bouillaguet and Brian G. Rogers. Paris: Champion, 2004, 512–14.
Leroy, Géraldi, and Julie Bertrand-Sabiani. "Les revues: traditions et innovations." *La vie littéraire à la Belle Epoque*. Paris: PUF, 1998, 117–56.
Leslie, Esther. *Walter Benjamin: Overpowering Conformism*. London: Pluto Press, 2000.
Lewis, Pericles. *Modernism, Nationalism, and the Novel*. Cambridge: Cambridge University Press, 2000.
Littré, Émile. *Dictionnaire de la langue française*. Paris: Hachette, 1872–77, https://artfl-project.uchicago.edu/content/dictionnaires-dautrefois.
Lloyd, David. "Valéry on Value: The Political Economy of Poetics." *Representations* 7 (1984), 116–32.
Lucey, Michael. *Gide's Bent: Sexuality, Politics, Writing*. Oxford: Oxford University Press, 1995.
———. *What Proust Heard: Novels and the Ethnography of Talk*. Chicago: Chicago University Press, 2022.
Lyons, Sara. *Assessing Intelligence: The Bildungsroman and the Politics of Human Potential in England, 1860–1910*. Edinburgh: Edinburgh University Press, 2022.

Macé, Marielle. *Le temps de l'essai: Histoire d'un genre en France au XXe siècle*. Paris: Belin, 2006.

Mackintosh, Nicholas. *IQ and Human Intelligence*. Oxford: Oxford University Press, 2011.

Mahuzier, Brigitte. "Proust, War, Intelligence, and Idiocy." *Contemporary French and Francophone Studies* 9, 1 (2005), 47–61.

Mairesse, Anne N. "Return to Teste? Or 'What is a Man Capable of?': Valéry, Anthropologist of Modernity." *MLN* 117, 5 (2002), 1003–27.

Malabou, Catherine. *Morphing Intelligence: From IQ Measurement to Artificial Brains*. Translated by Carolyn Shread. New York: Columbia University Press, 2019.

Margel, Serge. "Langage et politique: Le pouvoir critique des mots, de Brecht à Benjamin." *Lignes* 3, 42 (2013).

Marion, Jean-Luc. *God Without Being: Hors-Texte*. Translated by Thomas A. Carlson. Chicago: University of Chicago Press, 1991.

Marquer, Bertrand, *Naissance du fantastique clinique: la crise de l'analyse dans la littérature fin-de-siècle*. Paris: Hermann, 2014.

Marx, Karl. *Karl Marx: Selected Writings*. Edited by David McLellan. Oxford: Oxford University Press, 2000.

Marx, William. *Naissance de la critique moderne: La littérature selon Eliot et Valéry*. Arras: Artois Presses Université, Cahiers scientifiques, 2002.

Marx, William, ed. *Les arrière-gardes au XXe siècle*. Paris: PUF, 2008.

Massis, Henri. "Manifeste pour un parti de l'intelligence." *Figaro littéraire* (July 19, 1919).

Mauriac Dyer, Nathalie. "Paul Valéry." *Dictionnaire Marcel Proust*. Paris: Honoré Champion, 2004, 1019–20.

Maurras, Charles. *L'avenir de l'intelligence*. Paris: Albert Fontemoing, Éditeur, 1905.

Maya, Kazuko. "L'Anti-intellectualisme de Proust." *Revue de Hiyoshi. Langue et littérature française* 21 (September 1995), 81–100.

McDonald, Christie. *The Proustian Fabric: Associations of Memory*. Lincoln: University of Nebraska Press, 1991.

McGrath, Larry Sommer. *Making Spirit Matter: Neurology, Psychology, and Selfhood in Modern France*. Chicago: University of Chicago Press, 2020.

McGuinness, Patrick. *Poetry and Radical Politics in Fin de Siècle France: From Anarchism to Action Française*. Oxford: Oxford University Press, 2015.

Mehlman, Jeffrey. "Craniometry and Criticism: Notes on a Valeryan Criss-Cross." *boundary 2* 11, no. ½ (Autumn 1982-Winter 1983), 81–101.

Menninghaus, Winfried. *Walter Benjamins Theorie der Sprachmagie*. Frankfurt: Suhrkamp Verlag, 1980.

Merleau-Ponty, Maurice. *Phénoménologie du corps*. Paris: Gallimard, 1945.

———. *Recherches sur l'usage littéraire du langage: Cours au Collège de France, Notes, 1953*. Edited by Emmanuel de Saint Aubert and Benedetta Zaccarello. Paris: Metis Presses, 2013.

———. *L'union de l'âme et du corps chez Malebranche, Maine de Biran et Bergson*. Paris: Vrin, 1978.

———. *Le visible et l'invisible*. Paris: Gallimard, 1988.

Meschonnic, Henri. *Modernité, Modernité*. Paris: Folio Essais, 1994.

Mill, John Stuart. "Taine's *De l'intelligence*." *Collected Works of John Stuart Mill*, vol. 11. Toronto: University of Toronto Press, 1978, 441–8.
Milne, Anna-Louise. "*La Nouvelle Revue Française* in the Age of Modernism." *The Romanic Review* 99 (2008).
Mitchell, Allan. *The German Influence in France after 1870: The Formation of the French Republic*. Chapel Hill: University of North Carolina Press, 1979.
Mitchell, Stanley. *Understanding Brecht*. Translated by Anna Bostock. London: Verso Books, 1998.
Moriarty, Michael, and Jeremy Jennings, eds. *The Cambridge History of French Thought*. Cambridge: Cambridge University Press, 2019.
Morimoto, Atsuo. *Paul Valéry. L'imaginaire et la genèse du sujet: de la psychologie à la poïétique*. Caen: Lettres Modernes Minard, 2009.
———. "L'implexe chez Valéry: une notion de potentialité et la théorie motrice de la psychologie à l'époque de Valéry." *L'intelligence de la complexité: Épistémologie et pragmatique*. Edited by Jean-Louis Le Moigne and Edgar Morin. Avignon: Éditions de l'aube, 2007.
Nägele, Rainer. "Vexierbild einer kritischen Konstellation. Walter Benjamin und Max Kommerell." *Max Kommerell: Leben, Werk, Aktualität*. Edited by Walter Busch and Gerhart Pickerodt. Göttingen: Wallstein Verlag, 2003, 349–67.
Nattiez, Jean-Jacques. *Proust Musicien*. Paris: Christian Bourgois, 1999.
Nguyen, Victor. *Aux origines de l'action française: intelligence et politique vers 1900*. Paris: Fayard, 1991.
Nias, Hilary. *The Artificial Self: The Psychology of Hippolyte Taine*. London: Routledge, 2017.
Nicholls, Julia. *Revolutionary Thought after the Paris Commune, 1871–1885*. Cambridge: Cambridge University Press, 2019.
Nicholls, Peter. *Modernisms: A Literary Guide*. New York: Palgrave McMillan, 2008.
Nietzsche, Friedrich. *Kritische Studienausgabe*. 15 vols. Edited by Giorgio Colli and Mazzino Montinari. Berlin, New York: Walter de Gruyter, 1964–65.
———. *Beyond Good and Evil*. Edited by Rolf Peter Horstmann and Judith Norman. Cambridge: Cambridge University Press, 2002.
———. *The Anti-Christ, Ecce Homo, Twilight of the Idols, And Other Writings*. Edited by Alan Ridely and Judith Norman. Cambridge: Cambridge University Press, 2005.
Nizan, Paul. *Les chiens de garde*. Marseille: Agone Éditeur, 1998.
Nolan, Michael E. *The Inverted Mirror: Mythologizing the Enemy in France and Germany, 1898–1914*. New York: Berghahn Books, 2005.
Nordmann, Jean-Thomas. "Taine et le positivisme." *Romantisme* 8, 21–22 (1978), 21–33.
———. *Taine et la critique scientifique*. Paris: PUF, 1992.
North, Michael. "Afterlife of Modernism." *New Literary History* 50 (2019), 91–112.
O'Brien, Justin, ed. *N.R.F. Essays from the Nouvelle Revue Française 1919–1940*. London: Eyre & Spottiswoode, 1958.
Orlando, Francesco. *Obsolete Objects in the Literary Imagination: Ruins, Relics, Rarities, Rubbish, Uninhibited Places, and Hidden Treasures*. Translated by Gabriel Pihas, Daniel Seidel, and Alessandra Grego. New Haven: Yale University Press, 2007.

Oster, Daniel, *Monsieur Valéry*. Paris: Seuil, 1981.
Palmier, Jean-Michel. *Walter Benjamin: Le chiffonnier, l'Ange et le Petit Bossu*. Paris: Klincksieck, 2006.
Paul, Zakir. "Intellectual Equality." *Understanding Rancière, Understanding Modernism*. Edited by Patrick M. Bray. London: Bloomsbury, 2017, 245–50.
Paulhan, Jean. "Carnet du spectateur." *Nouvelle Revue Française* 185 (February 1929), 244–47.
——. *Paul Valéry ou, La littérature considérée comme un faux*. Brussels: Éditions complexe, 1987.
Pavel, Germaine. "Deux poètes du sommeil: Proust et Valéry." *Bulletin des amis de Marcel Proust* 10–11 (1960–61).
Perrin, Jean François. "Taine et la mémoire involontaire." *Romantisme* 82 (1993), 73–81.
Peteers, Benoît. *Valéry: Tenter de vivre*. Paris: Flammarion, 2014.
Pflug, Günther. *Henri Bergson, Quellen und Konsequenzen einer induktiven Metaphysik*. Berlin: De Gruyter, 1959.
Philippe, Gilles. *Sujet, verbe, complément: Le moment grammatical de la littérature française (1890–1940)*. Paris: Gallimard, 2002.
——. "Du 'Style NRF.'" *La Nouvelle Revue Française: Les colloques du centenaire*. Edited by Alban Cerisier et al. Paris: Gallimard, 2013, 155–66.
Phillipon, Michel. *Le vocabulaire de Valéry*. Paris: Éditions Ellipses, 2007.
Piaget, Jean. *La psychologie de l'intelligence*. Paris: Armand Collin, 1967. *Psychology of Intelligence*. Translated by Malcolm Piercy and D. E. Berlyne. Paterson, NJ: Littlefield, Adams & Co., 1966, 1968.
Pilkington, A. E. *Bergson and His Influence: A Reassessment*. Cambridge: Cambridge University Press, 1976.
Prendergast, Christopher. *The Classic: Sainte-Beuve and the Nineteenth-Century Culture Wars*. Oxford: Oxford University Press, 2007.
——. *Mirages and Mad Beliefs: Proust the Skeptic*. Princeton: Princeton University Press, 2015.
Prochasson, Christophe and Anne Rasmussen, eds. *Vrai et faux dans la Grande Guerre*. Paris: La Découverte, 2004.
Proust, Marcel. *Marcel Proust–Jacques Rivière: Correspondance, 1914–1922*. Edited by Philip Kolb. Paris: Plon, 1955.
——. *Correspondance de Marcel Proust*. 21 vols. Edited by Philip Kolb. Paris: Plon, 1970–93.
——. *Jean Santeuil, précédé de Les plaisirs et les jours*. Edited by Pierre Clarac and Yves Sandre. Paris: Gallimard, Bibliothèque de la Pléiade, 1971.
——. *Le Carnet de 1908*. Edited by Philip Kolb. Paris: Gallimard, 1976.
——. *À la recherche du temps perdu*, 4 vols. Edited by Jean Yves Tadié. Paris: Gallimard, Bibliothèque de la Pléiade, 1987–89. *In Search of Lost Time*, 6 vols. Translated by C. K. Scott Montcrieff and Terence Kilmartin. Revised by D. J. Enright. New York: Modern Library, 1981, 2003.
——. *Proust on Art and Literature*. Translated by Sylvia Townsend Warner. New York: Caroll and Graf, 1997.
——. *Swann's Way*. Translated by Lydia Davis. New York: Penguin, 2004.

———. *Essais*. Edited by Antoine Compagnon, Christophe Pradeau, and Matthieu Vernet. Paris: Gallimard, 2022.

Quaranta, Jean-Marc. *Le Génie de Proust: Genèse de l'esthétique de la "Recherche," de "Jean Santeuil" à la madeleine et au "Temps Perdu."* Paris: Honoré Champion, 2011.

Rabaté, Jean-Michel. *La penultième est morte: Spectographies de la modernité (Mallarmé, Breton, Beckett et quelques autres)*. Seyssel: Champ Vallon, 1993.

———. *1913: The Cradle of Modernism*. London: Blackwell, 2007.

———. "Modernism and the French Novel: A Genealogy (1888–1913)." *A History of the Modernist Novel*. Edited by Gregory Castle. Cambridge: Cambridge University Press, 2015, 86–109.

———. "French Modernism: Gide, Proust, and Larbaud." *The Cambridge History of Modernism*. Edited by Vincent Sherry. Cambridge: Cambridge University Press, 2017, 575–91.

Rabinbach, Anson. *In the Shadow of Catastrophe: German Intellectuals between Apocalypse and Engagement*. Berkeley: University of California Press, 1997.

Rabinow, Paul. *French Modern: Norms and Forms of the Social Environment*. Chicago, University of Chicago Press, 1995.

Rancière, Jacques. *La chair des mots*. Paris: Galilée, 1989.

———. *La parole muette: Essai sur les contradictions de la littérature*. Paris: Hachette, 1998. *Mute Speech: Literature, Critical Theory, and Politics*. Translated by James Swenson. New York: Columbia University Press, 2011.

Rasmussen, Anne. *Au nom de la patrie: Les intellectuels et la première guerre mondiale (1910–1919)*. Paris: Éditions la Découverte, 1996.

Ravaisson, Félix. *De l'habitude*. Paris: Allia, 2007.

Renan, Ernest. *L'avenir de la science: pensée de 1848*. Paris: Calmann Lévy, 1890.

Rentzou, Effie, and André Benhaïm, eds. *1913: The Year of French Modernism*. Manchester: Manchester University Press, 2020.

Ribot, Théodule. "De l'intelligence." *Revue philosophique de la France et de l'Étranger* (January–June 1884), 583–4.

———. *Les maladies de la personnalité*. Paris: Félix Alcan, 1885.

Richard, Jean-Pierre. *Littérature et sensation*. Paris: Seuil, 1954.

———. *Proust et le monde sensible*. Paris: Seuil, 1974.

Richard, Lionel. "Jacques Rivière et l'orientation idéologique de la *Nouvelle Revue Française* au lendemain de la Première Guerre mondiale." *Ethnopsychologie* 3–4 (September 1975), 431–5.

Richard, Nathalie. *Hippolyte Taine: Histoire, Psychologie, Littérature*. Paris: Éditions Classiques Garnier, 2013.

Rivière, Jacques. "Le roman d'aventure." *Nouvelle Revue Française* 53 (May 1913), 748–65; 54 (June 1913), 914–32; 55 (July 1913), 56–77.

———. *L'Allemand: Souvenirs et réflexions d'un prisonnier de guerre*. Paris: NRF, 1918, 1936.

———. "Histoire abrégée de *La Nouvelle Revue Française*" (1918). *La revue des revues*, 21 (1996), 73–96.

———. Editorial. *Nouvelle Revue Française* 69 (June 1919).

———. "Le parti de l'intelligence." *Nouvelle Revue Française* 72 (September 1919), 612–18.

———. "Catholicisme et nationalisme." *Nouvelle Revue Fançaise* 74 (November 1919), 975–8.
———. *Quelques progrès dans l'étude du coeur humain*. Paris: Gallimard, 1925, 1985.
———. *Correspondance Jacques Rivière et Alain-Fournier 1905–1914*, vol. 2. Paris: Gallimard, 1926.
———. "La *Nouvelle Revue Française*." *L'esprit NRF 1908–1940*. Edited by Pierre Hebey. Paris: Gallimard, 1990.
———. *Une conscience européenne*. Paris: Gallimard, 1992.
Robinson, Judith. *L'analyse de l'esprit dans les "Cahiers" de Valéry*. Paris: José Corti, 1963.
Rodic, Vesna. *Lyricism and Politics in Paul Valéry's Poetry and Poetic Theory and La Nouvelle Revue Française, 1909–1939*. Ph.D. Dissertation: University of California, Berkeley, 2008.
———. "Lyricism, Aesthetic Tradition, and the Debates on Nationalism in *La Nouvelle Revue Française* 1909–1914." *MLN* 127 (2012), 806–25.
Rogers, Gayle. "Death by Prefix? The Paradoxical Life of Modernist Studies." *Los Angeles Review of Books* (July 3, 2016).
Rolland, Romain. "Un appel: Fière déclaration d'intellectuels." *L'Humanité* (June 26, 1919).
Rubenstein, Dianne. *What's Left? The Ecole Normale Supérieure and the Right*. Madison: University of Wisconsin Press, 1990.
Rushworth, Jennifer. "Mourning and Intermittence between Proust and Barthes." *Paragraph* 39, 3 (November 2016), 269–87.
Ruskin, John. *The Works of John Ruskin*. London: George Allen; New York: Longmans, Green 1903–1912.
Sabin, Margery. "The Community of Intelligence." *Raritan*, 4, 3 (Winter 1985), 1–25.
———. *The Dialect of the Tribe: Speech and Community in Modern Fiction*. Oxford: Oxford University Press, 1987.
Said, Edward W. *Orientalism*. London: Penguin, 1978, 2003.
———. *Representations of the Intellectual*. New York: Vintage, 2012.
Sainte-Beuve, Charles Augustin. *Nouveaux portraits et critiques littéraires*, vol. 1. Brussels: Haumon, Cattoir et cie, 1836.
Samuels, Maurice. *Inventing the Israelite: Jewish Fiction in Nineteenth-Century France*. Stanford: Stanford University Press, 2009.
———. "Jews and the Construction of French Identity from Balzac to Proust." *French Global: A New Approach to Literary History*. Edited by Christie McDonald and Susan Rubin Suleiman. New York: Columbia University Press, 2010, 404–19.
———. "France." *Cambridge Companion to European Modernism*. Edited by Pericles Lewis. Cambridge: Cambridge University Press, 2011, 11–32.
Sapiro, Gisèle. *La responsabilité de l'écrivain: Littérature, droit et morale en France, XIXe–XXIe Siècle*. Paris: Seuil, 2011.
Sarraute, Nathalie. *Paul Valéry ou L'Enfant de l'Éléphant; Flaubert le précurseur*. Paris: Gallimard, 1986.
Sartre, Jean-Paul. *L'imagination*. Paris: PUF, 1936, 1950.
———. *L'imaginaire*. Paris: Gallimard, 1986.

Schlegel, Friedrich. *Kritische Schriften und Fragmente, 1789–1801*. Edited by Ernst Behler and Hans Eichner. Paderborn: Ferdinand Schöningh, 1988.

Schlumberger, Jean. "Sur le parti de l'intelligence." *Nouvelle Revue Française*, 73 (October 1919), 788–791.

———. "Considérations." *L'esprit NRF 1908–1940*. Edited by Pierre Hebey. Paris: Gallimard, 1990, 11–13.

Scholem, Gershom. *Walter Benjamin: the Story of a Friendship*. Translated by Harry Zohn. New York: NYRB Books, 2003.

Schuller, Kyla. *The Biopolitics of Feeling: Race, Sex, and Science*. Durham: Duke University Press, 2018.

Shattuck, Roger. *Marcel Proust*. Glasgow: Collins / Fontana, 1974.

———. *Proust's Way: A Field Guide to* In Search of Lost Time. New York: Norton, 2000.

Sherry, Vincent. *Modernism and the Reinvention of Decadence*. Cambridge: Cambridge University Press, 2015.

Shklovsky, Viktor. "Art as Device" (1917 / 1919), *Viktor Shklovsky: A Reader*. Translated and edited by Alexandra Berlina. London: Bloomsbury, 2016, 73–96.

Sirinelli, Jean-François. *Intellectuels et passions françaises: Manifestes et pétitions au XXe siècle*. Paris: Fayard, 1990.

Smock, Ann. *What is There to Say?* Lincoln: University of Nebraska Press, 2003.

Sommer, Christian. *Heidegger, Aristote, Luther*. Paris: PUF, 2005.

Sowerwine, Charles. *France Since 1870: Culture, Society and the Making of the Republic*. New York: Palgrave, 2009.

Spitzer, Leo. "Le style de Marcel Proust." *Études de style*. Edited by Jean Starobinski. Paris: Gallimard, 1970, 397–473.

Starobinski, Jean. "Brève histoire de la conscience du corps." *Genèse de la conscience moderne: Études sur le développement de la conscience de soi dans les littératures du monde occidental*. Edited by Robert Ellrodt. Paris: PUF, 1983, 215–29.

———. "Monsieur Teste face à la douleur." *Valéry pour quoi?* Edited by Michel Jarrety. Paris: Impressions nouvelles: 1987, 93–119.

Staum, Martin. *Nature and Nurture in the French Social Sciences, 1859–1914 and Beyond*. Montreal: McGill Queen's University Press, 2011.

Steiner, Uwe. *Walter Benjamin: An Introduction to his Work and Thought*. Translated by Michael Winkler. Chicago: University of Chicago Press, 2010.

Sternberg, Robert J. *Metaphors of Mind: Conceptions of the Nature of Intelligence*. Cambridge: Cambridge University Press, 1990.

Streuver, Nancy S. *Rhetoric, Modality, Modernity*. Baltimore: Johns Hopkins University Press, 2009.

Sussman, Robert W. *The Myth of Race: The Troubling Persistence of an Unscientific Idea*. Cambridge, MA: Harvard University Press, 2014.

Sutton, Michael. *Nationalism, Positivism, and Catholicism: The Politics of Charles Maurras and French Catholics 1890–1914*. Cambridge: Cambridge University Press, 1982.

Szondi, Peter. *On Textual Understanding and Other Essays*. Translated by Harvey Mendelsohn. Minneapolis: University of Minnesota Press, 1986.

Tadié, Jean-Yves. *Marcel Proust: biographie*. Paris: Gallimard, 1996. *Marcel Proust: A Life*. Translated by Euan Cameron. London: Penguin Books, 2001.

———. *Le lac inconnu. Entre Proust et Freud*. Paris: Gallimard, 2012.

Taine, Hippolyte. *Philosophie de l'art*. Paris: Germer Ballière, 1865. *Philosophy of Art*. Translated by John Durand. New York: Holt and Williams, 1873.
———. *Histoire de la littérature anglaise*. 5 vols. Paris: Hachette, 1866–73.
———. *De l'intelligence*. 2 vols. Paris: Hachette, 1870, 1892. *On Intelligence*. 2 vols. Translated by T. D. Haye. New York: Holt, 1875.
———. *Hippolyte Taine, sa vie et sa correspondence*. 3 vols. Paris: Hachette, 1904–05.
Thibaudet, Albert. "L'esthétique des trois traditions." *Nouvelle Revue Française* 49 (January 1913), 5–42; 50 (March 1913), 355–93.
———. "Sur la démobilisation de l'intelligence." *Nouvelle Revue Française* 76 (January 1920), 129–40.
———. "Renan et Taine." *Nouvelle Revue Française* 115 (April 1923), 71–81.
———. *Paul Valéry*. Paris: Bernard Grasset, 1923.
———. *La république des professeurs*. Paris, Geneva: Slatkine Reprints, 1927, 1979.
———. "Le centenaire de Taine." *Revue de Paris* (15 April 1928), 751–75.
———. "De la critique gidienne." *Réflexions sur la critique*. Paris: Gallimard, 1939, 231–7.
———. "A Discussion of the 'Modern' in Literature." *N.R.F. Essays from the Nouvelle Revue Française 1919–1940*. Edited by Justin O'Brien. London: Eyre & Spottiswoode, 1958.
———. *Réflexions sur la littérature*. Edited by Christophe Pradeau and Antoine Compagnon. Paris: Gallimard, 2007.
———. *L'histoire de la littérature française de 1789 à nos jours*. Paris: CNRS Éditions, 2007.
Tortonese, Paolo. "Taine: Art et Hallucination." *Relire Taine*. Paris: École Nationale Supérieure des Beaux-Arts, 2001, 51–78.
Turing, Alan Mathison. *The Essential Turing: Seminal Writings in Computing, Logic, Philosophy, Artificial Intelligence, and Artificial Life, plus the Secrets of Enigma*. Edited by Jack B. Copeland. Oxford: Oxford University Press, 2004.
Valéry, Paul. *Monsieur Teste*. Paris: Gallimard, 1946.
———. *Œuvres*. 2 vols. Edited by Jean Hytier. Paris: Gallimard, 1957–60.
———. *Lettres à quelques-uns*. Paris: Gallimard, 1962.
———. *The Collected Works of Paul Valéry*. 15 vols. Edited by Jackson Matthews. Princeton: Princeton University Press (Bollingen Series), 1971–5.
———. *Cahiers*, 2 vols. Edited by Judith Robinson. Paris: Gallimard, 1974.
———. *Cahiers 1894–1914*. 29 vols. Edited by Judith Robinson-Valéry and Nicole Celeyrette-Pietri, Paris: Gallimard, 1987–92.
———. *Cahiers / Notebooks*. 5 vols. Edited by Brian Stimpson. Translated by Brian Stimpson, Paul Gifford, Norma Rinsler, et al. Berlin: Peter Lang, 2000–2010.
———. *The Idea of Perfection: The Poetry and Prose of Paul Valéry*. Translated and edited by Nathaniel Rudavsky-Brody. New York: Farrar, Straus and Giroux, 2002.
———. *Correspondance: 1890–1942*. Edited by Peter Fawcett. Paris: Gallimard, 2009.
Vatan, Florence. "La 'puissance de l'image' Bouvard et Pécuchet, disciples de Taine?" *Gustave Flaubert—La revue des lettres modernes 6: "Fiction et philosophie"* (2008), 109–41.
Wais, Kurt, ed. *Die Gegenswartsdichtung der europäischen Völker*. Berlin: Junker und Dünnhaupt Verlag, 1939.

Walsh, Ian Alexander. *French Literature and the Philosophy of Consciousness.* New York: Saint Martin's Press, 1984.
Watt, Adam. "État Présent: Marcel Proust." *French Studies* 72 (2018), 412–24.
Watt, Ian. *Conrad in the Nineteenth Century.* Berkeley: University of California Press, 1981.
Watt, Robert. "The Naive Realism of Henri Bergson." *The Bergsonian Mind.* Edited by Mark Sinclair and Yaron Wolf. New York: Routledge, 2022, 158–74.
Weber, Eugen. *Peasants into Frenchmen: The Modernization of Rural France.* Stanford: Stanford University Press, 1976.
Weber, Samuel. *Benjamin's -abilities.* Cambridge, MA: Harvard University Press, 2005.
———. "Der Brief an Buber vom 17.7.1916." *Benjamin Handbuch: Leben—Werk—Wirkung.* Edited by Burkhardt Lindner. Stuttgart: J. B. Metzler, 2006, 603–8.
———. *Singularity: Poetics and Politics.* Minneapolis: University of Minnesota Press, 2021.
White, Edmund. *Marcel Proust: A Life.* London: Penguin, 1999.
Wiener, Anna. *Uncanny Valley: A Memoir.* New York: Farrar, Straus and Giroux, 2021.
Wilson, Edmund. *Axel's Castle: A Study in the Imaginative Literature of 1870-1930.* New York: Charles Scribner's Sons, 1931.
———. *To the Finland Station: A Study in the Writing and Acting of History.* New York: NYRB Classics, 1972, 2003.
Winock, Michel. *Le siècle des intellectuels.* Paris: Seuil, 1997, 1999.
Wizisla, Edmund. *Walter Benjamin and Bertold Brecht: The Story of a Friendship.* Translated by Christine Shuttleworth. New Haven: Yale University Press, 2009.
Wohl, Robert. *The Generation of 1914.* Cambridge, MA: Harvard University Press, 1979.
Wolf, Theta H. "A New Perspective on Alfred Binet: Dramatist of Le Théatre De L'Horreur." *The Psychological Record* 32, 3 (July 1982), 397–407.
Wood, Michael. *Literature and the Taste of Knowledge.* Cambridge: Cambridge University Press, 2005.
———. "Enemies: Proust's Intelligence." Unpublished manuscript of a lecture delivered at Harvard University.
———. *Unregistered Experience: The Habits of Distraction.* Eastbourne: Sussex Academic Press, 2018.
Wooldridge, Michael. *A Brief History of Artificial Intelligence: What It Is, Where We Are, and Where We Are Going.* New York: Flatiron Books, 2021.
Worms, Frédéric. "L'intelligence gagnée par l'intuition." *Les Études philosophiques,* 4, 4 (2001) 453–64.
Yeschua, Silvio. "Le Yalou: Enigmes, formes, signification." *Paul Valéry contemporain.* Paris: Klincksieck, 1974.
Zaccarello, Benedetta. "Pour une littérature pensée." Maurice Merleau-Ponty, *Recherches sur l'usage littéraire du langage: Cours au Collège de France, Notes, 1953.* Edited by Emmanuel de Saint Aubert and Benedetta Zaccarello. Paris: Metis Presses, 2013, 9–51.
Zhang, Dora. *Strange Likeness: Description and the Modernist Novel.* Chicago: University of Chicago Press, 2020.

INDEX

Action française, 13, 131–32, 135–36, 149
Adorno, Theodor, 88, 91, 94–96, 111, 154–55, 161, 171, 179–81
Agamben, Giorgio, 106
agency, 13, 35, 40, 100, 101, 150
algorithms, 189–90
anti-Fascism, 152, 168, 183
anti-modernes, 24
anti-Semitism, 75, 77
Apollinaire, Guillaume, 154, 165, 167–68, 171, 183; *Poète assassiné*, 163
Aragon, Louis, 175, 178
Arcades Project, The (Benjamin), 162, 170, 172, 181
Arendt, Hannah, 78
Aristotle, 16
arrière-garde, 23–24
artificial intelligence, 186–89; defined, 191; fake digital assistants, 193–94; superintelligence, 193; weak, 192
associationist psychology, 45
atavism, 34
"Author as Producer, The" (Benjamin), 162, 173–74

Balibar, Étienne, 9–10
Ball, Hugo, 17
Balzac, Honoré de, 4, 62, 104, 134; *Comédie Humaine*, 98.
Barbusse, Henri, 132, 148; *Le feu*, 140
Barrès, Maurice, 5, 43, 175, 181; *Les déracinés*, 164
Barthes, Roland, 55
Bataille, Georges, 9, 150, 152
Baudelaire, Charles, 20, 22, 161, 170
Beckett, Samuel, 71
Benda, Julien, 76–77, 137, 144, 161, 164, 175–76, 181; *Discours à la nation européenne*, 176; *La France byzantine*, 76; *La trahison des clercs*, 176
Benjamin, Walter, 2–3, 24–25, 34, 77, 88, 97–98, 141, 152, 153–54; *The Arcades Project*, 162, 170, 172, 181; boycotted in Germany, 179; German *Intelligenz* and, 160–62, 182–83; *Krise und Kritik*, 161; *Kulturkritik*, 160; on *Monsieur Teste*, 105; political style and, 162–66; on Proust *vs.* Valéry, 93–94, 164–65; pure bluff and magic in writing by, 179–84; on returned soldiers, 139–40; on revolutionary writers, 176–78; on Surrealism, 161; Surrealist Marxism, 172; on *Technik*, 169–70, 174; on techniques of political style, 166–71; on techniques of treason, 175–79; "The Author as Producer," 162, 173–74; "The Literarization of Living Conditions," 171–74; "The Present Social Situation of the French Writer," 162–63, 171–74, 178–84; "The Work of Art in the Age of its Technological Reproducibility," 174; *Ursprung des deutschen Trauerspiels*, 178; vulgar materialism of, 171–72
Bergson, Henri, 1–2, 14, 17–18, 38; on art, 44; challenges to meaning of intelligence and culture of scientism, 29–30; *Essai sur les données immédiates de la conscience*, 43, 45; formalism and, 43; on intelligence as creative force, 27–28; intuitive method of, 44–45; *La pensée et le mouvant*, 44; *L'Evolution créatrice*, 46–47; *Matter and Memory*, 45–46; on object of philosophy, 50; on perception, 39; philosophy of movement and, 44
Berl, Emmanuel, 161, 175, 176–77
Bernard, Claude, 28
Bersani, Leo, 56, 202n52
Binet, Alfred, 9–10, 28–29, 38, 187; common sense theory of intelligence, 34; emphasis on judgment, common sense, initiative, auto-critique, and adaptability, 35; intelligence test designed by, 31–34, *32*; *La psychologie du raisonnement*, 32; *Les idées modernes sur les enfants*, 35
Blanchot, Maurice, 10, 98, 102, 137
Bolshevik Revolution, 90, 148
bon sens, 37, 60

Bourdieu, Pierre, 9
bourgeoisie, 3, 61, 156, 163–64, 177, 178
Boutroux, Émile, 28
Bowie, Malcom, 97, 112, 130–31
Brecht, Bertold, 152, 161, 168, 171, 180
Breton, André, 98, 100–101
Broca, Paul, 32
Brooks, Peter, 117–18
Brunetière, Ferdinand, 5, 43, 133
Brunschvicg, Léon, 28
Buber, Martin, 166–67

Cahiers (Valéry), 51, 97, 104, 107, 109, 111–17, 128; on the implex, 113–14; on seeking-intelligence *vs.* finding-intelligence, 117; subject matter of, 112
Calvino, Italo, 128
Canguilhem, Georges, 46
capitalism, 173
Carson, John, 9, 27, 187; on definition of intelligence, 27
Cartesianism, 60, 154–55, 183
Céline, Louis-Ferdinand, 76, 164
cerebral localization, 45
Changeux, Jean-Pierre, 188
Charcot, Jean-Martin, 10
ChatGPT, 189
China, 126–27
civilization, 35, 94, 124, 148–49
Clarté group, 148
classicism, 96–97
Claudel, Paul, 130
Clemenceau, Georges, 5, 133
clichés, 41, 65, 68, 73, 98
Colucci, Gio, 87, 88
Communism, 165, 174, 177, 181–82
Compagnon, Antoine, 15, 24, 145
computers: Alan Turing and, 189–91; artificial intelligence and, 186–89; simulating intelligent processes, 191–92; synaptic and quantum computing, 188
Comte, August, 28
Condillac, Étienne Bonnot de, 17, 37–39
Congrès international des écrivains pour la défense de la culture, 152
consciousness, 41–42; Bergson on, 45–46; Nietzsche on, 155–56
Contre Sainte-Beuve (Proust), 53–54, 59, 61; Proust's view of intelligence in, 63; writing style of, 64–65

Copeau, Jacques, 130, 138
counterrealism, 117–21
Cousin, Victor, 28
craniometry, 34, 36
creation, 131–132, 145; aesthetic, 66, 113; Benjamin on, 180; creativity, 62, 66; defined, 146–47; intelligent criticism and, 146–7; process of, 67, 75
crisis of intelligence: Valéry on, 90, 121–25, 185
criticism, 1, 28, 38, 39, 145, 152, 153, 160–61, 184, 187; analytic, 132; art, 12, 19; Benjamin on, 171, 172, 174, 180–81; as disinterested exercise of intelligence, 16; formalist, 102; function of, 43–44; of intelligence, 59, 134–36; literary, 13–14, 24, 146; models of, 7; modern, 20, 23, 130, 162, 180; New French, 137–38; physiognomic, 141; politicization of, 183; professional, 22; Proust on, 64, 66; qualitative, 43; romantic novel, 97; as technique of treason, 175
Curtius, Ernst Robert, 93

Dada, 168
Dagan, Yaël, 139
Daston, Lorraine, 9, 11, 187
David, Jean, 8
Davis, Colin, 104
DeepMind, 191, 192
delayed coding, 75
Deleuze, Gilles, 18, 55, 76; "Postscript on the Societies of Control," 185–86; on intelligence and objectivity, 63; on style, 62
De l'intelligence (Taine), 29, 31, 38, 40, 42–43, 132
Derrida, Jacques, 114, 125, 183
Descartes, René, 36–37, 60, 84, 155
Descombes, Vincent, 58, 61, 79–80
determinism, 32, 89, 125, 172, 187, 194
Detienne, Marcel, 16
dialectical movement, 177–78
Dichtung, 158–59
Dictionnaire de l'Académie françoise, 27
Dorgelès, Roland, *Les croix de bois*, 140
Dreyfus, Alfred, 5, 8, 34, 177
Dreyfus, Hubert, 192
Duhem, Pierre, 28
Durkheim, Emile, 31; *Revue philosophique*, 175

eclecticism, 28, 38
École normal supérieure, 28
École polytechnique, 28
Eliot, T. S., 23; "The Perfect Critic," 16
Empson, William, 56
epistemology, 9–10
equality: intelligence and, 36–38; political, 11
Erskine, John, 17
esprit, 10, 39
Étiemble, René, 78
eugenics, 34, 36, 187
evolutionary biology, 187
exclusion: based on class, race, and gender, 36; of neurodivergent persons, 11, 34; of women, 11

Fascism, 152, 168, 183
Faulkner, William, 19
Faure, Félix, 4–5
Fechner, Gustav, 31
Fénelon, François de Salignac de La Mothe, 84
Fénéon, Félix, 141
Fenves, Peter, 172
fetishism, 32
First World War, 5–6, 129–30; Proust and, 6; Rivière and, 140–50, 152; literary changes during, 130–31; *Nouvelle Revue Française (NRF)* and outbreak of, 139; Versailles Treaty and end of, 144
Flaubert, Gustave, 59, 60–61, 156; *L'Éducation sentimentale*, 151
form, 2, 43; artistic, 22; and content in literary technique, 169; fragmentary, 117; of intelligence, 48, 64, 139, 156; literary, 12–13, 88–89, 91, 162, 164, 167, 169; narrative, 101–2; novelistic, 163; of speaking, 15; as substance, 100; writing as cultural, 172
formalism, 43, 89–90
Forster, E. M., 23, 152
Foucault, Michel, 5, 186, 202n52
Fournier, Alain, 130
Franco-Prussian War of 1870, 5–6; decline of rationalism after, 42
Freed-Thall, Hannah, 23
French literature, phases of, 13–14
French modernism, 19–24, 204n95

Freud, Sigmund, 109
Front Populaire, 3, 24
Futurism, 168

Gallimard, Gaston, 118, 130, 133, 136
Galton, Francis, 34, 187
Geist, 158–59, 184
genetic transformation, 187
genius, 37, 99, 137–38, 145, 191, 201n45; conceptual histories of term, 153; exceptional creativity and, 62; hereditary, 34; mock-romantic variants of, 164; reaction of intelligence against, 28; two aspects of, 7
German Idealism, 28, 61, 158–59. *See also* Benjamin, Walter
Germanophobia, 151
Ghéon, Henri, 138, 147–48, 149
Gide, André, 164, 165, 179; Benjamin's essays on, 162; Bergson and, 51; *Congrès international des écrivains pour la défense de la culture* and, 152; First World War and, 144; *NRF* and, 130–31, 136–40; Valéry and, 126
Goddard, Henry H., 34, 36
Google, 191; Alexa, 193
Gould, Stephen Jay, 34, 187
Greaney, Patrick, 165–66
Great War of 1914–1918. *See* First World War
Green, Julien, 164
Guerlac, Suzanne, 47, 89

Halévy, Daniel, 151
hallucination, 38–42
Hamacher, Werner, 15, 21
Hartman, Geoffrey, 23, 98–99, 113
Hegel, G. W. F., 28, 155
Heidegger, Martin, 153, 154, 161, 170, 183; on intellectualism, 157–60; *Introduction to Metaphysics*, 157–58; "On the Provenance of Art and the Destiny of Thinking," 194
Helmholtz, Hermann von, 39
Henry, Anne, 71
Herrenschmidt, Clarisse, 189
Hilbert, David, 189–90
Histoires brisées (Valéry), 100; counter-realism in, 117–21; love and beauty themes in, 119; slaves' memories as narrative in, 119–20

Hollier, Denis, 176
Horkheimer, Max, 180
Hughes, Edward, 151
Human Genome project, 188
Huxley, Aldous, 152

Idealism, 28
implex, the, 113–14
induction, 98–99
innocence of the eye, 69–70
insomnia, 123
intellect, the, 4, 47, 49, 61, 64, 98–99, 104, 109, 134, 175
intellectualism, 5, 157–58
intelligence, 1–2; artificial (*See* artificial intelligence); attention and reflection and, 71–72; as basis for social distinction, 9; beliefs about gender and, 11; *bon sens* and, 37, 60; as capacity to create medial effects, 69; claim of, 147; disarming, 14–17; creativity and, 62, 66, 146–47; crisis of, 90, 121–25, 185–96; critical, 146; demobilization of, 147–50; dominating the *esprit du temps*, 1870–1930, 10, 124–25; early definitions of, 27; essential ambiguity of, 50; establishment of the Third Republic and, 1–4; evolutionary biology and psychometric studies of, 187; exclusionary, 11; as faculty of understanding, 57; finding-intelligence, 117; Franco-Prussian War of 1870 and First World War impacts on, 5–7; Germanic reaction to, 153–162; intuition and, 44–47; involuntary, 18; measuring, 30–36, *33*; as mental capacity to register and interpret signs, 29; modes of knowing ascribed to, 9; music and, 70–72; neural plasticity and genetic transformation and, 187; psychophysics and, 42; racism of, 9; reaction against romanticism, 28; reflection and action as sword and mirror, 7–12, 24–26; reflective, 29; as reflex, 115; seeking-intelligence, 117; signaled through speaking, 78–84; spatial forms of, 46; subjectivization and naturalization and, 11; super-, 193; testing of, 9; theory of the sign and study of, 40–41; tied to equality and to distinction, 36–38
intelligence-cuirasse, 25
intelligence-glaive, 25

intelligence tests, 10–11, 187
intelligentsia, 123–24
Intelligenz, 153–55, 182–83; Heidegger and, 157–60; Nietzsche and, 155–57. *See also* Benjamin, Walter
intelligere, 10
intuition, 44–47, 72
involuntary psychology, 40

James, William, 40–41
Jameson, Frederic, 20, 118
Jarrety, Michel, 98, 103
Jefferson, Ann, 153
Jennings, Michael, 174
Jenny, Laurent, 12
Journal des deux mondes, 5
Joyce, James, 19
judgment, 41, 80, 82, 120, 139, 141, 201n45; aesthetic, 94, 135, 138; elevation of intelligence over, 14, 35, 134; moral, 142; of taste linked to aesthetic universal, 43; tautology as form of, 146
July monarchy, 28

Kafka, Franz, 95, 102, 157
Kant, Immanuel, 31, 46
Kaufman, Vincent, 107
Keynes, John Maynard, 144
knowledge, 9, 15; conscious, 54; cultural, 35; defined in mechanical and materialist terms, 41–42; different types of, 2; divine, 37; elements of, 41; faculty of, 32, 57; governed by laws of contiguity and resemblance, 41; institutionalized kinds of, 25; intelligence and, 16, 27, 46, 48–49, 66–67, 84, 108; literature's desire for, 13–14; as mechanical and materialist, 41–42, 187; as not proprietary, 66–67; origin of, 36–37; as potential or ability, 9, 29; as sequence of events, 39; sociology of, 161; specialized domains of, 5, 13
Koffeman, Maaike, 130, 138
Kommerell, Max, 141
Korsch, Karl, 172–73
Kristeva, Julia, 61
Kurzweil, Ray, 192

Lachelier, Jules, 28
Lagneau, Jules, 164, 175, 181
Lalande, André, 5

L'Aurore, 4–5
Leibniz, G. W., 74
Lenin, Vladimir, 177, 180
Le Temps, 5, 75
L'Humanité, 132, 148
literature, 1–7, 12–16; as anti-paranoid activity, 109; as bearer of truth, 104; Benjamin on, 162–63, 165, 172–74, 180; bourgeois stupidity exposed in, 156; classicism and, 139; contradictions of, 96; disarming intelligence, 25; French, 130, 134, 157, 160–61, 162, 179–80; as key to psychosis, 165; modernist, 20, 22, 23–24, 30; Nietzsche on, 156–57; *Nouvelle Revue Française*, 130, 145–47, 151–52; politically effective, 166; Proust on, 53, 55–56, 58, 59, 62, 73, 76–77, 84, 92; realist, 117–18; renewal of style in modern, 84; revolutionary, 182; Rivière on, 140; Taine on, 28–29, 43; Thibaudet on, 175–76; as transcription of logic of beings and events, 40; Valéry on, 96–97, 98–99, 109, 114
Littré, Emile, 9, 57, 69
Locke, John, 37
logical faculty, 58–59
logical relations, 1, 12, 14–15, 25; cause and effect, 70, 118, 184; intelligence and intuition and, 47; in realist novels, 40; truth and, 66–67
Louÿs, Pierre, 112
lyricism, 102, 103, 110, 129

machine learning, 188
Maine de Biran, François-Pierre-Gontier, 28, 38
Malabou, Catherine, 187–88, 194; *Morphing Intelligence: From IQ Measurement to Artificial Brains*, 187
Mallarmé, Stéphane, 89–90, 98, 110, 111
"Manifeste du parti de l'intelligence," 148–51
Mann, Thomas, 157
Marx, Karl, 161, 166; *Critique of Political Economy*, 172–73
Marx, William, 24, 43
Marxism, 161, 166, 171, 172–73, 179, 183; vulgar, 172
Massis, Henri, 132, 148, 152
materialism, 39, 43, 170, 171–72, 175, 176, 183

Maupassant, Guy de, 40
Maurras, Charles, 13–14, 43, 145, 146, 152; *L'avenir de l'intelligence*, 131, 132–36; "Manifeste du parti de l'intelligence," 148–51; *Nouvelle Revue Française (NRF)* and, 132–36, 138–39
McCarthy, John, 191–92
measurement of intelligence, 30–36, *33*
memory: Bergson on, 39, 45; cultural memory, 144, 148; Taine on, 29–30, 41–3, 45; Proust on, 18, 52, 55–6, 61, 64–66, 70, 73, 86; Valéry on, 93, 113, 120
Merleau-Ponty, Maurice, 98
metaphysics, 9–10, 157–58
metapsychology, 113
mētis, 16, 202n55
Mill, John Stuart, 39
Milne, Anna-Louise, 23
mimesis, 103
mind, 48, 74, 123, 144, 145–46, 150
mind-body dualism, 28
modern classicism, 129–30, 131
modernity, 11, 19, 160; conservatism versus, 132; contradictions in, 150; destructive forces of, 22; discourses of, 20; intelligence and, 17; literary periods in, 21; paradoxes of, 23–24; self-consciousness as cornerstone of philosophical, 155
Monsieur Teste (Valéry), 90, 98, 128, 164; anonymous narrator of, 107; character of Teste in, 106–7; counter-hysterical movement in, 109; death in, 108; language used in, 107–9; physical pain depicted in, 109; prose of intelligence in, 109–10; as series of writings, 106; violence of language in, 105–6
Moore's Law, 192
Morand, Paul, 164; *Tender Shoots*, 61
Morimoto, Atsuo, 110
Musil, Robert, 152, 157; *Man without Qualities*, 107

nationalism, literary, 139
Natorp, Paul, 142–43
Naturalism, 163
naturalization, 11, 187
Neumann, John von, 190
neural plasticity, 187
Newell, Allen, 191–92
Nias, Hilary, 29

Nietzsche, Friedrich, 155–57, 170, 183; *Beyond Good and Evil*, 156; *Genealogy of Morals*, 155; on intellectualism, 157–58; *Nachlass*, 155
Noegerrath, Felix, 179
non-contradiction, 15
Nouvelle Revue Française (NRF), 1–2, 14, 22–23, 51, 92; André Gide and, 136–40; Charles Maurras and, 132–36, 138–39; demobilization of intelligence after the war, 147–50; *Future of Intelligence* and, 131, 132–36; Jacques Rivière and, 140–50, 152; *l'esprit*, 137–38; literary impact of, 130–32, 150–52; modern classicism and, 129–30, 131, 136, 138–39; role in prewar literary movement, 144; wartime silence of, 144–46
novel, the: academy of, 138; contradiction in, 67; criticism of, 103–4; as a genre, 88–89, 117–18; internal stitching of, 23; mediocrity and rise of, 100; modern, 19; realism in, 40, 90, 98, 99; relationship to philosophy, 61; role of intelligence in, 73–74, 79

OpenAI, 189
Oracle, 193
Oster, Daniel, 89, 106
Ozenfant, Amédée, 11–12

Parti de l'intelligence, 148–52
Pasternak, Boris, 152
Paulhan, Jean, 98, 102, 110, 136–37; *Le guerrier appliqué*, 140
Péguy, Charles, 43, 130, 164, 181
perceptions, 39–42; as harmony with the outside world, 39–40; substitution of signs for, 40–41
philology, 15, 23–24
philosophy, 2, 5, 10, 12, 18, 90; Dasein and, 158; Derrida and, 114; Descartes and, 60, 84; as effort to mobilize thinking, 47; German, 84, 143, 157–58, 173; literary works and, 58, 59; of movement, 44; object of, 50; Platonic, 16; post-Cartesian, 17, 36–37, 188; Proust and, 61; terminology of new, 29; Third Republic, 129; university, 28
Piaget, Jean, 8, 32
Plato, 16, 165, 168

Poe, Edgar Allan, 40
poetry, 16, 36, 64, 165, 168; intelligence in, 16, 106, 128; political style and, 167–68; as prose, 97–98, 103; symbolist, 136; Valéry and, 97–98; validity of, 159; voice in, 102–3
Poincaré, Henri, 28
political style, 162–66; techniques of, 166–71
positivism, 38, 106, 159
"Present Social Situation of the French Writer, The" (Benjamin), 162–63, 171, 174; on Marxist theory, 172–73; pure bluff and magic in, 179–84; on treason, 178–79
primitive mind, 19, 31, 35
prophecy, 167–68, 172
prose: Benjamin on, 97–98; of intelligence, 109–10; lyricism and, 102, 103, 110; Valéry's attack on, 98–105
Proust, Marcel, 1–2, 13–14, 17–18, 43, 111, 150, 151–52, 162, 164, 179; on art and intelligence, 54, 66–69; on attention and reflection, 71–72; as contemporary of Valéry, 91–98; *Contre Sainte-Beuve*, 53–54, 59, 61, 63–65; critique of intelligence, 62–66, 85–86; depictions of Jewishness by, 76, 78; on epiphanic structure of time, 73; Étiemble's defense of, 78; on external objects, 63; on faith, 85; on the Franco-Prussian War, 6; French modernism and, 19, 23; on genius, 62; German *Intelligenz* and, 160–61; German translation of, 77–78; on hermeticism in contemporary literature, 84–85; *In Search of Lost Time*, 52–86, 170; labeled an anti-intellectual writer, 76–77; *Nouvelle Revue Française (NRF)* and, 130; on philosophers as readers, 59–60; physiology of society of, 165; on place of intelligence in literary and artistic creation, 75; *Sodom and Gomorrah*, 74; redemption and reparation and, 56–57; rejection of style of, 76; relations to philosophy, 61–62, 84; on sensibility *versus* intelligence, 74–75; on the sick body, 62; style of writing between critical essay and novel, 64–65; *Time Regained*, 54, 67, 96; on truth, 66–67, 72; use of literature to disarm intelligence, 55–56;

on value accorded to intelligence, 64; on words and logical faculty, 58–59. See also *Recherche*
psychology, 2, 8, 10, 11, 12, 26, 27; associationist, 45; experimental, 40, 76; Gestalt, 153; of intelligence, 30–32, 42, 44, 51, 184; involuntary, 40; meta-, 113; philosophy and, 188; Proust and, 77, 93, 99; quantitative, 43; terminology of, 29; Third Republic, 129; Valéry and, 99, 112
psychophysics, 42, 209n95

racism, 9
Rancière, Jacques, 91; *La parole muette*, 96
Ravaisson, Félix, 28
realism, 117–18, 156–57, 170
reason, Enlightenment, 8
Recherche (Proust), 52–86, 91, 170; depictions of Jewishness in, 76, 78; German translation of, 77–78; instinct and impressions in, 60–61, 67, 72; involuntary feelings and consciousness in, 67–68; manner of speaking in, 78–84; music in, 70–72; narrative device of translation in, 75; reimagined as a novel, 56; spectator's intelligence in, 70–71; Valéry on, 92
redemption, 56–57
reflective intelligence, 29
reflex theory, 113
relational modes, 202n52
Renan, Ernest, 28–29, 42; *L'avenir de la science*, 132; *La Vie de Jésus*, 135–36
Renoir, Pierre-Auguste, 140
Renouvier, Charles, 28
reparation, 56–57
representation: affective critiques of, 23; AI and cinematic, 193; humanism and, 110; of intelligence, 1–2, 71, 109, 132; perception and, 39, 104; in science, 47; spatialized, 30; of strength, 135; of subjective experiences, 118
Republicanism, 175–76
Revolution, of 1789, 21, 131; of 1848, 28
revolutionary writers, 176–78, 182
rhetoric, 2, 9, 15, 199n1
Ribot, Théodule, 28, 31–32, 38; *Erkenntnistheorie*, 31; *Essai sur l'imagination créatrice*, 31–32; *Les maladies de la mémoire*, 45

Rivière, Jacques, 24, 57, 130–31, 136, 138; call for demobilization of intelligence, 149–50; *L'Allemand: Souvenirs et réflexions d'un prisonnier de guerre*, 132, 140–41; on *la passion de la France*, 139; wartime service of, 140–50, 152
Robinson, Judith, 98, 104
Rolland, Romain, 132, 148
Romanticism, 28, 154
Rousseau, Jean-Jacques, 141
Ruskin, John: *Bible of Amiens*, 70; *Elements of Drawing, The*, 69; *Modern Painters*, 69
Russian Revolution, 90, 148

Sainte-Beuve, Charles Augustin, 7–8, 18, 24–25, 43, 54–55
Samuels, Maurice, 76
Sand, George, 134
Sarraute, Nathalie, 99
Saussure, Ferdinand de, 43
Schlumberger, Jean, 130, 137, 139, 147, 149
Scholem, Gershom, 171, 180–81
Schopenhauer, Arthur, 71; *The World as Will and Representation*, 62
Scottish Common-Sense Realism, 28
Second Empire, 28
Second World War, 145, 186
Sedgwick, Eve Kosofsky, 56
sensations, 39–40; absent, 41
sensorimotor theory, 114
services de renseignements, 8
Shklovsky, Viktor, 75
Simon, Herbert A., 191–92
Simon, Théodore, 29, 34
socialism, radical, 164
Socialist Realism, 169–70
social progressivism, 151
Soviet Union, 152, 159, 165–66, 169–70
Spearman, Charles, 34, 187
Spencer, Herbert, 39
Spiritualism, 28
Stern, Ludwig Wilhelm, 34
Stevens, Wallace, 23
Stimpson, Brian, 121
subjectivity, 2, 10, 19, 111, 120, 179, 184; affective logic of, 118; self-conscious, 49
superintelligence, 193
Surrealism, 101–2, 152, 161, 162, 164, 177, 179

surveillance and spying, 8
symbolic language, 40
symbolism, 21, 22, 58, 87, 89, 136, 146

Tadié, Jean-Yves, 111
Taine, Hippolyte, 1–2, 14, 17–18, 132; on *clichés*, 41; on consciousness, 41; decline of views of, 42–44; *De l'intelligence*, 29, 31, 38, 40, 42–43, 132; Gustave Fechner and, 31; on harmony, 39–40; *Histoire de la littérature anglaise*, 38–39; on intelligence as corrective force, 27; as leading figure in French philosophy, 38–39; on perceptive practices, 37–38; as principle avatar of intelligence, 28–29; on psychophysics, 42; on restriction of the self, 49, 51; *zoologie de l'esprit humain*, 38
Terman, Lewis, 34
Thibaudet, Albert, 22, 98, 130, 138–39, 161; Le parti de l'intelligence and, 149–50; on Republicanism, 175–76; *The Republic of Professors*, 175
Third Republic, 1–4, 17, 129, 176; Cartesianism of, 60; French modernism in, 19
Tracy, Antoine Destutt de, 39
treason, 175–79
Tretiakov, Sergei, 169
Turing, Alan, 189–91

unconscious, the, 7, 16, 29, 38, 61–62; alternative to, 113; cunning of, 156; dynamic role of, 32; struggle to control, 155; intelligence and, 55
understanding, 25, 156, 166; eye as source of, 120; faculty of, 27, 36, 46, 47, 57; intelligence as basis for, 2, 3, 9; linked to the real, 46; literary, 18; modes of, 37; as operation of linguistic substitution, 112; self-, 38, 111, 130; unique personal, 115

Valéry, Paul, 1–3, 13–14, 17–18, 87–128, 160, 162, 179; Adorno on, 154–55; on analytic power in intelligence, 116; attack on prose, 98–105; on authority of fiction, 100; *Cahiers*, 51, 97, 104, 107, 109, 111–17, 128; *Charmes*, 91; on classicism, 96–97; on consciousness, 113; as contemporary of Proust, 91–98; "Conquest of Ubiquity" 195; counterrealism of, 117–21; on crisis of intelligence, 90, 121–25, 185, 193, 195; critique of spontaneous meaning, 115; definition of intelligence, 90, 121–22; definition of philosophical problem, 105; doubts about the potential of the novel as a genre, 88–89; on European achievement, 124–27; formalism of, 89–90; French modernism and, 21–22; *Histoires brisées*, 100, 117–21; ideal novel of, 104; images of, 87; on the implex, 113–14; on impulse and reflex, thought and action, 112–13, 115–16; on induction, 98–99; on insomnia, 123; *La jeune parque*, 91; on law of continuity, 115; *Le Figaro littéraire*, 118; *Le problème des musées*, 94, 95–96; mental crisis and self-understanding in, 111; model of address/voice used by, 102–3; *Monsieur Teste*, 90, 98, 105–10, 109, 128, 164; *Nouvelle Revue Française (NRF)* and, 130; philosophy of, 43–44; on politics, 126–27; position in French literary history, 87–88; on the practice of writing, 99–100; process of poetry and, 97; on psychology, 112; resistance to philosophy, 114; resistance to realism, 100, 104, 117–18; skepticism of language to express truth, 104–5; surrealism and, 101–2; technical constructivism of, 164; *Tel quel*, 96–97, 99; on truth-value in fiction, 101–2
Vernant, Jean-Pierre, 16

Wais, Kurt, 77–78
Watt, Ian, 75
Weber, Samuel, 167
Winock, Michel, 139
Wood, Michael, 64, 74
Wooldridge, Michael, 190
World War I. *See* First World War
Worms, Frédéric, 46

Zola, Emile, 4–5, 163

A NOTE ON THE TYPE

THIS BOOK has been composed in Miller, a Scotch Roman typeface designed by Matthew Carter and first released by Font Bureau in 1997. It resembles Monticello, the typeface developed for The Papers of Thomas Jefferson in the 1940s by C. H. Griffith and P. J. Conkwright and reinterpreted in digital form by Carter in 2003.

Pleasant Jefferson ("P. J.") Conkwright (1905–1986) was Typographer at Princeton University Press from 1939 to 1970. He was an acclaimed book designer and AIGA Medalist.

The ornament used throughout this book was designed by Pierre Simon Fournier (1712–1768) and was a favorite of Conkwright's, used in his design of the *Princeton University Library Chronicle*.

GPSR Authorized Representative: Easy Access System Europe - Mustamäe tee
50, 10621 Tallinn, Estonia, gpsr.requests@easproject.com

www.ingramcontent.com/pod-product-compliance
Lightning Source LLC
Chambersburg PA
CBHW051212300426
44116CB00006B/540